RECENT DEVELOPMENTS IN TRANSPORT ECONOMICS

Recent Developments in Transport Economics

Edited by

GINÉS DE RUS
Department of Applied Economics, University of Las Palmas de Gran Canaria

and

CHRIS NASH
Institute for Transport Studies, University of Leeds

Ashgate

Aldershot • Brookfield USA • Singapore • Sydney

Published by
Ashgate Publishing Limited
Gower House
Croft Road
Aldershot
Hants GU11 3HR
England

Ashgate Publishing Company
Old Post Road
Brookfield
Vermont 05036
USA

British Library Cataloguing in Publication Data
Recent developments in transport economics
  1. Transportation
  I.Rus, Ginés de II.Nash, Chris
  388'.049

Library of Congress Catalog Card Number: 97-70342

ISBN 1 85972 500 7

Printed in Great Britain by The Ipswich Book Company, Suffolk

Contents

Figures and tables

List of contributors

Ginés de Rus, Department of Applied Economics, University of Las Palmas de Gran Canaria, Spain.

Chris Nash, Institute for Transport Studies, University of Leeds, England.

J. J. Bates, John Bates Services, England.

Tae Hoon Oum, Faculty of Commerce and Business Administration, University of British Columbia, Canada.

W. G. Waters II, Faculty of Commerce and Business Administration, University of British Columbia, Canada.

Jan Owen Jansson, Department of Transport Economics, University of Linköping, Sweden.

Stephen Glaister, Department of Geography, London School of Economics, England.

John Dodgson, Department of Economics and Accounting, University of Liverpool, England.

K. M. Gwilliam, Principal Transport Economist, The World Bank, Washington, USA.

Acknowledgements

We are grateful to Professor Antonio Marrero, Chairman of the V Spanish Congress of Economy, for his support and encouragement to publish this set of papers presented in the Transport Economics sessions of the V Congress, held in Las Palmas in December 1995. We also wish to express our gratitude to Jose Luis Quevedo, Candelaria Mateos and Liliana Toledo (University of Las Palmas de Gran Canaria) for their efficient production of the volume.

We are grateful to Professor Antonio Marrero, Chairman of the V Symposium of Economy, for his support and encouragement to publish this set of papers presented in the Transport Economics sessions of the V Congress, held in Las Palmas in December 1997. We also wish to express our gratitude to José Luis Quevedo, Canariana Marcet (Instituto Tirado Universitario of Las Palmas de Gran Canaria) for their efficient coordination of the volume.

1   Introduction

Ginés de Rus and Chris Nash

The provision of good transport services and infrastructures is widely believed to constitute a necessary condition for economic growth. Econometric estimations have shown a strong relationship between infrastructure and economic development (see Aschauer, 1989; Stern, 1991; Munnell, 1992). Although there remains much debate about the reasons why this relationship occurs, such as the direction of causation (see Gramlich, 1994 for a survey), it is difficult to imagine how a society with a high degree of specialization of its economy could function without a complex and effective transport system that makes possible the required flows of people and goods. It is not surprising that 7% of the gross national product and 40% of public investment in the European Union take place in the transport sector. The European Commission has analysed the crucial role of transport for the completion of a common market, the problems associated with capacity shortages and bottlenecks and has also stressed the contribution of transport infrastructure in the convergence of the regions (European Commission, 1993).

Although transport makes an important positive contribution to economic development, it also constitutes an important source of externalities, which are not internalised in many cases due to the failure of national and European policies in the aim of equalizing private and social costs. This is inefficient, leading to excessive growth of transport demand, distortion of modal split, and degradation of the environment.

Transport economics deals with the analysis of the transport system, the functioning of transport markets and in general with the economic problems associated with mobility of people and the shipment of goods. In many aspects transport economics is simply the application of microeconomic principles and methods to an economic activity consisting of the movement of freight and passengers. Transport economists however tend to argue that the transport sector deserves a specialized approach within economics for several reasons (Mohring, 1994; Winston, 1985):

1 Transport appears as a vital input in the majority of economic activities. Production in transport consists of changing the location of people and goods without physical transformation of their attributes. The spatial nature of transport services and the

impossibility of storage complicate the supply side of transport industries which have to face fluctuating demands and multiple combinations of origins and destinations. Since each combination of origin, destination and time may be considered as a separate good, the transport sector produces literally millions of different goods using the same inputs, so joint cost problems abound.

2 Quality of transport services is particularly relevant to the explanation of demand behaviour. Empirical evidence shows that consumers value transport quality highly, and that quality depends on the overall combination of speed, frequency and other attributes supplied by all the operators on a given route. The concept of generalized cost has been very useful in economic analysis, incorporating a richer modelling of the interaction of supply and demand in an activity in which travel time is very often more important than producer cost.

3 Pervasive role of government. Although with less intensity than in the recent past, entry, pricing and operating conditions are still determined by government in many transport services (i.e. buses, taxis and railways) all over the world. The provision of transport infrastructure is mainly in public hands. The way in which public infrastructure should be priced and the rules for investing in new capacity will continue in public hands in the coming years, despite the growing contribution of private capital in the financing of some particular projects.

4 Economies of scale and externalities. Indivisibilities, economies of scale or density are frequent in transport industries. Pricing has to reconcile the gap between low marginal cost and high average costs, with the added difficulty of allocating common costs in multiproduct industries. The divergence between marginal social cost and user marginal cost requires the design of a price mechanism to make compatible market freedom with allocative efficiency. Cost subaddivity and negative or positive external effects of public infrastructure and private vehicle use require a regulatory framework helping the market to allocate resources to the benefit of society.

What then are the major issues faced by transport economists at the end of the twentieth century? It appears that they still relate primarily to the two issues of the role and form of government intervention in the transport sector, and to the problems of transport pricing.

The introduction of more freedom in transport markets through liberalization and privatization has produced efficiency gains forecasted by economists (see Winston, 1993) and many problems connected with x-efficiency have found a quick solution through the working of market forces, avoiding complicated and expensive regulatory schemes. However, there remain conflicts between the achievement of allocative and productive efficiency, exemplified by U.K. bus deregulation and by the reorganization of the airlines, whilst it is hardly conceivable that the majority of transport infrastructure could be transferred to the private sector without continued regulation.

One of the areas in which the gap between theory and practice is particularly wide is in the treatment of congestion and other externalities. Transport economists made sound proposals 50 years ago in order to optimize the use of roads in presence of traffic congestion. The Smeed report was written in the fifties giving solutions for traffic congestion, and 40 years later, the allocation of space through queuing, a highly inefficient way of capacity rationing, is still the dominant way of adjustment between demand and supply. At the same time, concern about the environmental externalities produced by road traffic is rapidly growing. Some use of the pricing mechanism to deal with these problems has taken place, but much remains to be done to design practical schemes for the internalisation of externalities, and to win support for their introduction (see Small and Gomez Ibañez, 1994).

This volume deals with recent contributions in transport economics. The main subjects in the field are covered in a generic way. Demand and cost analysis, externalities, pricing of services and infrastructures, deregulation, evaluation of investment and the economics of transport and development are the issues covered in depth by a group of experienced transport economists.

Demand forecasting is an essential topic to the study of transport. It is necessary for the planning of infrastructure investment and, in general, in the assesment of different transport policies. The economic effects of the introduction of alternative pricing policies, railway closures, airline deregulation and many other policies need an estimation of demand response to changes in the generalized cost of travel.

John Bates argues that it is crucial to improve our understanding of supply-demand equilibrium. Although demand forecasting in any industry implies an equilibrium of supply and demand, prices are usually assumed fixed, and the supply side is not considered worth analysing in many cases. In transport, once the concept of generalized cost is substituted for the money price, it is impossible to leave supply effects aside, as demand variations may have significant effects on travel costs, even in the case of constant producer costs.

Demand forecasting usually requires a higher level of detail in transport than in other industries. Bates gives two reasons to explain this fact: firstly, the applications of specific policies require particular values in space and time; secondly, the above mentioned supply effects are strictly local. The assessment of the closure of late evening services, for example, needs the response of late evening demand in the space affected by the planned cut in services.

Bates discusses the elements which are required to forecast transport demand. The concepts of derived demand and generalized cost are the starting point for the estimation of the demand curve. Keeping fixed the external variables which determine transport demand (population, car ownership, etc.), an equilibrium is then derived between demand and unit generalized costs. Forecasts may then be derived for two alternative sets of changes in future conditions:

Firstly, changes in the external factors which makes the demand for travel a derived demand. Changes in household structure, employment and spatial patterns, for example, will shift the demand curve modifying the initial equilibrium with a new value of the unit generalized cost as long as the supply curve is not perfectly elastic.

3

Secondly, changes in policy variables; for example, the introduction of road pricing or the construction of a new road, will shift the supply function, and together with the shift in the demand curve due to changes in population, car ownership, etc., will lead to a new equilibrium.

Knowledge of **the cost structure of transport industries** is crucial for different policy issues. The nature of the returns to scale has important implications for the feasibility of competition, efficiency gains from mergers, financial implications of optimal pricing, etc. Tae Oum and Bill Waters II review the developments over the last fifteen years of aggregate cost functions in transport. These authors explain the origins of empirical cost function estimation in transport and give a summmary of conceptual and econometric developments.

Oum and Waters explain the concepts of economies of scale, density and scope, the introduction of flexible functional forms in the estimation of cost functions, the specification and treatment of multiple outputs, the importance of data quality and the use of panel data for estimating cost functions.

Their paper examines recent developments for improving the accuracy of estimating key indicators of cost structure in the presence of firm disequilibrium input adjustments in the short run. They survey recent estimates of returns to scale and advances in econometric work for measuring productive efficiency: cost function estimation with firm and time effect variables, decomposition techniques for total factor productivity and techniques for estimting frontier cost functions.

Pricing of transport services and infrastructure is a central issue in transport economics. There is a wide range of theoretical and empirical literature (see Winston, 1985) discussing optimal pricing for buses, railways and airlines and optimal road, port and airport charges. One of the key points in the theoretical treatement of pricing is the distinction between user and producer costs, and the modelling of the system as a trade off between the two. The presence of budget constraints, underpriced alternative modes of transport, externalities, etc, constitute additional complications in the determination of optimal prices.

Jan Owen Jansson in his paper offers a comprehensive and integrated analysis of optimal pricing for transport infrastructure and services. Jansson defines the basic framework as one consisting of transport vehicles and transport infrastructure, in which transport vehicles belong to private or public agents and the infrastructure usually belongs to the public sector.

The cost structure of the transport system is divided into three parts: total producer cost, total user cost and total external cost. The optimizaton of the resources supplied by producers and users, including the internalization of exernalities, gives the set of optimal prices for different transport modes.

Jansson introduces the concept of pricing relevant cost, equal to the marginal cost of the producer, the marginal change in average user cost multiplied by the quantity affected, and the external marginal cost. From this basic conceptual framework he derives optimal prices for two main different topics: public transport services (urban public transport and long distance public transport by rail and air) and infrastructure (urban and interurban road pricing).

Deregulation and privatisation policies have been applied widely in the transport sector. Britain is perhaps the country in which liberalization of transport industries has produced the broadest evidence to be contrasted with the expected results predicted by economists. Stephen Glaister offers a review of privatization and deregulation policies in the U.K. discussing the theoretical framework of these policies and offering an economic interpretation of the mixed results derived from their introduction.

Privatization and deregulation are not the same thing. It is possible to change the ownership structure of a regulated industry protected by legal barriers to entry. It is also possible to introduce competition in an industry with public and private companies coexisting. Glaister suggests that when people talk of competition they usually refer to competition in final product markets but competition in inputs markets is in his view at least as important. The promotion of competition in labour markets is according to Glaister the key to the success of deregulation.

Glaister reviews long distance coach deregulation and the privatization of British Railways, but the experience more deeply discussed in his paper is the deregulation of local bus services. British local bus service deregulation is particularly interesting because many cities and towns around the world have urban transport companies in a similar regulatory regime to that in Great Britain before 1986. The double experience of competition for the market (London) and competition in the market (Great Britain, London excepted) offers valuable information for other countries wanting to increase the efficiency and performance of their bus industries without incurring unnecessary risks. Glaister explains the economic results of both experiences and the lessons to be learnt.

Transport activities have associated with them serious negative effects (congestion, accidents, environmental damage) which are partly internalized by transport users and partly suffered by third parties. The share of these negative effects of transport borne by a different group of people from those that caused them are called **externalities**. The importance of externalities in transport, their valuation in theory and practice and the relevance of estimated values for policy decisions is the content of Chris Nash's paper.

Nash discusses the issue of whether congestion and accidents should be considered externalities. He concludes that the total cost of congestion and accidents cannot be accounted for as externalities. For congestion, the difference between marginal and average cost of congestion is the externality. In the case of accidents, for the vehicle to impose an externality requires the simultaneous presence of two conditions. Firstly, the accident would have been avoided, or its harmful effects reduced, in the absence of the vehicle in question. Secondly, some of the costs are paid by third parties.

In recent years, more attention has been paid to environmental effects. These are clear external effects in the case of noise and air pollution, and partly externalities in the case of land take, property destruction and the extraction of building materials.

Two different approaches are discussed by Nash in his paper. One is based on the measurement of the willingness to accept compensation for negative externalities or willingness to pay for positive externalities. The other is based on setting maximum levels of negative effects which must not be overcome. The standards are translated in money terms by means of an opportunity cost argument. Thus, if the externality is increased from one source, it must be reduced from another. The most cost-effective way of reducing the externality becomes the opportunity cost of additional emissions.

Nash describes the methods employed to value externalities and reviews some empirical work that shows totally different results in the valuation of the same external effects. Despite the difficulties in putting values on negative environmental impacts, Nash argues the importance of using monetary values for pricing, regulation and investment policy.

There are many investment decisions which are not taken in the private sector. This is particularly true in the case of transport, where road and railway networks, ports and airports have been built by the private sector but appraised and decided on by public agencies.

The economic evaluation of transport investment is well developed and is common practice. Despite its limitations, it has provided a sound way to compare costs and benefits to society as a whole, so introducing rationality into the public decision process. John Dodgson reviews this field in his paper **the economic appraisal of transport projects and policies**, discussing the theoretical foundations of social cost-benefit analysis, and presenting the main topics: shadow pricing, the valuation of non marketed goods, the determination of a social discount rate, how to deal with uncertainty and equity.

Once the principles and methods have been discussed, Dodgson illustrates their applications to highway investment projects and to different transport policies. The evaluation of road pricing, urban public transport subsidies and deregulation policy are assessed using the cost-benefit analysis framework.

Cost-benefit analysis has specific value as a tool in checking plans for public expenditures. As Dodgson points out if the rates of return which belong to a particular line of expenditure are systematically low, this suggest a change in the strategy of public expenditure priorities. This strategic role of cost-benefit analysis requires *ex post* evaluation of projects to allow the feedback from the appraisal of projects to the allocation of public funds.

The economics of transport and development is covered in the paper of Ken Gwilliam. Transport strategies for sustainable development of transitional and developing countries are considered. The idea is to broaden the scope of transport objectives in the design of transport projects. Economic rationality and a sound financial basis are considered necessary conditions for the development of broader sustainability. Gwilliam discusses the concept of sustainable development and its different dimensions when applied to transport.

The role of transport in economic growth is described, explaining the mechanisms through which transport contributes to economic growth. Several barriers to economically sustainable transport are identified in the paper (lack of maintenance, government intervention and lack of competition). Once the barriers are detected and analysed, Gwilliam discusses the role of private and public agencies in the provision of infrastructure and services.

6

The environmental and social dimensions of transport policy are treated with the recognition that the way in which these problems are perceived and the instruments to deal with them differ between the developing and developed world. The results of the analysis contained in this paper allow Gwilliam to discuss the key elements of the reform needed in developing countries to make the functioning of the transport system compatible with sustainable development.

References

Aschauer, D. A. (1989a): 'Is Public Expenditure Productive?'. *Journal of Monetary Economics*, 23(2), pp. 177-200.

Commission of the European Communities (1993): 'Trans-European Networks'. *Towards a Master Plan for the Road Network and Road Traffic* Directorate-General for Transport. Bruselas.

Gramlich, E. (1994): 'Infrastructure Investment: A Review Essay'. *Journal of Economic Literature,* Vol. 32, pp. 1.176-1.196.

Mohring, H. (1994): *The Economics of Transport*, Introduction, Edward Elgar, Vol I.

Munnell, H. A. (1992): 'How Does Public Infrastructure Affect Regional Economic Perfomance?' *Journal of Economic Perspectives*, Vol. 6, No.4, pp. 189-198.

Small, K. A. and I. Gómez (1994):'Road Pricing for Congestion Management: the Transition from Theory to Policy'. TRED conference, Lincoln Institute of Land Policy. Cambridge. Massachusetts.

Stern, N. (1991): 'The Determinants of Growth'. *The Economic Journal*, No. 101, pp. 122-133.

Winston, C. M. (1993): 'Economic Deregulation: Days of Reckoning for Microeconomist', *Journal of Economic Literature*, No. 31, pp. 1263-89.

Winston, C. M. (1985): 'Conceptual Developments in the Economics of Transportation: An Interpretative Study', *Journal of Economic Literature*, Vol. 23, March, pp. 57-94.

2 Forecasting travel demand and response

J. J. Bates

Introduction

Demand and supply

The notions of demand and supply are fundamental to economic theory, and it is natural for economists to apply them to particular contexts of interest. Within the field of transport economics, the terms are indeed widely used. Nevertheless, there are certain aspects of the transport problem which require demand and supply to be defined with rather more care than is generally the case in wider economic theory.

The aim of this paper is to throw some light on these issues while discussing the general points of demand forecasting. The paper is intended as a personal contribution, rather than a review, and for this reason contains only a limited number of direct references to other work. I must, nonetheless, acknowledge my indebtedness to a number of colleagues from whose work I have learnt much, both by direct collaboration and from their writings.

Questions of units

Economists can generally be fairly cavalier about units without encountering major problems. In particular, the units of time over which quantities are demanded and supplied are not usually relevant to the analysis: they can always be clarified when there is a specific need (for example, in making international comparisons). Nor is the **location** of consumption generally of great interest. Thus we may examine the equilibrium price of bananas without being too specific about where and over what period the consumption actually takes place.

With transport, on the other hand, both space and time are of the essence. And though statistics about aggregate travel demand (eg total annual vehicle-Km) may be produced, in themselves they tell nothing like the whole picture, since the **supply** considerations will depend precisely on where, and at what times, the demand occurs.

These issues are particularly important when we try to make forecasts, or introduce notions like elasticity. The elasticity of travel in urban areas is likely to be very different from that in rural, and the elasticity of peak travel different from that for off-peak travel. Further, when prices are assumed to vary either spatially or temporally, there are possible **substitution** effects, and these also affect the elasticities. What this implies, of course, is that, in addition to the issue of units, the variation of transport demand in space and time requires the notion of *ceteris paribus* to be carefully respected.

The underlying demand for travel

We must always remind ourselves that travel is a 'derived' demand. In other words, travel is not demanded *per se*, but as a consequence of the desire to partake in activities in different locations.

Since, in addition to costing money, travelling between different locations inevitably involves an expenditure of time, it has become standard in transport economics to deal with so-called 'generalised cost', which explicitly recognises both kinds of expenditure. In its simplest form, generalised cost is a linear combination of cost and time, the latter being converted to money units by means of the so-called 'value of time'. However, in wider formulations it can be represented by a multi-dimensional vector, capable of containing any variable which is likely to impact on travel decisions in the broadest sense. Thus it is a direct reflection of **indirect utility** (Deaton & Muellbauer, 1980).

Further, while certain aspects of the supply function do, of course, relate to the cost of providing services (whether it be the cost of highway infrastructure or a public transport service with a specified schedule), the **focus** of supply relationships in transport has very often been on the non-monetary items, and on time in particular. This is because many of the issues of demand with which transport analysts are concerned impinge on the **performance** of the transport system (in terms of travel times, waiting times, crowding etc.) rather than monetary costs.

This again is a reflection of the units question. While it might be of interest to consider the general question of the money cost of supplying different levels of national travel demand (in person-Kilometres, say), the particular problems that analysts are likely to address are localised in space and time. In various ways, the traveller can be insulated from the money costs associated with different levels of service: he cannot, however, be insulated from the time aspects.

Returning to the question of derived demand, there is a further issue as to whether travel should be conceived in terms of trips (journeys) or in terms of distance. In micro-demand terms it is more straightforward to conceive it in trips: this acknowledges the purpose of the journey (the associated activity) but does not require the journey to be confined to a particular location. This allows certain regularities to be exploited: for example, commuters tend to make the same number of trips to work in a week, even though the distances may differ greatly. From the supply side, however, the response is related to the volume of travel at different times and places, and is better conceived in terms of **flows** (past a point), or as loadings on particular

9

parts of the system, or as aggregate distances travelled. We will discuss the conflict between the units of demand and those of supply in the later sections of this paper

External influences on travel demand

Forecasts of Travel Demand require an appropriate set of input assumptions. Broadly speaking, these assumptions can be separated into two components: those that relate to the demographic composition of the population, together with other external changes (eg effects due to land-use, income, car ownership etc.), and those directly related to the transport system.

Both components, of course, need to be forecast, and both involve economic assumptions. However, the nature of the assumptions and the modelling implications are substantially different between the two components.

The population and land-use will vary over time, so that transport demand needs to be related to a particular point in time. In addition, there may be different views on how the future population and land-use will develop, so that different assumptions (often termed 'scenarios') may be conceived for the same year.

Fundamentally, of course, different persons have different basic demand for travel. For example, employed persons need to get to work, children need to get to school, retired people have more free time etc. In addition, as noted, different kinds of travel impact on the transport system in different ways, both in time and space. Because of the spatial implications, it is necessary to forecast not only how the number of different types of person will change over time, but also how they are located.

Hence, in estimating the level of travel demand, it is sensible to take reasonable account of this variation by person-type between areas, or 'zones': changes in the distribution of such person-types between the base and forecast year will have repercussions on total demand, as will changes in zonal populations. The demand model therefore has an essential input of external 'planning' data.

We can now consider what is known about these 'external' effects on total travel demand. It turns out that car ownership is a dominant factor.

Confining our attention first to trips, it is known that the most important categories influencing the level of personal trip making are age and employment status. However, looking at trips for **all purposes** by **all modes**, the variation is not large. For the general purposes of illustration we can use the four categories used in the START model of which an early description is provided in Bates *et al* (1991). These are:

1 children
2 employed adults
3 unemployed adults below retirement age
4 retired persons.

Based on data from the UK National Travel Survey, the approximate figures for trips per person per average week excluding weekend travel are:

Children 14	14	(12 - 15)
Employed Adults	18	(16 - 19)
Unemployed Adults	16	(14 - 17)
Retired	12	(9 - 12)

The figures in brackets show the variation between persons in households without cars and those in households with two or more cars. Thus, while car ownership does affect total trip making, it is not a major influence.

Except for the most aggregate kind of analysis, it is normal to distinguish travel by the purpose for which it is made. There are two main reasons for this. Firstly, there are institutional arrangements which lead to concentration of certain kinds of trips in time and space, of which peak hour commuting is only the most obvious example. Secondly, the sensitivity to changes in money costs and times etc. varies with trip purpose, in that certain kinds of travel are more or less mandatory (travelling to work) while others are more discretionary. It is standard practice to distinguish between Commuting trips, Business trips, and Other trips, and further distinctions (eg Education and Shopping) are often made.

In the context of the purpose for which trips are made, the variation by person type is much more important, of course. Of the 14 weekday trips made by children, about 6 are to and from school (NB this is an average over the whole year so the figures include an allowance for holidays), and of the 18 by employed adults, 7.5 are to and from work. As might be expected, these figures are hardly influenced at all by the level of car ownership. And while shopping trips vary with person type, for obvious reasons, there is little variation by car ownership.

On the other hand, trips on employers' business are significantly affected by car ownership: employed adults without a car make 0.65 trips a week, those in one-car households make 1.3 trips per week and those in multi-car households make 2.2 trips per week. And though these numbers are small, their above average journey length make them an important component of total travel.

The other purposes where car ownership effects are significant are Social and Recreational, and the general category of 'non-home-based' trips (movements between two places where neither is the home), which are of course greatly facilitated by the car ('trip chains'). In general terms, these are aspects of discretionary travel (as opposed to the mandatory elements of travel to work, education and (at least some types of) shopping). However, it should be borne in mind that the relative need for such kinds of trips could itself influence the level of car ownership, so that there is some circularity here.

Overall we may conclude that car ownership has some influence on the basic demand for trips, though the effect is not large. However, when we consider how the trips are made and **over what distance** they take place, the influence is much greater. These two aspects are, of course, interrelated, because trips by walk and cycle will not generally be made over long distances.

Figure 2.1, based on the same National Travel Survey data, shows how the number of trips made by non-mechanised modes changes with increasing car ownership: in all cases, while the total number of trips increases with car ownership, the number of those trips made on foot or by cycle falls. Since the cost of these non-mechanised trips is effectively zero, and their overall impact on the transport system is small, the economic consequences of car ownership on the transport system are much more important than the limited variation of trips by all modes might suggest. And when the trips are translated into **distance** travelled, the effects are even more marked.

Hence, a prerequisite for the estimation of travel demand is a forecast of the numbers of persons in (at least) each of the person-types referred to above, **cross-classified** by the level of car ownership. This is provided by the START model referred to above. A further useful categorisation is by the number of driving licence-holders in the households and by the individual licence-holding of each person type: this provides an indication of the level of access to the car within a household. A forecasting system which meets these additional requirements is the **Dutch National Model** (DVK, 1990).

These forecasts are, more or less, independent of the details of the transport system. As we shall discuss in the next Section, the level of car ownership varies in a consistent way with the level of urbanisation. Since many features of transport supply vary with the level of urbanisation (for example, the nature and extent of the public transport system, the road network density, the availability and cost of parking), it is reasonable to suppose that these factors may be affecting car ownership. There is, however, little or no evidence relating variation in car ownership to the **detail** of the transport network. For example, it is very difficult to adduce statistical evidence that an increase in public transport fares has a given influence on car ownership, though attempts have been made (see Goodwin, 1992 for a brief review).

In general, therefore, we refer to these basic forecasts of the demand for travel as **external**, based on a combination of demographics and car ownership. We shall consider the economic effects on car ownership in the following Section.

There is, of course, some debate about the extent to which the 'external' changes and the Transport changes really can be separated - in particular, transport changes may give rise to land-use changes, and, as just discussed, the demand for car ownership will be in some way conditioned by the availability and cost of travel opportunities. The majority of transport models **do** assume independence: however, there is a class of models termed 'land-use/transport interaction models' that attempt to link the two elements explicitly (see, for example, Simmonds (1987) and, for a detailed survey of recent work in this area, Webster *et al* (1988)).

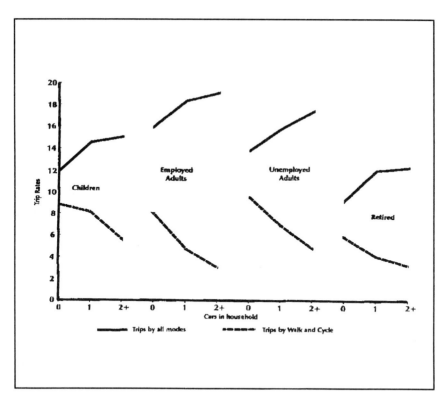

Figure 2.1   Variation in trip rates (all modes and non-mechanised only) by person type and household car ownership

The demand for car ownership

There is a large literature on the subject of car ownership, and many reviews are available (for example, de Jong (1989)): it is therefore not intended to provide a review here. Instead, some general principles will be enunciated.

In general, consumer durables are purchased for their use value, rather than *per se*. The demand for car ownership can be seen as a tradeoff between the additional accessibility conferred by the car and the costs of ownership, viewed in the light of available income. There are many ways in which this notion can be formulated, but the essential properties are clear, and can be illustrated along the following lines:

As was mentioned earlier, a standard convention of transport modelling is to make use of the concept of 'generalised cost' as a reflection of the disutility of travel. Thus we may write G_{ijm} as the generalised cost of travel between areas i and j, using mode m.

Assume a household living in area i. In general terms the household's utility from

13

travel will be dependent on the number of travel **attractions** X (which could be represented by employment opportunities, shopping floorspace etc.) at different generalised costs according to location. It is reasonable to define an 'accessibility index' A_i as

$$A_i = \Sigma_j X_j \, f(G_{ij})$$

where f is an appropriate declining function of G: a common assumption is to use a negative exponential form $\exp(-\lambda \, G_{ij})$. Thus A_i is an index of travel opportunities, weighted by the disutility of reaching them from the residential zone i. It will have a high value when there are many opportunities located close to i, and a low value when i is remote from the majority of opportunities.

We can give this simple concept some theoretical validity in terms of utility theory. Suppose that the (indirect) utility of a journey from i to j can be represented by the sum of the utility of the destination U_j and the (dis)utility of the travel from i to j U_{ij}. Recasting the accessibility index in these terms implies that

$$U_{ij} = -\lambda \, G_{ij}$$

and that the inherent attraction of the zone $U_j = \ln(X_j)$.

We now consider the modal effects. Suppose that there are three modes: 1 = walk/cycle, 2 = public transport, 3 = car. If we suppose in the first place that zone i is not served by public transport, then travellers in zone i without a car are **confined** to the 'slow' mode. Hence we write:

$$TU^{[1]}{}_{ij} = \ln(X_j) - \lambda \, G_{ij1}$$

where TU represents the 'total utility' (as usual, **indirect** utility) of the journey, and the [1] indicates that only the walk mode is available.

We now extend this to the case where the zone i is reasonably served by public transport. The general results of discrete choice theory suggest that we should substitute the appropriate **composite** generalised cost in this formula, and under reasonable assumptions we may write:

$$TU^{[12]}{}_{ij} = \ln(E_j) - \lambda \, G_{ij*[12]}$$

where the composite G is defined as:

$$G_{ij*[12]} = -1/\lambda \, \ln[S_{m=1,2} \exp(-\lambda \, G_{ijm})]$$

This is the well-known 'logsum' or 'inclusive value' used in hierarchical logit models (see, for example, Ben-Akiva & Lerman (1985)). Its properties imply that if public transport is **not** available, the value will be identical to G_{ij1}. Thus we view $TU^{[12]}{}_{ij}$ as a general measure of utility for persons without a car, **regardless** of whether public

14

transport is in fact available.

Finally, we consider someone who, in addition to slow modes and public transport, also has a car available. In an exactly comparable way we use the formula:

$$TU^{[123]}_{ij} = \ln (E_j) - \lambda\ G_{ij*[123]}$$

where the composite G is defined as:

$$G_{ij*[123]} = -1/\lambda\ \ln\ [S_{m=1,3}\ \exp (-\lambda\ G_{ijm}\ )\ ]$$

It can be shown theoretically that it is not possible for the composite Generalised Cost to **increase** as a result of more modes being available. The extent to which it decreases depends on both the value of λ and the relative performance of the added mode.

So far we have focussed on a single destination. We now need to extend the process, effectively by 'compositing' over all possible destinations available from a given origin. This again follows standard procedures, and we use the 'logsum' formula:

$$TU^{[K]}_{i*} = \ln\ [\ \Sigma_j\ \exp (TU^{[K]}_{ij})\ ]$$

where K represents the set of available modes.

[Note that on theoretical grounds it would be reasonable to insert an additional parameter, q say, to distinguish between the levels in the putative hierarchical structure relating to mode choice on the one hand and destination choice on the other. For expositional reasons we have omitted this complication.]

The additional utility gained from car ownership for residents at origin i can then be written as:

$$\Delta U[car]_i = TU^{[123]}_{i*} - TU^{[12]}_{i*}$$

and this can be re-written in a form which makes it directly interpretable as a **differential accessibility**:

$$\Delta U[car]_i = \ln A^{[123]}_i - \ln A^{[12]}_i$$

The fact that persons **without a car** will have different levels of accessibility from area to area is the primary reason for the locational variation in car ownership. It relates to (at least) a) the spatial concentration of opportunities and b) the alternative means of access to them, in particular the public transport provision.

The utility of this differential accessibility has then to be related to the underlying **need** for travel, and this, as noted in the previous section, is primarily a function of household structure, in particular the number of adults, the number of children, and the number of employed persons. Associated with this is the question of licence-holding, which is of course a pre-requisite for being able to **realise** the differential accessibility afforded by car ownership.

Finally, whether the utility of the differential accessibility is translated into car ownership will depend on the costs associated both with acquiring and with using the car, relative to available income. All this suggests that the **net indirect utility** of car ownership is a function of:

1 differential accessibility $\Delta U[car]_i$,
2 the costs associated with car ownership and use,
3 basic travel demand due to household structure, and
4 available income.

Models encapsulating these ideas have frequently been estimated on cross-sectional data relating to household car ownership, and demonstrate that the dominant influence is that of income. In most cases, however, the complexity of constructing the component $\Delta U[car]_i$ has led to the use of simpler indexes of 'urbanization', such as residential density, with little or no loss in explanatory power.

A further variant is to model car ownership and a broad indicator of car use (for example, annual Kilometres travelled) simultaneously, allowing car ownership to be partly influenced by the expected use to be made of the car. This approach has been used by Train (1986), de Jong (1989) and Hensher *et al* (1990) among others.

However, while these models of car ownership fit cross-sectional data well (in other words, they explain a considerable amount of the observed variation in car ownership levels), they do **not** typically predict more than about half of the observed growth over time. In other words, after taking account, as far as possible, of changes over time in the explanatory variables listed above, there remains some kind of 'trend' towards increasing car ownership.

It has proved generally difficult to introduce price terms into the models. Although on *a priori* grounds one would obviously expect them to influence demand for car ownership, it is difficult to find suitable datasets in which adequate variation in prices **over time** exists. It can certainly be said that there is no correlation between the **unexplained** growth over time and the movement of any general price indices relating to motoring. Thus it does not appear that the temporal stability would be improved by the inclusion of price effects.

The only way in which it has been possible to develop price effects on car ownership is by means of so-called 'car type' models, where the basic concept of 'car' is greatly expanded to consider engine size, age and other essential characteristics: an example is the work by Train (1986) cited above. However, while this level of detail can be significant in predicting **environmental** effects, it contributes little to the more general question of travel demand, where there is no strong reason to discriminate between different types of car.

The recent experience of the UK, which is reasonably in line with that of other Western European countries, is that the growth rate in cars per household has been about 2% p.a. Between 1976 and 1991 there was an overall growth of 29.3%, only 12.6% of which could be directly attributed to income growth, implying an income elasticity of 0.4. The fall in household size has actually had a negative effect on the growth of cars per household, amounting to - 6.8% over this period. The greatest effect turns out to be due to the shift in the function over time (instability), implying an increasing net indirect utility of car ownership, other things being equal: the UK data suggests that this effect is equivalent to an exogenous growth in cars per household of about 1.8% p.a.

Recent forecasts made by the UK Department of Transport (1989) envisage an annual growth rate in cars per household of just under 2% over the period 1986-2011.

Sensitivity of travel demand to changes in the transport system

Dimensions of travel categories

As noted, the majority of transport models assume that travel demand is a function of generalized cost and that any changes in the transport system can be represented by changes in the components of generalized cost between specific zones at specific times by specific modes.

In considering demand responses to changes in the transport system, there are two very different levels at which we can operate, depending on the objectives. One is at a more or less aggregate level, where the aim is to predict broad outcomes, such as the total passenger or vehicle Kilometres by different modes, possibly with some limited spatial information (eg urban *vs* rural). This may be useful for certain policy issues, in particular global pricing policies relating to fuel or public transport fares.

The majority of models, however, aim to recognise the spatial distribution of travel explicitly, by means of an appropriate system of zones. The modelling of 'demand' then implies a procedure for predicting what travel decisions people would wish to make, **given** the generalized cost of all alternatives. The decisions include choice of time of travel, route, mode, destination, frequency/trip suppression.

The various choices need to be linked together in an appropriate way. The usual approach is to set up 'choice hierarchies' making use of Discrete Choice theory. This allows the 'lower level' choices to made conditional on higher choices (for example, mode choice might be assumed to be conditional on the choice of destination) in a theoretically consistent way, ensuring sensible cross-elasticities. Such models have the property that the hierarchy of choices is defined so that the most cost-sensitive choices are at the **bottom**.

At any level in the hierarchy, the measure of generalized cost needs to reflect all the choices that are implicit beneath it. For this reason the **composite** cost is used for all levels, except the lowest, and is calculated according to the 'logsum' formula given earlier, which ensures that the choice process is consistent with theories of travel behaviour (see, for example, Ben-Akiva & Lerman, 1985).

Reactions to a change in generalized cost will differ according to the exact circumstances of the trip. Not only do people differ, but the same individual will react differently according to the purpose of the trip. In building a demand model, the modeller's task is to represent as much of this variation as is useful for the forecasting process. In general, this will depend on the use to which the forecasts will be put **and** the kind of policies which may be tested. For example, a demand model which needs to be sensitive to **large** price changes may well wish to distinguish between persons at different income levels: such a distinction will be less important if the policies largely relate to time savings (or losses).

The principal reasons for distinguishing categories of travel can be summarized as:

1 Variation in generalized cost formulation. Different purposes/person types may have, for example, different values of time, different resistance to walking, face different money costs (senior citizen/child concessions) etc; they may also have different overall sensitivities (elasticities).

2 Variation in choice sets. The alternatives available for certain choices may vary with purpose or person type: a particular, and well-known, example is the availability of the car mode depending on different levels of household car ownership.

3 Variation in hierarchy. Variation in the order in which the various travel choices should be structured is likely to be primarily due to purpose; for example, for commuting trips the choice of time of travel might be higher than the choice of mode, while being lower in the case of social trips. Similar arguments relate to the order in which mode choice and destination are dealt with. In principle, such variation could also apply to person types.

4 Sensitivity of output forecasts. Principally we are here concerned with **a)** the selective way in which different categories impact on the transport system (thus, we probably need to distinguish commuting because of its implications for peak travel as well as its journey length characteristics), and **b)** likely changes in relative contributions over time (for example, we may need to distinguish different leisure categories because of their different implications for growth). The need for such distinctions will occur particularly when the observed base pattern of travel differs between categories **and** the expected rates of growth are different: it is in such circumstances that aggregating categories will lead to the greatest errors.

In selecting the number of distinctions to make, there is a difficult balance between the requirements of consistency, which tend to push in the direction of greater disaggregation, and the quality of available information, which will typically not be sufficient to allow very fine distinctions to be made. A secondary consideration is whether excessive disaggregation will run up against computing constraints. A minimum requirement is probably to distinguish travellers by level of car ownership and a certain number of purposes (commuting, education, business, shopping and other). In addition, it will usually be necessary to make special arrangements for non-home-based movements.

We can write p for the purpose of the trip and k for the person characteristics that we wish to distinguish. In most cases, the demand model can be run **independently** for each traveller 'segment', so that the total demand is merely the sum of the demand from the individual segments {pk}. However, as will be clear from the preceding discussion, we do not estimate a single element of demand, but rather a matrix of elements. We now turn to the likely components of the matrix.

Dimensions of travel demand response

In order to represent the essential spatial component of transport, we will need to distinguish movements, at some level of detail, based on the area of origin and the area of destination, which we notate as i and j. As usual, the level of detail we actually recognise will depend on the use to which we put the result. The more we are concerned with detailed supply side response, which relates primarily to **networks**, the more detail we require about the location of the trip.

Since journeys are made by individuals, it is at the individual level that demand relationships are applied. However, the consequences of making a journey between i and j are different according to the **mode** that is used, which we notate as m. For a consistent account we are likely to need to distinguish at least the modes car, public transport and 'slow' (walk/cycle), and further subdivisions (eg between bus and rail) may be required in some cases.

Finally, there is increasing interest in distinguishing according to **when** the journey is made: we denote this by t. At the least a distinction between peak travel times and off-peak may be required: again, depending on the detailed requirements, much finer gradations may be used.

We may thus notate the general output of the demand model as T^{pk}_{ijmt}, without being explicit about the exact level of detail for each subscript and superscript. It will be clear from the above that an important determinant of detail is the level of application of the **supply** model. Although this is not directly the subject of this paper, we cannot avoid some of its implications, as we discuss later.

The distinction between the superscripts and the subscripts is that the subscripts relate to **choices** about travel that individuals may make. Since in general the selection of one {ijmt} option can be considered to be a rejection of others, there is an inherent interdependence between the elements of T^{pk}_{ijmt} for any given {pk} combination. It is this interdependence which is captured by the application of Discrete Choice theory.

An illustrative choice structure

For any given segment {pk}, we may consider that the **external** demand model described in Section 2 provides a base estimate of total trips (by all modes) generated from a given origin zone. Using the convention that an asterisk denotes summation

19

of the index whose place it takes, we may write this as T^{pk}_{i***}.

The extent to which this base total demand may be influenced by the costs of travel remains unknown: there is very little evidence for such an influence, and we may conclude that in any event it is small. However, we will assume that in theory at least there may be an effect, and we refer to it as a 'frequency' response.

The main travel choices which we are interested in are those of destination, mode and time of travel. For illustrative purposes we will assume the following hierarchy (notated F-D-M-T):

$$
\boxed{
\begin{array}{c}
\text{Frequency} \\
| \\
\text{Destination} \\
| \\
\text{Mode} \\
| \\
\text{Time of day}
\end{array}
}
$$

The description generally follows the approach of the START model (Bates *et al* (1991)). In order to construct the full demand matrix T^{pk}_{ijmt} we proceed as follows. We first take the generalized cost, which we write as C^{pk}_{ijmt}, for the lowest choice model (here assumed to be Time-of-Day). The generalized costs at the lowest level lead to an estimate of the proportion that choose time-of-day t, **given** origin i, destination j and mode m: we notate this as $p^{pk}_{t/ijm}$.

Assuming the standard **logit** formulation, we have:

$$p^{pk}_{t/ijm} = \exp(-\lambda^{pk}_T\, C^{pk}_{ijmt})/S_u \exp(-\lambda^{pk}_T\, C^{pk}_{ijmu})$$

This thus provides the estimate of the proportion of total travel in each time period, separately for each combination of origin, destination and mode, as a function of the costs in each time period.

As already noted, the general results of Discrete Choice theory show that we should make use of **composite** costs for all higher levels in the hierarchy. Because the composite cost at any level is in a sense a summation or average of the costs which lie beneath it, it is convenient to use the asterisk convention in this context also. Thus for example the cost element C^{pk}_{ij**} relates to the case where mode and time-of-day choices have already been considered, and would typically be the relevant measure for the consideration of Destination Choice.

Having dealt with the time-of-day choice, we require the appropriate composite cost for mode choice: this is C^{pk}_{ijm*}, given by the formula

$$\exp(-\lambda^{pk}_T\, C^{pk}_{ijm*}) = S_u \exp(-\lambda^{pk}_T\, C^{pk}_{ijmu})$$

Using a corresponding logit formula for mode choice, we obtain a new set of modal proportions $p^{pk}_{m/ij}$ and the composite cost C^{pk}_{ij**} for the next choice model, destination choice. In the same way, we go on to obtain the destination choice proportions $p^{pk}_{j/i}$, and composite cost $C^{pk}_{i\bullet\bullet\bullet}$. The process is illustrated in Figure 2.2.

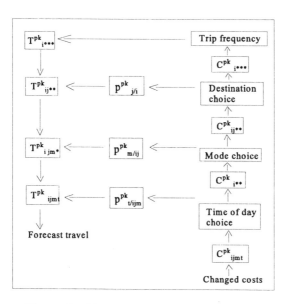

Figure 2.2   Illustrative hierarchical demand model

Finally, we reach the frequency model, where a simpler model may be more appropriate to modify the total base number of trips from origin i according to changes in the composite cost, to give a new estimate of total demand $T^{pk}_{i\bullet\bullet\bullet}$.

Once the top of the structure in Figure 2.2 is reached, the demand forecasts can be calculated, with increasing detail as we descend. First we combine the trip generations $T_{i\bullet\bullet\bullet}$ with the destination choice proportions $p_{j/i}$ to produce the **distribution** matrix $T_{ij\bullet\bullet}$. This is then combined with the modal split model $p_{m/ij}$ to produce the matrix of trips by mode $T_{ijm\bullet}$. Finally, these matrices are factored by the time of day proportions $p_{t/ijm}$ to give the full level of detail T_{ijmt}.

At the bottom, the full matrices for each purpose and person-type can be appropriately combined and passed to the supply model, as we discuss in a later section.

The elasticities implicit in such a model structure can be shown to depend on the relative values of the λ parameters that enter each level of the hierarchy, together with the tradeoffs between elements making up the generalised cost (in particular, the value of travel time). Note that with the hierarchy illustrated, it would be a structural requirement that $\lambda_T \geq \lambda_M \geq \lambda_D$, where the subscripts T M and D refer, respectively, to time of day, mode and destination choices.

Although the rigorous estimation of these parameters is a major task, there is now sufficient experience of the general properties of such models that reasonable 'default' values can be chosen. These then permit a reasonably straightforwardly 'calibration' to known sensitivities (for example, to available evidence on fuel price or public transport fare elasticities).

As an example of this, a recent modelling exercise in the London context for which the author had some responsibility implied the set of elasticities given in Table 2.1.

It can be seen that the overall own-elasticity for car petrol prices is -0.12, though there is considerable variation by purpose. For bus and rail, the own fares elasticity are, respectively, -0.46 and -0.41. These values will, of course, reflect the London context to which they apply.

Table 2.1
Cost elasticities from the 'APRIL' model

Policy compared with Base (10% increase in ..)	Mode	HBE d	HBE B	HB W	HBO	Overall incl NHB
pt fares	Car	+0.15	+0.07	+0.21	+0.14	+0.15
	Bus	-0.62	-0.36	-0.52	-0.48	-0.46
	Rail	-0.42	-0.16	-0.26	-1.02	-0.41
	MECH	-0.20	-0.01	-0.05	-0.14	-0.05
petrol costs	Car	-0.33	-0.00	-0.11	-0.10	-0.12
	Bus	+0.14	+0.08	+0.17	+0.07	+0.10
	Rail	+0.13	-0.03	+0.06	+0.06	+0.05
	MECH	-0.10	-0.00	-0.01	-0.05	-0.06

Source: The MVA Consultancy (1995)
Notes: The columns have the following interpretation:

HBEd: Trips between home and education
HBEB: Trips between home and Employers' Business
HBW: Trips between home and normal workplace
HBO: Trips between home and all other destinations
NHB: Trips between locations where neither is the home

The abbreviation 'MECH' refers to travel by mechanised modes, thus excluding walk and cycle trips

General considerations relating to the forecast of equilibrium in transport models

The motivation for forecasts

Although we have so far described the forecasting process as if its motivation was self-evident, the most likely reason for making forecasts is to assess different **policies**. The level of detail which we have outlined can be justified on two grounds: firstly, that the practical application of many policies is specific to certain elements of overall demand - for example, a policy imposing a surcharge on peak hour trips by road, or rail, and secondly, as already noted, that the **supply** effects are specific in space and time. For the purpose of evaluating the most global kinds of policy, such as changes in fare levels on public transport, or increases in motor fuel taxation, we **may** be able to dispense with some of the detail.

As a result of increasing concerns with congestion **and** environmental problems associated with high levels of transport activity, there has recently been a major change of emphasis in transport policy in the developed countries. Whereas earlier there was a concentration on infrastructure investment, predominantly outside the urban areas, there is now a general recognition that the external growth in demand is likely to be far higher than the ability to provide extra capacity. In any case, the possibilities of providing extra capacity in dense urban conditions have for a long time been very small, for a variety of social and physical reasons.

The result of this is a renewed emphasis on the topic of **managing** demand, and renewed interest in urban transport issues. A major component is the use of pricing policies for bringing about a better allocation of resources. The policy requirements lead in turn to the need for an enhanced understanding of supply-demand equilibrium.

Of course, **any** economic forecasting process implies an equilibrium between supply and demand. However, in many of the fields to which economic theory is applied, it is not necessary to devote much effort to the supply effects. This is because either the price can be assumed as given, on the basis of prevailing market conditions, or, in the case of taxation policies, it can be considered to be directly under the control of the relevant authority. In such circumstances, the forecasting process effectively begins and ends with the specification of the demand curve.

This is certainly not the case with most transport applications, and the reason is that while variations in demand probably do not have great impact on the supply price in direct **money** terms, the redefinition of the cost variable as **generalised cost** opens up the possibility of quite significant effects on non-monetary elements. The best known example is the effect of congestion on road travel times, but there are other areas within transport modelling where similar considerations apply.

Moreover, it is exactly in this area that the major **problems** for transport planners are encountered, problems which relate in general to system efficiency. The result is that an estimate of the demand curve alone is not sufficient for making forecasts in the majority of transport situations.

As noted above, however, it is only in the relatively recent past that the need for a full supply-demand equilibrium process has been widely acknowledged among transport planners. As long as the preoccupation of most transport planners was with infrastructure projects outside the urban context, it was generally thought acceptable to work with **fixed** demand, at a given point in time, although some aspects of supply were usually considered.

The recognition that the supply side also needs to be modelled has come about largely because of perceived need for changes in pricing policy, particularly in those areas where prices depart most from marginal social costs.

Thus while we have argued that in general economics it is often possible to make forecasts without explicitly modelling supply, the experience in transport planning has been precisely the opposite: apart from what we have termed the **external** effects on demand, demand has often been assumed fixed, and transport engineers have occupied themselves with supply issues (though they have not necessarily categorised them in that way).

The problems in modelling supply-demand equilibrium therefore need to be faced within the general topic of forecasting, and we must give some consideration to them in this paper. However, we cannot provide a complete treatment, since this is a major topic in its own right: a useful introduction is given in Chapter 11 of Ortúzar & Willumsen (1995).

Dealing with supply effects in transport models

Quite apart from the general issues of convergence common to all equilibrium processes, there are substantial issues of **interface** which need to be resolved when balancing demand and supply in the transport context. This is because the essential elements to which demand and supply relate are very different. Once again, this is a variant on the question of **units**.

In previous sections we have conceived the dimensions of demand essentially at the **person trip level**, and have allowed for differing response by purpose and person type, as well as allowing the travel choices to range over the indexes of origin, destination, mode and time of travel (ijmt). This appears unexceptionable: although there are certain 'linkages' which might be taken into account, both between trips and between, for example, persons within the same household, these can be viewed as extensions of the approach (even if in practice they may lead to considerable complexity). For a recent attempt to incorporate some of these linkages, see the SIMS model for Stockholm (Algers *et al* (1995)).

The dimensions of supply are very different. We can identify a number of crucial distinctions:

1 Supply models are not concerned with purpose or person-type distinctions.
2 At least as far as private transport is concerned, supply is concerned with **vehicle** rather than person movements (and to some extent this is true of public transport movements as well).

3 The details of origin and destination are only of concern inasfar as they impact on specific parts of the **network**: moreover, there is a whole dimension, relating to the links on chosen routes, which is crucial to the supply model but which plays virtually no rôle in demand forecasts.

If we notate this last dimension as l, then for each element of demand T^{pk}_{ijmt} there will be a set of chosen routes between i and j. For simplicity of exposition we will assume that there is in all cases a single best route, though the theory can deal with multiple routes at the cost of some additional complexity. In this case, we can define

e^{pk}_{ijlmt} = 1 if the journey from i to j uses link l,
= 0 otherwise.

To summarise, the demand model is **matrix**-based so that all calculations relate to individual i-j elements. The supply model is typically **link**-based so that the majority of calculations relate to individual links l. Hence an interface system is required in moving between Demand and Supply. In the next Section we sketch out the nature of the interface.

Essential aspects of the interface

For convenience and clarity we restrict the number of superscripts and subscripts in this section.

The demand model takes the cost C_{ij} as input and outputs a matrix of travel T_{ij}. The supply model takes, as input, link loadings or 'flows' F_l (that is, the volume of travel, measured in appropriate units, on a link of the transport network in a given period) and outputs new link costs C_l.

The interface in both directions is underlain by appropriate paths through the networks. We represent these by the quantity e_{ijl}.

Given the paths, there are two essential processes: **loading** the matrices T_{ij} to produce flows F_l, and '**skimming**' the costs C_l to produce the costs C_{ij}. We can represent this in the following figure:

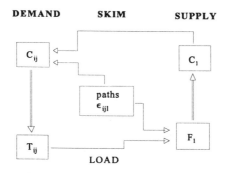

25

For any component of demand we will have a number of procedures:

Minimum Path. This procedure provides a defined path for each component in each time period by each mode and for each zone pair, thereby yielding e^{pk}_{ijlmt}. Underlying this is a generalised cost specification relevant to demand segment {pk}, a network appropriate to time period t {lt}, and the times and money costs (etc.) on the links {C_{lt}}.

Accumulate Matrix. Given an estimate of T^{pk}_{ijmt} from the Demand model, the aim of this procedure is to produce a total trip matrix (**vehicles**, in the case of highway), for each time period t: we refer to this as V_{ijt}.

$$V_{ijtm} = \Sigma_{pk}\, T^{pk}_{ijmt} / Occ^{pk}_{t}$$

where Occ is a correction for vehicle occupancy.

Load. This loads the matrix V_{ijt} to its appropriate set of links, thereby producing the flows F_{lt}.

$$F_{lt} = \Sigma_i \Sigma_j\, V_{ijt} \cdot \epsilon_{ijlt}$$

Skim. This cumulates the costs along the path in order to obtain the cost matrix for the Demand procedure.

$$C^{pk}_{ijmt} = \Sigma_l\, C^{pk}_{ltm} \cdot \epsilon^{pk}_{ijlmt}$$

Between procedures Load and Skim the Supply model is invoked. In practice there may be other aspects of the interface required for the Supply model, but the aim here is merely to sketch out the salient points. On the highway side this involves converting person trips between zones, for a number of segments, into vehicle flows on links. The link costs are then modified to reflect supply constraints, in particular the way travel times deteriorate as flows approach capacity. A readable description of the standard approach to this problem is given in Chapter 10 of Ortúzar & Willumsen (1994).

In practice the pure link elements (journey time etc.) will not vary with segment. However, the way these elements are combined to produce generalised cost is segment-specific, since the relative weights placed on different elements will vary with journey purpose and person-type.

An outline of the generalised cost specification

The formulae given here are intended only to be indicative of general modelling practice in this area. In the example the generalised cost is assumed to be given in units of **time**.

For **public transport** modes, a typical approach might be

$$C^{pk}_{ijmt} = f_{ijm}/v^{pk} + t_{ijmt} + w^{pk}_1 . w_{ijmt} + w^{pk}_2 . E_{ijmt}$$

where: f_{ijm} is the ordinary single fare (in pence)
t_{ijmt} is the in-vehicle travel time (mins)
W_{ijmt} is the waiting time (mins)
E_{ijmt} is the access/egress time (mins)
v^{pk} is the value of in-vehicle time savings (p/m)
w^{pk}_1 is the weighting for waiting time
w^{pk}_2 is the weighting for access/egress time

For the **car and commercial vehicle (CV)** modes, we require a function along similar lines:

$$C^{pk}_{ijmt} = (X^{pk}_{ijt} + P^{pk}_{jt} + Z_{ijt})/O^p/v^{pk} + w^{pk}_2 E_{jt} + w^{pk}_3 . S_{jt}$$ where the notation is as before, and additionally:

S_{jt} is the parking search time (mins),
P^{pk}_{jt} is the parking cost (pence),
O^p is the vehicle occupancy, and
X^{pk}_{ijt} is the sum of operating costs over each link l on the route.

Some of the elements in these formulae are fixed, while others are generated by the supply functions within the model. The modeller will decide which supply functions to implement in particular contexts, but some recent examples of urban applications in the UK have made use of supply functions affecting:

1 in-vehicle time for highway modes
2 parking search time for cars
3 waiting time for bus and rail
4 level of crowding on rail

Public transport operator response

The autonomous network responses to different levels of traffic are reasonably well understood. Congested conditions on the highway will affect public transport services which have to share the highway with other vehicles, leading not only to extended journey times but also to 'bunching' of vehicles as the regular frequency of the service is disrupted, with consequent unpredictable waiting times. Mechanisms have also been devised to reflect these phenomena (see for example Frerk (1984)).

Ultimately, however, the public transport operator has to respond in the light of the market situation and the institutional framework. While much work has been done of a global nature in constructing models of competition (for example, Evans (1987)), it is much more difficult to build such relationships into a supply-demand equilibrium. Two attempts, at somewhat different levels of detail, are the 'Glaister Model' (Department of Transport, 1982) and the London Area Model (Oldfield (1993). It is interesting briefly to consider the contributions made by these models. In both cases, however, they assume that public transport services are provided by a monopoly supplier operating under second-best conditions with some public subsidy.

Given a change in demand for public transport, the operator's response is likely to depend on capacity considerations. In general terms, rail systems behave rather differently from bus systems. The heavy capital costs of rail systems mean that small changes in service frequency can be achieved at relatively low marginal cost, except when the system is near capacity. In this latter case, the operator can either raise prices, to drive away additional demand, or allow crowding levels to rise (which will also have **some** downward influence on demand). Bus operators, on the other hand, have much greater flexibility to increase capacity, but the marginal operating costs are relatively high.

The Glaister model took absolute levels of subsidy as fixed, and examined the optimum combination of changes in service frequency and changes in fare, with the aim of maximising passenger benefit. The London Area Model followed similar lines, but allowed the modeller to test the effects of different operator responses - for example, increasing services in line with demand, or changing fare levels to achieve a fixed margin between operating costs and revenue.

Both these models fell foul of political considerations at a time when the UK Government was trying to bring about major institutional changes in public transport operation, and, in particular, to reduce levels of subsidy. As a result of the experience, this has been little enthusiasm for revisiting the topic within equilibrium models, and the usual assumption is that fares and services will **not** respond to changes in demand in the short term. However, this is a less than satisfactory situation, and it is to be hoped that there will be renewed interest in the financial conditions facing public transport operators and their consequent response to changes in demand.

We may conclude this Chapter with a diagrammatic description of the key elements determining the supply-demand equilibrium: see Figure 2.3.

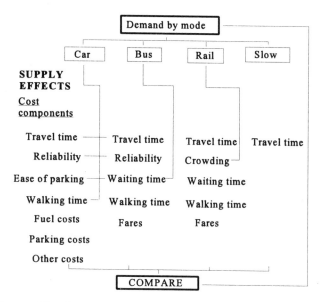

Figure 2.3   **Key factors in supply-demand equilibrium**

Conclusions

We have discussed the various elements that are required in making forecasts of the demand for transport. We conclude by illustrating the processes in a series of highly simplified diagrams.

We need to begin with a known level of 'generalised' transport activity assumed to be in equilibrium. If we can represent this by some suitable aggregate, such as person-Km of travel, we have a base estimate of demand. Then, on the basis of known data about costs and public transport service levels, together with appropriate supply models to provide the non-monetary components of generalised cost, we can determine the overall unit cost (eg, per person-Km) associated with the base point. This is shown in Figure 2.4.

Of course, the details of the simplification to a single aggregate dimension will be specific to the transport situation we are considering: the relation can be expected to be very different for a largely rural region as opposed to a dense conurbation. But while this will affect the shapes of the curves, and hence the sensitivities, it does not invalidate the overall description.

The next stage is to construct the demand curve, assuming fixed population, car ownership etc., as a function of unit generalised cost. It should be clear from the preceding discussion that such a demand curve needs to take account of all the main

29

responses to changes in generalised cost, hence allowing for changes in mode, destination, time of day etc. Since the levels of population etc. are assumed to be those compatible with the base position, the curve must pass through the point of equilibrium. This is shown in Figure 2.5.

Underlying such a model system in the base is, of course, a very large amount of detail along the lines described in this paper, relating to different types of person, household, journey purpose, and the representation of the transport system itself. The construction of the model is a substantial task. However, except for the most straightforward types of policies, having more or less global application, we have argued that such a system is needed for forecasting travel demand and response.

Actually to make the forecasts we now proceed at two levels. First, we take account of the expected external changes affecting the basic demand for travel (eg changes in household structure, employment, car ownership and spatial patterns) - this leads to a new demand curve, which in itself will imply a new equilibrium point (assuming, for the moment, no change in supply conditions). Note that unless the supply curve is horizontal in the base, the change in demand will itself be associated with a change in generalised cost, reflecting, for example, that increased car ownership will lead to more congestion.

Secondly, we introduce the 'policy' changes in the transport system. This leads to a modification of the supply curve reflecting price changes, network changes (including new infrastructure), changes in public transport frequency, changes in parking capacity etc. The combination of the changed demand curve and the changed supply curves yields the new forecast, as shown in Figure 2.6. In reality, of course, this forecast will be a large array of variables, representing the travel by different types of person at different times of day on different parts of the network.

The experience of the last ten years, greatly aided by recent quantum leaps in computing power, has allowed such systems to be developed in flexible ways. As a result a much greater range of policies can be tested in a consistent and informative way.

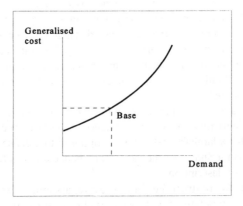

Figure 2.4   **Original equilibrium point and supply curve**

30

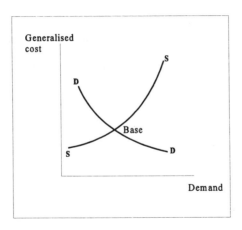

Figure 2.5   Base equilibrium system

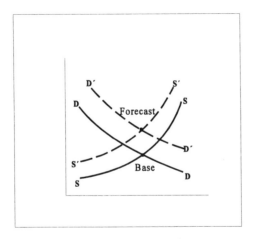

Figure 2.6   Forecasting with changed demand and supply

References

Algers S, Daly A J, Kjellman P & Widlert S (1995), 'Stockholm Model System
(SIMS): Application'. Paper presented at the 7th World Conference on Transport
Research, Sydney 1995.

Bates J J, Brewer M, Hanson P, McDonald D & Simmonds D C (1991), 'Building a
Strategic Model for Edinburgh', PTRC Summer Annual Meeting, Transportation
Planning Methods Seminar.

Ben-Akiva M E & Lerman S R (1985), *Discrete Choice Analysis: Theory and*

Application to Travel Demand, MIT Press.

Deaton A & Muellbauer J (1980), *Economics and Consumer Behaviour*, Cambridge University Press.

Department of Transport (1982), *Urban Public Transport Subsidies: An Economic Assessment of Value for Money*, LPT1 Division, London.

Department of Transport (1989), *National Road Traffic Forecasts (Great Britain) 1989*, HMSO.

DVK (1990), *Het Landelijk Modelsysteem Verkeer en Vervoer (Modelbeschrijving), Rapport C: Methoden en Modellen, Concept Versie*, Rijkswaterstaat, Dienst Verkeerskunde (DVK), August 1990, The Hague.

Evans A (1987), 'A Theoretical Comparison of Competition with Other Economic Regimes for Bus Services', *Journal of Transport Economics and Policy*, Vol. XXI, No.1, pp. 7-36.

Frerk M Y (1984), *The Disaggregated Strategic Model*, London Transport Executive, Group Planning Office TN 159.

Goodwin P B (1992), 'A Review of New Demand Elasticities with Special Reference to Short and Long Run Effects of Price Changes', *Journal of Transport Economics and Policy*, Vol. XXVII, No. 2, pp. 155-163.

Hensher D A, Milthorpe F W and Smith N C (1990), 'The Demand for Vehicle Use in the Urban Transport Sector', *Journal of Transport Economics and Policy*, Vol. XXIV, No.2, pp. 119-137.

de Jong G C (1989), *Some Joint Models of Car Ownership and Use*, PhD Thesis, Department of Economics, Universiteit van Amsterdam.

The MVA Consultancy (1995), *London Congestion Charging Study - Main Report*, HMSO, London.

Oldfield R H (1993), *A Strategic Transport Model for the London Area*, Transport Research Laboratory Research Report 376, Crowthorne.

Ortúzar J de D & Willumsen L G (1994), *Modelling Transport* (Second Edition), Wiley.

Simmonds D C (1987), 'Theory and Applications of a Land-use/Transport Interaction Model', in Young W (ed), *Proceedings of the International Symposium on Transport, Communications and Urban Form*, Monash University, Australia.

Train K E (1986), *Qualitative Choice Analysis: Theory, Econometrics and an Application to Automobile Demand*, MIT Press.

Webster F V, Bly P H & Paulley N J (eds), *Urban Land-Use and Transport Interaction, Report of the International Study Group on Land-Use/Transport Interaction (ISGLUTI)*, Avebury.

Williams I N & Bates J J (1993), 'APRIL - A Strategic Model for Road Pricing', PTRC Summer Annual Meeting, Seminar D.

3 Recent developments in cost function research in transportation

Tae Hoon Oum and W.G.Waters II

Introduction

The analysis of costs has been a central feature of transport economics since its inception. The earliest writers on railway transportation pondered the various costs associated with rail transportation and the problem of pricing the myriad of services being provided in a way which would sustain the enterprise (Lardner, 1850). But early writers were constrained due to limited knowledge of costs. More specifically, they had little knowledge about the extent to which costs varied with levels and varieties of output. The consensus was that large portions of rail costs were fixed or unallocable. As late as the 1920s, it was still thought that at least half of rail costs did not vary with traffic volumes (Ripley, 1921, discussed in Clark 1923).

Because a substantial portion of costs were deemed not to vary with traffic volumes, it was expected that marginal cost pricing would not be financially viable. This raised the whole question of how to price multiple products in the presence of unallocable costs. What we would call transport economics was the early literature on 'railway rate theory'; it was regarded as a separate branch of economics since it dealt with the theory of price setting based on demand factors as well as cost considerations, i.e. the problems of allocating joint and common costs.[1]

Over time, analysis of costs revealed closer links between volumes of rail activity and levels of costs, i.e., costs were not as fixed as had been thought previously. This was especially true as new transport modes arose where fixed investments such as railway track were less important. In addition to the problem of cost variability was the ability to separate costs among multiple outputs. In the literature on railway rate theory and overhead costs, this was essentially a pricing problem rather than a matter for costing. The standard measure of output (ton-miles) was always recognized as highly aggregative hence, in some cases, misleading. The ambiguity of measuring 'output' in transportation has been a long-standing controversy, from the Pigou-Taussig debate early in this century, to more recent authors notably Wilson (1962) (see also Waters, 1980, and more recently Jara-Diaz, 1982a, 1983, 1996). A major

33

advance in formulating cost functions is the explicit recognition of multiple outputs and the ability to estimate multiple parameters as well as other properties of multi-output cost functions such as complementarities or scope economies (see especially Baumol, Panzar and Willig (1982, 1977, 1981)). Estimation of multiple output cost functions are a major part of modern economic analysis of transportation costs.

Today, journals regularly contain empirical cost functions for transportation and other industries. This review concentrates on the developments in transportation cost functions over the last 15 years or so. There are some previous surveys. Walter's (1963) survey of econometric methods for production and cost functions remains a solid starting point for the theoretical and econometric issues in cost and production functions; McFadden (1978) is a more recent overview of the theory. The two most important and relatively recent reviews of transportation cost functions would be Jara-Diaz (1982a) and the brief review in Winston's survey of transportation economics (Winston, 1985).[2] Many researchers provide concise summaries of cost function developments as background to their specific papers; these have been very helpful in assembling this review. The continued advancement and proliferation of empirical cost studies in transportation suggests that a review of these developments would be useful.

The rest of the paper is organized in four main sections. Section 2 describes purposes of empirical cost measurement. An overview of the evolution and recent developments in transportation cost functions is given in section 3. The methodological issues for estimating cost functions for measuring key parameters for cost structure such as economies of scale, density and scope are treated in section 4. Section 5 discusses the recent developments in measuring and comparing productive efficiency via cost function estimation including frontier cost (production) functions. Finally, section 6 contains a summary and concluding remarks.

Purposes of empirical measurement of transportation costs

The long history of cost analysis in transportation is motivated by several purposes; these can affect what is measured and how. Aside from academic curiosity, the interest in cost analysis is motivated primarily by the implications for making decisions, either by transportation firms or, more often, implications for government policies regarding the industry. Most decisions require some analysis of costs. Estimates of the costs of handling and transporting individual traffic are needed for the myriad of individual pricing/service decisions made by transportation firms. If prices are regulated, regulatory agencies will also need cost estimates for specific services. Estimates of costs may be needed for determining whether a route is financially viable. Such cost analysis for parts of a firm's overall operations we refer to as *disaggregate costing*.[3]

In contrast to estimating the costs of specific movements, there has long been interest in the broader cost structure of the industry, notably whether or not there are economies of scale. These are important for assessing the feasibility of competition between firms of different size, and long run equilibrium industrial organization of an industry. Will mergers produce efficiency gains? Where scale economies are prominent, regulation may be necessary and issues of financial viability of regulated monopoly arise because efficient pricing (at marginal costs) will lead to financial deficits.

Another major purpose of estimating cost functions is to measure and compare productive efficiency across firms or over time. Many specific factors could explain why one firm's unit costs and/or observed productivity can differ from another's, or why unit costs or observed productivity might change differently between firms over the years. Since some of these factors are beyond managerial control, estimated cost or production functions are used to remove the effects of those variables from the observed unit cost or productivity in order to identify pure differences or changes in productive (and managerial) efficiency.

For identifying broad cost/production structure and/or measuring productive efficiency, transport researchers normally use firm-specific aggregate data on costs, output measures and other variables, hence the label *aggregate cost functions*.[4] The distinction between aggregate and disaggregate costing is important because these approaches to cost analysis have evolved quite separately. However, this survey confines itself only to recent developments in aggregate cost functions based on firm-specific data.

Development and analysis of aggregate cost functions

The majority of academic research on transportation cost analysis has focused on aggregate costing: the total costs of a firm are related to measures of total output, along with other variables influencing costs including input prices, output attributes, network or other firm-specific characteristics.

Before turning to the use of transportation cost functions, this section provides a brief review of the origins of empirical cost functions in transportation and a summary of important conceptual and econometric developments which have influenced the development of cost function research over the last twenty five years or so. These include the distinction between economies of scale and economies of density, the introduction of flexible functional forms, the specification and treatment of multiple outputs in transportation cost functions, the use of pooled cross-section and time-series data for estimating cost functions, and issues of data quality. Subsequent parts of the paper review specific recent empirical contributions and advances in cost function analysis.

The origins and refinements of aggregate cost functions

The origins of empirical cost functions grew out of rail cost analysis. The railroads preceded other transport modes, and because they were regulated, they became a source of publicly-available data, at least in the United States. Because railroads were a multi-product industry with attendant ambiguity in linking costs with output, this stimulated management, regulators and academics to explore ways of measuring cost-output relationships. Further, the question of scale economies – which was the central economic justification for regulation or public control over railways – was a major focus in the analysis of cost functions.

The earliest aggregate cost analysis of railways related total operating cost per gross ton mile (GTM) to GTM per mile of track (see Lorenz, 1916, which was re-examined in Clark's classic work, 1923). It is noteworthy that this earliest formulation saw traffic density as being an important determinant of unit costs. The earliest explorations also recognized that average length of haul would affect cost-output relationships (Lorenz, 1916, noted by Clark, 1924).

The early formulation of relating unit cost to output per mile of track was carried forward in the analysis of costs used by the Interstate Commerce Commission (ICC). The basic formulation adopted was TOC/MT = a + b GTM/MT where TOC is total operating costs and MT is miles of track. The ICC used this equation to calculate a 'percent variable' which was then used to develop estimates of unit costs of rail operations, i.e., the percent variable times total costs, divided by output, was taken as a measure of average variable (and marginal) costs. This formulation has been a major influence on rail cost analysis in the United States despite substantial criticism of the practice of dividing by miles of track (Meyer, et al., 1959 and Griliches, 1972).

The rail industry itself largely adopted linear functions applied on a disaggregate basis to portions of rail operations (e.g., see Appendices in Meyer, et al., 1959, and Stenason and Bandeen, 1965). One of the earliest econometric analyses (see also Klein, 1953) was Borts' (1952 and 1954) estimation of rail production functions for switching and line-haul operations. He used production functions rather than cost functions but he also published a thorough review of the problems involved in estimating cost functions (Borts, 1960). But industry and the ICC persisted in the use of linear cost functions.

An important break from linear cost functions for railways was put forth by Keeler (1974). He derived cost functions from Cobb-Douglas production functions for passenger and freight services for the U.S. railroads, and estimated the derived cost functions. His work was followed by Harris (1977) who introduced the following linear cost function which allows one to measure both economies of density and economies of longer haul. He estimated the following cost function for the Class I railroads in the US:

$$C = B_o \ RTM + B_1 \ RFT + B_2 \ MR \tag{1}$$

where C is firm's total cost, RTM is revenue-ton-miles, RFT is revenue freight tons, and MR is route miles. By dividing this cost function through by *RTM*, one obtains the following interesting equation:

$$AC = B_o \ + B_1 \ (1 \ / \ \text{average length of haul}) + B_2 \ (1/ \ \text{traffic density}) \tag{2}$$

This captures the influences of density and length of haul but shows no influence of scale per se. Although this form is convenient to obtain the effects of average length of haul and traffic density on average cost (AC), it remains a linear function and thus, constrains marginal costs of RTM, RFT or MR at constant values. Although Harris was careful not to include in his sample any railways which carry a significant amount of passengers, his formulation can not be modified easily to treat firms with two or more outputs (passengers and freight); more on output measures shortly.

There were other formulations of aggregate cost functions for railways, as well as for other modes. Cobb-Douglas, or equivalently, log-linear functions (i.e., linear model with variables transformed into natural logarithms) were used in numerous transport cost work including Nerlove (1961), Keeler (1964), Koenker (1977), Good et al (1993). It is well known that the log-linear function is restrictive in that elasticities of cost with respect to its arguments are constant at all ranges of the data, as well as limiting elasticities of substitution at unity. Particularly, the log-linear model constrains the degree of increasing (or decreasing) returns to scale to remain unchanged between very small and very large firms.

Distinguishing between returns to scale and returns to traffic density, and re-thinking the measurement of economies of scale

Contrary to the belief of many practitioners at the time, empirical researchers of transportation costs began to question the existence of returns to scale. This is important because if scale economies were not present, this undermined the traditional rationale for regulation of inevitable monopoly due to increasing returns to scale.

The debate was sharpened by the distinction between economies of scale and density. Papers making this distinction most clearly were Caves, Christensen and Swanson (CCS: 1981), and Caves, Christensen, Tretheway and Windle (1987) for railways and Caves, Christensen and Tretheway (1984) for airlines. Returns to Traffic Density (RTD) referred to the impact on average cost of expanding all traffic, *holding network size constant*, whereas Returns to Scale (RTS) refers to the impact on average cost of equi-proportionate increases in traffic *and* network size. More specifically, CCS distinguishes Returns to Traffic Density and Returns to Scale as follows:

$$\text{RTD} = \frac{1}{\sum_{i}^{m} \epsilon_{Y_i}^{C}} \tag{3}$$

$$\text{RTS} = \frac{1}{\sum_{i}^{m} \epsilon_{Y_i}^{C} + \epsilon_{N}^{C}} \tag{4}$$

where $\epsilon_{Y_i}^{C}$ is the elasticity of cost with respect to output Y_i, and ϵ_{N}^{C} is the elasticity of cost with respect to network size. There are increasing returns to density (i.e., average cost decreases as traffic density increases) if the sum of output (Y_i) cost elasticities is less than unity. Most empirical studies supported the existence of increasing RTD. There were economies of scale if the sum of output cost elasticities plus the cost elasticity with respect to network size (N) was less than unity. Their studies showed increasing returns to density but the estimated returns to scale was not significantly different from unity.

Evidence of the absence of economies of scale was confirmed in many other empirical studies for various modes e.g., Keeler (1974), Harmatuck (1981) and Wang and Friedlaender (1984) for trucking; Keeler (1972), Douglas and Miller (1974), Caves, Christensen and Tretheway (1983), Gillen, Oum and Tretheway (1985) for the air mode; Gillen and Oum (1984) for bus mode. These and earlier studies (e.g., see the review in Winston, 1985) were influential in calls for deregulation of transportation. For the most part subsequent studies confirm the early findings of constant returns to scale (Table 3.2, below).

However, the measurement of economies of scale from transportation cost functions has come under re-examination recently. Traditionally, multi-product scale economies has been measured by the reciprocal of the sum of cost elasticties with respect to output, as in Caves, et al. (1981, 1984, 1987) cited above. Gagne (1990) questioned the measurement of scale economies in trucking noting that there were interrelationships among arguments of the cost function hence limiting the calculation of scale economies to the sum of partial cost-elasticities of output categories was incomplete. This issue was further discussed by Ying (1992). Xu, et al. (1994) provided further empirical analysis of scale economies which showed statistically that output and market characteristics change with firm size, and they incorporated the elasticities with respect to these characteristics in computing returns to scale.

A more rigorous reconsideration of the question of measuring scale economies is Jara-Diaz and Cortes (1995, 1996). Building on earlier formulations of transportation output and cost functions (Jara-Diaz, 1982a, 1982b, 1983 and 1988), they point out that all transportation cost functions work with highly aggregative measures of output and other attributes, in contrast to the precise notions of output in the theory of cost functions. The appropriate measure of economies of scale requires explicit analysis of the output measures along with output attributes such as length of haul, average load, etc. The behaviour of total costs with respect to proportional changes in all outputs (the definition of economies of scale) will be measured as a weighted sum of the (reciprocal of) elasticities of the cost function, where the weights depend on aggregation properties of the various arguments of the cost function. For example, Jara-Diaz and Cortes argue that the elasticity of costs with respect to average length of haul should *not* be included in calculating scale economies because this is already captured by the elasticities with respect to the individual outputs. On the other hand, changes in average load may be relevant in calculating the total cost elasticity depending on firms' practice at increasing load relative to frequency of service as output expands (Jara-Diaz and Cortes, 1996, p.164-5). However, Oum and Zhang (1996) point out that Jara-Diaz and Cortes explicitly ignore network changes in their analysis, but this would make changes in length of haul relevant. As a result, Oum and Zhang argue that Jara-Diaz and Cortes' calculations actually measure economies of density rather than scale. Nonetheless, Jara-Diaz and Cortes' analysis indicates that measures of economies of scale from previous studies need to be reexamined to ensure proper measurement and interpretation.

Flexible functional forms

Probably the most widely recognized innovation in cost function research was the introduction of so-called *flexible* functional forms. From the early 1970s, mainline economics journals began to publish empirical papers using flexible functional forms such as the generalized Leontief function proposed by Diewert (1971), the translog function proposed by Christensen, Jorgenson and Lau (1971 and 1973), the quadratic mean of order-r functions (Denny, 1972, 1974) and the generalized Cobb-Douglas function (Diewert, 1993). The translog function quickly proved to be the most popular, probably because it is easier to estimate and interpret as it is a quadratic function with all arguments in natural logarithms. The disadvantage of the translog and other flexible functions is the large number of coefficients to estimate. For this reason, it can only handle a few categories of outputs and other variables.[5]

The translog cost function for the case of m outputs and n inputs can be written as:

$$
\begin{aligned}
\ln C = a_0 &+ \sum a_i \ln Y_i + \sum b_j \ln W_j \\
&+ \frac{1}{2} \sum \sum a_{ij} (\ln Y_i \ln Y_j) \\
&+ \frac{1}{2} \sum \sum b_{ij} \ln W_i \ln W_j \\
&+ \sum \sum d_{ik} \ln Y_i \ln W_k
\end{aligned}
\tag{5}
$$

where C is total cost, Y_i is *i*th output, and W $_k$ is *k*th input. Normally, symmetry conditions on the second-order parameters are imposed on estimation. The translog cost function is estimated jointly with the cost-minimizing input cost share functions, typically for labour, energy, capital, and 'other purchased services and materials' (normally referred to simply as 'materials') in order to improve efficiency of estimation.

Note that the first line of the expression (5) corresponds to a Cobb-Douglas or log-linear specification. That is, if all of the second-order coefficients are zeros (are statistically insignificant), the equation reduces to the simpler Cobb-Douglas form. The second-order terms allow for possible cross-relationships among the variables, and for possible non-linearities in the relationships between cost and the variables. The *flexible* functions have desirable properties for empirical work in that they are capable of providing a quadratic approximation to an unknown form of a true twice continuously-differentiable function.[6] Furthermore, they allow for free variation of elasticities, including cost elasticities with respect to outputs, and elasticities of substitution. Therefore, the translog allows for economies of traffic density, scale, and scope, to be dependent on the data point at which they are evaluated.

Brown, Caves and Christensen (1979),[7] Oum (1977, 1979), Spady (1979), Spady and Friedlaender (1978), and Friedlaender and Spady (1980) were the first to use translog functions for transport cost and/or demand modelling. Since then numerous studies have estimated translog cost functions. Other early examples include Caves, Christensen and Swanson (1981a, 1981b) and Friedlaender and Spady (1981) for rail cost studies, Gillen and Oum (1984) for intercity bus cost function, Caves, Christensen and Tretheway (1980, 1983), and Gillen, Oum and Tretheway (1985) for airline cost functions, and Harmatuck (1981), Friedlaender, Spady and Wang Chiang (1981) and Wang and Friedlaender (1984) for motor carrier cost functions Today it is an exception when a cost function does not employ a translog formulation.

Output specification and output attributes

From the earliest research, the multiproduct nature of transportation hampers a proper specification of cost functions. The most common measure of ton-miles has obvious shortcomings in that it assumes that the cost of moving one ton over hundred miles is identical to that of transporting 100 tons over one mile. The single product aggregate approach results in biased estimation of the indicators of cost structure such as the degree of scale economies, unless all components of the output vector vary equi-proportionally (see Griliches, 1972; Panzar and Willig, 1977; and Jara-Diaz, 1982a,b). The ideal response is to incorporate a number of output measures, although data and computational constraints limit what can be done. For practitioners and regulators, who demand highly disaggregate output-specific measures of costs, this led to the development of disaggregate costing mentioned earlier.

For firm-specific aggregate cost functions, basically there are two approaches to deal with the multi-product nature of transport firms:

1 increase the number of outputs in the cost function;

2 develop a measure of aggregate output(s), usually an output index, by aggregating multiple outputs properly into a limited number of output categories and incorporate firm or output attributes in the cost function.

The seemingly obvious improvement is to directly increase the number of outputs in the cost function. Even if data would permit (which it usually does not), only a limited number of outputs can be included because there are a limited number of observations (firms' and/or years' data) from which to estimate the parameters of the cost function. Where feasible, researchers have included some disaggregation. For railways, passengers and freight are the most important output categories to separate (e.g., Keeler, 1974; Hasenkamp, 1976; Friedlaender and Spady, 1981; Caves, Christensen and Swanson, 1981b), but this still leaves the heterogeneity of freight output. Separating bulk traffic from other cargo would be desirable. In trucking, it is common to distinguish truckload (TL0) from less-than-truckload (LTL) cargos (see Harmatuck, 1981, 1989; Ying, 1990a and 1990b; Grimm, Corsi and Jarrell, 1989, among others). For airlines, passenger and freight services usually can be distinguished, sometimes different classes of passengers can be included such as charter versus scheduled passengers (Gillen, Oum and Tretheway, 1985, 1990), and 'other' miscellaneous non-airline business activities can be another output category.[8] But all of these still risk bias in parameter estimates because of the remaining high aggregation. A rare exception is the rail cost function of Jara-Diaz and Winston (1981) who incorporated an origin-destination specific commodity trip as separate output in a cost function. Although this type of output specification can reveal much more information about joint production of two or more O-D traffic, it can be applied only to firms with a very small network (i.e. firms that serve a small number of O-D markets) in order to have a reasonable number of degrees of freedom for estimation and hypothesis tests (Winston, 1985).

Another approach to deal with the multiple output problem is to construct an aggregate output index by properly aggregating multiple outputs, and to incorporate it along with attributes of outputs such as average length of haul, average load, percent of bulk traffic (for railroads) in the cost function. The output index is normally constructed by aggregating multiple outputs with respective revenue shares as the weights of aggregation. This is better than just adding up tonne-kilometres because outputs which are costly to produce will be given higher weights (assuming that relative revenues reflect relative production costs).

Output attributes to include in the cost function along with the output index might include variables which indicate the mix of outputs (percentage of passenger, freight, charter, etc.), average length of haul, load factor, shipment size, etc. Adjustments can be made simply by incorporating these output attribute variables directly into the cost function, as was done, for example, in Caves, Christensen and Tretheway (1984), Friedlaender et al. (1993), Baltagi, Griffin and Rich (1995), Xu et al. (1994), Oum and Yu (1995).

Note however, if multiple outputs are specified and each output has its own attributes, it is not easy to include all the attributes of all outputs as full arguments in a cost function, especially when a flexible functional form is used. Nor is it justified to include all of these attributes without imposing some structure in their relationships with outputs. An alternative approach to incorporate output attributes is called a hedonic approach. The hedonic approach was first introduced into cost function literature by Spady and Friedlaender (1978).[9] It attempts to control the effects of output quality and/or attributes on total cost by adjusting output measures.

Although hedonic theory was developed to adjust price or output indices for quality changes (or differentials),[10] in cost function research, it has been adopted largely for adjusting outputs for changes in output attributes such as average length of haul, load factor, etc. These are often referred to as 'quality-adjusted' outputs, although this is somewhat of a misnomer. But because the quality of outputs may be different across firms and/or changes over time within a firm, it would be desirable to also adjust for quality changes of output by using a hedonic output specification.[11] For example, it would be possible to adjust for on-time performance records of transportation firms in their cost functions.[12] We are aware of only one study which has explicitly incorporated quality into the cost function. Allen and Liu (1995) employ a shipper-based quality rating in an LTL (less-than-truckload) motor carrier cost function. The quality coefficients are highly significant, and the cost elasticity of output (aggregate ton-miles) is about 0.9 indicating scale economies when the quality coefficient is included. Excluding the quality measure produces an output cost elasticity not signficantly different from unity. Large firms realize scale economies but instead supply a higher quality more costly service (comprehensive network coverage and service) so that ignoring the quality dimension mistakenly underestimates economies of scale. (Ying and Keeler, 1991, had noted that larger firms obtain higher revenues per ton-mile which is consistent with the higher quality of service). There is one potential unresolved issue in Allen and Liu: they do not control for network coverage hence their model does not distinguish between economies of scale and density.

The hedonic cost function is typically specified as

$$C=C(\phi^1(y_1, q_1), \phi^2(y_2, q_2), --, w; t) \tag{6}$$

where $\phi^i(y_i, q_i)$ represents ith hedonic, quality-adjusted or attribute-adjusted output which depends on y_i (ith nominal aggregate output) and q_i (vector of attributes or quality variable for ith output), w is the vector of input prices, and t is the vector of technological conditions of the firm such as number of airports served for airlines, route miles for railroads, etc.[13] The hedonic specification is a convenient way of incorporating the effects of output attributes in a cost function. This saves valuable degrees of freedom in estimation. Therefore, the hedonic output specification has been used in many studies including Spady and Friedlaender (1978), Friedlaender and Spady (1980,1981), Gillen and Oum (1984), and Gillen, Oum and Tretheway (1985, 1990). Oum and Tretheway (1989) compare the number of parameters necessary to estimate in hedonic vs. general specification of output attributes in cost functions, and concludes that there are empirical and theoretical reasons for preferring the hedonic specification, especially when the sample size is small.

But as indicated earlier, virtually no empirical cost function has been able to truly reflect the heterogeneity of transportation outputs. High levels of aggregation are unavoidable. Jara-Diaz et al.[14] review the underlying aggregation problems of output classifications and output attributes included in various empirical transportation cost functions, and the implications for measuring scale economies (discussed above). Their work has significantly extended our theoretical understanding of output specification and interpretation of results in calculating returns to scale and density, but there is no escaping a high level of aggregation in empirical transportation cost functions.

A majority of transportation cost functions are estimated on panel data, i.e., a time-series data for a cross-section of firms. Since estimation of cost function on a panel data requires special attention, this section will focus on those econometric issues.

A panel data set normally leads to one or more of the following violations of the standard assumptions on the error structure for ordinary least squares application:

1 uneven distribution of residuals across firms in the panel data: usually gives negative or positive residuals for the time-series of each firm;
2 at times, errors are heteroscedastic;
3 residuals exhibit autocorrelation within each firm.

A good resolution of (1) also reduces the extent of the problems (2) and (3). One-sided (positive or negative sign) residuals for each firm occur primarily because of omitted variables (often they are inefficiency terms) in the cost model. The total cost function is usually specified in the following form:

$$C = C(Y, W, N, t) \tag{7}$$

where Y is the output vector, W is the vector of input prices, N is the vector of network variables, and t refers to the technology indicators, which includs time trend or time dummy variables.

When a cost function is estimated jointly with input cost share equations, Friedlaender et al. (1993) have shown that each error term can be decomposed into three components as shown in equations (8 and 9): a firm-specific error (α_r, α_{ir}), an error that exhibits first-order autocorrelations within a given equation (γ_t, γ_{it}), assuming that there is no autocorrelation across equations), and a normally distributed error term (white noise).

$$\varepsilon_{rt} = \alpha_r + \gamma_t + \omega_{rt} \tag{8}$$

$$\mu_{irt} = \alpha_{ir} + \gamma_{it} + \omega_{irt} \tag{9}$$

The firm-specific errors can be handled either by adding firm effect variables (firm dummy variables and/or firm-specific time-trend variables) in the cost function or by specifying stochastic inefficiency terms for firms. Intra-equation intertemporal effects are introduced by permitting γ_t and γ_{it} terms to follow first-order autoregressive processes, which are usually equal across all firms. However, the first-order autoregressive parameters in the cost function, γ_t, are different from those of input cost share equations, γ_{it}. To ensure the adding-up consistency of the share equations, it is necessary to specify that the autoregressive parameter for each share equation is equal across shares (see, Berndt and Savin, 1975). Most multi-equation econometric routines automatically handle the cross-equation contemporaneous covariances.

So far, the discussion is limited to conceptual and methodological issues. However, even if state-of-art methodologies are available for specification and estimation of the model, the results may be useless if the data used in the research is of poor quality. Too often, researchers pay less attention to the quality of the data they use than learning about fancy methodology. To our surprise, some authors do not even bother describing their data, but charge ahead applying sophisticated techniques to the data, and then try to interpret their results for important policy questions. In our view, such papers do more harm than good to the profession. The quality of data can be more important than applying the most sophisticated methodologies.

There are several data issues which can be raised regarding cost functions. The problem of high aggregation of output categories has already been mentioned. There are also issues in input measurement. Cost functions employ input prices rather than input quantities, but short run functions need to include a measure of fixed capital. Measurement of capital is always a contentious issue. Many researchers rely too heavily on firm's accounting data and financial reports. The firm's accounting data, especially published data, is designed to serve the firm's interests of tax savings and public relations with shareholders, creditors, stock markets, and a regulatory authority. It is well known that the book value of capital stock is very different from the economic value of capital input (stock), and interest payments and depreciation reported in books are very different from the opportunity costs of using existing capital stock. Therefore, from the early 1960s many economists began to generate their own capital stock series for target firms (and industries) in their study. This is done by picking a benchmark capital stock early on, applying economic depreciation every year, and adjusting for net investment during the year (i.e., the perpetual inventory method). In addition, prudent researchers compute the yearly user cost of dollar's worth of capital stock taking into account such factors as economic depreciation, interest cost, capital gains and losses, the tax effect of capital investment on firm's real cost (property tax, investment tax credit, and corporate profit tax, etc.). Christensen and Jorgenson (1969) derived a formula for computing a proper measure of the rental price of capital stock, which accounts for all of these factors. Their procedure has been used very widely for computing user cost of capital for cost function research. We note that many transport cost functions have been estimated without proper caution on capital stocks and capital input costs. Some researchers use the firm's reported operating costs or total costs as dependent variables for estimating cost functions. Their empirical results are not trustworthy.

An input often overlooked in productivity and cost research is land. It is particularly important for railways. Current dollar valuations of land holdings are even more difficult to reconstruct than way and structures capital, but they can be reconstructed via the Christensen-Jorgenson (1969) perpetual inventory method, excluding any allowance for depreciation because land does not depreciate. Railways present a further problem because many of them have valuable land holdings which are not being used for rail operations hence should not be included in data for rail cost functions.

When estimating cost functions using data from different countries, extra caution needs to be exercised in measuring some input quantities and price indices. Specifically, because 'materials' input is a catch-all input category, its quantity index must be created by deflating total materials expense with a multilateral materials price index. Since materials input consists of uncountably large numbers of items, one normally uses a PPP-adjusted (purchasing power parity) consumption price index which allows for inter-country as well as time-series comparisons of general consumer prices (see, for example, Good et al., 1993, Oum and Yu, 1995, for applications on international airline cost functions). Because of the complexity involved in measuring materials input costs and its price index, some studies have excluded materials inputs from their cost function estimation.

An additional data issue arises specifically because of widespread deregulation of the transportation industry. Deregulation has reduced the availability of data for economic analysis. Regulated firms were required to file a variety of data on operations and costs. Indeed, the availability of public data on regulated companies enabled the pioneering efforts in cost functions. These data may become more difficult to obtain in the future, and as a result, analysts are likely to find increasing barriers to doing econometric work for cost analysis.

Cost function estimation for identifying cost structure characteristics

In this section, we describe the recent advances in methodologies for measuring the key indicators of the cost structure of transportation firms including economies of scale, traffic density and scope. As described earlier, economies of scale exist when unit cost decreases with size of the firm (outputs *and* network size) while economies of traffic density exist when unit cost decreases as traffic density increases (output increases on a given network size). Economies of scope exist when it is cheaper to produce two or more outputs jointly by a single firm than producing each of them separately by an independent firm.

The most long-standing reason for estimating aggregate cost functions has been to test for economies of scale. The belief in existence of scale economies has been a primary justification for government ownership and operation of natural monopoly firms, or economic regulation of private firms. The degree of scale economies and the minimum efficient scale are also important. If economies of scale are slight, then smaller more nimble firms may be able to compete with large carriers. If scale economies are exhausted at relatively low levels of output, then competition can still be feasible in all but small markets.

The presence of economies of scale, traffic density and scope is also an important consideration in deliberation of merger policy. If there is evidence that being larger is more cost efficient, governments are more likely to approve mergers between firms than otherwise.[15]

45

In economics, the term 'long-run' is defined as the sufficient amount of time which will allow firms to adjust all of their inputs optimally to changes in their outputs. If outputs are constantly changing it is not possible for a firm to ever reach its long-run equilibrium. Nonetheless, the concept of 'long-run' is useful for identifying and measuring the total impact of a major change in a firm's output on inputs and input costs because, in the long run, all inputs are variable. The need for short-run vs. long-run distinction exists because of the fact that some inputs are not fully adjusted during the data period in which output is changed. Economists call these inputs as 'fixed' or 'quasi-fixed' inputs. In fact, what constitutes quasi-fixed factors depends really on the researcher's choice of data observational period. If a researcher choses a week as the time unit of observation, then virtually all inputs are fixed. On the other hand, if 10 years were chosen as the time unit of observation, then virtually all inputs are variable. Since it is convenient to use a year as the unit of observation for econometric analysis, plant size or production capacity is treated commonly as quasi-fixed input. Morrison (1988) treated both capital and labour as quasi-fixed inputs in a comparative study of U.S. and Japanese manufacturing sectoral study. However, most papers treat only the capital inputs (way and structure capital and/or rolling stock for railroads, and aircraft fleet for airlines) as quasi-fixed.

The presence of quasi-fixed inputs makes short-run costs deviate from long-run costs. This poses problems for estimating a long-run cost function which is required for public policy and other analysis. Outright estimation of a cost function using annual or quarterly data would not give the long-run cost function. For this reason, transport economists have tried different approaches. The first approach is to average three to five years together as the time unit of data observation. The rationale for this approach is that firms can adjust most of their inputs fully within three to five years (although this may be questionable for rail track). This approach may be acceptable if all of the changes in output occur at the beginning of the period, say during the first year of the three-year data period, and the firm adjusts their inputs during rest of the period. But this is a questionable assumption, and the use of averaged data over a few years could bias the cost function estimation. Outputs usually change from year to year. Averaging a series of disequilibrium points will not necessarily solve the disequilibrium problem. There is a further concern about averaging years' data together: it reduces the degrees of freedom for estimation.

A second approach is to estimate short-run disequilibrium total cost functions, and use it to derive the long-run cost function by minimizing the short-run total cost with respect to the quasi-fixed factors (i.e. enveloping the short-run cost functions). This is an improved method which was used in many transport cost studies including Eads, Nerlove and Raduchel (1969) for airline costs and Keeler (1974) for his Class I U.S. railroad cost study.

$$TC = C^S (Y, W, Z, K, t) \qquad (10)$$

$$C = \min_{\text{w.r.t. K}} \{ C^S(Y, W, Z, K, t) \} \tag{11}$$

where TC is observed (disequilibrium) total cost, $C^S(Y, W, T, K, t)$ is the short-run (disequilibrium) cost function conditional on the level of capital stock (K), Y is the output vector, W is the input price vector, Z represents technology and network variables which influence variable costs for the firm, and t is the indicator for technical change over time. C is the long-run equilibrium total cost.

A third approach to deal with disequilibrium adjustment in quasi-fixed inputs comes from Caves, Christensen and Swanson (1981a). They suggest estimating the following form of the variable cost function rather than estimating the total cost function when firms are suspected of being in disequilibria with respect to one or more quasi-fixed inputs.

$$VC = C^v(Y, W^V, Z, K, t) \tag{12}$$

where VC is total variable cost which excludes the cost of quasi-fixed input (capital), $C^v(Y, W^v, T, K, t)$ is a variable cost function conditional on the level of capital stock (K), W^v is the vector of variable input prices (it excludes the rental price of capital), Z refers to network variables and t stands for technology indicators.

Then the short-run disequilibrium total cost function is formed by adding the expression for capital input cost to the estimated variable cost function as follows:

$$TC = C^v(Y, W^V, Z, K, t) + r. K \tag{13}$$

where r is rental price of the capital stock. The long-run cost function C can be formed by minimizing equation (13) with respect to capital stock (K).

$$C = \min_{\text{w.r.t. K}} \{ C^V(Y, W^V, Z, K, t) + r.K \} \tag{14}$$

This approach has been used by, for example, Caves, Christensen and Tretheway (1984), Morrison (1988), and Gillen, Oum and Tretheway (1985, 1990), Friedlaender et al (1993).

Christensen and Swanson (CCS, 1981) derived formulae for computing Returns to Traffic Density (RTD) and Returns to Scale (RTS) directly from a variable cost function.

$$RTD = \frac{1 - \epsilon_K^{vc}}{\sum_i^m \epsilon_{Y_i}^{vc}} \tag{15}$$

$$RTS = \frac{1 - \epsilon_K^{vc}}{\sum_i^m \epsilon_{Y_i}^{vc} + \epsilon_N^{vc}} \tag{16}$$

where ϵ_K^{VC} is elasticity of variable cost (VC) with respect to capital stock, $\epsilon_{Y_i}^{VC}$ is elasticity of VC with respect to output Y_i, ϵ_N^{VC} is elasticity of VC with respect to network size.

However, a qualification to the CCS formulae for computing RTD in (15) and RTS in (16) is that they are valid only for homothetic production technology which is characterized by a firm's straight-line expansion path (e.g., a Cobb-Douglas cost function). However, many empirical studies including CCS themselves apply the RTS formula when the estimated cost function is not homothetic. Oum, Tretheway and Zhang (1990) modified the CCS formula for RTS by substituting the long-run equilibrium values of quasi-fixed inputs into the formula.[16] They show analytically that the CCS formula is likely to underestimate true measure of RTS, and empirically verify this result with their Canadian airline data (the CCS formula gave RTS value of 0.84 while the modified CCS gave 0.942 at the sample mean).

There is a further issue in the treatment of a fixed capital stock in estimating cost functions. Oum and Zhang (1991) observed that most of the variable cost functions in the transport literature had wrong (positive) signs for the capital stock, implying that the shadow value of capital input is negative.[17] They then show analytically that the wrong sign for capital stock is caused by a common mis-specification of the variable cost function. The mis-specification occurs because of a kink in the cost associated with capital stock shown in Figure 3.1.

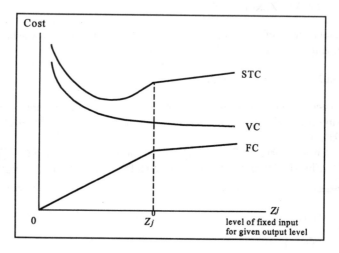

Figure 3.1   **Behaviour of variable cost, quasi-fixed input cost, and short run total cost**

The kink in the relationship between the annualized cost of capital and the quantity of capital occurs at Z_j° (the level of utilization of the existing capital stock to produce a specified output). This is because the cost of the quasi-fixed input (capital stock) increases linearly at the combined rate of depreciation d and the opportunity cost of capital r until its level reaches Z_j^o, after which the user cost of capital changes to the opportunity cost only (r) because the unutilized portion of the capital stock does not depreciate.

In order to solve this problem Oum and Zhang (1991) suggest that one should replace the capital stock (K) by a measure of the service flow from the capital stock as the argument in variable cost function, $C^V(.).$[18] The capital service flow can be computed by multiplying the capital stock (K) by its utilization factor (u).[19] For example, Oum and Zhang used 'average number of hours flown per aircraft per year' as the utilization factor for aircraft capital stock in their airline cost function estimation. This approach is consistent with the general approaches suggested in the economics of slack capacity developed in the productivity measurement literature (see, for example, Berndt and Morrison, 1981). All variable cost functions estimated with this modification had the correct signs for the capital input coefficient (see, for example, Oum and Zhang, 1991, Oum and Yu, 1995).

Table 3.1
Comparison of returns to scale and density estimates
(Standard errors in parentheses)

Cost Function Specification	RTS	RTD
Short-run total cost function method	0.971 (0.061)	1.211 (0.061)
Variable cost function with capital service flow	0.906 (0.061)	1.301 (0.123)
Long-run equilibrium cost function method	0.904 (0.061)	1.279 (0.119)
CCS Variable cost function method	0.836 (0.060)	1.433 (0.171)

Sources: Oum and Zhang (1991) and Gillen, Oum, Tretheway (1990)

Table 3.1 compares estimates for returns to traffic density and economies of firm size (scale) estimated by the alternative methods: the disequilibrium total cost function method, CCS variable cost function method, Oum-Zhang utilization rate adjusted variable cost function methods, and the long-run equilibrium method described above. All estimates are evaluated at the point of sample means of their panel data on Canadian air carriers. Table 3.1 shows that the Returns to Traffic Density (RTD) and

49

Returns to Scale (RTS) measures estimated from the variable cost function by the Oum-Zhang method were very close to those estimated by the long-run equilibrium method discussed earlier, while the CCS formula unestimates RTS and overestimates RTD.

Estimates of returns to scale

The distinction between returns to scale and density was thought to reconcile the common recognition that most firms would encounter less than proportionate change in costs with output increases, yet they still could have constant returns to scale production technology. The latter meant that regulation would not be necessary, and the empirical estimates of scale economies were important evidence in the debates which led to deregulation and privatization.[20]

The findings of Oum and Zhang (1991) that most cost functions have not treated fixed inputs properly could undermine the reliability of the estimates of economies of scale and density. Nonetheless, it is useful to summarize the empirical results in the cost function literature. Table 3.1 summarizes the estimates of returns to scale which appeared in the literature subsequent to Winston's survey (1985).

The numerous recent empirical studies of transportation costs are difficult to summarize and compare. Because of differences in the formulated cost functions (e.g., different definitions of outputs and attributes), and because of the absence of the standard errors associated with the Returns to Scale measure in some cases, it is not possible to discuss exact numerical results without extended discussion of specific differences between studies. Therefore, Table 3.1 simply reports their conclusions about economies of scale for various modes, with brief annotation about their sample data. Although most studies find constant returns to scale, not surprisingly, the results can differ depending on specific industry segments or for different formulations of cost functions. Several studies report apparent changes in cost structure after deregulation (see, for example, McMillan and Stanley, 1988, and Ying, 1990a). In some cases, different conclusions about RTS were obtained from the same data set simply by changing the specification of the cost function. Our conclusion from reviewing many studies is that it is essential to look closely at the data and specification of the cost function in drawing conclusions about economies of scale, and it is quite possible that different results may be found in different market segments.

The interpretation of estimates of scale economies is further complicated by whether total or partial output elasticities are included in the calculation. Traditionally, scale economies have been calculated using the sum of partial elasticities of costs with respect to outputs. As noted earlier, several authors have questioned the traditional approach (Gagne, 1990; Ying, 1992; Xu, et al., 1994) and Jara-Diaz et al. By incorporating output attributes where relevant and interrelationships among output categories and attributes, the revised calculations of scale economies may be changed from those reported in Table 3.2.

Economies of scope

Economies of scope exist when it is cheaper to produce two or more outputs jointly by a single firm than producing each of them separately by an independent firm. The concept of economies of scope can be used to evaluate whether it is desirable to separate passenger business from freight (air or rail mode), charter services from scheduled services (air, bus or shipping), and less-than-truck load business from truck load business (trucking). Baumol, Panzar and Willig (1982, p.70) define economies of scope for the case of two products as follows:

$$C(Y_1, Y_2) < [C(Y_1, 0) + C(0, Y_2)]$$ \hfill (17)

where $C(Y_1, Y_2)$ is the total cost of producing both outputs (Y_1 and Y_2) jointly by a single firm, $C(Y_1, 0)$ is the cost of producing output Y_1 only by a single firm, and $C(0, Y_2)$ is the cost of producing output Y_2 only by another single firm. If the above condition holds, it would be profitable for the two firms to merge. If the opposite inequality is true (i.e., diseconomies of scope), no arrangement involving multiproduct firms could be stable because separation would be profitable. Using the same notation as in (17), economies of scope for the two-product case can be computed by:

$$SC = \{[C(Y_1, 0) + C(0, Y_2)] - C(Y_1, Y_2)\} / C(Y_1, Y_2)$$ \hfill (18)

The above economies of scope measure is the percentage of additional cost required to produce each product separately by an independent firm as compared to the cost of joint production of both products by a single firm (see Panzar and Willig, 1981).

Table 3.2
Recent estimates of returns to scale (post 1984)

Authors (date)	Data	Returns to scale?
Airline Cost Functions		
Caves, Christensen and Tretheway (1984)	x-s, 1970-81	constant or slight increasing returns
Gillen, Oum and Tretheway (1990)	Cdn x-s, 1964-81	constant returns
Bauer (1990)	x-s 12, qtrly, 1970-91	constant returns
Kumbhakar (1990)	x-s 19, 1970-84	increasing returns
Oum and Zhang (1991)	1964-81 Cdn x-s	constant or slight decreasing returns
Good, Nadiri and Sickles (1991)	x-s 16, 1977-83	short run returns to scale
Kumbhakar (1992)	x-s 19, 1970-84	most firms constant or decreasing returns
Keeler and Formby (1994)	x-s 15, qrtly, 1984-5,89-90	constant returns
Atkinson and Cornwell (1994)	x-s 13, qtrly, 1970-81	increasing returns
Baltagi, Griffin and Rich (1995)	x-s 24, 1971-86	constant returns

Rail Cost Functions

Caves, Christensen, Tretheway and Windle (1985)	43 Class I RR,1951-75	constant returns
De Borger (1992)	1 Blgm. RR,1950-86	constant returns
Friedlaender, Berndt, et al. (1993)	Class I RR, 1974-86	increasing returns
Berndt, Friedlaender, et al. (1993)	Class I RR, 1974-86	increasing returns [not discussed]
De Borger (1991)	Belgian RR 1950-86	constant returns
Kim (1987)	56 Class I U.S.RR, 1963	constant returns
Filippini and Maggi (1991)	48 Swiss Rails, 1985-88	constant returns

Motor Carrier Cost Functions

Wang-Chiang and Friedlaender (1984)	x-s 1976	constant returns
Friedlaender and Bruce (1985)	85 general,1974-79	increasing returns for large carriers
Daughety, Nelson and Vigdor (1985)	85 gen., 1974-79	slight decreasing returns
Kim (1987)	1979 Cdn regional	increasing returns
McMullen (1987) (log linear fct.)	splized carriers 1977,83	constant returns
Christensen and Huston (1987)	splized carriers	constant returns
Daughety and Nelson (1988)	x-s 1953-1982	const. or increasing returns
McMullen and Stanley (1988)	splized carriers,1977-83	increasing returns 1977, const. returns 1983
Grimm, Corsi and Jarrell (1989)	LTL trucking	constant returns
Thomas and Callan (1989)	splized carriers	constant returns
Ying (1990a)	x-s 1975-84	increasing returns
Ying (1990b)	x-s 1975-84	decreasing returns after adjusting for deregulation
Winston, Corsi, Grimm and Evans (1990)	LTL trucking	constant returns
Harmatuck (1991)	TL & LTL, qrtly, 1974-82	const. or mild increasing returns
Harmatuck (1992)	9 LTL firms, 1974-88	increasing returns
McMullen and Tanaka (1992)	LTL trucking	constant returns
Thomas and Callan (1992)	splized carriers	constant returns
Callan and Thomas (1992)	splized carriers	constant returns
Allen & Liu (1995)	LTL trucking	increases rtns adjusting for quality

[broader interpretations of scale]

Xu, Windle, Grimm and Corsi (1994)	LTL, 1988-90	increasing returns once interaction effects included
Keeler (1989)	1984 HH goods	economies of firm size indicated by 'survivor principle'

U.S. data unless specified otherwise; x-s refers to cross-section cost elasticities or returns to scale evaluated at sample mean or mean of individual firms in the data set.

Note that, to be useful for policy purposes, the economies of scope will need to be evaluated at each data point (a particular firm of our consideration). For example, in order to evaluate the existence of economies of scope for a railroad producing Y_1 units of freight services and Y_2 units of passenger services, it is necessary to have information on the cost of producing Y_1 freight services and 0 passenger service, and the costs of producing 0 freight service and Y_2 units of passenger services. This can be done only if we can extrapolate a multiple output cost function to points where one of the two outputs are zero. Unless the sample data with which the cost function is estimated includes many single product firms as well as multiple product firms, it is risky to extrapolate the cost function to zero values. This is the main reason most transportation researchers have not attempted to measure economies of scope.[21] Kim (1987) attempted to measure economies of scope between passenger and freight services using cross-sectional data of U.S. railroads for 1963. He reports a scope economy estimate of -0.410 (standard error not reported) at the sample mean data, implying that the joint production of passengers and freight together by a single railroad imposes 41% extra cost to the sytem. However, since his data did not include any passenger-only railroad firm his finding on the extent of diseconomies of scope should be taken cautiously.

Some researchers evaluated the following inter-product cost complementarity condition between each pair of products (e.g., scheduled and charter services in airlines) at the sample mean and each data point:

$$\frac{\partial^2 C}{\partial Y_i \partial Y_j} < 0 \qquad (19)$$

If the above derivative is negative, then cost-complementarity exists between outputs Y_i and Y_j because the marginal cost of producing Y_i decreases as Y_j increases (see, Panzar and Willig, 1978, proposition 2). Gillen, Oum, Tretheway (1990) find that, for the case of Canadian carriers, cost complementarity exists between scheduled and charter passenger services if the proportion of charter services in an airline's total output is smaller than seven percent. In other words, the marginal cost of scheduled passenger services decrease as an airline increases charter services only up to seven percent of the total airline revenue. J.P. Keeler and Formby (1994) conducted a similar analysis on the 1984-85 and 1989-90 quarterly data of 15 major U.S. passenger airlines, and found existence of strong cost complementarity between passenger and freight services. Keeler and Fomby refer to this as 'economies of scope' but strictly speaking economies of scope refers to co-production being less costly than each product produced by itself rather cost-complementarities which could exist over a narrow range of production combinations.

The concept of economies of scope is important, and the flexible form of cost functions enable scope economies to be estimated. However, it appears that the data sets used to test for scope economies are too limited. It is imperative to have a greater diversity of firms for estimation. Ideally we would have data for some firms *not* producing all outputs. Of course, if economies of scope are important, then that might explain the scarcity of specialized firms; but differences in regional markets could allow very different firms to exist. In any event, greater diversity among firms in a data sample would improve estimates of scope economies.

Cost function estimation and analysis for measuring productive efficiency

The previous sections focused on using cost functions to identify characteristics of cost structure such as economies of scale, density or scope. Cost (or production) functions can also be used to measure and compare productive efficiency across firms and/or over time within a firm. Although non-parametric methods such as data envelopment analysis (DEA) and total factor productivity are also used to assess productive efficiency, in this review we focus our attention on the cost function approaches.[22]

The conventional approach: firm and time effects models

In order to measure changes in productive efficiency of a firm over time or to compare it across different firms, researchers often include a time trend or time dummy variables in a cost function of the following form:

$$C = C(Y, W, Z, t, F)$$ (20)

where C is total cost, W is the input prices, Z represents network and market variables which influence cost, t represents variables representing state of technology (a time trend or time dummy variables), F represents the variables representing firm-specific effects on costs which are unaccounted for by other arguments in the cost function (firm dummy variables and/or firm-specific time trend variables).The time trend or time dummy variables (t) are used to measure the extent of shift in cost function, i.e., the change in firm's efficiency over time, and the firm dummy variables (F) and any firm-specific trend variable in t are used to compare the difference in (residual) productive effiency across firms and over time. See Caves, Christensen and Tretheway (1984) and Friedlaender et al. (1993) for examples of firm-effect models.

When estimating a cost function of the type in (20), there may be high collinearity between firm dummy variables (F) and output or network variables (Y or Z), especially in a panel data which includes both very large and very small firms. Although theoretically high collinearity does not lead to biased parameter estimates, in a finite sample size it often affects point estimates of the parameters, especially for outputs (Y), and network variables (Z: e.g., average flight stage length for airlines or average length of haul for rail or trucking firms) very seriously. This situation gets worse as the amount of between-firm variation in Y and Z relative to the amount of within-firm variation in the same variables gets larger. Since the firm-dummy variables 'take away' a portion of cost variation which can be legitimately explained by Y and Z, it will reduce the statistical significance and size of coefficients for Y and Z. In particular, this leads to underestimation of cost elasticities with respect to outputs and network size which, in turn, results in an over-estimation of Returns to Traffic Density (RTD) and Scale (RTS). For example, the RTD estimates (1.5 - 4.3 at firm's mean data) reported in Friedlaender et al. (1993) appear to be too high. Similarly, when Oum and Yu (1995) estimated a translog variable cost function on a panel data of the world's major airlines (23 airlines for the 1986-93 period), the firm dummy variables obscured the coefficients for stage length and output variables. In fact, stage length variables become either statistically insignificant or have a wrong (positive) sign. This happened because the variations in the output and stage length across different airlines in the data set is very large relative to their variations over time within each firm, and firm dummy variables pick up a large portion of variations in cost which could be legitimately explained by the variations in output and stage length. Therefore, we question inclusion of firm dummy variables in a cost function without carefully examining its impacts on other coefficients. This calls for an alternative approach to deal with firm-effects. Identifying the variables which would explain the residual firm effects is a good avenue to pursue. Another promising way of dealing with the problem may be the stochastic frontier error specification, where positive (or non-negative) error distribution indicating the extent of firm-specific inefficiency relative to the efficient cost frontier, is estimated for each firm iteratively. The estimation of frontier cost functions is discussed later in this section.

Decomposition of TFP or costs into sources

An alternative approach to productivity measurement is to compute a total factor productivity (TFP) index and decompose the TFP growth rates into sources via regression analysis leaving a residual measure of productive efficiency. Denny, Fuss, and Waverman (1981) derived the following formula for decomposing TFP growth into effects of output scale, non-marginal cost pricing of outputs, and residual productive efficiency, and applied this to Bell Canada data:

$$\dot{TFP} = \dot{Y}^P - \dot{F} = (1-\epsilon_y)\dot{Y}^C + [\dot{Y}^P - \dot{Y}^C] + E \qquad (21)$$

where TFP is the TFP growth rate, Y^P is the growth rate of the output aggregated by using revenue shares as the weight for aggregation, Y^C is the growth rate of the output aggregated by using cost elasticities as the weight for aggregation, F is the growth rate of inputs, and

$$\{ \epsilon_y = \sum_i (\partial \ln C / \partial \ln Y_i) \}$$

is sum of the cost elasticities with respect to outputs which needs to be estimated via a cost function. The first term on the RHS of (16) is the effect of output growth (scale) on TFP growth. The second term is the effect of the change in the extent of non-marginal cost pricing of outputs on TFP growth. The last term E is the TFP growth due to residual productive efficiency. The TFP decomposition formula tells us that even if one computes TFP growth non-parametrically, it is necessary to estimate a cost function in order to identify TFP growth caused by productivity efficiency because the decomposition formula (21) requires information on the elasticity of cost with respect to outputs.

Note that formula (21) can be adapted to decompose observed cost changes or TFP changes into any number of sources included in the cost function one estimates. Bauer (1990a) applied this decomposition approach to airlines, and decomposed TFP growth of the airline industry into the effects of changes in output scale, extent of non-marginal cost pricing of outputs (he incorporated only passenger and freight outputs), changes in network variables (stage length and load factor), deviation of observed input shares from the least cost input shares, and a residual efficiency effect.[23] It is noteworthy that Bauer attempts to distinguish the effects of allocative efficiency (deviation from the least cost input combinations) from technical efficiency (shift in isoquant). Schmidt and Lovell (1979) and Kopp and Diewert (1982) have introduced methodologies for decomposing frontier cost function deviations into technical and allocative inefficiencies. Since then, many economists have attempted to measure allocative efficiency separately from technical efficiency (see, for example, Kumbhakar, 1987, 1989; Huang and Liu, 1994; and Oum and Zhang, 1995).[24] For example, Huang and Liu (1994) demonstrate that the effects of technical efficiency on productivity may be greater on some inputs than on others, thus conventional techniques may not be appropriate in identifying the sources of productive inefficiency.

As noted earlier, transport economists often estimate a variable cost function rather than total cost function. The variable cost function normally takes the form in equation (12). Drawing on the properties of a translog variable cost function, Caves and Christensen (1988) show that the (total) unit cost differential (including capital costs) between any two observations, 1 and 0, can be decomposed into various arguments included in the variable cost function:

$$
\begin{aligned}
C^1 - C^0 = {} & S[1/2(d_y^1 C_v + d_y^0 C_v) \cdot (Y^1 - Y^0) - (Y^1 - Y^0)] \\
& + S[1/2(d_k^1 C_v + d_k^0 C_v) \cdot (K^1 - K^0)] \qquad \Big\rangle \quad \text{scale} \\
& + (1 - S)[(K^1 - K^0) - (Y^1 - Y^0)] \\
& + S[1/2(d_w^1 C_v + d_w^0 C_v) \cdot (W^1 - W^0)] \qquad \Big\rangle \quad \text{input prices} \\
& + (1 - S)(W_k^1 - W_k^0) \\
& + S[1/2(d_z^1 C_v + d_z^0 C_v) \cdot (Z^1 - Z^0)] \quad \text{operating characteristics} \\
& + S[1/2(d_t^1 C_v + d_t^0 C_v) \cdot (t^1 - t^0)] \qquad \qquad \text{time effects} \\
& + E
\end{aligned}
$$

(22)

where S denotes the average share of variable cost in the total cost for observations 1 and 0, and $d_x^i C_v$ denotes the partial derivative of the variable cost for observation i with respect to variable x, and E represents the residual difference.

Oum and Yu have adopted this formula to decompose the unit cost differential between the benchmark airline (American) and other airlines into sources: input prices, scale of output, composition of outputs, capital stocks, stage length, load factor, ownership form, and residual technical efficiency. Furthermore, they illustrate that the observed TFP differential can be approximated by removing the effect of input prices from the observed unit cost differential. In a similar manner, Bhattachargya et al.(1995) decompose the residual of their cost function for bus companies to obtain firm and time-specific measures of inefficiency with ownership type, rates of vehicle utilization and breakdown as explanatory variables.

Frontier cost functions

Traditional econometric methods for estimating cost or production functions have implicitly assumed that all firms are successful in reaching the efficient frontier. If, however, the firms are not equally efficient, then the average relationships estimated by ordinary least squares would not reflect the (efficient) cost or production frontier against which to measure efficiency (or inefficiency) of each firm. For this reason, researchers now estimate frontier production or cost functions which recognize that some firms may not be on the efficient frontier. This is done essentially by specifying the following form of error terms of the cost (production) function:

$$\epsilon = u + v \tag{23}$$

where u is the inefficiency term resulting from a firm deviating from the efficient cost (production) frontier, and v is clean error term. Depending on whether u is assumed to be a deterministic or stochastic value, the method is called a 'deterministic' or 'stochastic' frontier method. The deterministic frontier can be estimated via a variety of methods including the corrected ordinary least squares (COLS) method[25] or even by including firm dummy and/or firm-specific time trend variables in the cost (production) function.[26]

Aigner, Amemiya and Poirier (1976), Aigner, Lovell and Schmidt (ALS,1977) and Meensen and van den Broeck (1977) specified the inefficiency term (u) to have a probability distribution, which is consistent with existence of a stochastic frontier and variable efficiency among firms. In particular, ALS explicitly set forth a joint density function based on the error form $\epsilon = u + v$ where u is usually assumed to be a 'half normal' or exponential distribution.[27]

Although the stochastic frontier methods have been widely applied in the electric utility and telecommunications area, to date only a few applications have been made to transportation (Bauer, 1990, and Good et al., 1993 on airlines, Grabowski and Mehdian, 1990 on railways, Forsund, 1992 on ferries, and Bhattacharyya, Kumbhakar and Bhattacharyya, 1995 on bus companies). For example, Bauer (1990) estimated a frontier translog cost function on the quarterly data of the U.S. airlines for the 1970-81 period[28] and used it to decompose the observed TFP growth into the effects of changes in output scale, extent of non-marginal cost pricing of outputs (incorporating only passenger and freight outputs), neutral technical change, changes in stage length and load factor, deviation of observed input shares from the least cost input shares, and the efficiency effect (one-sided distribution). Bauer observed increasing returns to scale for small U.S. airlines while observing constant returns to scale for large U.S. carriers. His results show that most of the observed TFP growth is accounted for by changes in output scale, load factor, stage length and neutral technical change. The effects of firm-specific inefficiency (u) on TFP are relatively small.

Good, Nadiri, Roller and Sickles (1993) estimated Cobb-Douglas stochastic frontier production functions (single-output measured in RTK) on the four largest European air carriers and the eight largest U.S. air carriers for the 1976-86 period.[29] The distinguishing feature of their model from Bauer (1990) is that their model takes into account endogeneity of the output and capital attributes such as stage length, load factor, network size (they used route-miles rather than number of airports served), percentage of turboprop aircraft, percentage of wide-body aircraft and firm-specific stochastic errors. They focused on measuring technical efficiency in order to identify effects of the U.S. deregulation on efficiency and to predict the size of efficiency improvement expected after European air liberalization. Their results show that the four largest European carriers are significantly less efficient than most of the large U.S. carriers, while British Airways has improved technical efficiency the most between 1976 and 1986.

Gong and Sickles (1992) use a Monte Carlo study to compare the performance of the stochastic frontier method and data envelopment analysis (DEA) in measuring firm-specific technical inefficiency. Yu (1995) conducted a similar Monte Carlo study for comparing performance of the stochastic frontier method, DEA, and a deterministic frontier method computed by Corrected Ordinary Least Squares (COLS) method. Both studies concluded that the stochastic frontier method is superior to other methods for measuring firm-specific productivity efficiency.

The stochastic frontier cost/production function is computationally complex and time-consuming to estimate. However, because user-friendly econometric programs for estimating stochastic frontier cost and production functions are likely to be available in the future, this is a promising area of future development in transport cost analysis which may refine some of the empirical results on scale economies estimated via conventional econometric specification. In sum, the stochastic frontier method appears to be the direction toward which empirical researchers in transportation need to move in order to improve accuracy in measuring productive efficiency.

Summary and concluding remarks

This paper reviews recent developments in aggregate cost function research in transportation. The major improvements in formulating transportation cost functions are threefold:

1 The ability to distinguish between economies of scale and economies of density econometrically helped sharpen the debates on various public policy issues such as

regulation, deregulation, mergers, etc. In addition, recent work indicates that the calculation of scale economies in multiproduct cost functions may have been interpreted too narrowly and overlooked interrelationships among output categories and output attributes which could explain cost advantages of larger firms.

2 A major improvement was the introduction of 'flexible' functional forms including the *translog function*, which allows for free variation of the cost elasticities with respect to outputs, network size and other variables. This in turn allows returns to scale, density and scope to depend on the data point at which they are evaluated.

3 There has been improved specification of outputs and output attributes which recognizes differential costs among heterogeneous outputs. Different approaches exist. The methods for improved specification include (a) inclusion of multiple outputs as arguments of cost function; or (b) inclusion of a single output measure (properly aggregated output index) and output attributes as arguments in the cost function; or (c) hedonic specification of output measures which allows the attribute-adjusted outputs to be included in the cost function.

In addition, we also examine some econometric issues associated with estimating cost functions using a panel data (pooled cross-section and time-series), and discuss importance of data quality especially for capital stock and some input prices.

In section 4, we examined recent developments for improving the accuracy of estimating key indicators of cost structure (economies of scale, density and scope) in the presence of the firm's disequilibrium input adjustments in the short run. Three alternative methods were examined: (a) the method of estimating a short-run total cost function and finding the long-run cost function by enveloping the short-cost functions with respect to the quasi-fixed input (capital); (b) the method of estimating a short-run variable cost function, and use the formulae proposed by Caves, Christensen and Swanson (CCS, 1981) in order to compute economies of scale and density directly from the variable cost function; and (c) a variant of method (b) for which the flow of capital services (utilized capital stock) replaces the capital stock variable as an argument in variable cost function. In terms of closeness of the returns to scale and density estimates to those computed from the long-run equilibrium cost function properly derived by using the variable cost function and the expression for capital cost, the method (b) proposed by Caves, Christensen and Swanson (CCS) is worse than method (a). Method (c) is shown to be the best.

Section 4 also presents a short survey of recent estimates of returns to scale (RTS). As in Winston's survey (1985), most of the recent studies find constant returns to scale. A few find increasing returns, primarily for railways or LTL trucking. Several studies reports apparent changes in cost structure after deregulation. Studies have attempted to measure economies of scope or inter-product complementarity. These studies show the existence of diseconomies of scope between passenger and freight services in the early period of the U.S. rail industry while showing existence of product complementarity between scheduled and charter services as well as between freight and passenger services in the airline industry.

In section 5, we discuss recent advances in econometric work for measuring productive efficiency: specifically, (a) cost function estimation with firm and time effect variables; (b) decomposition techniques for TFP or cost changes into potential sources; and (c) techniques for frontier cost functions.

We caution the use of firm dummy variables in a panel data especially when outputs and network size variables are highly correlated with firm dummies and the variations in these variables across firms are very large relative to their variations over time within each firm. Blind application of firm dummy variables could obscure the results on returns to scale, density and scope as well as estimates of productive efficiency.

The methods of decomposing unit cost changes into potential sources have been advanced rapidly in recent years, and this allows researchers to correctly identify the change in productive efficiency after removing the effects of the variables beyond managerial control.

Finally, recent advances in the stochastic frontier method make it easier for researchers to estimate frontier cost functions, which recognize econometrically that firms may not be on the efficient frontier. We believe that in the future, there will be an explosion in the use of frontier cost functions for transportation studies.

Notes

1   The debate held the attention of the most prominent economists, e.g. Pigou (1912, 1913) and Taussig (1913). Locklin (1933) provides a review of the literature.

2   Johnston's textbook (1960) provides a number of cites for early applications of statistical cost analysis for various industries. The development of cost functions in rail transportation are reviewed by Keeler (1983) and Waters and Woodland (1980). Caves (1962, pp.55-83) reviews early studies of airline costs; see also Straszheim (1969) and White (1979). Chow (1978) reviews early cost studies on trucking. Waters (1976) cites a number of statistical costs studies for various modes.

3   The disaggregate costing has been developed primarily by practitioners in regulatory authority or transportation firms, especially railways, without explicit linkage to the economic theory of production. For an exploration of the linkage between disaggregate and aggregate cost functions, see Waters and Tretheway (1989).

4   Many economists estimate cost functions using industry aggregate data instead of that for individual firms. Because the industry as whole does not make optimal choices, the validity of estimating models from industry-wide is questionable. In his survey article on production/cost functions, Walters (1963) concludes that, for sensible aggregation, the production function must be additively separable, and goes on to say 'one may easily

doubt whether there is much point in employing such a concept as an aggregate production function'. Fortunately, most transportation cost functions have been estimated on firm-specific data.

5   Some economists have criticized the translog function as being less flexible than some of the other flexible functions, and because it is difficult to impose curvature conditions for a well-behaved production technology in estimation. See, for example, Guilkey and Lovell (1980), Guilkey, Lovell and Sickles (1983), and Wales (1977). Diewert and Wales (1987) suggest methods for imposing curvature conditions globally in the context of cost function estimation including use of the generalized McFadden cost function which, under certain conditions, possesses a superior flexibility property. Also, Diewert and Wales (1988) discuss a normalized quadratic semiflexible functional form. Nonetheless, thus far the translog has been the most popular choice of flexible form for empirical application in transportation.

6   See Denny and Fuss (1977) for a concise proof of this property for the translog function.

7   They fitted a translog function to Klein's (1953) study of 1936 U.S. railroad data.

8   Among the airline cost studies we examined, only Good et al (1993) and Oum and Yu (1995) included the non-airline business outputs in the cost functions. Other papers appear to have ignored the presence of non-airline business output the airlines produce, although it accounts for a substantial portion to airlines' total revenues (average 8%).

9   Oum (1977, 1979) introduced the hedonic demand function in the transport demand literature by imbedding hedonic price functions for transportation services in shipper's transportation cost function and by deriving the corresponding demand functions for rail and truck modes.

10   Research on hedonic price theory originated from by the need to measure quality-corrected cost of living indices. The seminal works by Court (1939), Lancaster (1966, 1971), Fisher and Shell (1968, 1972) and Sherwin Rosen (1974) have provided the necessary micro-economic foundations for conducting the formal analysis and measure of quality attributes.

11   In a rail/truck demand study, Oum (1979) estimated shippers', not the carriers', cost functions with hedonic adjustment in order to compute the quality-adjusted rail and truck rates. He incorporated speed and reliability of service as quality variables.

12   U.S. Department of Transportation now publishes on-time performance records for airlines.

13   The weak separability of each hedonic aggregator with respect to other arguments in the cost function requires $\phi^i(y_1, q_i)$ to take a log-linear form if the (macro) cost function is specified in a translog form (see Blackorby, Primont and Russell, 1977, and Denny and Fuss, 1977).

14   Jara-Diaz and Cortes (1995, 1996), which build on earlier works by Jara-

Diaz (1982a,b; 1988) and Jara-Diaz, Donoso and Araneda (1991, 1992). See also Oum and Zhang (1996) and discussions earlier in this paper.

15   It is now well-known that increasing returns to scale is not a sufficient condition for government control or regulation. The concept of contestable markets focuses more on barriers to entry and the existence or non-existence of sunk costs. Even if economies of scale were substantial, if the assets were mobile then entry of new firms is possible and apparent monopoly due to scale economies can be benign and the threat of entry will prevent firms from exploiting market power. We do not pursue these issues here.

16   Similarly, Scrot (1993) notes that the productive efficiency measure will be biased if the data are drawn from observations that do not reflect long-run equilibrium. He uses the translog frontier cost function to present a method for adjusting data on inputs and outputs to the values they would be in long-run equilibrium, given the fixed inputs and input prices.

17   The coefficient for the capital stock variable was estimated to be (counter-intuitively) positive in variable cost functions reported in Caves, Christensen and Swanson (1981a,1981b), Caves, Christensen and Tretheway (1984) Caves, Christensen, Tretheway and Windle (1987), Nelson (1989), and Gillen, Oum and Tretheway (1990).

18   The amount of capital service flow can be computed by multiplying the capital stock times its utilization rate. When the capital stock is under- or over-utilized, the capital *stock* is not a proper indicator for the amount of *service flow* from capital stock.

19   See Nelson (1989) for a comprehensive treatment on measurement of capacity utilization. The practice of including the capital stock in a variable cost regression implicitly assumes that a fixed flow of capital services is derived from the capital stock; this is equivalent to assuming that the consumption of capital is purely a function of time. Adjusting the capital stock by its utilization rate might be thought of as capital flows determined by total use rather than the passage of time.

20   Even if scale economies were not present, economies of density would still give an advantage to established firms in a market. The concept of and belief in contestable markets was an important further factor in reconciling transport cost behaviour with the belief that regulation would not be necessary. See Bailey and Friedlaender (1982) for an extensive discussion on this issue.

21   Even when the data on multiple product firms and single product firms are available for cost function estimation, it is not straight-forward to estimate a cost function, especially a translog cost function. This is because of the presence of zero output values which make it impossible to do logarithmic transformation. In this case, researchers use a Box-Cox transformation of the variables rather than taking logarithms (see Caves, Christensen and Tretheway, 1980).

22	See Oum, Tretheway and Waters (1992) for an overview of various productivity measures; a more rigorous review is Diewert (1992).
23	See Oniki et al (1994) for another example of TFP decomposition.
24	See the seminal paper by Farrell (1957) for clear definitions of technical efficiency and allocative (price) efficiency.
25	COLS is done usually by shifting the cost function estimated via ordinary least squares method by the amount of the largest negative residual, and thus form the deterministic cost frontier.
26	Aigner and Chu (1968) made the first attempt to estimate a parametric functional form for a (Cobb-Douglas) production frontier within the theoretical framework of Farrell (1957).
27	See Stevenson (1980b) for generalized stochastic frontier estimation in which 'mode' of the probability distribution for stochastic inefficiency term (u) can occur at any point. Bauer (1990b) describes recent develoments in estimation of frontier functions.
28	Bauer does not show how he measured capital and materials costs. Nor does he show how he allocated costs to quarters.
29	The authors use firm dummy variables and the interaction terms between firm dummy and time trend variable in order to identify the firm-specific technical inefficiencies relative to Nortwest Airlines.

References

Aigner, D.J. and S.F. Chu (1968), 'On Estimating the Industry Production Function', *American Economic Review*, 58, pp.826-839.

Aigner, D., C.A.K. Lovell and P. Schmidt (1977), 'Formulation and Estimation of Stochastic Frontier Production Function Models', *Journal of Econometrics* 6, pp.21-37.

Aigner, D.J., T. Amemiya and D.J. Poirier (1976), 'On the Estimation of Production Frontiers,' *International Economic Review* 17 (June), pp. 377-396.

Allen, W.B. and D. Liu (1995) 'Service Quality and Motor Carrier Costs: An Empirical Analysis,' *Rev. Econ. and Stat.* (August), pp. 499-510.

Atkinson, S.E. and C. Cornwell (1994), Estimation of Output and Input Technical Efficiency using a Flexible Functional Form and Panel Data, *International Economic Review*, Vol.35, No.2. Feb., pp. 245-255.

Baltagi, B., Griffin, J., and Rich D (1995), 'Airline Deregulation: The Cost Pieces of the Puzzle,' *International Economic Review,* vol. 36, No.1, pp. 245-259.

Barla, P. and S. Perelman (1989), 'Technical Efficiency in Airlines under Regulated and Deregulated Environments', *Annals of Public and Cooperative Economics*, 60, No.1, pp. 103-124.

Bauer, P.W. (1990a), 'Decomposing TFP Growth in the Presence of Cost Inefficiency, Nonconstant Returns to Scale, and Technological Progress', *The Journal of Productivity Analysis*, 1, pp.287-299.

Bauer, P.W. (1990b), 'Recent Developments in the Econometric Estimation of Frontiers', *Journal of Econometrics*, 46(1/2), pp. 39-56.

Baumol, W., J. Panzar and R.Willig (1982), *Contestable Markets and the Theory of Industry Structure,* Harcourt Brace Jovanovich Inc.

Berndt, E.R., Friedlaender, A.F., J.S. Wang Chiang, and C.A. Vellturo (1993), 'Cost Effects of Mergers and Deregulation in the US Rail Industry,' *J. of Productivity Analysis*, 4.

Berndt, E.R., and Morrison C. (1981), 'Capacity Utilization Measures: Underlying Economic Theory and an Alternative Approach', *The American Economic Review*, pp. 48-57.

Berndt, E.R. and N.E. Savin (1975), 'Estimation and Hypothesis Testing in Singular Equation Systems with Autoregressive Disturbances,' *Econometrica*, 43, pp.937-58.

Bhattacharyya, A., S.C. Kumbhakar and A. Bhattacharyya (1995), 'Ownership Structure and Cost Efficiency: A Study of Public Owned Passenger-Bus Transportation Companies in India', *The Journal of Productivity Analysis*, Vol. 6, No. 1, pp. 47-61.

Blackorby, C., D. Primont, and R. Russell (1977), 'On Testing Separability Restrictions with Flexible Functional Forms,' *Journal of Econometrics*, 5, pp. 195-209.

Borts, G.H. (1952), 'Production Relations in the Railway Industry,' *Econometrica* (January), pp. 71-79.

Borts, G.H. (1954), 'Increasing Returns in the Railway Industry,' *Econometrica* (January), pp. 316-33.

Borts, G.H. (1960), 'The Estimation of Rail Cost Functions,' *Econometrica* (January), pp. 108-31.

Brown, R.S., D.W. Caves and L.R. Christensen (1979), 'Modelling the Structure of Cost and Production for Multi-product Firms', *Southern Economic Journal*, 46, pp. 256-273.

Callan, S.J. and J.M.Thomas (1992), 'Cost Differentials among Household Goods Carriers: Network Effects, Operating Characteristics and Shipment Composition,' *Journal of Transport Economics and Policy*, January, pp. 19-34.

Caves, D.W., L.R. Christensen, and W.E. Diewert (1982), 'Multilateral Comparisons of Output, Input, and Productivity Using Superlative Index Numbers', *Economic Journal*, 92, March, pp. 73-86.

Caves, D.W., L.R. Christensen, and J.A. Swanson (1981a), 'Economic Performance in Regulated and Unregulated Environments: A Comparison of U.S. and Canadian Railroads,' *Quarterly Journal of Economics*, Vol.96, November, pp. 559-81.

Caves, D.W., L.R. Christensen, and J.A. Swanson (1981b), 'Productivity Growth, Scale Economics, and Capacity Utilization in U.S. Railroads, 1955-1974', *American Economic Review*, Vol.71, December, pp. 994-1002.

Caves, D.W., L.R. Christensen, and M.W. Tretheway (1980), 'Flexible Cost Functions for Multi-product Firms', *Review of Economics and Statistics*, 62, pp. 477-481.

Caves, D.W., L.R. Christensen, and M.W. Tretheway (1984), 'Economies of Density versus Economies of Scale: Why Trunk and Local Service Airline Costs Differ',

64

Rand Journal of Economics, Vol.15, No.4, Winter, pp. 471-489.

Caves, D.W., L.R. Christensen, M.W. Tretheway, and R.J Windle (1987a), 'As Assessment of the Efficiency Effects of U.S. Airline Deregulation via an International Comparison' in E.E. Bailey ed. *Public Regulation: New Perspectives on Institutions and Policies*, Cambridge, Mass: MIT Press, pp. 285-320.

Caves, D.W., L.R. Christensen, M.W. Tretheway, and R.J Windle (1987b), 'Network Effects and the Measurement of Returns to Scale and Density for U.S. Railroads,' in A.F.Daughety, ed., *Analytical Studies in Transport Economics*, Cambridge: Cambridge University Press, pp. 97-120.

Caves, R.E. (1962), *Air Transport and Its Regulators: An Industry Study*, Cambridge: Harvard University Press.

Chow, G. (1978), 'The Current Status of Economies of Scale in Regulated Trucking: A Review of the Evidence and Future Directions,' *Proceedings*, Transportation Research Forum, Oxford, Indiana: Richard B. Cross, pp. 365-72.

Christensen, L.R. and J.Huston (1987), 'A Reexamination of the Cost Structure for Specialized Motor Carriers,' *Logistics and Transportation Review* 23:4, pp. 339-352.

Christensen, L.R. and D.W. Jorgensen (1969), 'The Measurement of U.S. Real Capital Input, 1929-1967', *The Review of Income and Wealth*, Series 15, No.1, pp. 293-320.

Christensen, L.R., D.W. Jorgensen and L.J. Lau (1971), 'Conjugate Duality and the Transcendental Production Function', *Econometrica*, July 1971, pp. 255-256.

Christensen, L.R., D.W. Jorgensen and L.J. Lau (1973), 'Transcendental Logarithmic Production Frontiers', *Review of Economics and Statistics*, February, pp. 28-45.

Clark, J.M. (1923), *Studies in the Economies of Overhead Costs*, Chicago, IL: Unviersity of Chicago Press.

Compagnie, I., H. Gathon and P. Pestieau (1991), 'Autonomy and Performance in Public Enterprises: the case of Railways and Postal Services', a paper presented at CIRIEC Seminar *Public Versus Private Enterprises: In Search of the Real Issues*, Liége, April 4-5.

Court, A.T. (1939), 'Hedonic Price Index with Automobile Examples', in *The Dynamics of Automobile Demand*, New York: General Motors Corporation, pp. 98-119.

Daughety, A.F. and F.D. Nelson (1988), 'An Econometric Analysis of Changes in the Cost and Production Structure of the Trucking Industry, 1953-82,' *Review of Economic and Statistics*, pp. 67-75.

Daughety, A.F., F.D. Nelson and W.R.Vigdor (1985), 'An Econometric Analysis of the Cost and Production Structure of the Trucking Industry,' in A.F. Daughety, ed., *Analytical Studies in Transport Economics*, Cambridge: Cambridge University Press.

De Borger, B. (1991), 'Hedonic versus Homogeneous Output Specifications of Railroad Technology: Belgian Railroads 1950-1986', *Transportation Research*, Vol 25A, No.4, pp. 227-238.

De Borger, B. (1992), 'Estimating a Multiple-Output Generalized Box-Cox Cost

Function: Cost Structure and Productivity Growth in Belgian Railroad Operations, 1950-1986', *European Economic Review*, 36, pp.1379-1398.

Denny, M. (1972), *Trade and the Production Sector; An Exploration of Multi-Product Technologies*, Ph.D. Dissertation, University of California, Berkeley.

Denny, M. (1974), 'The Relationship between Functional Forms for the Production System,' *Canadian Journal of Economics*, 7, pp. 21-31.

Denny, M., and M. Fuss (1977), 'The Use of Approximation Analysis to Test for Separability and the Existence of Consistent Aggregates,' *American Economic Review*, vol.67, no.3, pp. 404-418.

Deprins, D. and L. Simar (1989), 'Estimating Technical Inefficiencies with Correction for Environmental Conditions with an Application to railway companies', *Annals of Public and Cooperative Economics*, 1989, pp. 81-101.

Diewert, W.E. (1971), 'An Application of the Shephard Duality Theorem: a Generalized Leontief Production Function,' *Journal of Political Economy*, May-June, pp. 481-507.

Diewert, W.E. (1973), 'Separability and the Generalized Cobb-Douglas Utility Function,' Ottawa: Department of Manpower and Immigration, January, mimeo.

Diewert, W.E. (1987), 'Index Numbers', in J. Eatwell, M. Milgate and P. Neuman eds. *A Dictionary of Economics*, Vol.2, London: The MacMillan Press, pp. 767-780

Diewert, W.E. (1992), 'The Measurement of Productivity,' *Bulletin of Economic Research*, 44, pp. 169-98.

Diewert, W.E., and T.J. Wales (1987), 'Flexible Functional Forms and Global Curvature Conditions, *Econometrica*, vol.55, No.1, pp. 43-68.

Diewert, W.E. and T.J. Wales (1988), 'A Normalized Quadratic Semiflexible Functional Form', *Journal of Econometrics*, Vol. 39, pp. 327-342.

Distexhe, V. and S. Perelman (1993), 'Technical Efficiency and Productivity Growth in an Era of Deregulation: the Case of Airlines', a paper presented at the *Third European Workshop on Efficiency and Productivity Measurement*, CORE, Belgium, October.

Eads, G.C., M. Nerlove and W. Raduchel (1969), 'A Long Run Cost Function for the Local Service Airline Industry', *Review of Economics and Statistics*, Vol. 51, Aug., pp. 258-270.

Encaoua, D. (1991), 'Liberalizing European Airlines: Cost and Factor Productivity Evidence', *International Journal of Industrial Organization*, 9, pp. 109-124.

Färe, R., S. Grosskopf, and C.A. K. Lovell (1985), *The Measurement of Efficiency of Prodution*, Kluwer-Nijhoff.

Farrell, M.J. (1957), 'The Measurement of Productive Efficiency', *Journal of the Royal Statistical Society*, Series A (General), 120, Part III, pp. 253-281.

Filippini, M. and R. Maggi (1991), 'Efficiency and Ownership in the case of Swiss Private Railways', a paper presented at CIRIEC Seminar *Public Versus Private Enterprises: In Search of the Real Issues*, Liege, April 4-5.

Fisher, F.M. and K. Shell (1968), 'Taste and Quality Change in the Pure Theory of the True Cost-of-Living Index,' in *Value, Capital and Growth: Essays in Honour of Sir John Hicks*, edited by J.N. Wolfe, Univ. of Edinburgh Press.

Försund, F.R.(1992), 'A Comparison of Parametric and Non-parametric Efficiency Measures: the Case of Norwegian Ferries', *The Journal of Productivity Analysis*, Vol.4, No. 1/2, June, pp. 25-43.

Forsyth, P.J., R.D. Hill, and C.D. Trengove (1986), 'Measuring Airline Efficiency', *Fiscal Studies*, Vol.7, No. 1, February, pp. 61-81.

Freeman, K.D., T.H. Oum, M.W. Tretheway, W.G. Waters II (1987), *The Growth and Performance of the Canadian Transcontinental Railways 1956-1981*, Centre for Transportation Studies, University of British Columbia, Vancouver, B.C, Canada.

Friedlaender, A., and S.S.Bruce, 'Augmentation Effects and Technical Change in the Regulated Trucking Industry, 1974-79,' in A.F.Daughety, ed., *Analytical Studies in Transport Economics*, Cambridge: Cambridge University Press.

Friedlaender, A., and Spady, R.H. (1980), 'A Derived Demand Function for Freight Transportation', *Review of Economics and Statistics*, (August), pp. 432-441.

Friedlaender, A., and Spady, R.H. (1981), *Freight Transportation Regulation: Equity, Efficiency, and Competition in the Rail and Trucking Industry*, MIT Press., Cambridge, Mass.

Friedlaender, A., Spady, R.H., and S.J. Wang Chaing (1981), 'Regulation and the Structure of Technology in the Trucking Industry,' (eds.) T.G. Cowing and R. E. Stevenson in *Productivity Measurement in Regulated Industries*.

Friedlaender, A. Berndt, E.R.; Chiang, J.S; Showalter, M; Vellturo, C.A.; (1993), 'Rail Costs and Capital Adjustments in a Quasi-Regulated Environment', *Journal of Transport Economics and Policy*, pp. 131-152.

Gagne, R. (1990), 'On the Relevant Elasticity Estimates for Cost Structure Analysis of the Trucking Industry,' *Review of Economics and Statistics* 72, pp. 160-64.

Gathon, H. and S. Perelman (1990), 'Measuring Technical Efficiency in European Railways: a Panel Data Approach', an unpublished paper, University de Liege.

Gillen, D.W., and Oum, T.H. (1984), 'A Study of the Cost Structures of the Canadian Motor Coach Industry,' *Canadian Journal of Economics*, Vol. XVII, No. 3 (May, 1984), pp. 369-385.

Gillen, D.W., T.H. Oum and M.W. Tretheway (1985a), *Airline Cost and Performance: Implications for Public and Industry Policies*, Centre for Transportation Studies, University of British Columbia, Vancouver, B.C., Canada

Gillen, D.W., T.H. Oum and M.W. Tretheway (1985b), *Canadian Airline Deregulation and Privatization: Assessing Effects and Prospects*, Centre for Transportation Studies, U.B.C..

Gillen, D.W., T.H. Oum and M.W. Tretheway (1990), 'Airline Cost Structure and Policy Implications', *Journal of Transport Economics and Policy*, Vol. XXIV, No.2, May, pp. 9-34.

Gong, B.H., and R.C. Sickles (1992), 'Finite Sample Evidence on the Performance of Stochastic Frontier and Data Envelopment Analysis Using Panel Data', *Journal of Econometrics*, 51, pp. 259-284.

Good, D.H., M. I. Nadiri, and R.C. Sickles (1991), 'The Structure of Production, Technical Change and Efficiency in a Mutinational Industry: an Application to US airlines', NBER working papers Series No. 3939.

Good, David H.; Nadiri, M.I.; Roller, L.H.; Sickles, R.C.; (1993), 'Efficiency and Productivity Growth Comparisons of European and U.S. Air Carriers: A First Look at the Data', *The Journal of Productivity Analysis*, No 4, pp. 115-125.

Good, D.and Rhodes, E. (1990), 'Productive Efficiency, Technological Change and the Competitiveness of U.S. Airlines in the Pacific Rim', *Journal of the Transportation Research Forum*.

Grabowski, R. and S. Mehdian (1990), 'Efficiency of the Railroad Industry: A Frontier Production Function Approach', *Quarterly Journal of Business and Economics*, Vol.29, Issue 2, Spring, pp. 26-42.

Griliches, Z. (1972), 'Cost Allocation in Railroad Regulation,' *Bell J. of Economics*, Vol.3, No.1, pp. 26-41.

Grimm, C.M., T.M. Corsi and J.L. Jarrell (1989), 'U.S. Motor Carrier Cost Structure under Deregulation,' *Logistics and Transportation Review*, 25(3), pp. 231-49.

Guilkey, D. K., and C.A.K. Lovell (1980), 'On the flexibility of the translog approximation,' *International Economic Review*, Vol. 21, No.1(Feb), pp. 137-147.

Guilkey, D. K., C.A.K. Lovell and R. C. Sickles (1983), 'A Comparison of the Performance of Three Flexible Functional Forms', *International Economic Review*, Vol. 24, No.3(Oct), pp. 591-616.

Harmatuck, D.J. (1991), 'Economies of Scale and Scope in the Motor Carrier Industry,' *Journal of Transport Economics and Policy*, May, pp. 135-151.

Harmatuck, D.J. (1992), 'Motor Carrier Cost Function Comparisons,' *Transportation Journal*, Summer, pp. 31-46.

Harris, Robert G.; (1977), 'Economies of Traffic Density in the Rail Freight Industry', *Bell Journal of Economics*, pp. 556-564.

Hasenkamp, G. (1976), 'A Study of Multiple-output Production Function, Klein Railroad Study Revisited', *Journal of Econometrics*, 4, pp. 253-62.

Huang,C.J. and J. Liu (1994), 'Estimation of a Non-Neutral Stochastic Frontier Production Function', *Journal of Productivity Analysis*, Vol.5, pp. 171-180.

Jara-Diaz, S. (1982a), 'The Estimation of Transport Cost Functions: A Methodological Review,' *Transport Reviews* 2, pp. 257-78.

Jara-Diaz, S. (1982b), 'Transportation Product, Transportation Function and Cost Functions,' *Transportation Science* 16, pp. 522-39.

Jara-Diaz, S. (1983), 'Freight Transportion Multioutput Analysis,' *Transportation Research* 17A, pp. 429-38.

Jara-Diaz, S. (1988), 'Multioutput Analysis of Trucking Operations Using Spatially-Disaggregated Flows,' *Transportation Research* 22B, pp. 159-71.

Jara-Diaz, S., P.Donoso and J.Araneda (1991), 'Best Partial Flow Aggregation in Transportation Cost Functions,' *Transportation Research* B25, pp. 329-39.

Jara-Diaz, S., P.Donoso and J.Araneda (1992), 'Estimation of Marginal Transport Costs Using the Flow Aggregation Approach,' *Journal of Transport Economics and Policy,* 26, pp. 35-48.

Jara-Diaz, S. and C.E.Cortes (1995), 'Calculation of Scale Economies from Transport Cost Functions,' paper presented at the World Conference on Transport Research, Sydney.

Jara-Diaz, S. and C.E.Cortes (1996), 'On the Calculation of Scale Economies from Transport Cost Functions,' *Journal of Transport Economics and Policy* 30, pp. 157-70.

Jara-Diaz, S. and C. Winston (1981), 'Multiproduct Transport Cost Functions: Scale and Scope in Railway Operations', in N. Blattner (ed.) *Eighth European Association for Research in Industrial Economics*, Vol. I, University of Basel, pp. 437-469.

Jha, R. and B.S. Sahni (1992), 'Towards Measuring Airline Technical Inefficiency: the Case of Canadian Airlines Industry', *International Journal of Transport Economics*, Vol. XIX, No. 1, February, pp. 45-59.

Johnston, J.J. (1960), *Statisical Cost Analysis*, New York: McGraw-Hill.

Keeler, T.E. (1974), 'Railroad Costs, Returns to Scale and Excess Capacity,' *Review of Economics and Statistics*, Vol. 56, pp. 201-208.

Keeler, T.E. (1983), *Railroads, Freight and Public Policy*, Washington D.C.: The Brookings Institute.

Keeler, T.E. (1989) 'Deregulation and Scale Economies in the U.S. Trucking Industry: an Econometric Extension of the Survivor Principle,' *Journal of Law and Economics*, 32, pp. 229-253.

Keeler, J.P. and J.P. Formby (1994), 'Cost Economies and Consolidation in the U.S. Airline Industry', *International Journal of Transport Economics*, Vol.XXI, No.1, February 1994, pp. 21-45.

Kim, M.Y. (1987), 'Multilateral Relative Efficiency Levels in Regional Canadian Trucking,' *Logistics and Transportation Review* 23:2, pp. 155-72.

Klein, L.R. (1946), 'Remarks on the Theory of Aggregation,' *Econometrica*, vol.14, pp. 303-312.

Klein, L.R. (1953), *A Textbook on Econometrics*, Evanston, Illinois: Row, Peterson and Company.

Koenker, R. (1977), 'Optimal Scale and the Size Distribution of American Trucking Firms', *Journal of Transport Economics and Policy*, Vol.11, No.1, pp. 54-67.

Kopp, R. and W.E. Diewert (1982), 'The Decomposition of Frontier Cost Function Deviations into Measures of Technical and Allocative Efficiency', *Journal of Econometrics*, 19, pp. 319-331.

Kumbhakar, S. (1987), 'The Specification of Technical and Allocative Inefficiency in Stochastic Production and Profit Frontiers', *Journal of Econometrics*, 34(3), pp. 335-348.

Kumbhakar, S. (1989), 'Modelling Technical and Allocative Inefficiency in Translog Production Function', *Economics Letters*, 31(2), pp. 119-124.

Kumbharkar, S.C. (1990), 'A Reexamination of Returns to Scale, Density and Technical Progress in U.S. Airlines', *Southern Economic Journal*, 57, pp. 428-442

Kumbharkar, S.C. (1992), 'Allocative Distortions, Technical Progress, and Input Demand in U.S. Airlines: 1970-1984', *International Economic Review*, Vol.33 No.3, Aug., pp. 723-737.

Kumbhakar, S. (1994), 'A Multiproduct Symmetric Generalized McFadden Cost Fucntion', *J of Productivity Analysis,* 5, pp. 349-357.

Lancaster, K. (1966), 'A New Approach to Consumer Theory', *Journal of Political Economy*, 74, pp. 132-157.

Lardner, D. (1850), *Railway Economy: a Treatise on the New Art of Transport, Its Management, Prospects and Relations*, New York: A.M. Kelley, (1968 reprint).

Locklin, D.P. (1933), 'The Literature on Railway Rate Theory', *Quarterly Journal of Economics*, 47, pp. 167-230.

Lorenz, M.O. (1916), 'Cost and Value of Service in Railroad Ratemaking', *Quarterly Journal of Economics*, 21, pp. 205-218.

McFadden, Daniel (1978), 'Cost, Revenue and Profit Functions,' in M.Fuss and D. McFadden, eds., *Production Economics: a Dual Approach to Theory and Applications*, Vol. 1, The Theory of Production (New York: North Holland Publishing).

McGeehan, H. (1993), 'Railway Costs and Productivity Growth', *Journal of Transport Economics and Policy*, Vol. XXVII, No.1, January 1993, pp. 19-32.

McMullen, B.S. (1987), 'The Impact of Regulatory Reform on Motor Carrier Costs,' *Journal of Transport Economics and Policy*, September, pp. 307-19.

McMullen, B.S. and L.R.Stanley (1988), 'The Impact of Deregulation on Production Structure of the Motor Carrier Industry,' *Economic Inquiry*, 26, pp. 299-316.

McMullen, B.S. and H. Tanaka (1992), 'Structural Differences between Large and Small U.S. Motor Carriers Folllowing Deregulation: Implications for Market Structure,' mimeo, Oregon State University.

McShane, S. and R. Windle (1989), 'The Implication of Hub-and-Spoke Routing for Airline Costs and Competitiveness, *Logistics and Transportation Review*, vol.25, no.3, pp. 209-230.

Meeusen, W. and J. van den Broeck (1977), 'Efficiency Estimation from Cobb-Douglas Production Functions with Composed Error', *International Economic Review*, 8, pp. 435-444.

Meyer, J.R., and Kraft G.(1961), 'The Evaluation of Statistical Costing Techniques as Applied to the Transportation Industry,' *American Economic Review*, Vol.51, pp. 313-340.

Meyer, J.R., Peck, M.J., Stenason, J., and Zwick, C. (1959), *The Economics of Competition in the Transportation Industry,* Harvard Univ. Press.

Morrison, Catherine (1988), 'Quasi-Fixed Inputs in U.S. and Japanese Manufacturing: A Generalized Leontief Restricted Cost Function Approach', *The Review of Economics and Statistics*, pp. 275-287.

Nataf, A. (1950), 'Sur la Possibilite de Construction de certains Macromodeles,' *Econometrica*, Vol. 16, pp. 232-244.

Nelson, R.A. (1989), 'On the Measurement of Capacity Utilization,' *Journal of Industrial Economics*, 37, pp. 273-286.

Oniki, H., Oum, T.H., Stevenson, R. and Zhang Y. (1994), 'The Productivity Effects of the Liberalization of Japanese Telecommunications Policy' *Journal of Productivity Analysis*, vol.5, No.1 (1994), pp. 63-79.

Oum, T. H. (1977), 'Derived Demand for Freight Transportation and Inter-modal Competition in Canada,' *Transportation Research Forum Conference Proceedings*, pp. 56-67, a substantially revised version published in *Journal of Transport Economics and Policy*, (May, 1979), pp. 149-168.

Oum, T. H. (1979), 'A Cross Sectional Study of Freight Transport Demand and Rail-Truck Competition in Canada', *Bell Journal of Economics*, Vol 10, No. 2, pp. 463-482.

Oum, T. H. and Tretheway, M.W. (1989), 'Hedonic vs General Specifications of the Translog Function', *Logistics and Transportation Review*, Vol 25, No 1, pp. 3-21.

Oum, T. H., M.W. Tretheway and W.G. Waters (1992), 'Concepts, Methods, and Purposes of Productivity Measurement in Transportation', *Transportation Research A*, Vol.26A, No. 6, pp. 493-505.

Oum, T.H., Tretheway, M.W., and Zhang, Y. (1990), 'A Note on Capacity Utilization and Measurement of Scale Economies,' *Journal of Business and Economic Statistics*, 9, pp. 119-123.

Oum, T.H. and C. Yu (1994), 'Economic Efficiency of Railways and Implications for Public Policy: A Comparative Study of the OECD Countries' Railways', *The Journal of Transport Economics and Policy*, Vol.28, No.2, May, pp. 121-138.

Oum, T.H. and C. Yu (1995), 'A Comparative Study of Productivity and Cost Competitiveness of the World's Major Airlines', a Working Paper, Faculty of Commerce, Univ. of British Columbia, Vancouver, Canada.

Oum, T.H., and Zhang, Y. (1991), 'Utilization of Quasi-Fixed Inputs and Estimation of Cost Functions', *Journal of Transport Economics and Policy*, Vol.25, No.2, pp. 121-134.

Oum, T.H. and Zhang, Y. (1995), 'Competition and Allocative Efficiency: The Case of Competition in the U.S. Telephone Industry,' *Review of Economics and Statistics,* vol.77, no.1 (Feb, 1995), pp. 82-96.

Oum, T.H. and Zhang, Y. (1996), 'A Note on Scale Economies in Transportation,' working paper, Faculty of Commerce and Business Administration, The University of British Columbia, Vancouver.

Panzar, J.C. and R.D. Willig (1977), 'Economics of Scale in Multi-output Production', *Quarterly Journal of Economics*, 91, pp. 481-494.

Panzar, J.C. and R.D. Willig (1981), 'Economics of Scope', *American Economic Review, Papers and Proceedings*, 71, pp. 268-272.

Perelman, S. and P. Pestieau (1988), 'Technical Performance in Public Enterprises: A Comparative Study of Railway and Postal Services', *European Economic Review*, 32 (1988), pp. 432-441.

Pigou, A.C. (1912), *Wealth and Welfare*, London: MacMillan.

Pigou, A.C. (1913), 'Railway Rates and Joint Costs,' *Quarterly Journal of Economics*, 27, pp. 687-92.

Ripley, W.Z. (1923), *Railroads: Finance and Organization*, New York: Longmans, Green and Co.

Rosen, S. (1974), 'Hedonic Prices and Implicit Markets: Product Differentiation in Pure Competition,' *Journal of Political Economy*, Jan/Feb., pp. 34-55.

Sarndal, Carl, T.H. Oum, and W.B. Statton (1978), 'Further evidence on Factors Influencing Operating Costs of U.S. Commercial Airlines'; *Journal of Transport*

Economics and Policy, Vol XII No. 1, pp. 47-55.

Schmidt, P. and C.A.K. Lovell (1979), 'Estimating Technical and Allocative Inefficiency Relative to Stochastic Production and Cost Frontiers', *Journal of Econometrics*, 9(3), pp. 343-366.

Sickles, R.C. (1985), 'A Nonlinear Multivariate Error Components Analysis of Technology and Specific Factor Productivity Growth with an Application to the U.S. Airlines, *Journal of Econometrics*, 27, 1, pp. 61-78.

Spady, Richard H.(1979), *Econometric Estimation for the Regulated Transportation Industries.* NY: Garland Press.

Spady, Richard H.; Friedlaender, A.F. (1978), 'Hedonic Cost Functions for the Regulated Trucking Industry', *Bell Journal of Economics*, pp. 159-179.

Stenason, J. and R.A.Bandeen (1965), ' Transportation Costs and Their Implications: an Empirical Study of Railway Costs in Canada,' in *Transportation Economics* (National Bureau of Economic Research).

Stevenson, R.E. (1980a), 'Measuring Technological Bias', *American Economic Review*, 70, pp. 162-173.

Stevenson, R.E. (1980b), 'Likelihood Functions for Generalized Stochastic Frontier Estimation', *Journal of Econometrics*, 13, pp. 57-66.

Straszheim, M.H. (1969), *The International Airline Industry* (Brookings: Washington, D.C.).

Summers, R. and A. Heston (1991), 'The Penn World Table (Mark 5): An Expanded Set of International Comparisons, 1950-1988', *Quarterly Journal of Economics*, Vol. 106, Issue 2, May, pp. 327-368.

Taussig, F.W. (1913), 'Railways Rates and Joint Costs', *Quarterly Journal of Economics*, 27, pp. 378-84.

Thomas, J.M. and S.J.Callan (1989), 'Constant Returns to Scale in the Post-Deregulatory Period: the Case of Specialized Motor Carriers,' *Logistics and Transportation Review*, 25(3), pp. 271-88.

Thomas, J.M. and S.J.Callan (1992), 'Cost Analysis of Specialized Motor Carriers: An Investigation of Aggregation and Specification Bias,' *Logistics and Transportation Review*, 28(3), pp. 217-29.

van de Broek, J., F.R. Forsund, L. Hjalmarsson and W. Meeusen (1980), 'On the Estimation of Deterministic and Stochastic Frontier Production Functions: a Comparison', *Journal of Econometrics*, 13, pp. 117-138.

Wales, T.J. (1977), 'On the Flexibility of Flexible Functional Forms', *Journal of Econometrics*, 5, pp. 183-193.

Walters, A. A. (1963), 'Production and Cost Functions: An Econometric Survey', *Econometrica*, Vol 31, No 1-2, pp. 1-65.

Wang, J.S. and A. Friedlaender (1984), 'Output Aggregation, Network Effects, and the Measurement of Trucking Technology,' *Review of Economics and Statistics*, 64, pp. 267-76.

Waters, W.G.II (1976), 'Statistical Costing in Transportation,' *Transportation Journal*, Spring, pp. 49-62.

Waters, W.G.II (1980), 'Output Dimensions and Joint Costs,' *Int'l. Journal of*

Transport Economics (April), pp. 17-35.

Waters, W.G.II and M.W. Tretheway (1989), 'The Aggregate Econometric Approach versus the Disaggregate Activity Approach to Estimating Cost Functions,' paper presented at the World Conference on Transportation Research, Yokohama, Japan.

White, L.J. (1979), 'Economies of Scale and the Question of 'Natural Monopoly' in the Airline Industry,' *Journal of Air Law and Commerce* 44, pp. 545-73.

Wilson, G.W. (1962), *Essays on Some Unsettled Questions in the Economics of Transportation* Indiana Business Report No. 42, Foundation for Economic and Business Studies, Indiana University, Bloomington.

Windle, R.J. (1991), 'The World's Airlines: A Cost and Productivity Comparison', *Journal of Transport Economics and Policy*, Vol.XXV, No.1, January, pp. 31-49.

Winston, C. (1985), 'Conceptual Developments in the Economics of Transportation: An Interpretive Survey', *Journal of Economic Literature*, Vol. XXIII, Vol. 1, March, pp. 57-94.

Winston, C., T.M. Corsi, C.M. Grimm and C. Evans (1990), *The Economic Effects of Surface Freight Deregulation*, Washington, D.C.: Brookings.

Xu, K., R. Windle, C.Grim and T. Corsi (1994), 'Re-evaluating Returns to Scale in Transport,' *Journal of Transport Economics and Policy,* Sept., pp. 275-286.

Ying, J.S. (1990a), 'Regulatory Reform and Technical Change: New Evidence of Scale Economies in Trucking,' *Southern Economics Journal* 56(4), pp. 996-1009.

Ying, J.S. (1990b), 'The Inefficiency of Regulating a Competitive Industry: Productivity Gains in Trucking Following Reform,' *Review of Economics and Statistics*, 72(2), pp. 191-201.

Ying, J.S. (1992), 'On Calculating Cost Elasticities,' *Logistics and Transportation Review* 28, pp. 231-35.

Ying, J. and T.E.Keeler (1991), 'Pricing in a Deregulated Environment: the Motor Carrier Experience,' *Rand J. of Econ.* 22 (Summer), pp. 264-73.

Yu, C. (1995), *A Comparative Study of Alternative Methods for Efficiency Measurement With Applications to Transportation Industry*, unpublised PhD Dissertation, University of British Columbia, Vancouver, B.C., Canada.

4 Theory and practice of transport infrastructure and public transport pricing

Jan Owen Jansson

Introduction

Background, problem and purpose

The part of the transport sector which belongs to the public sector of the economy consists of the transport infrastructure - TI for short - and in most countries the lion's share of public transport as well. By public transport is to be understood all scheduled passenger transport services along given routes, irrespective of the type of vehicle and bearer of the transport vehicles. The TI and public transport sub-sector is as a whole a main source of net revenue for many, in particular European governments. However, within this sub-sector public transport by road and rail is with few exceptions a heavily subsidized activity. This implies that individual motorized transport by road is also much more a milch cow for the Treasury. In Sweden, for example, road transport generates some 10% of central government total revenue, of which only a fraction goes back to the sector.

The pricing of transport infrastructure and public transport services is, consequently, not just an issue of economic efficiency. A central question in Transport Economics is therefore whether the existing structure of prices of TI and public transport services, for which public finance and equity considerations could be expected to play important roles, would be very different from an efficient structure? The purpose of this paper is to take up this old issue by a modern approach, which, hopefully, will give some new insight.

Efficiency is a complex concept. A main division which may help to prevent confusion is between allocative efficiency and X-efficiency. Economists know a lot about the former, and much less about the latter. X-efficiency concerns the achievement of the least-cost solution to problems of individual organizations, which economists take for granted when looking for the optimal allocation of resources between the organizations in the economy. It has been pointed out many times, most forcefully in the original contribution by Leibenstein 1966, that in a world-wide

74

perspective, X-inefficiency seems to be a greater problem than allocative inefficiency. This is, of course, important for the division of labour in economic research, but no problem per se for the limited band of transport economists looking for improvements in the allocative efficiency. These tasks are important enough. A serious problem would arises if solutions to allocative ineffeciency problems and solutions to X-inefficiency problems were in conflict. A case in point is the famous British bus deregulation. It seems that allocative efficiency has suffered, but possibly that the slack (X-inefficiency) in the public transport industry has been reduced. What the net result has been seems to be difficult to sum up.

Both allocative efficiency and X-efficiency in the TI and public transport part of the transport sector are to be aimed at. There is no inherent conflict between these two goals. It is just that the institutional framework and organizational structure have to be designed with both goals in mind, which is seldom done. One part of this multi-objective analytical process is the search for the unconstrained optimum as regards the level and structure of prices of TI and public transport services.

The transport system definition and the pricing-relevant costs of public transport and TI and public transport services

So far as investment theory for transport infrastructure (TI) is concerned, it has long been clear that, analytically, it is advantageous to define the system to include the user costs i.e. the costs of the vehicles with occupants making use of the TI-service concerned, since TI optimization is to a large degree a matter of trading off producer costs against user cost savings by adjusting different facility design variables.

A similarly wide system definition is appropriate for discussing optimal pricing. The transport system considered in the following discussion consists of transport vehicles and transport infrastructure - bearers of moving vehicles, terminals for change of mode of transport, and parking facilities for idle vehicles. The transport vehicles in the system are either owned or hired by the trip-makers and owners of goods, or belonging to a public transport company. From a price theoretical point of view, the total system costs are naturally divided into three parts:

$$TC = TC^{prod} + TC^{user} + TC^{ext} \tag{1}$$

The definition of the producer and user costs depends on which service is in focus. When we are discussing optimal pricing of the TI-services, the service producer is the TI-owner, the service users are different vehicles, and the system output is traffic volume normally measured by vehicle-kilometers (Q).

The external (to the transport system) costs comprise all possible costs falling on 'third parties', i.e. the rest of society. It is not always obvious where the line should be drawn between TI-users and external subjects. In road transport, for example, it can be argued that pedestrians and bicyclists are external if separate lanes are provided for them. It is really a matter of modelling convenience, of selecting the most natural transport production function for facility optimization and pricing in each particular case.

When public transport pricing is taken up for discussion, we are looking at a subset of the TI-service users, constituted by one or more public transport enterprises. The producer costs are now the costs of these enterprise(s). In the main case the public transport volume is relatively so small that the traffic conditions from the point of view of the public transport enterprise(s) in question are exogenously given, independent of the public transport vehicle input. The exceptional case is railway transport systems, where all vehicles in the system belong to the same owner/operator. An additional train in the system may affect running times and/or the safety of other trains, and this is naturally taken into account by the operator. The users of public transport services are, of course, the passengers, and the (sub)system output is measured by passenger-kilometers and/or number of trips (B).

Pricing with a view to maximizing the sum of producers' and consumers' surplus as well as internalizing all possible negative externalities is 'optimal pricing'. It is traditionally thought of as 'marginal cost pricing', and in spirit, if not quite formally, that is what the present discussion is all about. However, with a system definition including 'users' in the double role of suppliers of essential inputs as well as consumers of the output, optimal price will be strictly different from the social marginal cost.

To avoid confusion, a different cost concept is introduced, which is called 'the pricing-relevant cost' and generally designated PC, and which should be equal to the price in optimum. Its definition is the following in the case of TI-services (for a complete derivation and discussion, see Jansson 1984, 1993):

$$PC = MC^{prod} + Q \frac{\partial AC^{user}}{\partial Q} + MC^{ext} \tag{2a}$$

For the discussion of pricing of TI-services, it is appropriate to regard the transport infrastructure as fixed. The relevant cost and output relationship to be considered is thus that between the costs of wear and tear, traffic control, etc. and the traffic volume, so far as the producer costs are concerned. As is well known, far more important for optimal pricing is the relationship between the user costs of time (and accidents, so far as road transport is concerned), various external costs and the traffic volume.

The middle term of (2a) represents the influence on the costs of fellow TI-system users that an additional user has. Mathematically the product of Q and the derivative of AC^{user} with respect to Q equals the difference between MC^{user} and AC^{user}, and the latter formulation makes, of course, economic sense, too: AC^{user} is perceived as the private marginal cost when a good number of independent transport consumers make use of the transport facility concerned, and it is the difference between the social and private marginal user costs that is pricing-relevant.

In the exceptional case, the 'fellow TI-system users' belong to the same concern as the additional vehicle considered, which means that the middle term vanishes from the PC expression (2a). To be more specific, rail track charges on the trains of the National Railways should not contain a congestion cost component, where no other

76

train operators exist.

The same basic formula for PC applies to public transport optimal pricing. Superficially the only difference is that the number of trips, B, replaces Q in the middle term of (2a): the pricing-relevant cost of public transport services is likewise the sum of the producer marginal cost, the difference between the user marginal and user average costs, and the external marginal cost.

Here, however, the similarities end. It is now appropriate to take up the public transport and TI-service pricing problems in turn. The following discussion is basically divided into two sections. First, public transport pricing is dealt with. Urban bus transport is the main focus, but also long-distance public transport by rail and air is discussed. Afterwards, TI-service pricing is taken up for discussion, where urban and interurban road pricing, respectively, are the main topics.

Optimal public transport pricing

When it comes to public transport system optimization and pricing (with the exception of the National Railways) the natural procedure is to limit the system analysis to a subset of the total transport system defined at the outset. Obviously the design and capital costs of the transport infrastructure are taken as given, and conveniently kept outside the cost picture.

On the other hand, it is equally obvious that the vehicle input of the public transport enterprise(s) should be regarded as more or less variable. This means that the first term of the general expression for the pricing-relevant cost in its public transport version, (2b) below, represents the marginal cost of public transport capacity, and the middle term can be a negative cost, i.e. a benefit in the form of reduced waiting time for the original passengers in the case where additional public transport output is produced by putting in another vehicle:

$$PC = MC^{prod} + B \; \frac{\partial AC^{user}}{\partial B} + MC^{ext} \qquad (2b)$$

The external marginal cost of a public transport sub-system has to some extent the same character as the external marginal cost of the whole transport system, i.e. noise, pollution, and accident externalities accruing to 'third parties'. In addition, by the sub-system definition, the wear and tear of the TI caused by the public transport vehicles, and their contribution to traffic congestion (affecting private cars in the first place) are external to the sub-system in question. Charges on the public transport vehicles on account of the marginal external costs are included in the producer marginal cost in the present case. If the externality charges are perfect, the third term of (2b) disappears; only if the externalities are imperfectly internalized, MC^{ext} in the PC expression is a relevant component.

The outline of the following discussion is governed by two main lessons learnt from my experience in dealing with the complex matter of optimal pricing of public transport:

77

1 Transport system design and optimal pricing should be determined simultaneously in reality as well as in theoretical analysis.

2 The two issues of the optimal level and the optimal structure of prices are each very important and complicated enough to be dealt with in separate steps.

The main model underpinning the discussion of the optimal level of public transport prices is of an urban bus transport system of 'Circletown'. To be able to take a system viewpoint and yet keep the model reasonably simple, a number of real life complexities are ignored, e.g. the heterogeneous structure of urban travel demand.

In later sections the peakiness of travel demand in time and space is taken into full consideration in discussions of peak-load pricing of urban bus services as well as interurban train services.

The Circletown model of urban bus transport system optimization and pricing

Urban bus transport cost analysis is not so much a matter of econometrics as an exercise in geometry. The characteristics of Circletown and the bus travel of its population are as follows:

r = radius of Circletown
B = total number of bus trips per day
l = average trip length
lB = total passenger-kilometres per day
X = trip density, i.e. number of trips generated per km^2 ($X = B/\pi r^2$).

Circletown is a markedly centralized city. It is assumed that if, starting from the centre, the town is divided into successively larger rings of equal width, the population as well as the number of bus trips generated in each ring is the same. This assumption yields a reasonably realistic distribution of the population of Circletown. It can then be assumed that travel demand is homogeneous in time and space in Circletown.

The Circletown bus transport system consists of a number of equi-distant radial lines of similar length (equal to the city radius). The characteristics of the system are summarized thus:

n = number of radial bus lines
N = total number of buses
S = bus size (= pax max)
V = speed of bus transport (taking stop time into account), km/hour
H = effective service-time (hours) per busday
φ = average occupancy rate (load factor).

From the above parameters and variables the frequency of service can be derived assuming that the same service is offered in each direction.

$$F = \frac{NV}{2nr} = \text{frequency of bus services}$$

The total capacity constraint can be written thus:

$$lB = \phi SNVH \qquad\qquad (3)$$

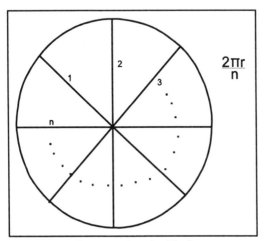

Figure 4.1   **Network of bus services in Circletown**

The total cost for the bus company can be given in a very simple way under the following assumptions. First, let us assume that all buses are in all-day service: the same time-table applies the whole day. Let us also assume that overall speed, V is constant, given by street design, traffic conditions, etc., which means that the mileage of each bus per day is constant. Then the total bus company costs can be expressed as the product of the number of buses, N, and an all-inclusive daily cost per bus. The daily bus cost depends on bus size, S. In Jansson 1984 is it shown that both the running cost per kilometre, and the standing cost per day are approximately linear functions of S. The total cost per busday can consequently be written $a_1 + b_1 S$. It has been demonstrated in several studies that the overhead costs of public transport companies are proportional to the size of the fleet of transport vehicles (see e.g. Jansson 1984). It is not known, however, to what extent the vehicle size, if at all, influences the overhead costs. It is likely that most overhead costs are contained in the constant a_1, and relatively little in the bus size-dependent constant b_1. Anyway, it is possible to express the total bus company (producer of transport services) cost of Circletown per day as:

$$Tc^{prod} = N(a_1 + b_1S) \tag{4a}$$

The constant a_1, which includes the cost of the driver, and the lion's share of the overhead costs, dominates over the bus size-dependent cost component b_1S up to the very largest bus sizes.

The user cost component of the model is built up from the following values of time (time costs per hour).

c = walking time cost per km
w = waiting time cost per hour
$g(\phi)$ = riding time cost per hour; this is not a constant, but depends on the occupancy rate. The more crowded the bus is, the higher the riding time cost per hour.

The user costs of bus travellers thus consist of a walking time cost to/from stops, a waiting time cost at stops, and a riding time cost. These costs are influenced by city characteristics and the service design variables in the following way:

$$\frac{c\pi r}{2n}$$

* the average walking time cost per trip is proportional to the city radius, r, given the number of bus lines, and inversely proportional to n, given the city radius;

$$\frac{w}{2F}$$

* the average waiting time cost per trip is inversely proportional to the frequency of service (equals half the headway);

$$\frac{1 \cdot g(\phi)}{V}$$

* the average riding time cost per trip is a product of trip time, l/V, and riding time cost per hour $g(\phi)$.

Taking into account that the service frequency $F = NV/2nr$, total user costs per day are written:

$$TC^{user} = B \left(\frac{c\pi r}{2n} + \frac{wnr}{NV} + \frac{1 \cdot g(\phi)}{V} \right) \tag{4b}$$

Relative to individual car travel, public transport is normally at a marked advantage so far as negative externalities are concerned. They could be ignored. However, for completeness the total external costs are included, too. To keep the model as simple as possible, it is assumed that TC^{ext} can be expressed in the same way as TC^{prod}, i.e.

as a product of the number of buses, N, and a daily cost per bus, $a_2 + b_2S$. Road wear and tear, congestion and accident costs, as well as noise and exhaust fume emissions, depend both on total bus-kilometers and bus size. The total social cost of bus travel per day can then be written as follows:

$$TC = TC^{prod} + TC^{user} + TC^{ext} = N(a+bS) + B\left[\frac{c\pi r}{2n} + \frac{wnr}{NV} + \frac{l \cdot g(\phi)}{V}\right] \qquad (4c)$$

where $a = a_1 + a_2$, and $b = b_1 + b_2$.

The model should now be used to optimize the bus system in respect of capacity as well as quality of service as a preparation for discussing optimal pricing. The design variables concerned are N, S, ϕ, n and F, of which the service frequency, F, follows from N and n, as shown above.

Optimal design along the expansion path. In analogy with general production and cost theory, the purpose is to explore optimal input combinations, or service design along the 'expansion path', i.e., to express N^{opt}, S^{opt}, n^{opt}, F^{opt} and ϕ^{opt} as functions of the level of output, factor prices, and exogenous city characteristics.

The most interesting output measure in the present context is trip density, X i.e. the number of trips generated per square kilometre, $B/\pi r^2$, rather than the total number of trips, B, or total passenger-kilometres in Circletown, lB. Trip density is decisive for the quality of service. As will be demonstrated presently, both the optimal frequency of service and average walking distance to/from stops are determined by X, irrespective of the size of Circletown (r), or the average trip length (l).

The solution to the problem of optimal design is found by trip cost minimization. A Lagrangian expression, L, is formed that consists of the total social cost per trip, $AC = (TC^{prod} + TC^{user} + TC^{ext})/B$, and the capacity constraint.

$$L = AC - \lambda(lB - \phi SNVH) \qquad (5)$$

The cost minimization conditions are obtained by taking the derivatives of (5) with respect to the design variables and the Lagrangian multiplier, setting them equal to zero:

$$\frac{\partial L}{\partial N} = \frac{a+bS}{B} - \frac{wnr}{N^2V} + \lambda\phi SVH = 0 \qquad (5a)$$

$$\frac{\partial L}{\partial S} = \frac{bN}{B} + \lambda\phi NVH = 0 \qquad (5b)$$

81

$$\frac{\partial L}{\partial n} = -\frac{c\pi r}{2n^2} + \frac{wr}{NV} = 0 \tag{5c}$$

$$\frac{\partial L}{\partial \phi} = \frac{1 \cdot g'(\phi)}{V} + \lambda SNVH = 0 \tag{5d}$$

$$\frac{\partial L}{\partial \lambda} = -1B + \phi SNVH = 0 \tag{5e}$$

Multiplying (5b) by S/N we obtain:

$$\frac{bS}{B} + \lambda \phi SVH = 0 \tag{6}$$

By substituting -bS/B for the third term of (5a) we obtain:

$$\frac{a + bS}{B} - \frac{wnr}{N^2V} - \frac{bS}{B} = 0 \tag{7}$$

$$\frac{a}{B} - \frac{wnr}{N^2V} = 0 \tag{7a}$$

Combining (7a) and (5c) both n and N can be solved for

$$N^{\text{opt}} = \pi r^2 \left(\frac{cw}{2V}\right)^{\frac{1}{3}} \left(\frac{X}{a}\right)^{\frac{2}{3}} \tag{8}$$

$$n^{\text{opt}} = \pi r \left(\frac{c}{2}\right)^{\frac{2}{3}} \left(\frac{VX}{aw}\right)^{\frac{1}{3}} \tag{9}$$

From the formula for the average walking distance per trip (d), d^{opt} is obtained as follows:

$$d^{\text{opt}} = \frac{1}{2} \left(\frac{2}{c}\right)^{\frac{2}{3}} \left(\frac{aw}{VX}\right)^{\frac{1}{3}} \tag{9a}$$

From N^{opt}, n^{opt}, and the definition on page 77 the optimal frequency of service can be obtained:

$$F^{opt} = \left(\frac{w}{2}\right)^{\frac{2}{3}} \left(\frac{VX}{ac}\right)^{\frac{1}{3}} \tag{10}$$

Given N^{opt} it is possible to calculate optimal bus size from the capacity constraint:

$$S^{opt} = \frac{1}{\phi H} \left(\frac{a}{V}\right)^{\frac{2}{3}} \left(\frac{2X}{cw}\right)^{\frac{1}{3}} \tag{11}$$

As long as the riding time cost function is specified no further than $g(\phi)$ per hour, S^{opt} has to be given conditional on ϕ. It is interesting to note that the previously derived design variables are independent of ϕ, and consequently also of the exact shape of the function $g(\phi)$. This conclusion can be drawn more directly by combining optimality conditions (5b) and (5d), and the capacity constraint (5e). In this process λ is eliminated, and the following relationship is obtained:

$$\phi^2 \cdot g'(\phi) = \frac{b}{H} \tag{12}$$

The optimal occupancy rate is found by balancing the riding time cost per hour, which is increasing with increases in ϕ, and the bus size-dependent producer cost per hour, b/H.

Looking at the result of the optimization, it is apparent that total capacity has to keep abreast with an increasing trip density X along the expansion path; two thirds of the required capacity augmentation is achieved by increasing the number of buses, and one third by increasing bus size. It is interesting to note that a traffic volume increase caused by a lengthening of each trip, given the number of trips, should be met by a corresponding increase in bus size (and no number increase).

The quality of service is continuously improving as trip density is increasing. The elasticities of n^{opt} and F^{opt} with respect to X are both 1/3.

The factor prices have the expected effects on the design variables. An increase in the size-independent bus transport cost 'a' (e.g. a driver's wage cost increase), ceteris paribus, reduces N^{opt}, n^{opt}, and F^{opt}, and raises S^{opt}. The size-dependent bus transport cost 'b' is a determinant of the occupancy rate, and consequently of bus size, but neither of the number of buses, nor of density and frequency of service. The walking time and waiting time costs per hour, 'c' and 'w', have the same positive influence on N^{opt} and negative influence on S^{opt}, whereas, as expected, they have symmetrically opposite effects on n^{opt} and F^{opt}.

Keeping trip density constant, while increasing the total number of trips by making Circletown successively larger, has an expected effect on the required bus transport capacity: N^{opt} should increase in proportion to the city area, πr^2, while S^{opt} remains the same. The quality of service is likewise constant with respect to city size as long as trip density remains the same: 'F^{opt}' is independent of 'r', and n^{opt} should increase in proportion to 'r', which means that the average walking distance, d^{opt}, is kept constant.

In Table 4.1 a numerical example is given of the bus service design in Circletown along the expansion path. The necessary parameter values used for the illustration are taken from Swedish manuals for road, rail and public transport investment calculation, and rounded off as shown below. In addition it is assumed that the average trip length is 4 kilometers, the mean journey speed on the bus is 20 kilometers per hour, the effective service-time per busday is 10 hours and the occupancy rate is one half.

$a = 700$ ECU/day
$b = 4$ ECU/day
$c = 2$ ECU/km
$w = 8$ ECU/hour
$l = 4$ km
$V = 20$ km/h
$H = 10$ hours
$\phi = 0.5$
$g(\phi) = 4$ ECU/hour

Table 4.1
Service characteristics along the expansion path

Trip density; number of trips per km² and day	Bus size; pax max	Frequency of service; buses per hour	Average walking distance to/from stops; km
100	20	3	0.35
250	27	4	0.26
500	34	5	0.21
750	39	6	0.18
1000	43	6	0.16
2000	54	8	0.13
4000	68	10	0.10
8000	86	12	0.08
15000	105	15	0.06

The total number of bus trips in Circletown is inconsequential for the design variables picked out. It is the trip density that matters. This is the same as saying that the size of the city area does not matter for the optimal quality of service. It can be noted that if average trip length, 'l', were positively related to the size of Circletown - in large cities trips may be longer, on average, than in small towns - the optimal bus size, S, will increase with increases in the size of the city area, given the trip density, since S is proportional to 'l', as seen from (11). However, this would not make any difference to the above conclusion that the frequency of service and walking distance to/from stops are independent of city size.

Bus transport cost along the expansion path. The above observations about capacity and quality of service along the expansion path indicate that both the producer cost and user cost per trip (AC^{prod} and AC^{user}) are falling with increases in trip density. It is instructive to derive the cost-output relationship by inserting the values given above of the parameters involved in the cost function.

The relationship between total social cost per trip and output is obtained by inserting the values for N^{opt}, S^{opt}, n^{opt}, and $g(\phi)$ in TC as given in (4c) above, and dividing by the total number of trips, B. It is interesting and easy to separate, on one hand, the producer cost and the external cost, of which the latter takes the form of charges on buses and their fuel, and on the other hand, the user cost:

$$AC^{prod} + AC^{ext} = \left(\frac{acw}{2VX}\right)^{\frac{1}{3}} + \frac{bl}{\phi VH} \tag{13}$$

$$AC^{user} = 2\left(\frac{acw}{2VX}\right)^{\frac{1}{3}} + g(\phi)\frac{1}{V} \tag{14}$$

$$AC = 3\left(\frac{acw}{2VX}\right)^{\frac{1}{3}} + \left[g(\phi) + \frac{b}{\phi H}\right]\frac{1}{V} \tag{15}$$

It can be noted that the total average cost per trip consists of two terms, of which one falls with increases in X, and the other is constant, independent of X. The total cost-elasticity, E, is apparently to be found in a range between 2/3 and unity; the larger the constant, second term is relative to the first term, the closer to unity E will be, and vice versa.

As can be seen in Table 4.2, the user cost is between two and three times higher than the sum of the producer and external costs. Both items are falling with increases in X; the user cost, AC^{user} at a slightly lower rate than the sum of AC^{prod} and AC^{ext}. The total social cost per trip, AC at a trip density of 15000 is only one third of the value of AC at a trip density of 100.

Table 4.2

Total social cost components along the expansion path, ECU per trip

Trip density; number of trips per km² and day	AC^prod + AC^ext	AC^user	AC = AC^prod + AC^user + AC^ext
100	1.57	3.62	5.19
250	1.20	2.88	4.08
500	0.98	2.45	3.43
750	0.88	2.24	3.12
1000	0.81	2.11	2.92
2000	0.68	1.84	2.52
4000	0.57	1.62	2.19
8000	0.49	1.45	1.94
15000	0.43	1.33	1.76

The optimal price level. To find the optimal factor combination and least social cost for each trip density, as illustrated in the preceding analysis, is a necessary but not sufficient condition for net social benefit maximization. The optimal price has to be levied, too. Otherwise the optimal input combination including user time inputs along the expansion path are unfeasible. The pricing-relevant cost PC will be derived below; this cost constitutes the optimal price at every equilibrium level of demand. (See e.g. Jansson 1993 for a more complete derivation, where the demand function is explicitly brought into the analysis.) An expression for PC was discussed in general terms on page 75, and given as (2b). For convenience it is repeated here:

$$PC = MC^{prod} + B\frac{dAC^{user}}{dB} + MC^{ext} \tag{16}$$

In the Circletown model the sum of the first and the third term of (16) can be calculated from (13). It comes to:

$$MC^{prod} + MC^{ext} = \frac{2}{3}\left(\frac{acw\pi r^2}{2VB}\right)^{\frac{1}{3}} + \frac{bl}{\phi VH} \tag{17}$$

The middle term of (2b), the user cost component of PC, is negative because AC^user is falling as B increases. From (14) the product of B and the derivative of AC^user with respect B is easily calculated:

$$B \frac{dAC^{\text{user}}}{dB} = -\frac{2}{3}\left(\frac{acw\pi r^2}{2VB}\right)^{\frac{1}{3}} \tag{18}$$

$$LRPC = \frac{bl}{\phi VH} \tag{19}$$

Remember that b/H is the size-dependent bus cost per seat and hour, l/V is the trip time, and ϕ the occupancy rate, and this surprisingly simple result makes sense. The optimal price should equal the cost (capital cost, running cost and external cost) of increasing the bus size by $1/\phi$ units (seats) spread over all additional trips that could be produced by such a capacity increase. With the parameter values used in the illustrations of Tables 1 and 2, the optimal price comes to 0.16 ECU per trip, which is to be compared to $AC^{\text{prod}} + AC^{\text{ext}}$ in table 4.2 to get an idea of the financial result of optimal pricing of bus services in Circletown.

Treating buses like putty is repellent to practical men. Alternatively the pricing-relevant cost could be calculated by the time-honoured approximation afforded by 'the average cost of the marginal plant'. An additional plant in this case is another bus. The crucial fact to bear in mind is, however, that an additional bus will cause an appreciable lowering of the user costs of the original trip-makers besides being a capacity addition. This cost reduction has to be deducted from the incremental producer (and external) cost of another bus to arrive at a correct proxy for PC. Formally the approximation suggested takes this shape:

$$PC^{\text{proxy}} \approx \frac{d(TC^{\text{prod}} + TC^{\text{ext}})}{dN} : \frac{dB}{dN} + B\frac{dAC^{\text{user}}}{dN} : \frac{dB}{dN} \tag{20}$$

On the basis of the total cost expression (4a-c) the proxy for PC takes this shape:

$$PC^{\text{proxy}} \approx \frac{al}{\phi SV} + \frac{bl}{\phi VH} - \frac{w}{2F} \tag{21}$$

As long as we are on the expansion path, i.e. the optimality conditions are fulfilled, this proxy should give the same result as in (19): on the expansion path any factor increment should give the same marginal cost, and that goes, of course, also for dN. Inserting the values for S^{opt} and F^{opt} from (11) and (10) in (21), it is found that the first term and third term of (21) just offset one another. Only the middle term remains, and, as seen, this equals the pricing-relevant cost according to (19).

A third alternative of calculating PC could be to change nothing but the capacity utilization ϕ. In the present model only the user cost is affected in this case.

$$SRPC = B \cdot \frac{\partial AC^{user}}{\partial \phi} \frac{\partial \phi}{\partial B} = \frac{1}{V} \phi g'(\phi) \qquad (22)$$

In the spirit of the received short run marginal cost school of thought on optimal pricing, it could be argued that this is the only correct way of calculating the pricing-relevant cost. Before further comments on this long-standing issue are offered, let us just observe that as long as the function $g(\phi)$ is unspecified, SRPC cannot be calculated. However, if this function could be estimated, it would nevertheless be insufficient on its own as a cost basis for pricing policy. Off the expansion path, $\phi g'(\phi)$ can take almost any value. Before taking a stand on pricing policy, a wise bus company manager will first see to it that the bus line network and the frequency of service are optimal. Pricing policy and service design should be determined simultaneously. Following a sudden leap in demand it would be ill-advised to charge a very high price on account of crowded buses. The right thing to do is to adjust the bus fleet to the new level of demand, and fix the price at a level consistent with an optimal design of the bus transport system.

Going back to (12) it is seen that the product $\phi^2 g'(\phi)$ takes a value of b/H at the expansion path. Inserting that value in (22), it is found that the pricing-relevant cost per trip comes to:

$$SRPC = \frac{bl}{\phi VH} \qquad (23)$$

The same expression for PC as in (19) and (21) reappears, as expected.

The need to tackle the tricky problem of estimating the function $g(\phi)$ has not been conjured away by the handy approximation to the pricing-relevant cost given by 'the average cost of the marginal plant'. The occupancy rate ϕ appears, as seen, in the expression for PC in all cases. However, even if one has great difficulties with $g(\phi)$, it should not stop a sound pricing policy. A proxy for ϕ^{opt} has to be found by 'fingerspitzgefühl', if no better way is at hand. And that is enough for easily fixing the right level of fares.

The financial result of optimal pricing

Taking the ratio of PC to $AC^{prod} + AC^{ext}$, it is found that the revenue from optimal pricing would cover only a small fraction of the costs. At a trip density of 100 the pricing-relevant cost is only a tenth of the bus company cost. At the other end of the scale, at a trip density of 15.000, cost recovery is raised to 37%.

This result is affected by a number of conditions which are not inherently stable, but vary from one case to another, like the average trip length (l), and the occupancy rate (ϕ). The latter has been assumed to take a value of 1/2 in the numerical example. This value is on the high side compared to real life bus services in urban areas, where a value of 1/4 is thought to be representative. Drawing on the following discussion of peak-load pricing, the assumed higher value seems justified. Here we have not gone into the matter of the structure of fares, but only discussed the optimal level of fares. By proper peak-load pricing it should be possible to raise the occupancy rate quite substantially above what is at present common in practice.

It can be noted that because $lb/\phi VH$ is the second term of the expression for the sum $AC^{prod} + AC^{user}$, PC appears both in the numerator and the denominator of the ratio representing the financial result of optimal pricing of bus services in Circletown, which means that this ratio is not very variable. It is rather low in a wide range of relevant parameter values.

Possible extensions of the Circletown model

To be sure, a number of simplifying assumptions are made in the Circletown model. The main idea of the model is to explore the broad lines of the development of the basic design-variables and the pricing-relevant cost along the expansion path. One characteristic of the design of the model system, which may appear too unrealistic, is that routes are perfectly straight, even in situations of very low trip density. The normal policy is to make routes rather winding in order to increase the catchment area, when trip density is on the low side. Therefore a neglected economy of trip density may be that travel time on the bus (and not just walking and waiting time) also falls along the expansion path. To complicate matters further, mention should be made of a possible effect on travel time working in the opposite direction: as buses get bigger, hold more passengers, overall speed V tends to go down. The total effect of raising bus size, S, is in fact rather complicated. On one hand, taking the stochastic nature of demand for bus travel into account, there is an additional economy of bus size, which might be realized by the possibility to slightly increase the occupancy rate, ϕ with increases in S, with impunity as to the probability of being left behind because the bus is full. On the other hand, with more passengers per bus, boarding/alighting time will constitute an increasing proportion of total bus time with successive increases in bus size.

There are thus several possible total travel time influences along the expansion path as a result of bus size increases. The net effect on V is uncertain. The last mentioned effect is the most obvious one in a modelling context, and it is possible to accommodate it fairly easily within the Circletown model. It is also relevant to the following discussion of optimal train and airline fares. Therefore the previous model is modified by calculating additional 'boarding/alighting charges' on top of the previously calculated pricing-relevant cost.

Completing the pricing-relevant cost by boarding/alighting charges. In goods transport pricing, and especially liner shipping freight rate-making, it is natural and practical to divide the costs underlying freight rates into 'handling charges' and space 'occupancy charges'. The former consists of two components: stevedoring charges for loading and unloading services, and the costs of laytime of the ship. These are both relatively important; the occupancy charges for taking up space in the ship's hold are often the minor part in shipping freight rates. In passenger transport this proportion is completely different. First, passengers do not need help to board or alight, and, secondly, the acts of boarding and alighting take, relatively speaking, very little time.

Herbert Mohring (1972) is the pioneer in the field of optimal bus transport pricing, and his contribution is rightly acknowledged by naming the crux of the matter, the relationship which makes public transport pricing special, the 'Mohring effect' (i.e. the fact that an increase in capacity, by putting in additional buses on a line, will simultaneously improve the service frequency and lower the user costs of the original bus riders). A remarkable feature of Mohring's original model (in the 1972 paper) is, however, that he only considered boarding/alighting charges. Some years later when I asked him why he ignored occupancy charges, he conceded in his reply (in a letter) that it was 'heroic' to assume that the capacity constraint is always non-binding, but that it made sense in the United States at that time; buses were rather big and were running with a lot of spare capacity (which is typical of a declining industry).

Under the circumstances assumed in the Circletown model there is no need to distinguish boarding/alighting charges and occupancy charges. Now is the time to look closer at that issue. (For a more detailed analysis, see Mohring, 1972 and Jansson, 1984.)

Total travel time from start to end of each route in Circletown, R (=r/V), is the sum of a fixed time component, T, and the product of the average boarding/alighting time, 't', and the total number of passengers served by one bus along the route. The fixed component T equals the time it would take to run a bus from start to end, stopping at every bus stop, without letting any passengers in or out. The passenger number-dependent component is proportional to bus size, given the occupancy rate, and the fact that passengers board only through the front door, where they pay or show a pass to the driver. How important is the latter component? It is the act of boarding that is the main determinant of boarding/alighting time, and if most passengers have passes, the total boarding/alighting time on a 10 km route, where the average trip length is 4 km, will be about 3 minutes out of a total time from start to end of about 30 minutes for a bus holding on average 30 passengers. If the bus size is halved, the total boarding/alighting time goes down to 1.5 minutes, and if the size is doubled, it goes up to 6 minutes. If most passengers pay cash, these figures are doubled or trebled.

From a social point of view, a time-consuming fare collection system is an anomaly. In the Circletown model it is assumed that passed and pre-paid tickets are dominating. In that case the neglect so far of the influence of the bus size on boarding/alighting time is probably not a very serious omission in the search for optimal fares. For completeness, however, an addition to the previously calculated PC should be derived, taking account of the fact that the required capacity expansion along the expansion path involves successive increases in bus size S, which in turn raises the boarding/alighting time.

The new assumption introduced in the Circletown model requires the following additional symbols:

R = total bus travel time from start to end
T = total time with doors closed
t = boarding/alighting time per passenger

The total number of passengers served along the route per bus trip from start to end equals BR/HN.

$$R = T + t \frac{BR}{HN} \tag{24}$$

which gives

$$R = \frac{TN}{N - tB/H} \tag{25}$$

$$V = \frac{r}{R} = \frac{r(N - tB/H)}{TN} \tag{26}$$

The additions to the previously derived pricing-relevant cost PC is now calculated by raising S to accommodate some more passengers, dB, and, as an inevitable consequence, slightly reducing V in accordance with the relationship (26). The capacity requirement (3) and total social cost function (4c) still apply as they stand; it is just that V is no longer assumed to be fixed.

As was mentioned, in a position on the expansion path, the pricing-relevant cost comes out the same irrespective of the number of factors assumed to be variable; so let us assume N, n, and ϕ to be fixed. The pricing-relevant cost has three components according to (16), of which the first and third are merged in the present model. The calculation proceeds in the following way:

$$MC^{prod} + MC^{ext} = \frac{\partial (TC^{prod} + TC^{ext})}{\partial S} / \frac{\partial B}{\partial S} \tag{27}$$

and

$$B \frac{\partial AC^{user}}{\partial B} = B \frac{\partial AC^{user}}{\partial V} \cdot \frac{\partial V}{\partial B} \tag{28}$$

A comment on the user cost component is appropriate: from (26) it is seen that B has a negative influence on V, everything else remaining equal ($\partial V/\partial B < 0$). To accommodate more passengers, S has to be raised. Since S does not appear directly

91

in the user cost function, there is no need to take explicit account of the fact that it is the increase in S that made the increase in B possible in the first place.

The results of the calculations are as follows:

$$MC^{prod} + MC^{ext} = \frac{bl}{\phi VH}\left(1 + \frac{R-T}{T}\right) \tag{29}$$

$$B\frac{\partial AC^{user}}{\partial B} = \left(\frac{wnr}{NV} + \frac{lg(\phi)}{V}\right)\frac{R-T}{T} \tag{30}$$

The previously derived pricing-relevant cost is equal to $bl/\phi VH$. According to the new results, two additions to that should be made, one is a factor $(R-T)/T$ of $bl/\phi VH$, and another is the same factor $(R-T)/T$ of the user cost per trip of waiting time (wnr/NV) and riding time $(l\cdot g(\phi)/V)$.

The factor in question is recognized as the ratio of the passenger number-dependent time to the fixed time component of total bus time, R. As was suggested previously, this factor is in the range of 0.05 - 0.2 depending on, in the first place, the fare collection technique and the length of passenger trips. In Circletown the low end of this range is applicable because efficiency has higher priority than revenue raising.

Optimal level of train and airline fares

The preceding discussion leads naturally to the problems of optimal pricing of the other two main modes of public transport - rail-borne and air-borne scheduled transport services.

Commuter trains. Modelling urban train services is in one important respect similar to the Circletown bus transport model: the frequency of service is in the high range, where headways are short enough that travellers do not bother to learn the time-table, but arrive to stations more or less at random. The main, relevant differences are (i) that separate track is used, which makes it possible to go much faster; the journey speed of commuter trains is typically three times higher than for urban buses, and (ii) that the size of vehicles in terms of number of seats is much bigger because of the possibility to add carriages to the train, and (iii) the average trip length is typically substantially longer than for urban bus services.

A good grip on the issue of optimal pricing of commuter train services is obtained simply by modifying some parameter values in the Circletown model like journey speed (V) and average trip length (l), and extending the range of vehicle size (S) considered in the cost calculation up to 600 or even more passengers. Without going further into this matter, let us just note that the same expression for the pricing-relevant cost, PC, as for urban bus services is relevant, and PC will be at an equally low level, since the vehicle-size independent traffic operation cost component 'a' is, like for buses, relatively high, and both 'l' (appearing in the numerator of the PC expression) and V (appearing in the denominator of the PC expression) are trebled, or something like that, compared to what is normal for bus services.

Long-distance public transport. In long-distance public transport, where time-tables are used by prospective riders, the 'Mohring effect' is much more difficult to estimate compared to the case of urban travel. The handy proxy for the pricing-relevant cost of 'the average cost of an additional vehicle', which works fine in urban bus transport, is not so attractive, because the (negative) user cost component is not as easily calculated as where travellers arrive at random to bus stops and suffer waiting time at the stop, which can be assumed, on average, to equal half the headway. The right approach for long-distance public transport is instead to calculate PC by assuming that additional passenger demand is met by vehicle size increases. This approach avoids most of the difficulties of user cost estimation. Not quite, however. As was pointed out before, one effect of raising S is that travel time can be affected.

For both train transport and airline transport service, the type of additional boarding/alighting charges discussed in the preceding section should play a relatively minor role, since tickets are bought in advance. In addition, it is important in the train case that the number of inlets and outlets is increasing proportionally to vehicle size, as capacity is expanded by train lengthening. This makes it possible to keep total time at stations (almost) constant irrespective of the number of train carriages.

Aircraft are like buses insofar as there is just one gate for letting passengers in. However, in the airline case there is often only one destination, and rarely no more than one stop on the way to the final destination, which should mean that the passenger volume-dependent boarding/alighting time makes up a relatively small part of total airline travel time, at least on long-distance routes. (The same is true about many interurban bus/coach services.)

In other words, the pricing-relevant cost is in both cases close to the producer marginal cost calculated on the assumption that vehicle size is increased to accommodate additional traffic. The result of calculating PC in this way can be deduced from the preceding discussion of the complete pricing-relevant cost of urban bus travel.

$$PC = \frac{\partial TC^{prod}}{\partial S} \Big/ \frac{\partial B}{\partial S} \left(1 + \frac{R-T}{T} \right)$$

$$+ AC^{user} \frac{R-T}{T}$$

(31)

Remember that the ratio (R-T)/T stands for passenger number-dependent travel time over passenger number-independent travel time. The main part of PC is clearly the linked derivative of TC^{prod} with respect to B. In the case of railway passenger transport there is an extremely simple way of calculating this part: vehicle size is increased in this case by train lengthening.

The only more demanding bit in the calculation of the incremental social cost of adding another carriage to a train is to find out how energy cost develops as a train is made successively longer. In a joint study with SJ, a Linköping University research team found that, given train speed, energy consumption will increase linearly with train length in the whole range of observations (Jansson, et.al. 1992). On the well-founded assumption that R-T is practically zero, because the number of passenger inlets and outlets are increasing in proportion to the train holding capacity, the pricing-relevant cost can be formulated in the same simple way as the optimal fare in Circletown, $bl/\phi VH$. The only difference in the train case is that the least unit of supply is another carriage carried from the point of departure, say the central station of Stockholm, to the final destination, for example Malmö, and back again. The incremental cost of producing this additional capacity constitutes the numerator of the pricing-relevant cost, and the number of additional passengers thus accommodated constitutes the denominator:

$$Pc_{ti}^{train} = \frac{\mu_{ti} + \alpha D}{\beta} \qquad (32)$$

Pc_{ti}^{train} = pricing-relevant cost per occupied seat day 't' train departure i (t = 1...365, and i = 1......m)
μ_{ti} = opportunity cost day 't' train departure 'i' of the marginal carriage
α = additional running cost of a train per kilometer caused by coupling up another carriage
D = round voyage distance
β = target number of occupied seats per carriage

This formulation of the pricing-relevant cost presupposes that the train on the route concerned only makes one round voyage per day. On a shorter route it may be possible to carry out two rounds, which would mean that the denominator is increased by a factor of two.

Note that the pricing-relevant cost is given per occupied seat of a round voyage. This cost should be shared out among all passengers successively occupying a particular seat during a round voyage. The number of passengers per seat and round voyage should be at least two, one in each direction, and more often more than two, each passenger travelling less than the whole distance from start to end.

An efficiency condition is that summed over all departures all days of a year the opportunity cost of a carriage should equal the annual capital cost.

The financial result of optimal pricing of passenger train services is easily imagined. The revenue will cover the capital and operating costs of carriages including guards' wage costs, but no contribution will be made towards covering the costs of engines including engine-drivers' wage costs, nor to the major part of overhead costs which are independent of train length. Only about half the total costs of passenger services will be covered by optimal train fares.

For airline services much the same result of optimal pricing is indicated. Computationally the main difference is that the derivative of TC^{prod} with respect to B via an increase in S has to be found by cross-section analysis of the total costs of airplanes of different capacity, including the costs of passenger and baggage handling on the ground. In the long-distance airline transport sector the ratio of $(R-T)/T$ can be very small, if the in-checking and baggage handling capacity, as it should, is expanded commensurately to airplane holding capacity.

Peak-load pricing in time and space

The attractive simplicity of the theory of the optimal level of prices of scheduled transport services disappears to a large extent when the structure of prices is considered in the face of the pronounced peakiness of demand both in time and space. The broad lines, however, of the peak-load pricing structure of the different modes of public transport are straightforward enough. Let us take up the story where we finished in the preceding section, and look at interurban railway transport.

Peak-load pricing of interurban train services. With reference to expression (32) for the level of the pricing-relevant cost of railway passenger transport, an additional efficiency conditions, which is useful in the derivation of the peak-load pricing structure, can be written like this:

$$\mu_{t1} = \mu_{t2} = \ldots \mu_{ti} \ldots = \mu_{tm} = \mu_t \qquad (33)$$

The rolling stock of a particular line can be assumed as given one particular day. The number of engines and carriages can only be changed from one day to another. An efficiency condition is then that each day the given number of carriages should be distributed between the 'm' trains such that the capacity utilization is constant. This means in turn that the opportunity cost of a carriage is the same every departure a particular day, as shown in (33) above.

The stochastic element in railway travel demand is substantial, so a very high occupancy rate should not be aimed at. At present for SJ the mean occupancy rate of SJs trains is about 1/3, but is systematically rather different in different sub-markets. By eliminating the systematic differences by means of peak-load pricing, aiming basically at equalization in time and space of the train occupancy rate, it should be possible to raise the mean occupancy rate to at least 1/2, which would be a very considerable improvement.

The first demand equalization to aim at should be to make the Monday-Thursday and Saturday (off-peak) level of demand nearly equal to the Friday and Sunday (peak) level. A representative example of the time profile of train travel demand by day of the week in Sweden is given in Figure 4.2.

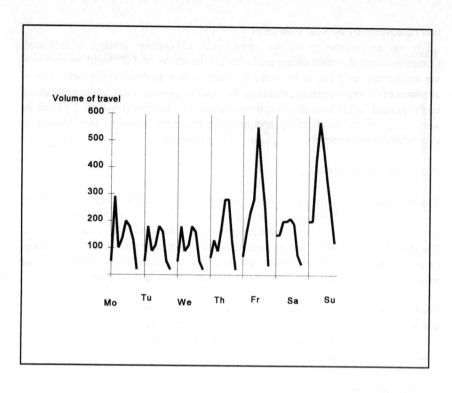

Figure 4.2   **Rail travel between Stockholm and Gävle on different days of the week**

It was found in Jansson et.al 1992 that $\mu_i = 0$ in off-peak, i.e. if fares in off-peak were based on just the running cost component αD of the pricing-relevant cost (see equation (32) above), the level of demand would just fall short of the peak level as it would be when peak traffic alone pays the carriage capital costs.

The second demand equalization to aim at should be to level out spatial peaks and troughs. We have not gone into this matter very deeply. A lot remains to be done. Take just as a rather typical example the line between Stockholm and Sundsvall in the north of Sweden. Dividing it into three segments, the daily passenger flow in peak and off-peak, respectively, in the three segments was as follows:

Table 4.3
Passenger flow per day in peak and off-peak on the Stockholm-Sundsvall line in 1984

Line segment	Fri, Sun	Mon-Thur, Sat
Stockholm - Gävle	3307	1751
Gävle - Söderhamn	2490	1240
Söderhamn - Sundsvall	1494	734

The peak/off-peak price differentiation advocated above would equalize the flow figures in each particular row in Table 4.3. The spatial demand equalization would imply a price differentiation with the aim of making the passenger flow figures equal also in each column. This aim will never be completely attained. The pattern of demand is such that, even if zero-prices would be applied here and there, the level of demand would not reach the spatial peak level everywhere.

Numerical comparison of optimal fares and SJ fares. In the illustrative comparison below of SJ fares and optimal fares according to the principles laid down in this paper, the focus is on the fare differentiation by day of the week. As seen in Table 4.4, in both cases investigated (with and without a budget constraint), off-peak fares should be only about one third of the peak fares. Fares examples are given for a rather short, a medium-distance, and a fairly long-distance line. Never mind the absolute values of the figures; they are in Swedish currency at the end of the 1980s. It is the structure of fares which is interesting. Since the elasticity of demand for rail travel differs somewhat between routes with and without airline competition, both cases are considered in the illustration.

Table 4.4

Comparison of optimal rail fares for different days of the week, and SJs fare structure

Line distance	Day of the week	Optimal fares				SJ fares	
		without budget constraint		with budget constraint			
		Air comp	No air comp	Air comp	No air comp	Black	Red
170 km	Fri, Sun	113	113	154	154	128	64
	Mon-Thu, Sat	30	30	56	57		
335 km	Fri, Sun	187	202	240	303	242	121
	Mon-Thu, Sat	50	58	87	123		
550 km	Fri, Sun	254	294	292	462	342	171
	Mon-Thu, Sat	72	96	104	204		

As seen, the route distance makes little difference so far as the peak/off-peak differentiation is concerned. It is interesting to note that where air transport is no alternative, the distance-dependency is about the same as in SJs current tariff, and where air transport is an alternative, fares more markedly tape off in both cases of optimal fares.

The comparison with SJs fares is made a little difficult by the fact that SJ has abandoned the differentiation of fares by day of the week, which was the basic feature of the 1979 'low-fares policy'. As from 1989, SJ has introduced a new fare differentiation by departure in one and the same day. Some 20% of departures every day are 'red', which means that the fares are only half the fares applying to the remaining 80% 'black' departures.

The low off-peak fares in the optimal tariff would apply to 70% of total travel, which means that the weighted average fare level is substantially lower than the current level, even in the case where the financial result is constrained to be the same as at present.

We made a rough calculation of the likely travel volume increase as a result of changing over to the optimal fares structure. In the unconstrained case the travel volume would double. Most of the increase would, of course, occur in the off-peak period. In the constrained case the price level has to be substantially higher, and as a consequence, the increase in the total volume of travel is down to 40%. It is interesting to note that the net welfare gain in the latter case is as high as 75% of the net welfare gain of peak-load pricing in the case where no budget constraint is assumed.

Peak-load pricing of urban bus services. In urban bus transport, where travel to/from work is the most important travel purpose, it is the morning and afternoon peaks that stand out in the time-profile of demand. In addition, the spatial peaks of each round voyage is just as marked. It is not only on the backhaul that the occupancy rate is low, but also on the main haul the bus is fully occupied only in the 'critical section', which may constitute just a fraction of the whole route.

In OECD 1985 a model was designed by the present author with a view to determine the optimal differentiation of peak and off-peak fares in urban bus transport. In that model bus size was kept out of consideration. The idea was not to study optimal design along the expansion path, but to pinpoint the basic elements of peak-load pricing. A summary of the model results is given below.

Consider an urban area served by N buses in the peak period. If these buses were in operation all day, Case a, the total cost of the bus company can roughly be expressed like this:

$$TC_a^{prod} = \beta N \qquad\qquad (34a)$$

In the case where off-peak capacity is less than peak capacity, Case b, two categories of buses are used - 'peak-only buses' and 'all-day buses'. As the names suggest, a peak-only bus is in operation only in the morning and afternoon peaks manned by a driver on a 'split shift', or by two half-day working drivers. An all-day bus is in operation during two straight shifts. The total producer cost is in this case written thus:

$$TC_b^{prod} = \beta N_{ad} + \beta_1 N_{po} \qquad\qquad (34b)$$

where

N_{ad} = number of all-day buses
N_{po} = number of peak-only buses
$N = N_{ad} + N_{po}$ = total peak vehicle requirement

The total costs of the users of bus services are also a function of N in the first place.

The more buses there are, all other things remaining equal, the higher the frequency of service and/or density of bus lines will be, with consequent reduction in waiting times and/or walking distances. More buses in the system can also lead to less devious routes being chosen for individual lines, which should result in reduced riding times, too. In Case a where the number of buses in peak and off-peak periods is the same, we can write, denoting the total number of bus trips per day by B,

$$TC_a^{user} = f(N)B \tag{35a}$$

In Case b where the number of buses are different in peak and off-peak, the total user cost comes to:

$$TC_b^{user} = f(N) \cdot B_{peak} + f(N_{ad}) \cdot B_{off-peak} \tag{35b}$$

The external costs of bus traffic can be assumed to be proportional to the number of buses in operation:

$$TC_a^{ext} = eN \tag{36a}$$

$$TC_b^{ext} = eN_{ad} + e_1 N_{po} \tag{36b}$$

We now have a complete, very simple expression for the total social cost of bus services per (work)day:

$$TC_a = \beta N + f(N)B + eN \tag{37a}$$

$$TC_b = \beta N_{ad} + \beta_1 N_{po}$$

$$+ f(N) B_{peak} + f(N_{ad}) B_{off-peak}$$

$$+ eN_{ad} + e_1 N_{po} \tag{37b}$$

The pricing-relevant cost of peak trips. The pricing-relevant cost of bus traffic should be calculated per bus in the first step. In the second step we arrive at a cost per bus trip simply by dividing the pricing-relevant cost per bus by the number of trips made on a marginal bus.

For Case a the cost and benefit (= negative cost) of another bus in the system is easily obtained as:

$$\frac{dTC_a}{dN} = \beta + B\frac{\delta f}{\delta N} + e \qquad (38a)$$

In Case b we have, in principle, two costs of additional buses, depending on whether a peak-only or all-day bus is added, although only the former alternative would be relevant when it comes to peak-price calculations.

The incremental cost difference between adding an all-day bus and withdrawing a peak-only bus has some interest in that it represents the marginal off-peak capacity cost in Case b. If one wants to increase the number of buses in off-peak, keeping the peak capacity constant, this is the way to go about it: add an all-day bus and take a peak-only bus out of operation, or, which happens in practice of course, put a peak-only bus into all-day service.

$$\frac{dTC_b}{dN_{po}} = \beta_1 + B_{peak}\frac{\delta f}{\delta N} + e_1 \qquad (38b1)$$

$$\frac{dTC_b}{dN_{ad}} = \beta + B_{peak}\frac{\delta f}{\delta N} + B_{off-peak}\frac{\delta f}{\delta N_{ad}} + e \qquad (38b2)$$

$$\frac{dTC}{dN_{ad}} - \frac{dTC}{dN_{po}} = \beta - \beta_1 + B_{off-peak}\frac{\delta f}{\delta N_{ad}} + e - e_1 \qquad (38b3)$$

The next question is: by what should the incremental cost of an additional bus be divided to get the pricing-relevant cost per trip? The first thought, that the incremental cost should be shared by all passengers using the additional bus while it is in operation, is wrong. Only those passengers that are on the bus in the 'critical section' of the route concerned have 'cost responsibility' for an additional bus. This may be only something like half the total number of passengers travelling by the bus; for example, all passenger trips made on the back-haul put hardly any demand on capacity. We assume that a given proportion (α) of the total peak trips, B_{peak}, are capacity-demanding in the sense that they occupy seats and standing space on buses when the buses traverse the sections of each individual route which constitute 'spatial peaks'.

Dividing the incremental cost of another bus by the number of capacity-demanding peak trips per bus employed in the peak periods, $\alpha B_{peak}/N$, we get the pricing-relevant cost, PC_{peak} in two versions:

$$PC_{peak}^a = \frac{(\beta + e)N}{\alpha B_{peak}} + \frac{Bf(N)}{\alpha B_{peak}} \cdot E_{fN} \qquad (39a)$$

101

$$PC_{peak}^{b} = \frac{(\beta_1 + e_1)N}{\alpha B_{peak}} + \frac{1}{\alpha} f(N) \cdot E_{fN} \qquad (39b)$$

$$\text{where} \quad E_{fN} = \frac{\delta f}{\delta N} \cdot \frac{N}{f(N)}$$

The pricing-relevant cost of off-peak trips. The normal off-peak case should be that buses practically never run fully occupied, and it is irrelevant to pursue the preceding 'average cost of the marginal bus' argument. Increased off-peak patronage should not require additional buses.

The acts of boarding and alighting of additional passengers will reduce overall bus speed. If bus travel were free in off-peak, this pricing-relevant cost would be almost negligible. On the other hand, if a ticket were to be bought from the bus driver, the pricing-relevant cost would be doubled or trebled. However, it is nonsensical to charge a price with the main rationale that the very collection of the price, and nothing else, causes the pricing-relevant cost. Perhaps the best compromise is to introduce extremely cheap monthly or yearly passes for off-peak travel. Passengers with passes cause hardly any additional cost (over and above the cost of a free rider) and a yearly pass at the cost of, say 30 ECU would not (as it should not) discourage any person in need of bus transport in off-peak periods, and it could have a desirable, preventive effect on children's or others' riding for fun or mischief.

The case of off-peak capacity being scarce: Under certain, not very likely circumstances, it can be right to reduce off-peak capacity enough that the capacity constraint becomes binding in the critical sections also in off-peak. Or in other words, the number of all-day buses, N_{ad} is made just sufficient to meet the off-peak demand in the spatial peaks on individual routes.

In this case, Case c the pricing-relevant cost of off-peak trips in the critical section becomes:

$$PC_{off-peak} = \frac{\left(\dfrac{dTC}{dN_{ad}} - \dfrac{dTC}{dN_{po}} \right) N_{ad}}{\alpha B_{off-peak}}$$

$$= \frac{\left(\beta - \beta_1 + e - e_1 \right) N_{ad}}{\alpha B_{off-peak}} + \frac{1}{\alpha} \cdot \frac{\delta f}{\delta N_{ad}} N_{ad} \qquad (40)$$

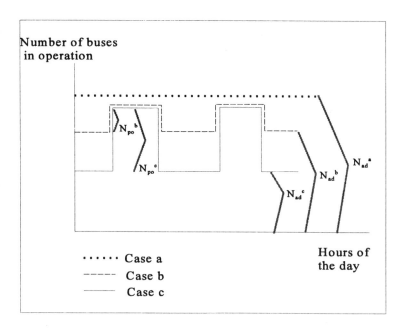

Figure 4.3   Bus inputs during the day in three cases

It is interesting to note that it matters very little for the pricing-relevant cost whether or not off-peak capacity can be assumed to be a binding constraint. The pricing-relevant cost is very low all the same. This is a reflection of the fact that the benefit to all off-peak passengers of increasing the frequency of service is so relatively great (when the frequency is at a low level initially) that the incremental cost of another peak-only bus extending its operation to all-day service is practically offset by cost savings for the original off-peak passengers.

With the parameter values used previously, it turns out that, for peak trips, the level of the pricing-relevant cost is substantially higher in Case a than in Case b. This is not a general characteristic of running only all-day buses versus differentiating the peak and off-peak frequency of service, but a result of the fact that, given the circumstances of the model example, both alternatives cannot be optimal.

Table 4.5

Examples of pricing-relevant costs and bus company average costs per trip in peak and off-peak, excluding night, Saturday and Sunday services, ECU per trip

Different cases as to off-peak frequency of service	AC^{prod}	PC peak		PC off-peak	
		critical section	other sections	critical section	other sections
Case a: Peak = off-peak	1.12	3.30	0.20	0.08	0.08
Case b: Peak > off-peak	1.04	2.40	0.20	0.08	0.08
Case c: Peak >> off-peak	0.94	2.40	0.20	0.10	0.08

Concluding remarks

It is somewhat daring to claim that, as a general rule, optimal pricing of public transport services - irrespective of mode - should cover less than half the total costs. In practice such a financial situation applies in urban public transport in many towns and cities of the world. Many national railways are also showing red figures, and require subsidies of the same relative order of magnitude. This state-of-affairs is seldom justified by politicians or civil servants by the fact that the ratio of PC to AC^{prod} speaks for a large financial deficit. Other motives are held up like distributional considerations. In my view, however, the main reason is simply that these public transport enterprises cannot show black figures. Look at the different position of airlines. The same principle of optimal pricing applies, but since airlines normally are in a position to be able to break even, they are seldom or never encouraged to pursue a low-price policy requiring substantial subsidization. Instead airlines practice far-reaching price dicrimination with economy class fares down to the charging floor of the pricing-relevant cost as defined in the present analysis.

It is important, finally, to pinpoint the fundamental cause of this grave conflict between allocative efficiency and financial stringency. This will also indicate the limits for the applicability of the 'general' theory.

At bottom is the Mohring effect. It is not quite enough, however; something else has to apply, because otherwise it would be possible to nullify the Mohring effect by employing sufficiently small vehicles in such a large number that the 'frequency delay' (Panzar 1979) would be negligible. The concurrent factor is the pronounced diseconomy of vehicle smallness. Generally speaking it is true for passenger transport that the smaller a transport vehicle is, the higher AC^{prod} will be in a very wide range of trip densities.

As the density of public transport demand along a route is increasing, economies of density are reaped both in the form of user cost lowering, by increasing the number of vehicles (the Mohring effect), and in the form of producer cost lowering, by increasing the size of vehicles. Will this continue to be possible for ever?

If there is no limit to the economies of vehicle size, the pricing-relevant cost will remain at a constant low level, constituting just a fraction of AC^{prod}. On the other hand, if the economies of vehicle size are petering out to cease altogether sooner or later, a corresponding exhausting of the vehicle number economies will happen along the expansion path.

The limit to further exploiting vehicle size economies is in many cases set by an exogenous factor like the infrastructure. For example, a fairway is not deep enough for employing larger ships, a road is not strong enough for heavy vehicles, or a terminal is not spacious enough for vehicles that take up a lot of space.

The last-mentioned example is relevant for railway transport. Trains can be very long before energy consumption diseconomies set in, which freight trains bear witness to, but well before that point is reached, platforms of railway stations become too short. In the case of railway passenger transport it is therefore rather easy to tell for which services the pricing-relevant cost as formulated in (32) applies, i.e. which services are well on this side of the output range, where the economies of trip density start to taper off more appreciably. Just look around to see where train lengths are less than the possible maximum!

Optimal TI-service pricing

In the previous models of public transport systems, the TI-service user charges should be contained in the public transport service producer costs. Now we are going to look in detail at those charges. The system definition is therefore widened so that all motor vehicles using the TI-services concerned are included.

The general formulation of the pricing-relevant cost was given already in section 1. It is repeated here with the slight modification of including a factor α in the middle term.

$$PC = MC^{prod} + \alpha Q \frac{\partial AC^{user}}{\partial Q} + MC^{ext} \qquad (41)$$

$$0 \leq \alpha \leq 1$$

Normally α is unity. In the opposite extreme case of the National Railways being the sole user of the railways, α is zero. All possible in-between cases are conceivable, but, of course, not very common in reality.

For most TI-facilities it is right to regard the capacity and other facility design characteristics as given when discussing optimal pricing. Then the second and third terms of (41) are the potentially important ones. These are to be discussed below under the sub-titles 'congestion tolls' and 'accident externality charges'. Other pricing-relevant externalities exist, too, needless to say, but these will be covered elsewhere.

Looking at TI-service facilities in general, it is appropriate to make a distinction between common facilities and departmentalized facilities when considering the nature of the short-run costs of TI-services. The latter facilities consist of one or more 'service stations', in which each customer is being served one at a time. The interference between users of departmentalized facilities typically takes the form of queuing at times when all service stations are occupied. In the service sector of the economy, departmentalized facilities are legion. In the transport sector, the berths of a seaport, the runways of an airport, various parking facilities, and the ticket office at a railway station are typical examples. The railways is an in-between case. Roads, airways, fairways, and the back-up areas of terminals are clearly common facilities.

There is no space here for anything like a full treatment of the short-run user costs at different TI-facilities. However, the two aspects taken up for discussion are central to the main policy issue at stake in this area: the issue of urban road pricing. Again it is impossible to deal with all important aspects of road pricing. (A recent comprehensive survey is Ramjerdi 1995.) The two chosen aspects are both important and controversial, and therefore worth much more attention than they have received in the literature so far.

Congestion tolls

The congestion cost component in the pricing-relevant cost is obtained by (i) ascertaining the appropriate relationship between traffic volume and speed, and (ii) determining the applicable values of time. A large amount of literature exists on both topics, neither of which we will go into. A number of good summaries exist. An excellent book covering both topics is Small (1992).

The relevant relationship between travel time and trip volume. A problem that has intrigued some authors on road pricing theory and which still seems to be a puzzle, is connected with the backwards-bending shape of the relationship between travel time and traffic flow [see Jansson (1969), Else (1981, 1982, 1986), Nash (1982), Button and Pearman (1983) and Kawashima (1988)].

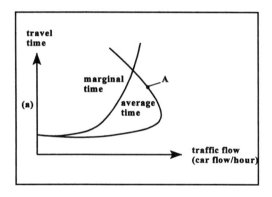

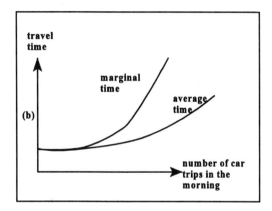

Figure 4.4   (a) Travel time - traffic flow relationship, and (b) Travel time - number of car trips relationship

When traffic density in a city road network is very high, a point like A in figure 4.4.(a) is obtained: it is a very bad situation because the production of car-kilometers per unit of time is below capacity, and yet travel time per kilometer is substantially higher than at full capacity. Starting from a moderate flow level, where speed limits rather than traffic volume determine travel time, it seems that the marginal cost goes towards infinity as the capacity flow is approached, and at some stage it appears that somehow the marginal cost will become negative.

This intricacy is hair-splitting. High capacity utilization occurs in peak-hours, and what happens, as the demand for road space goes up, is that the peak period becomes wider and wider. It is not the relationship between travel time and traffic-volume per hour that should be the basis for the congestion cost calculation, but the relationship between travel time and the number of car travellers completing their trips in the morning peak, taking into account that the morning peak is not of fixed duration, but will expand into the previous off-peak time. The pricing-relevant relationship between travel time and the number of car trips in the morning rises more gently - like the one depicted in Figure 4.4 (b) - than the relationship between travel time and flow per hour.

Will the fact that the morning peak is preceded by a long period of light traffic make a substantial difference to the optimal congestion toll for using the road system in the morning?

Some simple calculations suggest that a substantial difference may well exist compared to the theoretical case, where the same level of traffic prevails all day long. A comparison of two pure cases is revealing:

In the imaginary case where the number of cars in the system N is the same all the time, the traffic output per unit of time in terms of car kilometers is $Q = N/T(N)$, where T is travel time per kilometer. The crucial relationship is obviously travel time as a function of traffic density, i.e. the number of cars, N. The elasticity of T with respect to N is designated 'e'. This elasticity is zero for low densities, and is increasing continuously as traffic grows denser, and takes a value of unity at the flow maximum. The total time cost per hour is vN, and the time cost per kilometer, AC^{user} is $vT(N)$. The optimal congestion toll is written:

$$Q\frac{\partial AC^{user}}{\partial Q} = \frac{e}{1-e} AC^{user} \qquad (42)$$

On the other hand, in a case where there is no traffic on the roads until the morning peak commuters enter the system, the relevant output measure is simply N, the number of car commuters. (This traffic is assumed to disappear at, say eight o'clock, when they all have reached their destinations, i.e. their workplaces). The same travel time-traffic density relationship as before is applicable. The optimal congestion toll is now written:

$$N\frac{\partial AC^{user}}{\partial N} = e\ AC^{user} \qquad (43)$$

The ratio of (42) to (43) goes from unity to infinity. In the former conventional but imaginary case the optimal congestion toll is infinite at the point of flow maximum, because the range of traffic density, where output is continuously diminishing, has to be shunned like the plague. In the latter case, however, the optimal congestion toll takes the more modest value of AC^{user}, i.e. the private trip cost should be doubled to equal the social marginal cost, when flow is at its maximum. Contrary to the

108

conventional wisdom, total output can continue to grow well beyond this point because output is measured in terms of the number of car commuters completing their journeys to work in the morning (before eight).

Accident externality charges

A simple and straightforward view of accident costs and optimal pricing in different transport systems is that, if a user accidentally causes harm to other users of the system or 'third parties', for that matter, the user in question should pay for all the damages.

Since very substantial sums of money may be claimed, transport system users wisely insure themselves, and the insurance premium is the proper accident externality charge. For example, the owner of an oil tanker that may run aground, spring a leak, and cause oil spills spoiling sea and shore flora and fauna, should be insured against such a catastrophe so that he can afford to pay all the costs of cleaning up.

For accidents constituted by collisions between different transport system users, it is more complicated, because it is often hard to tell ex post who caused the accident. Looking at a road transport system, it is true to say that, ex ante, all road users can cause accidents. If it can be statistically ascertained that in a particular situation additional road users will affect the risk for an accident of the original road users, there is a case for accident externality charges on top of the present traffic insurance premium.

In addition, if the insurance does not cover all costs to society caused by traffic accidents (which it does not), the case for accident externality charges remains, even if the accident risk is unaffected by additional road users.

Therefore, besides paying traffic insurance premiums, Swedish motorists pay about 0.3 ECU per litre of petrol (as part of the petrol tax) allegedly constituting the proper accident externality charge. This is two thirds of the total petrol tax. It is apparently important that the underlying theory of accident externality charges makes sense.

Total accident costs. On a road, users' interference with each other takes two related forms - a reduction in speed to avoid collisions when traffic density goes up, and (multi)vehicle accidents that occur in spite of speed moderation. That more cars on the road sooner or later means increasing time costs per vehicle is obvious. Is a similar progressivity characteristic of the total accident costs with respect to traffic volume?

Empirical studies with a view to establishing a functional relationship between traffic accidents and probable determinants such as traffic flow are very difficult because of the fortunate fact that accidents are rare occurrences. In a cross-section study where traffic and traffic accidents on different roads constitute the observations, the observation period has to be rather long in order to arrive at a reasonably representative number of accidents in each particular case (road). And during that long observation period, explanatory variables such as weather conditions, the state of the road, the composition of traffic as well as the traffic flow do not stay constant.

A lot of averaging is inevitable, which greatly reduces the accuracy of the data.

So far the weight of evidence speaks for a constant risk for accidents per unit of traffic with respect to traffic flow, in a range from rather high traffic density to free flow, all other things remaining equal. Or at least, there is no sufficiently substantial evidence consistently speaking against the convenient constancy hypothesis. This hypothesis is the somewhat shaky basis for the current treatment of accident costs in calculations of optimal road user charges.

Traffic accident costs are traditionally and conveniently divided into 'cold-blooded' costs of the expected loss of net production of persons killed or crippled in traffic accidents, hospital treatment of injured victims, etc. and 'warm-blooded' costs borne by the road users themselves and their dependants. Nowadays the latter are rightly considered to be some ten times greater than the former i.a. according to national CBA manuals for road investment in different countries. It is the warm-blooded costs that make accident externality charges potentially very important. The problem is that they are very difficult to determine accurately, as distinct from the cold-blooded costs, which are relatively easily calculated per accident.

The warm-blooded costs should not be valued directly per accident, but indirectly approached via observations of the willingness to pay for risk reductions. In the introductory model below the following traffic accident cost definitions and notations are used:

A = number of accidents in a given road traffic system per unit of time

n = average number of road users involved per accident

Q = traffic volume (vehicle-kilometers per unit of time)

r = nA/Q = risk for road users of meeting with a traffic accident, i.e. the ratio of the total number of road users involved in accidents to total exposure

c = the cold-blooded cost per victim of traffic accidents

W(r) = total willingness to pay of a representative road user and his/her dependants for reducing the actual risk to zero per tripkilometer

It is now possible to give the total accident cost, TC:

$$TC = W(r) \cdot Q + cnA \qquad (44)$$

The willingness to pay for complete safety is obviously highly dependent on the actual risk level, 'r'.

The assumed general shape of the willingness to pay function W(r) is depicted in Figure 4.5. In particular, the assumption is made in the following analysis that this function is linear for small risks, i.e. that $W = (a + b)r$ up to $r = \breve{r}$, where $\breve{r}$ takes a very small value, but big enough to exceed most actual risk levels in road transport. The latter assumption is by no means necessary for the main point of the following discussion. It facilitates the exposition and seems harmless enough.

110

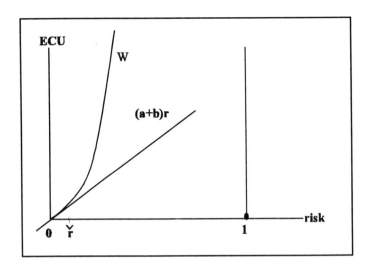

Figure 4.5   Willingness to pay (W) for complete safety at different risk levels (r)

The two components comprising the total willingness to pay are defined as follows under the simplifying assumption made:

ar = willingness to pay per tripkilometer of a representative road user for reducing the actual risk to zero

br = willingness to pay per tripkilometer of the dependants of a representative road user for reducing the actual risk to zero.

The total cost expression (44) can now be further specified to get the following final form:

$$TC = (a + b)rQ + cn = (a + b + c)rQ \qquad (45)$$

In case the accidents we are talking about were all fatalities, the sum of $a + b + c$ would represent the cost of a 'statistical life', as the term goes in the traffic safety literature. In round figures representative for Sweden and a number of other countries $a + b$ would in that case come to some 1.5 million ECU, and 'c' to 0.15 million ECU. The risk of a fatality in the Swedish road transport system per tripkilometer has in the 15 years since 1980 been nearly 10^{-8}. (Fortunately it is on the decrease in the 1990s, whether temporarily or for good is too early to say.) Current total tripkilometers are 10^{11} per annum. This means that the expected total fatal accident costs in Swedish road transport are in the order of magnitude of 1.5 milliard ECU per annum.

It is good to have a rough idea of the orders of magnitude of the main cost items involved. However, the present discussion is not aimed at a well-founded empirical estimation of traffic accident costs and externality charges. Too many theoretical cruxes remain to be solved before this would be possible. The aim is instead to tackle some of the major, rather controversial issues by a theoretical model.

An appropriate starting-point for the discussion is established by deriving optimal accident externality charges in the simplest case of homogeneous traffic and just one type of accident. For this purpose the total accident cost function (45) above has to be supplemented by an assumed relationship between the risk of accidents and the traffic volume:

$$r = r(Q) \tag{46}$$

As was pointed out in among others Newbery (1988) and Jansson (1994), the main weakness of the state of the art of traffic accident externality charges is the deplorable shakiness of the empirical evidence as regards the function $r(Q)$, which tends to lead to assuming 'r' to be independent of Q, i.e. regarding the total number of accidents as basically proportional to the traffic volume.

The level of the pricing-relevant accident cost. The homogeneity assumptions made above as to both the traffic and the traffic accidents in the road transport system concerned can, alternatively, be viewed as an 'averaging' approach, where a traffic unit is a composite unit of different kinds of road users in given proportions, and an accident and the associated accident costs are weighted averages of many different types of accidents and costs. Then it can be argued that the simple basic model will do for a discussion of the general level of the pricing-relevant accident cost.

In the total accident cost expression (45) three groups of cost bearers are distinguished, corresponding to the three items 'a', 'b' and 'c'. It is common to reduce the three groups to two, assuming that road users fully take into account the sufferings of dependants in case a traffic accident happens. This assumption is made here, too (for a further discussion of this crucial assumption, see Jansson 1994).

Then the average accident cost can be divided like this between the road users (and their dependants), and the rest of society:

$$AC^{user} = (a + b)r(Q) \tag{47a}$$

$$AC^{ext} = cr(Q) \tag{47b}$$

The pricing-relevant accident cost, PC, which should equal the accident externality charge, is obtained by taking the derivative of TC with respect to Q, and deducting AC^{user}.

$$PC = \frac{\partial TC}{\partial Q} - AC^{\text{user}} =$$

$$= \frac{\partial r}{\partial Q}(a+b+c)Q + cr \tag{48a}$$

Introducing the risk-elasticity, $E_{rQ} = \dfrac{\partial r}{\partial Q}\dfrac{Q}{r}$, the pricing-relevant cost can also be written:

$$PC = E_{rQ} AC^{\text{user}} + \left(E_{rQ} + 1\right)AC^{\text{ext}} \tag{48b}$$

The crucial importance of the shape of the relationship between the accident risk and the traffic volume is clear from this formulation: if 'r' is constant, independent of Q, the pricing-relevant accident cost is reduced to $AC^{\text{ext}} = cr$, since E_{rQ} comes to zero. Taking only motorized road transport into account, the product of 'c' and 'r' in the Swedish (and similar) road transport systems amounts to no more than about 0.02 ECU per 10 tripkilometers, which is a far cry from the present values (cited above) underpinning the high level of fuel taxes. Current values of the allegedly pricing-relevant accident cost exceeds 'cr' by more than a factor of ten.

How come? The explanation closest to hand would be that E_{rQ} in reality is greater than zero. If the true value of this elasticity were unity rather than zero, PC would be in the neighbourhood of the current 'official' value. This would mean that the number of (equally costly) accidents increases in proportion to the squared value of the traffic volume, which however, is a completely unrealistic assumption. Such an assumption is not made in the Swedish case. An implicit, assumed value of $E_{rQ} = 0$ can, as a matter of fact, be deduced from various relevant committee reports. The high 'official' value is instead arrived at by taking into account the fact that road users are generally rather heterogeneous, and, in particular, when divided into protected and unprotected road users, stand very different chances in a collision.

The way this fact is taken into account, unfortunately, leaves a great deal to be desired. The purpose of the next section is to discuss how the crucial and controversial fact that different categories of road users constitute systematically very different threats to each other should be taken into proper consideration. It can be anticipated that a drastic differentiation of the accident externality charges is indicated, but let us first conclude this section by holding up the main result as a bench-mark for the level of the pricing-relevant accident cost.

On the assumption that $E_{rQ} = 0$, the pricing-relevant accident cost, $PC = cr$, and the total revenue from the corresponding charges will amount to no more than the total external accident costs, $TC^{\text{ext}} = crQ = cnA$. In the Swedish case this total is in the order of magnitude of 0.3 milliard ECU, which can be compared to the current motor vehicle fuel tax revenue of some 5 milliard ECU.

The structure of the pricing-relevant accident cost. Differentiation of accident externality charges is warranted for a number of reasons. The following discussion is focused on one: the fact that road traffic is a mixture of light cars, heavy lorries, buses, trams, and unprotected road users (pedestrians, bicyclists and motorbike riders), and that collisions, as well as less direct confrontations, between road users of these different categories have systematically more or less unequal consequences. Mention can also be made in this connection of the fact that where the road transport system and the rail transport system overlap - at road/rail-crossings - accidents happen too often, and it is almost always the road transport vehicle that is demolished.

In Jansson (1994) a model was developed for calculating pricing-relevant accident costs of a mixed traffic system of just two road user categories - protected and unprotected (vulnerable) road users. In that case the simplifying assumption could be made that all crashes between road users of different categories were inconsequential for the protected, and more or less damaging only for the unprotected road user. Here a somewhat more general assumption is made, namely: there are two main kinds of traffic accidents occurring in the road traffic system under consideration, the numbers of which are designated A and X. The number of the former kind of accidents, A, is a function of the traffic volume of just one category of road users, whereas the latter, X, which is now to be dealt with, is a function of the volumes of two different, for the time being, unspecified road user categories:

$X = f(Q_1, Q_2)$ = number of accidents, the determinants of which are the traffic
  volumes of two different user categories.

$$r_1 = \frac{f(Q_1, Q_2)}{Q_1} = \text{accident risk of road user category 1}$$

$$r_2 = \frac{f(Q_1, Q_2)}{Q_2} = \text{accident risk of road user category 2}$$

For expository reasons the willingness to pay for complete safety on the part of the road users themselves and their dependants are merged:

$$(a_1 + b_1)r_1 = z_1 r_1$$
$$(a_2 + b_2)r_2 = z_2 r_2$$

The total costs of accidents of the kind at issue are written

$$TC = z_1 r_1 Q_1 + z_2 r_2 Q_2 + (c_1 + c_2)X$$
$$= (z_1 + z_2 + c_1 + c_2) \cdot f(Q_1, Q_2) \tag{49}$$

The pricing-relevant costs, PC_1 and PC_2 are derived by taking the difference between the social and private marginal cost. The latter is equal to the average user cost,

$$AC_1^{user} = z_1 r_1 \text{ and } AC_2^{user} = z_2 r_2.$$

The pricing-relevant costs, consequently, come to:

$$PC_1 = \frac{\partial TC}{\partial Q_1} - AC_1^{user}$$

$$= \left(z_1 + z_2 + c_1 + c_2\right)\frac{\partial f}{\partial Q_1} - z_1\frac{f}{Q_1} \tag{50}$$

$$PC_2 = \frac{\partial TC}{\partial Q_2} - AC_2^{user}$$

$$= \left(z_1 + z_2 + c_1 + c_2\right)\frac{\partial f}{\partial Q_2} - z_2\frac{f}{Q_2} \tag{51}$$

Introducing the following partial elasticities of the accident risk with respect to the traffic volumes, Q_1 and Q_2.

$$E_1 = \frac{\partial r_1}{\partial Q_1}\frac{Q_1}{r_1},$$

$$E_2 = \frac{\partial r_2}{\partial Q_2}\frac{Q_2}{r_2},$$

and defining the average external accident cost as well as total accident cost of each road user category like this:

$$AC_1^{ext} = c_1 r_1$$

$$AC_2^{ext} = c_2 r_2$$

$$TC_1 = \left(z_1 + c_1\right)X$$

$$TC_2 = \left(z_2 + c_2\right)X,$$

the pricing-relevant cost can be reformulated in a perhaps more intelligible way:

$$PC_1 = E_1 AC_1^{user} + \left(E_1 + 1\right)\left(AC_1^{ext} + \frac{TC_2}{Q_1}\right) \tag{50a}$$

$$PC_2 = E_2 AC_2^{user} + \left(E_2 + 1\right)\left(AC_2^{ext} + \frac{TC_1}{Q_2}\right) \tag{51a}$$

The interpretation of this result is made easier by multiplying PC_1 by Q_1 and PC_2 by Q_2 to get the total revenue from accident externality charges, TR.

$$TR = TC^{ext} + (E_1 + E_2 + 1)TC \qquad (52)$$

The sum of the two risk-elasticities E_1 and E_2 plays the same critical role for the level of the pricing-relevant accident costs as E_{rQ} in the preceding discussion. If this sum is minus unity, total revenue from accident charges comes to the total external accident cost, TC^{ext}. When we set $E_{rQ} = 0$ in the previous analysis, it means that the accident risk is constant, independent of the traffic volume. Setting $E_1 + E_2 = -1$ corresponds to such a state of affairs, but since two different risks, r_1 and r_2 are involved there is a certain difference. Minus unity of the sum of E_1 and E_2 implies that when the traffic volumes, Q_1 and Q_2 are both increasing at the same rate, the number of accidents X is increasing in the same proportion, too. So in an overall perspective, it can then be said that the accident risk stays constant in such cases, and it is logical that total revenue from accident charges would just cover TC^{ext}.

Irrespective of whether or not $E_1 + E_2$ sum up to minus unity the relative size of the two partial elasticities matters for the structure of the pricing-relevant accident costs. This is seen from expression (50a) and (51a) for PC_1 and PC_2. From (50) and (51) it is clear that the relative size of z_1 and z_2, and c_1 and c_2 matters, too.

When applied to the ill-matched pair of hard motor vehicles and soft pedestrians and bicyclists, the results of the model for calculating accident externality charges raise a number of difficult questions, which will be taken up in the following attempt to get urban road pricing into perspective. Before that a generalization of the model results concerning mixed traffic systems is offered.

Generalization. The road transport system and the other transport systems, which are partly overlapping, comprise a relatively large number of different traffic categories interfering with each other. Accidents of the X-type may happen, in principle to any pair of the different traffic categories, which motivate differentiated accident externality charges. The empirical problems of estimation, in particular of the applicable partial risk elasticities, which are the crucial entities in this connection, are very great indeed, and a number of practical/political snags are easily imagined before implementation, even if the empirical problems were solvable. This should not prevent us from spelling out fully the implications of a consistent adherence to the principles derived.

Suppose that there are 1...i... m traffic categories that should be distinguished for the present purpose. A-accidents occur within each category, which can be of single- as well as multi-vehicle character. By definition, the risk and the expected accident costs of each party involved is the same, so far as A-type accidents are concerned. There are $(m - 1)^2/2$ conceivable pairs of traffic categories producing X-accidents.

Let us single out a particular category 'k', and sum up all the pricing-relevant accident costs that arise due to the fact that this category mixes with categories 1.....j...m (j $\neq$ k) as well as produces internal accidents of the A-type. The designations used are listed below. The notations used in the previous homogeneous traffic model are adjusted to the present wider scope:

$r = r(Q_k)$ = risk of road users of category 'k' to meet with an accident involving no other traffic categories but 'k'

$E_{rQ} = E_k^r$ = elasticity of 'r' with respect to Q_k

$r_{kj} = \dfrac{(Q_k, Q_j)}{Q_k}$ = risk of road user of category 'k', to meet with an accident involving a road user of category 'j'

E_{kj}^r = elasticity of r_{kj} with respect to the volume of traffic of category 'k'.

TC_{kj}, AC_{kj}^{user}, AC_{kj}^{ext} = total cost, average user cost and average external cost of road users of category 'k' of accidents involving also road users of category 'j'.

The total pricing-relevant accident cost of category 'k' is now written in this way:

$$PC_k = E_k^r \, AC_k^{user} + \left(E_k^r + 1\right) AC_k^{ext} + \sum_{j \neq k}^{m} E_{kj}^r \, AC_{kj}^{user}$$
$$+ \sum_{j \neq k}^{m} \left(E_{kj}^r + 1\right)\left(AC_{kj}^{ext} + \frac{TC_{kj}}{Q_k}\right) \tag{53}$$

When it comes to empirical estimation of PC_k, there are two main types of problem. One is the aforementioned, severe difficulties of estimating all the various risk-elasticities; a very fine division of the total traffic into categories 1.....i.....m is, of course, impossible to maintain in that empirical work. To make it worse, a certain categorization of the traffic is not the only necessary disaggregation. The cost parameters 'a', 'b' and 'c' take very different values for different kinds of accidents within each of the two only types of accidents distinguished so far - A-type and X-type accidents. Within each type it is necessary to distinguish (at least) fatalities, accidents causing serious personal injury and light personal injury, respectively, and accidents only causing material damage, because in the stated preference studies of values of risk reduction, it is necessary to carefully specify the type of accident concerned.

To paraphrase Churchill, this theoretical discussion is not the end, it is not even the beginning of the end, but possibly the end of the beginning of tackling the problems of accident externality charges.

Getting urban road pricing into perspective

In the road pricing literature the unprotected road users play a secondary role. This is right and proper so far as the interurban road network and the main urban arteries are concerned. Those roads are meant for medium- and long-distance travel by fast motor vehicles, and to the extent that the slow, short-distance traffic by foot and two-wheelers take the same routes, separate lanes should be provided alongside the roadway. An 'industrial economics' view of the transport work produced by the motor vehicles in the road system is appropriate, by which the pricing objective is to ensure that an optimal rate of capacity utilization of the transport production plants is obtained in terms of traffic flow and travel time.

In the streets of the central city things can look quite different, at least in the cities of the old world. Short-distance trips dominate. (Through traffic should use by-passes.) A substantial proportion of the trips could be made by foot or bike, if it is safe, and if pedestrians and bicyclists are not too hampered by traffic lights and other restrictions. Speed limits for cars are applied in the interest of unprotected road users in the first place. 'Traffic calming' is nowadays equally prominent as traditional traffic management, by which the travel time of car trips should be minimized. The extreme of car-free streets is no longer exceptional but a steadily more prominent feature of the central city.

The theory of road pricing should be similarly differentiated between motor traffic roads and central city streets. This will be automatically achieved by paying proper attention to the component in the pricing-relevant cost constituted by the accident externality charges.

The mixed traffic problem. The streets and squares of the central city are not primarily a production system for car, bus, and lorry transport. 'Livable streets' (Appleyard 1981) are essential parts of urban life, where people meet, take walks, as well as transport themselves by different modes of transport in pursuit of various businesses. The problem is that protected and unprotected road users do not mix very well. In the classic Buchanan-report (Traffic in Town, 1963) it was envisaged that future generations may see our careless acceptance of unprotected people mixing with heavy vehicle traffic, and our obduracy for the inevitable result in a similar way as we see earlier generations' indifference to basic sanitary needs.

Has a change in attitude happened in the subsequent thirty years? There is no question about that: traffic safety is a high-priority goal in developed countries, but it does not mean that a generally accepted solution to the mixed traffic problem has appeared. In terms of number of casualties the problem is as great as ever.

X-accidents involving motor vehicles and unprotected road users are, by far, the most common type of fatalities of the latter traffic category. In Sweden more than 90% of cyclists and pedestrians killed in traffic have been knocked down by motor vehicles. The fatalities involving unprotected road users occur in urban areas to a large extent - about 90% of cyclist and 70% of pedestrian fatalities.

Is the solution that everybody should protect themselves, i.e. stop walking or biking in the streets? That may enhance traffic safety, but it will also make streets much less 'livable'. Or is the solution that far-reaching separation of protected and unprotected road users is to be aimed at? This can be done in widely different ways. On one hand, this option may mean that pedestrians are fenced off, and cyclists scared off the streets. This will make the road system more efficient for the car traffic and most

118

likely improve road safety, but other less measurable qualities of the complex concept of urban amenity will be set aside. On the other hand, separation can also mean car-free streets and so called pedestrianized areas in the central city. Which are the preferences of the majority of urban dwellers, workers, and visitors?

This is a difficult question which needs careful weighing up. It is close to hand to ask whether the market mechanism could be a means of weighing up the pros and cons of different parties.

Would accident externality charges solve the problem? Let us consider what kind of solution would be afforded by applying accident externality charges, on top of optimal congestion tolls and polluter payments.

It is clear that the crucial relationship in a mixed traffic system of protected and unprotected road users is the following:

$X = f(Q_1, Q_2) = f(Q, M)$ = number of collisions (and similar accidents) between protected and unprotected road users.

What is the nature of this relationship? In Jansson 1994 it was argued that assuming $f(Q, M)$ to be homogeneous of degree one is a convenient specification of the function, which is consistent with the general notion that 'the number of accidents is proportional to the traffic volume': if both Q and M are increasing by k%, X goes up by the same percentage. The empirical support for this assumption is not very impressive. The big problem is the measurement of total exposure of unprotected road users. Travel surveys usually ignore a good deal of the trips by foot or bike. The only relevant evidence to my knowledge with a bearing on the nature of the function $f(Q, M)$ are the results of a large study of accidents at junctions in Swedish urban areas, where either pedestrians or cyclists are involved (Brüde and Larsson 1993).

Data were collected from some 30 towns and cities with populations ranging from 25000 to 1.5 million (Stockholm). Only junctions with more than 100 cyclists or pedestrians crossing per day were included. Some 400 different junctions were studied. The accident data consisted of accidents reported to the police from 1983 to 1988.

Applying a Cobb-Douglas function for the regression analysis, the results, separate for pedestrian and cyclist accidents involving motor vehicles, were as follows:

Pedestrian accidents:

$$X_{12} = aQ_1^{0.50} Q_2^{0.72} \tag{54}$$

Cyclist accidents:

$$X_{13} = bQ_1^{0.52} Q_3^{0.65} \tag{55}$$

Accidents at junctions is an important type of accidents where protected and unprotected are conflicting. In Sweden it is estimated that 85% of collisions between motor vehicles and pedestrians, and 80% of collisions between motor vehicles and cyclists occur at crossings and junctions.

Nevertheless, we need far more empirical evidence before it is possible to calculate the pricing-relevant cost of central city road users in different urban areas. However, the cited evidence will do for the purpose of getting urban road pricing into a new perspective.

Illustrative example. A specific example is the best illustration of the problems that may meet when accident externality charges are to be applied. The X-accident function is assumed to take this shape:

$$X = kQ^\alpha M^\beta \tag{56}$$

The risk of an unprotected road user of being hit by a motor vehicle is:

$$r = \frac{X}{M} = kQ^\alpha M^{\beta-1} \tag{57}$$

In the numerical illustrations below, the elasticities α and β take the values of $\frac{1}{2}$ and $\frac{2}{3}$, respectively. (The latter is an average of the two elasticities found for pedestrian-accidents and cyclist-accidents.) The constant k determines the general risk level.

Since total exposure of unprotected road users is very difficult to measure, it is common to give the number of casualties of unprotected road users relative to motor vehicle traffic volume, i.e. the risk of a protected road user to hit an unprotected road user.

$$\frac{X}{Q} = kQ^{\alpha-1} M^\beta \tag{58}$$

Over time the latter risk has, fortunately, been steadily falling in most places during the process of motorization, at least in the later stage of maturity of the car-society. A cross-section comparison of fatalities per motor vehicle in different European countries by NTF (Nationalföreningen för trafiksäkerhetens främjande) in 1995 shows that risk levels can be very different even in groups of relatively homogeneous countries. However, the differences between groups of countries are astonishing. Compared to the safest group including the Scandinavian countries, the UK, and Holland, the emerging car-societies in the former communist block have four times more fatalities per car. If countries in Africa, South America and Asia (apart from Singapore and Japan) are included in the comparison, the risk figures rise into a range ten to twenty times higher than in Northern Europe. The same pattern appears when the comparison is restricted to city traffic.

The main explanation for these large differences seems to be that the countries showing wide differences in risk levels are in different stages of the evolution of the car-society. This means most likely both that 'k' takes much higher values in cities of the developing countries (including East European countries) and that the traffic mixture (Q/M) is unfavourable for road safety as measured by the ratio of X to Q. With the X-accident function assumed for the present discussion, the ratio X/Q is falling with increases in Q (given the value of 'k'). However, the risk of unprotected road users, 'r', measured in the usual manner, is increasing with increases in Q, all other things remaining equal.

The optimal accident externality charges on motor vehicles and unprotected road users, respectively, come to:

$$PC_Q = \alpha(c+z)k \; Q^{\alpha-1} \, M^{\beta} \tag{59}$$
$$PC_M = (\beta-1)(c+z)k \; Q^{\alpha}M^{\beta-1} + rc \tag{60}$$

It is easily checked that the total revenue from the accident externality charges amounts to cX, i.e. the total accident costs falling on 'third parties' are just covered in case $\alpha + \beta = 1$. In the present numerical example this sum equals 1.17 in accordance with the scanty empirical evidence to hand. Then the total revenue from optimal accident externality charges is almost trebled; it comes to $[(c + z)/6 + c]X$ in the present example.

Still this is not a very large amount. It is no more than a fourth of the total accident cost. It should be remembered, however, that the total revenue is the result of PC_Q being a charge, and PC_M a subsidy, which are nearly offsetting each other. The really remarkable feature of the structure of charges is that each one of PC_Q and PC_M takes very different values for different mixtures of protected and unprotected road users.

In Table 4.6 accident externality charges are calculated, assuming such conditions that exist in large Scandinavian cities, that is the α- and β-values assumed above, and a value of 'k' which is consistent with the total number of X-accidents involving protected and unprotected road users.

Table 4.6

X-accident externality charges for different mixtures of protected and unprotected road users; risk level for unprotected road users typical of Scandinavian cities; ECU per carkilometer and walking/biking-kilometer, respectively

Q/M	PC_Q	PC_M	PC_Q- $PC_M/5$
1/100	0.20	-0.001	0.20
1/10	0.06	-0.003	0.06
1/5	0.04	-0.005	0.05
1/2	0.03	-0.007	0.04
1	0.02	-0.01	0.04
2	0.02	-0.02	0.03
3	0.01	-0.02	0.02
4	0.01	-0.02	0.02
5	0.01	-0.02	0.02
10	0.006	-0.03	0.01
100	0.002	-0.1	0.02

Given the parameters of the X-accident function (56), the main determinant of the values of the charges is the ratio of Q to M. Looking first at PC_Q in Table 4.6, it is seen that, given the number of unprotected road users in the road transport system, the charge on protected road users starts at a high level, and falls relatively steeply to a more modest level as the car traffic volume goes up, and the ratio of protected to unprotected road users becomes more akin to existing mixtures. When car traffic becomes very dominant, PC_Q is down to a rather low level, where, alone, it will have a negligible effect on demand.

The optimal subsidy to unprotected road users PC_M, on the other hand, is at its highest where motor vehicle traffic is dominating. The idea of a subsidy to unprotected road users may seem far-fetched as a practical measure of traffic control. One can perhaps regard the providing of new bicycle lanes, wider side-walks (pavements), etc. without any payment from users in return as a subsidy to unprotected road users, indicated by the theory of accident externality charges.

Another idea is to assume that the sum of central city road users is approximately constant: if you do not appear as a protected road user, you will appear as an unprotected road user; the purposes for which you need to transport yourself in the central city are indispensable. In this case, it is correct to take the difference between PC_Q and a certain fraction of PC_M as a charge on motor vehicles in the central city. Car trips can be assumed to be some five times longer than trips of unprotected road users. The interesting thing about this difference is that it is U-shaped rather than L-shaped like PC_Q. Since the absolute value of PC_M, unlike PC_Q is increasing with increases in the ratio Q/M, the combined charge will not be really low for any traffic mixture.

Finally it should be remembered that the examples of accident externality charges given in Table 4.6 apply to cities with the safest traffic in the world. In cities where the accident risk of unprotected road users is much higher, the level of charges should be at a correspondingly higher level, whereas the structure may well be similar.

Interior solutions and corner solutions to the mixed traffic problem. The relationship between the optimal accident externality charges on motor vehicles and the volume/capacity ratio takes apparently the very opposite shape to that between the optimal congestion toll and the volume/capacity ratio. The optimal congestion toll is zero in a relatively wide range of the traffic volume/capacity ratio, and begins to rise when traffic density is such that the speed limit is difficult to reach. It will accelerate as the volume/capacity ratio approaches unity.

This may cause some unexpected problems in finding the true optimum. If car traffic demand is fairly elastic, the demand curve may well intersect the total pricing-relevant cost - (2) in Figure 4.6 - from below the first time (intersection point B), and a second time from above (intersection point C). Point B corresponds to a minimum of the net benefit and point C to a maximum. However, a third point of interest is the starting point A, where the net benefits are zero. Although point C corresponds to a maximum, it may still represent a negative net benefit, in which case the corner solution A is to be preferred. Complete freedom from motor vehicle traffic may turn out to be the true optimum in many cases.

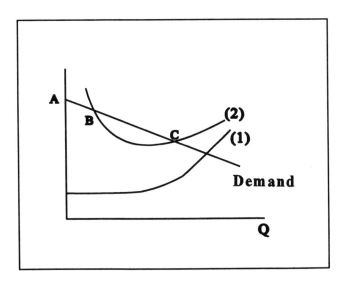

Figure 4.6   Accident externality charges on top of congestion tolls and polluter payments

This possibility complicates the already complicated and controversial issue of urban road pricing, but I think it is an important reminder that it is not just in certain residential areas that freedom from car traffic is very natural. 'Pedestrianization' is a measure as worthy of attention as road pricing also in the central city. When the possibility to prohibit car traffic in certain areas is up for discussion, many road pricing enthusiasts argue that it is most unlikely that a corner solution could be optimal anywhere, since threshold costs are absent. This is plainly wrong. The truth is instead that when accident risks are considered, a substantial threshold cost exists, which under certain circumstances speaks for complete freedom from car traffic.

In this connection it is pertinent to ask the question whether a similar corner solution can exist in the markets for travel by foot or bicycle? The typical position of the travel demand and pricing-relevant cost in these markets is indicated in Figure 4.7. The demand curve gives the (hypothetical) marginal willingness-to-pay of pedestrians and cyclists for using the road system (in the appropriate way, it may be added) on the assumption that their own accident costs are internalized, i.e. that they are fully aware of the risk involved. The pricing-relevant cost, which in this case is a subsidy, is falling in absolute terms as the volume M of unprotected road users is increasing.

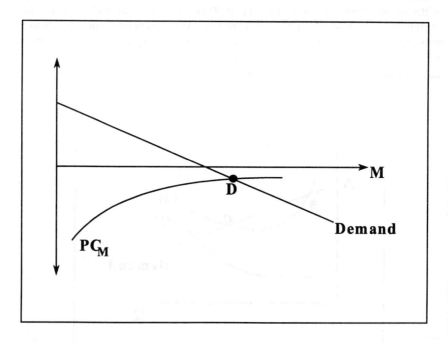

Figure 4.7   **The optimal accident externality subsidy to unprotected road users**

The point of intersection D gives a net benefit maximum, and as long as only accident costs are considered, a corner solution seems unlikely. A critical assumption is that their own accident costs are internalized. It is perhaps more common to take the opposite view, and argue that pedestrians and cyclists are often unaware of the accident risk. In that case the result may be that all positive net benefits are wiped out at any level of M greater than zero. It is also too restrictive to consider only traffic safety consequences of mixing protected and unprotected road users. Cyclists and pedestrians will in some road transport systems force motorists to slow down and take care much more than is necessary on roads where unprotected road users are wholly absent. There is a threshold time cost in many cases e.g. on motorways, which speaks for complete separation by prohibition of unprotected road users.

Concluding reflections

The nature of the X-accident function induces a last reflection on the development of the modal split and traffic safety in urban transport.

As is suggested by the diagram of Figure 4.8, the main change in the pattern of urban transport in the postwar period is the very considerable substitution of motorized individual transport for walking and biking. Roughly speaking public transport seems to have maintained its market share. However, it should also be pointed out that in the same period the population density of the central city has diminished.

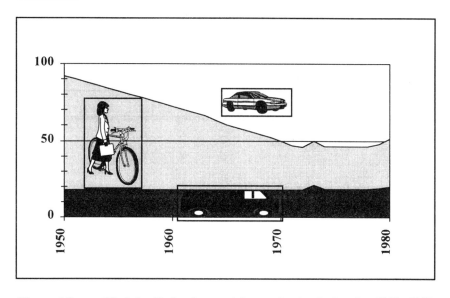

Figure 4.8   Modal split development for work trips in Sweden 1950 -1980

125

The central city has lost a good deal of its population, which has moved out from overcrowding to the suburbs. Car travellers in the central city are in the end of the transition period suburbanites to a large extent. They make longer trips compared to trip-makers in the initial situation, partly because they have a car at their disposal, partly because they live farther away from their destinations.

How has this radical, multi-dimensional change affected urban traffic safety? This is a complex and controversial issue, which is very relevant, bearing in mind that the cities of the developing countries are in the beginning of the transition period. They have a choice.

One attitude is to whole-heartedly welcome the change from unprotected to protected road use, because accident risks are much higher for the former than for the latter traffic category. Figures like those in Tables 4.7 and 4.8 below are quoted in support of such an attitude. The first table gives average risks of death and injury in the Swedish road system in the last decade.

Table 4.7
Risks of death and injury in road traffic in Sweden

Mode of transport	Casualties per 100 million person km		
	Death	Injuries	
		requiring a stay in hospital	not requiring a stay in hospital
Car	$5 \cdot 10^{-9}$	$7 \cdot 10^{-8}$	$3 \cdot 10^{-7}$
Bicycle	$3 \cdot 10^{-8}$	$15 \cdot 10^{-7}$	10^{-5}
Walk	$5 \cdot 10^{-8}$	$5 \cdot 10^{-7}$	10^{-5}

Source: Vägverket 1995

In the following figures for risks of traffic casualties in Denmark of different road user categories, an example of the safest of all modes of transport - public transport - is also included.

Table 4.8
Risk of death and injury in road traffic in Denmark

Mode of Transport	Death	Injuries
Bus	$5 \cdot 10^{-10}$	$2 \cdot 10^{-8}$
Car	$5 \cdot 10^{-9}$	$8 \cdot 10^{-8}$
Bicycle	$3 \cdot 10^{-8}$	$9 \cdot 10^{-7}$
Walk	$14 \cdot 10^{-8}$	$12 \cdot 10^{-7}$

Source: Elbek 1995

Although this is the conventional way of presenting relative risks of protected and unprotected road users, these figures can be very misleading unless the large differences in trip distance are taken into account. The modal substitution that occurs is not one personkilometer by car for one personkilometer by foot or bike. In particular, in the long run, it is a trip by car that is substituted for a trip by foot or bike, and because of the large speed difference, the trip purpose is fulfilled at a much longer distance when the trip is made by car. Looking at relative risks on a per trip basis, quite a different picture emerges: the risk of death in traffic is more or less the same for car travellers and cyclists and pedestrians (but obviously much less for public transport riders). The risk of slight injuries, on the other hand, is greater for unprotected road users than for car travellers, because pedestrians slip and cyclists fall down as well as being hit by objects other than motor vehicles.

All in all it is not possible to say that road traffic safety has improved thanks to the fact that most road users nowadays are protected. First, trip distances have grown much longer, and secondly, A-accidents are increasing in proportion to the volume of motor vehicle traffic. A different matter is that in many cities of the developed countries a general improvement in traffic safety has, fortunately, been experienced in the postwar period. This has had many causes, like better road and street design. In the risk function (14) for unprotected road users the accumulated effect of all different measures to raise traffic safety is represented by a successively decreasing value over time of the constant 'k'. This development could probably have occurred irrespective of the development of the modal split Q/M.

During the whole transition period, a significant difference between protected and unprotected road users has all the time been that only one party is a threat to the other party. This is equally true today. As was mentioned, more than 90% of the deaths of pedestrians and cyclists in Sweden occur as a result of collisions with motor vehicles. The empirically estimated X-accident functions (54) and (55) indicate that the risk for unprotected road users will increase by 5% as car traffic goes up by 10%, and will decrease by 3% as the volume of travel by foot and bike goes up by 10%.

This is the basic justification for the accident externality charges discussed.

Optimal pricing of inter-urban TI-services

Sweden is a sparsely populated country with few interurban routes where traffic volumes are really substantial. The contrast between the urban traffic intensity and the relative quietness of rural and interurban transport systems is so striking that a division of TI-service pricing theory between urban and non-urban conditions is self-explanatory. In densely populated countries it is more a difference of degree. Alan Walters who pioneered urban road pricing theory (Walters 1961 is a milestone) also made a lasting impression on interurban road investment and pricing theory by work commissioned by the World Bank with first-hand relevance for developing countries (Walters 1968). Sweden is a highly developed country with a good interurban and rural road network, but light traffic on those roads is the normal condition, which makes the optimal congestion tolls close to zero. Few unprotected road users are to be found in the main interurban road network, which speaks for rather low accident externality charges too. Optimal road user charges would cover only a fraction of the capital costs of the non-urban road network. Polluter payments from road traffic might be substantial, depending on the fuels used, and the (in)efficiency of the exhaust emission control devices of the road vehicle fleet, but like the accident externality charges intended to cover 'third party' costs, this revenue should not be regarded as a potential source of road financing.

The same cost conditions apply to small-town airports versus big-city airports, to all the minor seaports versus one or two major seaports, and to railway branch lines versus the relatively few, main railway lines. (As was mentioned, in the latter case congestion tolls on trains are irrelevant, where a national railway monopoly runs all the trains; it is the train operator that should levy a surcharge on passengers in critical sections in peak periods.)

The pricing issue could be left at that. By pointing at the contrast between the extremely low level of optimal prices of non-urban/low traffic density road services, and the much higher level of optimal prices of urban/high traffic density road services, the main point is made. However, one may ask for an explanation. Why are the pricing-relevant costs very low in one case? Why not adjust capacity fully to the lower level of demand in that case, which would raise the pricing-relevant costs to more 'normal' levels? Is the omission to do so evidence of inoptimal overinvestment in the non-urban TI?

The theory of optimal pricing of TI-services should be capable of giving satisfactory answers to this kind of question. That this can be done will be demonstrated in the last part of this paper.

The division of labour is limited by the extent of the market. To create the mental preparedness for accepting the following points, let us start by considering the general shape of the long-run average cost (LRAC) of industrial goods and services. Many studies have confirmed the L-shape of the LRAC-curve, or, as the classical work by

Haldi and Whitcomb 1967 concluded, there seems to be no limit to the economies of industrial plant size in production.

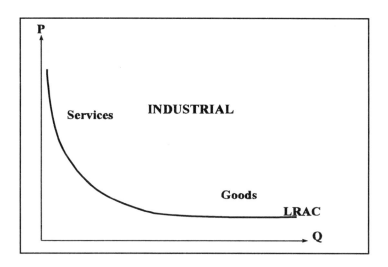

Figure 4.9   **General shape of the long run average cost of industrial goods and services**

'The division of labour is limited by the extent of the market' was observed already by Adam Smith in chapter 3 of the *Wealth of Nations*. At that time, when horse-waggon was the main inland mode of goods transport, the market could not be extended very widely, and sparsely populated regions without access to water could reap little benefit of the industrial revolution, until, in this century, motor transport on paved roads opened up also more remote areas to the market economy. Today when market areas for most manufactured goods are global thanks to the 'transportation revolution', the average production costs of all plants and/or firms of a particular industry should be more or less at the same level, that is in the plane interval of LRAC. A high-cost plant or firm could not survive, where all plants in the industry serve the same national or international market. (Technological change over time makes, of course, a modern 'best-practice' plant superior to older plants, but this will be balanced by faster capital write-offs than in the case where only wear and tear determines the depreciation.)

Transport infrastructure services are 'industrial' so far as the production technology is concerned. However, being immaterial goods, which neither can be stored nor transported to different places of use, their markets are geographically extremely limited. The road services between A and B cannot be bought for use elsewhere, e.g. on the route between C and D. No matter how cheap or high-quality the TI-services are in one particular relation, this is of no avail to people and freight with destinations in other relations. The general strong limitations of individual markets for TI-services explain the fact that a small road between two villages and a motorway in a different part of the country, which produces road services at a fifth of the cost per vehicle-kilometer of the small road, can co-exist in the transport industry.

Equality of the short-run and long-run pricing-relevant costs. The total cost of TI-services written as a sum of three components in (1) can be further specified by introducing vectors of design variables and characteristics of the physical conditions at the location of the facility concerned

$$
\begin{aligned}
TC &= TC^{prod} + TC^{user} + TC^{ext} \\
&= f(X,Y,Z) + g\left(X, \frac{Q}{K}\right)Q + h(X,Q)
\end{aligned}
\tag{1a}
$$

where $TC^{prod} = f(X,Y,Q)$ is the total cost for the producer of transport infrastructure services as a function of facility design, physical conditions for the construction and the traffic volume; $AC^{user} = g(X,Q/K)$ is the average cost of users of transport infrastructure services as a function of facility design and the rate of capacity utilization; $TC^{user} = g(X,Q/K)Q$; $TC^{ext} = h(X,Q)$ is the total cost of the rest of society (apart from actors within the transport production system) as a function of facility design and the traffic volume; $K = k(X)$ is the capacity of the facility as a function of facility design; X is the vector of facility design variables (width, curvature etc.); Y is the vector of physical conditions at the location of the facility (piece of transport infrastructure); Q is the output in terms of traffic volume; and $Q/K = \phi$ is the rate of capacity utilization.

The long run average cost, TC/Q, is steeply falling initially for two basic reasons: there are a number of more or less marked indivisibilities in the capacity costs, and, as a rule, TI facilities of higher capacity offer a higher quality of service than facilities of lower capacity, given the rate of capacity utilization. In Walters 1968 it is argued that capacity and quality are 'joint products'. Some well known examples from different TI sectors support this argument, which in the specification above of the total cost function is represented by the vector X being the determinant of both capacity K, and the level of service, i.e. the user cost, given the capacity utilization. A double-track railway has not only much more than the double capacity of a single-track railway, but enhances also railway traffic safety. Another berth in a seaport raises capacity as well as reduces expected queuing time per ship, keeping the berth occupancy rate constant. If road traffic visibility is improved by removing bushes and trees blocking the view, and/or building broader shoulders of the road, capacity will be higher, because the speed-flow relationship will shift upwards, which, of course, also will reduce the average user time cost.

The efficiency condition for road design is written like this in the cost model:

$$\frac{\partial TC}{\partial X} = \frac{\partial f}{\partial X} + Q\left(\frac{\partial g}{\partial X} - \frac{\partial g}{\partial \phi}\frac{Q}{K^2}\frac{\partial K}{\partial X}\right) = 0 \tag{61}$$

A general expression for the pricing-relevant cost is obtained, after total differentiation of TC, as follows:

$$\frac{dTC}{dQ} - AC^{user} = \frac{\partial f}{\partial Q} + \frac{\partial g}{\partial \phi}\frac{Q}{K} + \frac{\partial h}{\partial Q}$$

$$+ \frac{dX}{dQ}\left[\frac{\partial f}{\partial X} + Q\left(\frac{\partial g}{\partial X} + \frac{\partial g}{\partial \phi}\frac{Q}{K^2}\frac{\partial K}{\partial X}\right)\right] \tag{62}$$

It is observed that the expression within brackets of (62) equals zero under the efficiency condition that each level of output should be produced at minimum social costs. The pricing-relevant cost is then reduced to the three first terms, which corresponds to the general PC expression. It can be confirmed that PC is independent of the degree of factor fixity assumed, as long as the actual factor combination is on the expansion path. This is, of course, a reflection of the well known theorem of micro economics that the short run marginal cost is equal to the long run marginal cost under the usual efficiency conditions.

By combining (61) and (62) an alternative, 'long-run' formulation of PC is obtained, which further elucidates this relationship. An expression for the 'congestion toll', $\phi\partial g/\partial\phi$ obtained from (61), can be substituted for that component in (62). The final result of this substitution is:

$$LRPC = \frac{\partial f}{\partial Q} + \frac{\partial h}{\partial Q} + \frac{1}{\phi}\left(\frac{\partial f}{\partial K} + Q\frac{\partial g}{\partial K}\right) \tag{63}$$

In the long run the pricing-relevant cost should be equal to the sum of the marginal cost of wear and tear, the external cost on third parties, and the marginal capacity cost minus the total user cost savings obtained by a marginal increase in capacity, via a marginal increase in X, given the rate of capacity utilization.

For relatively low traffic volumes, where the long-run average cost is steeply falling, the two terms within the brackets of (63) tend to offset each other, confining the pricing-relevant cost to the marginal cost of wear and tear, and the marginal external cost.

The 'development cost' of interurban road services. The expression for the pricing-relevant cost above applies to a particular TI facility, e.g. road link in the interurban road network. Empirically it would be quite demanding to calculate with precision the pricing-relevant cost of each link in the network. In Sweden, like in many other countries without toll-roads, the fuel taxation constitutes the pricing of road services. Taking this institutional fact as given, it seems rather pointless to make the large effort of separate calculations for each link. An alternative, empirical approach would be to study by time series analysis how the total cost of the interurban road transport system has developed as traffic has been growing, thereby aiming at an average (for the whole system) pricing-relevant cost, which could be the basis for the fuel tax rate. This idea is not new. It has been used empirically, often referred to as 'development cost' calculations. For example in Norway some thirty years ago, such a calculation was made, which allegedly should produce the long-run marginal cost of road services (Hiort 1964): what appears as a marked indivisibility on an individual road link being improved is smoothed out in the context of the whole road network. This study was strongly criticised by a competing school of thought at that time of mainly Swedish economists, which dogmatically pointed out that nothing but the short run marginal cost is pricing-relevant. Since the short-run and long-run marginal costs coincide on the expansion path according to well established micro-economic theory, the heavy criticism seemed somewhat misdirected. The error of the 'development cost' school of thought is instead that one, decisive term of the long-run pricing-relevant cost expression is overlooked. (Compare expression (63) for LRPC.) Only under the unrealistic assumption that the road investments are purely capacity-expanding, without any joint quality-raising effect, would it be reasonable to take the ratio of the annual capital costs of new investments to the additional traffic on these roads as a proxy for LRPC. Since, on the contrary, non-urban road investments are almost wholly justified by cost savings for the existing traffic, a large error is made by ignoring the negative user cost term in the LRPC expression. The correct proxy for the average pricing-relevant cost of the inter-urban road services has the following form:

$$LRPC^{\text{proxy}} = \frac{C_t - B_t}{\Delta Q_t} \tag{64}$$

C_t = Capital cost of new investment year 't'
B_t = Benefits for existing traffic year 't' in the form of user cost savings thanks to the new investments.
Δq_t = Annual addition to the traffic on road links improved in year 't'.

As is well known, the traditional praxis of the national road administration for calculating the benefits of prospective investment projects is to disregard newly generated traffic; only cost savings to existing traffic and the forecasted, autonomous traffic growth are included on the benefit-side. Provided that the selected projects have a positive net benefit/cost-ratio, it follows that B_t is equal to, or greater than C_t, which means that the pricing-relevant cost is zero or negative.

There are, of course, in-between cases. In particular, in more populous countries than Sweden, it is presumably less rare that road investments (outside urban areas) are made partly because capacity is truly scarce. Then it is likely that the benefits to existing traffic, B_t, fall well short of the capital costs, C_t, and a positive value of the LRPC proxy comes out, which is consistent with a positive congestion toll in this case.

Notes

1   It is assumed that the same number of trips is generated in each city ring. Suppose further that trip-makers are distributed equally within each ring, and walk on 'ring-roads' to the radial bus lines. Then the average walking distance per trip follows from this formula, bearing in mind that each trip requires two walks.

$$2 \cdot \frac{\frac{1}{4} \cdot \frac{2\pi r}{n} + 0}{2} = \frac{\pi r}{2n}$$

References

Appleyard, D. (1981): *Livable Streets*. University of California Press. Berkely.

Brüde, U. and Larsson, J. (1993): 'Models for predicting accidents at junctions where pedestrians and cyclists are involved. How well do they fit?' *Accident Analysis and Prevention*. No. 5.

Elbek, B. (1995): *Transportmidlernes belastning af samfundet... og afgiftspolitikken. Niels Bohr Instituttet*. Københavns Universitet.

Else, P. (1981): 'A reformulation of the theory of optimal congestion taxes'. *Journal of Transport Economics and Policy*.

Else, P. (1982): 'A reformulation of the theory of optimal congestion taxes. A rejoinder'. *Journal of Transport Economics and Policy*.

Else, P. (1986): 'No entry for congestion taxes'. *Transportation Research*.

Haldi, J. & Whitcomb, D. (1967): 'Economies of scale in industrial plants'. *Journal of Political Economy*. August.

Jansson, J.O. (1969): 'Optimal congestion tolls for car commuters'. *Journal of Transport Economics and Policy*. September.

Jansson, J.O. (1984): *Transport System Optimization and Pricing*. John Wiley & Sons. New York.

Jansson, J.O. (1993): 'Government and transport infrastructure - Pricing,' chapter 8 in *European Transport Economics*. ed by Polak and Heertje. Blackwell, Oxford.

Jansson, J.O. (1994): 'Accident externality charges'. *Journal of Transport Economics and Policy*. January.

Jansson, J.O., Andersson, P., Cardebring, P. and Sonesson, T. (1993): Prissättning och finansiering av järnvägens persontransporttjänster. TFB och VTI Forskning/Research 5, Newbourg (1988).

Kawashima, T. (1988): 'Optimal congestion toll of expressway: A.A. Walters reexamined, P.J. Else re-appraised, and demand-surface paradigm re-considered'.

Gakushuin Economic Papers. September.

Leibenstein, H. (1966): 'Allocative efficiency and X-efficiency'. *American Economic Review*.

Mohring, H. (1972): 'Optimization and scale economies in urban bus transportation'. *American Economic Review*. September.

Nash, C. (1982): 'A reformulation of the theory of optimal congestion taxes: A comment'. *Journal of Transport Economics and Policy*.

OECD (1985): *Coordinated urban transport pricing. Road Transport Research*. Paris.

Panzar, J. (1979): 'Equilibrium and welfare in unregulated airline markets'. *American Economic Review*, Papers and Proceedings.

Small, K. (1992): 'Urban Transportation Economics.' Harwood academic publishers. Chur Traffic in Towns (1963): HMSO London, 'The Buchanan report'.

Vägverket (1995): *Vägverkets trafiksäkerhetsrapport 1994*. Borlänge.

Walters, A. (1961): 'The theory and measurement of marginal private and social costs of highway congestion'. *Econometrica*. October.

Walters, A. (1968): 'The economics of road user charges'. *World Bank Staff Occasional Papers*, No. 5, Washington D.C.

5 Deregulation and privatisation: British experience

Stephen Glaister

Introduction

The British experience of privatisation and deregulation since the war has been tremendously varied. We have had examples of just about every possible combination of change of ownership and change of regulation.

In this paper I will illustrate most of the possible combinations of privatisation and deregulation by reference to the UK experience in the transport sector. Road haulage was moved many years ago from a regulated, publicly owned industry to a privately owned and fully competitive one. Inter-city, long distance coaches were deregulated in 1980 but not privatised until 1985. Between 1985 and 1994 buses in London were neither privatised nor deregulated, but considerable competition was introduced in labour markets through competitive tendering. Buses outside London were both privatised and deregulated in 1985 and there is competition in both final markets and input markets. The proposals for British Railways are complex. The fixed infrastructure provider was encouraged to foster competition in labour market whilst initially remaining in the public sector. It was privatised in Spring 1996. Train operations are being privatised and they are free to take advantage of competition in their labour markets, but, for the time being, not permitted to indulge in widespread competition amongst themselves in the markets for passengers.

It is important to distinguish clearly between the issues of (a) private versus public ownership and (b) competition versus no competition. When people talk of competition in this context they often have in mind competition in *final* product markets: for example competition between modes for freight traffic or for passengers. But, within (b) there is competition in final product markets and competition in *input* markets. A constant theme in this paper is that competition in input markets - and especially in labour markets - is important, and possibly more so than competition in final product markets.

If British experience of privatisation and deregulation in the transport industry is extraordinarily wide, the degree of success is varied. I shall argue in this paper that where there have been successes, these are largely attributable to promotion of competition in labour markets. The question arises as to whether competition in labour markets can be achieved without some form of privatisation. In principle it can, and I will illustrate, it can be in practice. But it can be impossible in some political environments - in which case privatisation of the enterprise may be a solution.

We need criteria by which to judge success. These will include what happens to:

1 fares and charges
2 support from the tax-payer
3 service availability (including the provision of unremunerative services)
4 service quality
5 terms and conditions of employees
6 fulfilment of other political objectives.

The evolution of policy under Mrs Thatcher's Governments. The privatisation and deregulation philosophy developed considerably over the thirteen years of Mrs Thatcher's Conservative governments. When the party came to power in 1979 a main concern was to remove barriers to competition: to foster the free market in the belief that this would encourage efficiency. This was illustrated by a pamphlet written in 1977 by Mr Norman Fowler (then a senior conservative MP in the Opposition), arguing that there was no reason to maintain the strict system of quantity regulation that then applied to the bus industry. Mr Fowler duly became the first Secretary of State for Transport, and one of the new government's first pieces of legislation was to deregulate long distance bus services. There was a strong wish to reduce the involvement of the state to a bare minimum.

Later in the several Tory governments' programmes new motives for privatisation were discovered. British Telecom was the first major utility to be sold. The experience alerted the government to the fact that privatisation yielded substantial sums which were counted as negative public expenditure. These helped deal with a pressing problem of funding the cost of rapidly increasing social security claims without greatly increasing taxation. The notion was also developed that privatisation could be used as a way of introducing the experience of share ownership to a much wider range of people. The hope was that they would continue to hold shares and thus become more sympathetic to the values espoused by the Tory Party.

It was discovered that there is a conflict between the desire to promote competition and the desire to sell public utilities at a good price for the benefit of the Exchequer. This is well illustrated in the cases of buses in London and the privatisation of British Rail.

Market failure

If all markets functioned according to the paradigm of perfect competition then there would little justification for economic regulation. The traditional literature on 'market failure' identifies situations where the conditions for welfare to be optimised through

136

the free operations of markets are absent in some respect or other. Subsidy, regulation, or public enterprise operation with non profit maximising objectives are responses which might correct for such imperfections.

Decreasing costs. If an individual's consumption of transport does not affect the welfare of any other individual then the price paid will accurately reflect both the benefit to him of transport and the social benefit. Welfare will be optimised if the price of each trip is everywhere equal to marginal cost of producing the trip. If an industry faces long run decreasing costs (i.e. where there are unexhausted economies of scale) then a price set equal to long run marginal cost will be below average cost and a deficit will ensue.

This argument amounts to the assertion that if you have a technology with indivisibilities, and which is not fully utilised, then it may seem sensible to offer subsidies in order to use that available capacity at a cost which is exceeded by the benefit. The unit costs will thereby be reduced.

That has been one of the traditional arguments for rail subsidy. It may be a valid argument, if capacity genuinely cannot be reduced to eliminate spare capacity. It is not valid if carrying more passengers requires more investment in capacity to the extent that long run marginal costs are above average costs, as in the peak. It is less likely to be valid for buses than rail because buses are inherently more flexible than railways. Hence total costs tend to be more nearly proportional to output. However, it will still happen that certain parts of routes or times of day will have under-utilisation and hence marginal costs per passenger below the average.

In any case, if an industry has declining costs with size it will be a natural monopoly: competitive forces will tend to produce monopolistic ownership. Once this has happened then there will be a case for economic regulation in order to prevent exploitation of the monopoly position at the consumers' expense.

Externalities. If any third parties not involved in a transaction incur costs or benefits as a result of it, then the amount of output or activity will not necessarily be optimal.

Those who damage the environment, cause congestion or cause costs to society in some other way should not be allowed to benefit without recognising the costs to others.

One solution to this problem is internalisation - the setting of charges and compensation payments so that the impacts are converted into monetary terms by means of taxes and subsidies. The practical difficulties of both identifying the appropriate prices and arranging the appropriate payments have usually been so great that alternative approaches have been adopted, such as the setting of physical standards.

Public goods. A public good is one which is non competing in consumption (that is, the cost of using an extra unit is zero) and non excludable in use (that is, once provided it is impossible to stop people from using it). An example is the lighthouse. A public good may be rather more loosely interpreted as a good or service for which it is too difficult, or costly, or wasteful to organise through the market mechanism so it must be funded entirely by subsidy.

It is sometimes argued that roads have many of the characteristics of public goods. But the technological means to charge for their use are available if we choose to employ them.

Second best and the correction of distortions. Ideally, price should equal marginal cost everywhere. If that condition is not applied in one part of the economy then welfare may
be best achieved by creating a compensating distortion elsewhere. An example of this is the case for subsidising public transport to combat congestion.

Information. Imperfections of information can provide grounds for regulation. An obvious case is safety: if consumers correctly perceived the risks they faced then one might be able to argue that a competitive market would automatically provide the level of safety that consumers were willing to pay for. But consumers cannot be assumed to have the raw information or the ability to process it. Further, safety has some public good-like characteristics. Incomplete information or information held asymmetrically by different parts of the market can also lead to market failure.

Distribution and equity. Labour is a factor of production with a price which is determined by the balance of supply and demand in an imperfect market. The distribution of wealth and income which emerges from this market mechanism may be one which is not seen as ethically acceptable.

The proposition may be put much more simply as the existence of some categories of person - the old, the young and the infirm, as well as the poor - for whom the provision of subsidised public transport may be seen as an instrument to overcome their disadvantage.

Incentives to operate at minimum cost[1]

Technical inefficiency. It is often assumed that those who produce public transport services do so at the minimum possible cost, so that increased subsidy is fully applied to either improve services or reduce their costs to users. However, if subsidy in response to alleged market failure has the unintended effect of weakening the incentives to minimise costs then resulting increased costs will greatly reduce the benefits.

The following discussion concentrates on the relationship between ownership, competition and internal (or production) efficiency. A firm is internally efficient if it produces a given output using the minimum cost combination of inputs.

Objectives. Consider a firm in the public sector with objectives set by the government. Assume that the government is a social welfare maximiser and further that it seeks to maximise social welfare in a partial equilibrium context. We note that the partial equilibrium approach is limited: social welfare maximisation in a partial equilibrium context does not necessarily lead to a socially optimal outcome in the economy as a whole. However, the partial equilibrium approach provides a useful basis upon which to proceed. Assume that lump sum transfers are not possible, rather that the raising of government funds involves taxation which changes the decisions of individual agents in the economy. In this situation there are deadweight losses associated with the raising of public funds so that a £1 government transfer requires output losses elsewhere in the economy in excess of £1. We will refer to the difference between a £1 transfer and the associated output loss elsewhere in the economy as the shadow price of public funds. The very simplest arguments suggest a loss of 10 to 18 percent of each £1 or $1 levied by indirect taxation and about 20 per cent for income tax. More sophisticated analyses yield estimates ranging all the way up to a loss of 56 per cent.

The government's objective for the firm can be said to be to maximise $W = CS + \Pi - \lambda T$ where W = social welfare, CS = consumer surplus, Π = producer surplus, λ = the shadow price of public funds, T = transfer payment from the government to the firm. That is, social welfare is the sum of consumer and producer surplus net of the deadweight loss associated with raising the transfer payment. Given a welfare maximising government and assuming that the government and the firm share the same objective function then a socially optimal outcome will ensue. In particular, the firm will achieve internal efficiency.

Vickers and Yarrow (1988) drop the assumption that the public firm will act to maximise social welfare. The reason for this is that the objectives for a public firm are set by politicians. They assume that a politician seeks to maximise chances of re-election and that this does not result from the maximisation of social welfare. Say that a politician considers a policy with potential benefits that are distributed unevenly amongst the population. An example of this is a cost reduction effort which will adversely affect workers and benefit either taxpayers or consumers. Assume that the benefits of the cost reduction effort exceed the costs ie engaging in cost reduction would increase social welfare. Assume also that the benefits will be highly dispersed. Then the impact of the policy will be more visible to workers than to taxpayers/consumers. In this situation a vote maximising politician might avoid reducing costs to socially optimal levels.

We may then rewrite the government's objective function for the firm as $W = CS + \Pi - \lambda T - \beta x$ where x is a measure of effort applied to cost reduction. Now maximisation does not lead to an internally efficient outcome; internal efficiency is sacrificed in order that political objectives may be fulfilled. Haskel and Szymanski (1993) analyse a case where the objective function for the public firm incorporates political factors. They show that if the government attaches positive weight to union utility, for a given level of employment, wages will be higher in a public sector than a private sector firm. The implication here is that the public sector firm does not produce a given output at minimum cost ie it is not internally inefficient.

139

The principal and agent problem. There is another possible source of inefficiency if we drop the assumption that the government and the public firm share the same objectives. Say that the public firm is run by a utility maximising manager whose unfettered behaviour will not lead to maximisation of social welfare. Hay and Morris (1991) discuss the various factors which may influence a manager's utility. Amongst the variables that they suggest are income, status and power. Say that the utility of a public firm manager is a positive function of status. If status increases with the size of the workforce that the manager controls then he may expand it beyond the efficient level and as a result fail to maximise social welfare. Assume a manager of a public firm has utility that decreases as his effort increases. The utility maximising manager may choose a level of effort which is below that consistent with internal efficiency and hence maximisation of social welfare.

If manager utility maximisation is not consistent with social welfare maximisation then the government must attempt to create incentives for the manager to maximise social welfare. Whether this is possible can be analysed in a principal agent framework. See Rees (1985) for a discussion. In brief, the principal employs the agent to carry out a task. Standard neoclassical theory predicts that under profit maximisation the agent will be rewarded in accordance with his marginal product. Say that this is not possible because the principal does not observe the marginal product of the agent. An example of a situation where the principal does not observe the agent's marginal product is when the agent's output depends both on effort and random factors and the latter are observed only by the agent. There is scope here for the agent to pursue his own objectives rather than those of the principal. The principal recognises this and identifies the self interest of the agent. A contract between the principal and agent is then designed so that the principal's objectives are pursued contingent upon utility maximisation by the agent.

Bös (1986) adopts a principal agent approach to analyse the public firm where government and management objectives diverge. Here the government is the principal and the manager of the firm is the agent. Bös assumes a government with the objective of maximising social welfare and a utility maximising manager. The manager's utility function is increasing in income and decreasing in effort. If the government can observe the input of effort by the manager then it is possible for the government to reward the manager so that the public firm achieves internal efficiency. However, assume that the manager has private information, that he is a utility maximiser and that utility is an increasing function of income and a decreasing function of effort. Bös shows that in these circumstances there does not exist a practically implementable incentive scheme such that internal efficiency will ensue.

The models analysed by Bös are based on idealised situations. The assumptions required for these models may not be practically tenable. Further deviations from internal efficiency than are predicted in the models might *actually* have occurred. Bös assumes that the government sets clear objectives for the firm. The manager then pursues these objectives subject to any discretion which he may have due to asymmetries of information. Kay and Thompson (1986), and Glaister and Travers (1995) in the context of London Underground, argue that public firms' objectives actually tended in the past to be ill-defined. Ill-defined objectives are hard to pursue, thus even a manager sharing government objectives might face difficulties in achieving good performance. Ill-defined objectives are also hard to monitor and less effective monitoring provides more scope for managers to pursue personal objectives. Foster (1992) puts a similar point of view. He suggests that it was often the case in the public sector that objectives were confused, complicated and varying and as a result effective management was difficult and precise monitoring was prevented. Foster explains poor performance in the public sector in these terms.

The private firm. Consider now the private firm. Kay and Thompson (1986) argue that privatisation of a public firm will promote internal efficiency. Beesley and Littlechild (1986) put a similar view; they suggest that the substitution of market discipline for public influence which results from privatisation leads to a better use of resources. There are forces which may cause a tendency towards internal efficiency in a private firm. If a firm acts as a profit maximiser then it will be internally efficient. Whether or not a firm acts as a profit maximiser depends on the extent to which the firm's manager can be made to act as a profit maximiser. In the same way that the manager of a public sector firm may not act to fulfil government objectives in the absence of monitoring, the manager of a private firm may not act to pursue the profit maximising objectives of the firm's owners.

Vickers and Yarrow (1988) analyse the outcome for a private firm with a utility maximising manager and profit maximising owners. They assume a private firm with ownership in the form of dispersed share holdings. In the absence of monitoring or if the level of monitoring is inadequate the manager of the firm may pursue personal non profit maximising objectives. The motivations for this type of behaviour are the same as in the case of the public firm *ie* the manager may gain disutility from increased effort and increased utility through status or power. If the level of monitoring is sub optimal then internal inefficiency will result.

Monitoring may be absent or at least inadequate for two reasons. The first of these is that when share ownership is dispersed individuals gain only a fraction of the benefit they create by undertaking monitoring, in other words there is a beneficial externality associated with monitoring. It is a standard result that in this situation sub optimal levels of activity will take place. The second reason is that there are economies of scale in monitoring which are not exploited when share ownership is dispersed. Dispersed share ownership will raise monitoring costs relative to the case of a monopoly monitor and hence the level of monitoring will be lower in the former situation.

There are however ways in which effective monitoring can be carried out when share ownership is dispersed, for example through a board of directors. Vickers and Yarrow (1988) conclude that it is not clear in a context of dispersed ownership whether the optimal level of monitoring will be undertaken. Assume that the optimal level of monitoring is undertaken. It was stated above that in the case of a public firm monitoring does not lead to an outcome which is internally efficient. Bös (1986) analyses the monitoring of a manager by a profit maximising owner and shows that the firm's outcome will tend towards though not be synonymous with internal efficiency.

An alternative pressure affecting managers in the private sector, again examined by Vickers and Yarrow (1988), is the threat of takeover. These authors consider the case of a non profit maximising manager who is vulnerable to takeover after which optimal monitoring would take place and internal efficiency would ensue. Incentives towards takeover increase as pre and post raid share prices diverge. Assuming that the manager tries to avoid a takeover, he will aim to achieve internal efficiency in order that the share price of the firm does not fall below its post raid level. However, internal efficiency via this mechanism is not guaranteed. Say for example that shareholders anticipate raids and hold on to shares until prices reach post raid levels. At this point a takeover will yield negative profit due to transactions costs; takeovers will not take place. Another example given by Vickers and Yarrow is the case where the raider is not a profit maximiser. In this case the achievement of internal efficiency does not prevent a takeover, thus incentives to internal efficiency are undermined.

Product market competition. Product market competition may act as a pressure towards internal efficiency. Consider the case of a monopoly firm owned privately by shareholders. Assume that the shareholders' objective is to maximise profits and that the manager of the firm is monitored in pursuit of this end. It was stated above that even when monitoring is effective the outcome is not internally efficient. The reason for this is that the manager exploits his information advantage over the shareholders and follows personal non profit maximising objectives. Say that the market is opened up to competition. Vickers and Yarrow (1988) argue that competition in product markets leads to revelation of information about managerial effort. The information advantage of the manager is eroded relative to the case of monopoly and more effective monitoring can take place. The result is an increase in internal efficiency. However, competition in the product market is not a sufficient condition for internal efficiency. In the extreme case of perfect competition firms make normal profits and non profit maximising firms cannot survive. In this situation firms will be internally efficient.

To summarise, in a private sector firm monitoring can lead to a situation which is close to internal efficiency. When share ownership is dispersed it is not clear that the level of monitoring will be optimal. In the absence of monitoring takeover threats might lead to internal efficiency although this is not the only possible outcome. Competition in product markets may spur performance because it reveals information about managerial performance and allows more effective monitoring. Under perfect competition firms will be internally efficient.

Competitive tendering

Competitive tendering is a process through which services formerly supplied by the public sector are made potentially open to supply by the private sector. Competition here is *for the market* as opposed to *in the market* so that, for example, there will be one piece of work which firms compete for the right to carry out. Competition typically takes place between firms from the public and private sectors.

The tendering process works in the following way. Consider a service formerly produced 'in-house' (*ie* by the public sector) which is to be put out to competitive tender. The first step in the tendering process is to specify precisely the output and quality of the work to be tendered. Criteria for award of tenders must be devised. These must fulfil the objective of the tendering authority to achieve the desired level of output and quality at minimum cost. It is common to award tenders through some kind of auction process, usually a first price sealed bid auction. In this case a tender generally represents a fixed payment from the tendering authority to the tenderer agreed before work is undertaken and contingent upon carrying out the specified work. An in-house provider may compete with private sector firms for the tender. Rules must be set to govern bids from the former in-house provider to ensure that it has no advantage or disadvantage in comparison with private sector firms. After the tender is awarded the tenderer can increase profits by not carrying out the specified work. For this reason the tendering authority must monitor the tenderer to ensure that the specified work is carried out satisfactorily.

Hartley and Huby (1986) suggest that competitive tendering was introduced to the public sector as a solution to the problem of inefficiency. In the previous section sources of internal inefficiency in the public sector were discussed. It was suggested that lack of clearly defined objectives would lead to internal inefficiency, as might clearly defined but non commercial objectives. Thomas (1987) presents competitive tendering as a process of work specification, performance management and cost allocation. This can be related to the literature on the relationship between firms' objectives and internal efficiency. It seems implicit in what Thomas says that competitive tendering involves the introduction of new objectives and monitoring systems. If these objectives are consistent with internal efficiency and can be monitored effectively then on this basis alone we might expect to lead to efficiency gains. This is not however the only source of possible efficiency gains. Domberger, Meadowcroft and Thompson (1986) argue that it is the competition inherent in a system of competitive tendering which drives efficiency gains.

Consider a service which is provided by a local authority and produced in-house. Assume that there exist asymmetries of information between voters and the local authority and that as a result political factors are allowed to influence supply of the service. Assume also that asymmetries of information exist between the local authority and the manager of the service. We have seen earlier that internal inefficiency in the supply of the service may result from either of these asymmetries. Now say that competitive tendering is introduced. The old objectives of the in-house provider are replaced and geared towards cost minimisation for a given level of quality. If managerial performance can be effectively monitored then we would expect to see a move towards internal efficiency.

It might be argued that the public sector firm has an advantage over the private sector firm as regards monitoring because of economies of scale in monitoring and dispersed share ownership in the private sector. In the absence of competition however it cannot be guaranteed that internal efficiency will be achieved. First of all it is not clear that monitoring will be effective in the absence of competition. Change within an organisation is likely to be subject to resistance and gradual in pace. It may also be the case that the expertise required to achieve internal efficiency may not be present in the public sector firm. It is the introduction of lower cost private firms that forces the in-house provider to adopt new objectives and monitoring systems and to search for new methods in production. Vining and Boardman (1992) argue that in a system of competitive tendering an in-house provider must act as if it were a private firm. This is intuitive: if the in-house provider does not act as a private firm then it will not survive in a system of competitive tendering.

In a situation where former in-house provision was not efficient, competitive tendering leads to efficiency gains. Two early studies of the impact of competitive tendering on costs suggested that this was the case: Domberger, Meadowcroft and Thompson (1986, 1987) analysed refuse collection and ancillary hospital services and estimated that the introduction of competitive tendering had reduced costs by around 20%. Domberger (1987 p.76) states that: 'There is no longer a debate about whether competitive tendering yields cost savings. There is no question that it does'.

Road freight

Road freight was regulated in 1930 under a system which closely parallelled that in force for buses until 1985. It was a quasi-judicial system of quantity licensing. Applicants for licences had to prove a need for new licences and incumbents (including the railways) could object. Licences were often refused on the grounds that new services would abstract revenues from the railways. The system caused distortions, with rather few, over-large firms. Own-account operation was less severely quantity restrained than contract hire.

After the War much of the industry was state-owned. As early as 1953 the then Conservative government attempted to privatise long distance road freight but not all the vehicles found buyers. Under the 1968 Act (an important piece of *Labour* legislation) the sector was effectively deregulated altogether, except for price control which was finally removed by the Tories in 1980. The remainder of the state holding was sold in a remarkably successful management buy out in 1982. Now there is only a requirement to hold an Operator's Licence and to meet vehicle safety and drivers hours regulations. The industry now enjoys many of the classic characteristics of a constant return to scale, free entry, competitive industry: low profits, a substantial turn-over of firms because of entry to and exit from the industry, widely varying firm sizes. A large proportion of output is produced by single vehicle, owner-driver firms.

Distance per vehicle increased from 60,000 km to 75,000 km per year during the 1980s. Tonne km carried per vehicle also increased rapidly in the 1980s. Real operating costs decreased by an average of 2.5% per year followed closely by haulage prices to users.

There have been policy reviews of the sector but no strong arguments have been

144

advanced recently for making further changes to the economic regulation of the system.

Long distance (express) coaches

One of the first acts of Mrs. Thatcher's first Conservative Government in 1980 was to deregulate long distance coach services (as distinct from local services, also referred to as stage carriage services) defined to be those with a minimum passenger journey length of 15 miles.

Most services were operated by the state owned, National Bus Company. This also ran the majority of local services. Like the old road freight industry, services had to have a route service licence which was issued by a quasi-judicial body, the Traffic Commissioners. They restricted quantity and controlled fares.

In the new legislation all quantity and price restrictions were removed - the residual regulation related to relatively uncontroversial safety regulation. However, the NBC was not privatised.

Initially there was large scale competitive entry to the business. Fares fell markedly and the volume of service increased. Other attributes of service quality also changed - product differentiation emerged with the introduction of luxury vehicles with TV and stewardess service on board.

However, the competition was quite quickly defeated by the NBC who re-emerged as the dominant operator. This was because of three factors. First, the NBC were good, experienced bus operators and they were able to respond to the spur of competition by improving their own efficiency. Second, they were left with exclusive rights to use the existing major coach terminals, in particular, Victoria in central London where 25% of passengers interchanged. Third, it was alleged that they used profits earned in some of their local businesses to cross-subsidise the long distance business.

These last two features were clear failings of the deregulation: failures to recognise that if one is going to rely on competitive forces to police a market then one must take care that there are no substantial barriers to competition.

The failings were corrected under the 1985 Act: the NBC was broken into a large number of distinct companies and all hidden cross-subsidy was prevented. Equal access was granted to terminal facilities.

Since then the benefits of the deregulation of express coaching seem to have stabilised. Fares are generally lower and service levels have improved, relative to the pre-deregulation situation, as illustrated in the graphs shown in Thompson and Whitfield (1995).

British Rail responded to coach competition by aggressive fares cutting, especially where it had spare capacity, and by marketing initiatives in those markets in which coach is particularly strong: the young and the elderly.

The deregulation and privatisation of long distance bus services can be counted as a success by our criteria, unless one wishes to argue that railway finances were significantly damaged and that was, in itself a bad thing. As in the case of freight, it was achieved by promoting the free market for *both* final product markets and for inputs.

UK bus deregulation

In order to come to a view on the success of the policy of bus deregulation, it is important to understand the context and the *primary* problem that it was intended to solve. The impetus was primarily a result of a determination to reduce overall government expenditure - both central and local authority. Thus it was not only the result of a desire on the part of the Thatcher Government to introduce competition into markets as a matter of principle. Nor was it primarily in order to increase private ownership of public sector assets through privatisation, nor to secure government income by non-tax means.

Most of the controversy about the merits and demerits of bus deregulation and much of the subsequent evaluation has concerned the effects on passengers; that is, the effects on the demand side. Although the Government did express hopes of increased demand and lower fares (which, as we shall see, have not yet been realised) the prime motivation for the policy was actually to change things on the supply side in order to meet global requirements for subsidy reduction whilst minimising damage to passengers through fares increases and service reductions.

Nonetheless, a full evaluation of the success of deregulation must include effects on both the supply and demand sides. There are sound economic efficiency arguments which demonstrate that *external* bus subsidies can generate net economic benefits *if* they are not associated with reductions in operating efficiency.

On the other hand *internal cross* subsidy is difficult to identify, not economically efficient, often perverse in its effects and not subject to political scrutiny (Annex 2B of the White Paper *Buses* is a critique of internal cross subsidy). The Government expected competition to drive fares closer to avoidable costs, by route and period of the day. Cost levels would themselves be generally reduced. This would imply fares reductions on heavily loaded routes, except to the extent that peak load pricing modified this. Conversely, fares might rise on routes then in receipt of generous cross subsidy.

The 1984 bus policy

The philosophy, aims and means of the new bus policy are well encapsulated in paragraph 1.12 of *Buses:*

'The total travel market is expanding. New measures are needed urgently to break out of the cycle of rising costs, rising fares, reducing services, so that public transport can win a bigger share of this market. We must get away from the idea that the only future for bus services is to contract painfully at large cost to

146

taxpayers and ratepayers [ie local property tax payers] as well as travellers. Competition provides the opportunity for lower fares, new services, more passengers. For these great gains, half measures will not be enough. Within the essential framework of safety regulation and provision for social needs, the obstacles to enterprise, initiative and efficiency must be removed. The need to act is urgent'.

The White Paper proposed:

1 *Abolition of road service licensing*. Instead of having to apply for a road service licence operators would be required to register the route and timing of their services with a new licensing authority and to give adequate notice of intent to commence, make a significant modification to, or withdraw from a service. (The registration function was subsequently left with the existing Traffic Commissioners and the length of notice was fixed at 42 days.) A competitive market would thus be created resulting in lower fares, reductions in costs, greater variety and responsiveness in services to demand and new opportunities for operators. Overall patronage would increase as a result.

2 *Competition and cross subsidy*. In order to facilitate and foster this competition the industry was to be restructured. The nationalised National Bus Company was to be broken into separate companies and then sold to the private sector. The remaining publicly owned operators, in the metropolitan counties and the Municipals, were to be made into regular, 'arms length' companies, owned by the local authorities and with normal company accounts so that any subsidy was visible and explicit. The extensive system of cross subsidy of unremunerative services by remunerative ones, a deliberate function of the route licensing system under the 1930 Act, would thus be removed. The previous, anomalous exemption of the bus industry from the provisions of competition law was to be removed.

3 *Subsidy*. After operators had registered commercial services local authorities would be required to secure such additional, subsidised, services as they believed necessary by competitive tendering with equal access to any who would care to bid. Local authority-owned companies would be in equal competition with the private sector, including the ex-National Bus Companies. If a local authority chose to operate a system of allowing particular groups to travel at concessionary rates - the elderly for instance - then all operators would have to be given access to monies in compensation on the same terms.

4 *Safety*. The system of quality regulation in the name of safety was not greatly changed. Operators licences would be required and vehicles subject to regular and random inspection. The Traffic Commissioners would have limited powers to 'stop operators who behave foolishly on the road from running local services at all' and, where there are problems with traffic, to 'impose conditions about routes

and stopping places, so as to produce a result which is both orderly and fair to all operators involved'.

In interpreting the UK experience it is important to bear in mind that there were three distinct and simultaneous changes:

1 a substantial reduction in subsidies
2 removal of quantity regulation
3 privatisation of the nationalised undertakings and separation of the others from their local authorities.

Care must be exercised in attributing any one effect to a particular cause. It is also important to note that it is, in principle, possible to adopt a policy of changing any one of these three without changing the others. In the case we consider here it was decided that, in practice, it was necessary to change all three in order to achieve the Government's objectives.

The primary problem: subsidy reduction without cutting output

Figure 5.1 (on page 189) shows the situation as it would have looked in Spring 1984, when 1983 data were available. The dotted lines show Treasury provision for revenue support in the annual public expenditure budgeting process ('Cmnd' refers to the Command reference number of the respective annual Public Expenditure White Paper). The solid line shows the outturn - ie what was being shown in the official accounts as actually having been spent. Bus revenue support was seen to be growing very rapidly. The figure shows official public expenditure provisions for revenue support in successive years: bus subsidy appeared to be running out of *central* Government's control as a result of deliberate policies of *local* authorities. The Government of the day was determined to reduce public expenditure for reasons of macroeconomic policy. There was also a long-standing desire to put the industry on a sounder, more commercial footing.

Thus the problems to be addressed were:

1 local bus subsidies were running far ahead of central government provision
2 there was no effective control mechanism in the existing system
3 the bus industry was not considered to have a sufficiently commercial outlook.

The cost reduction solution. The prospect of closing the gap shown in Figure 5.1 must have seemed daunting. Simple calculations show that if this were to be achieved by removing subsidy at constant service levels and constant unit costs then fares would have to increase by at a factor of at least 2.5 on average in the metropolitan areas and much more in some of them. To do this by reducing output at constant fares would have implied an outcome which would have been just as politically difficult.

Salvation was offered by the observation that unit costs had increased in the industry, especially where subsidies had increased. Evidence was found by investigating differences within and between the National Bus Company (public sector; the major, or only, operator in most country areas, small to medium towns and cities) and metropolitan county operations, and between public and private operators at home and abroad (see *Buses* chapter 5 and Annex 2a). There were also investigations of the earnings of workers in the bus industry and those in similar industries such as road haulage. The conclusion was that (*Buses* paragraph 4.10) the potential exists for cost reductions of up to 30 per cent of total costs of public operators.

Having established that the only feasible solution lay in cost reduction the issue became one of how best to secure it.

The front-running alternative to the line actually adopted by the Government was some system of authorities putting routes out to competitive tender, but disallowing competition on the road. This became summarised as 'competition *for* the route rather than competition *on* the route'.

This alternative was pressed by many of the operators and most of the scholars who had expertise in transport also advocated this approach; Gwilliam, Nash and Mackie (1985a, b) give a good contemporary statement of the arguments.

In brief, the argument is that tendering would avoid the risks perceived of deregulation, of bad behaviour on the road in the attempt to win passengers; and it would allow local authorities to keep control of fares and allow them to plan an integrated set of services with cross subsidy, perhaps optimally adjusted according to the principles of the second best familiar to economists. At the same time competition for tenders would provide the required pressure on costs (Glaister and Beesley, 1985a, b gave counter arguments and responses).

In the event the view was taken that the method most likely to succeed, and the *only* one with a chance of acting quickly enough to meet the timetable set by the public expenditure requirements, was to introduce genuine competition into bus labour markets by creating a competitive industrial structure - that is, to both deregulate and privatise. However, the tendering alternative *was* adopted in London and I compare the way in which the two systems have turned out below.

The effect on costs and subsidies. Deregulation proper occurred in January 1987, although a transitional arrangement started in October 1986.

Figures 5.2 to 5.7 show the outcome at current prices including London.

Viewed simply in terms of the objective of bringing revenue support back to the public expenditure plan levels, the policy worked better than many people would have dared to hope at the time. In the English metropolitan areas fares rose by an average of only 23% real, 1984 to 1988/89. They did not rise at all in the English shire counties. On average they rose by 10% in England as a whole[3]. There has been a remarkable increase in output where a decrease might have been expected. There has been a 15% increase in total vehicle kilometres, 1985/86 to 1988/89 (but the average vehicle size has fallen, see below). There is now almost as much vehicle kilometreage operated as *commercial* service as the *total* in 1985/86; out of the big metropolitan areas there is more. The proportion of the routes extant before deregulation which carried on afterwards as commercial propositions - well over 80% - was far more than anybody had predicted (see Gomez-Ibanez and Meyer (1989)).

This has been possible because of the predicted fall in bus operating costs per vehicle-kilometre. Excluding depreciation, the real fall, 1985/86 to 1988/89 is around the predicted 30% with the exception of London at 14%. One source of these savings is wages, with real weekly and hourly earnings in the industry falling, against an increase in other industries. Another source of savings was the fall in numbers employed which, together with the increases in output, suggest considerable increases in output per employee. These are superficial comparisons and one needs to conduct careful analyses to understand what has happened in detail. Several authors have done this, see Gwilliam (1989), White and Turner (1990), White (1990), Gomez-Ibanez and Meyer (1989), Tyson (1989)[4], and they confirm the general impression given by the aggregate statistics. White and Turner do note that there was a 'windfall' reduction in costs due to the substantial reduction in fuel prices - worth 2 to 3 percentage points in cost saving. On the other hand, real labour costs have moved unfavourably, so that relative to general male weekly earnings costs per bus mile have fallen by much more than 30%. The predictions in the White Paper were relative to the earnings levels then ruling, not to present real levels.

This outcome was consistent with the general strategy of the administration at the time: to weaken the power of the labour unions and break up nationally negotiated agreements on terms and conditions. In the case of the bus industry before deregulation the dominance of the National Bus Company together with a relatively few large companies serving metropolitan areas made it easy for the Transport and General Workers' Union to keep a firm grip on negotiations. Deregulation and fragmentation of ownership were recognised as a means of loosening this grip and facilitating the development of new and individual labour contracts. Hibbs (1990) and Hesseltine and Silckock (1990) give accounts of how this has, in fact, happened. They estimate that roundly one third of the labour cost savings have been due to deterioration of terms and conditions and two thirds due to increased productivity. Hibbs[5] reports that there was general agreement among the managers he interviewed that one of the biggest advantages of the post-1986 situation arose from the managerial side walking out of the two negotiating bodies that had for many years arrived at the National Agreements on pay and conditions. The result was the growth of plant bargaining and pay now reflects the local market for labour. Without this the spread of minibus operation at specific rates could not have developed. Hibbs also notes that Municipal operation had always been constrained by the power of the unions through their influence in the Council Chamber and its committees. This was clearly most significant in Labour councils, but was not unknown elsewhere. Management authority was undermined and moves to improve productivity were often blocked by this route.

Two caveats are necessary here. A significant contribution to the cost reduction has been the introduction of new pay scales associated with small vehicles which have been growing in number. Therefore the fall in cost per vehicle kilometre overstates the fall in cost per seat kilometre - according to White and Turner (1990) by about one third. Secondly, the estimates quoted here exclude depreciation. It has been alleged that operators have been failing to renew their vehicle stock (for instance, White and Turner, 1990). If so then there are some missing components which will inevitably appear in the cost accounts sooner or later. This is a difficult issue to resolve. There has been considerable purchase of new vehicles. There has been a significant growth of leasing which must have affected the depreciation issue. It is also becoming more widely recognised that operators were initially over cautious in assuming a life of only four to five years for the new, smaller vehicles. Seven or eight years may now seem to be more appropriate (Banister and Mackett, 1990). In that case the depreciation will be substantially less than was previously thought.

It may not be legitimate to attribute all of the subsidy reduction to deregulation. In real terms and excluding London revenue support had peaked before 1984. No doubt this was due to other measures to limit local authority expenditure, such as precept control and the system of Protected Expenditure Limits under the 1983 Act. Supporters of deregulation will claim that the rapid increase in the rate of decline of revenue support after 1984 is largely attributable to deregulation because they will point to the reduction in labour costs after 1984 which was, itself largely attributable to deregulation.

As Figure 5.2 illustrates the overall fall in public expenditure on local buses in England, excluding London, 1984 to 1988 was over 25% at constant retail prices. White and Turner (1990) point out that there are some additional administrative and other costs in local authorities, connected, for instance, with the tendering process. If one accepts their estimate of these and assumes there were not offsetting administrative savings from deregulation and privatisation, then the saving is reduced from about 26% to about 16%.

The cost reduction must be counted as the success of the 1985 Act. Public expenditure has been reduced in the face of rising real costs of labour in a labour intensive industry. Yet physical output increased, fares rose only moderately and fares concessions were protected. The primary objective was achieved.

John Hibbs (1990) has conducted a series of structured interviews with managers in the bus industry. The managers are very clear that they would not wish to see a return to the system as it was before the 1985 Act. They prefer competition in the market to a tendering or franchising system because that gives them freedom to manage and develop their businesses in their own way, without the fuss of having to deal with a higher authority. Their greatest complaint about the former system was not regulation in itself, but the increasing interference from political bodies which inevitably accompanied the rapid increase of subsidy in the context of route licensing.

The secondary expectations of the 1984 bus policy

The summary of the *Buses* White Paper given above contains several secondary propositions and it is to these to which I now turn. I cannot attempt a complete recital of all the effects of bus deregulation. Here I wish to mention a few matters where I think the literature poses some interesting questions, or where there have been recent developments.

A competitive market would be created. It is difficult to say 'how much' competition has in fact occurred, beyond conceding that is has, so far, been less than the more optimistic of us expected. There is plenty of on the road competition to be witnessed in particular places. Evans (1990) notes that about 9% of bus kilometres were involved in direct competition at one time but says that this 'now appears to be declining'. But he goes on, 'active competition has been common enough and varied enough to have provided the industry with a wide range of experience'. Tyson (1989) says of the metropolitan areas, 'competition has been on a much larger scale than anticipated by many people, with at least 30 operators in the market in each area and an average of three bids for each tender for subsidised services'. Generally, competition increased in the second year of deregulation. Against this is observed a tendency amongst operators to form larger companies or to create and expand groups of companies. In a more recent paper Tyson (1990) says that 'whilst there are surprisingly few instances of two of more operators running identical routes there are many instances of two or more operators serving substantial segments of a corridor.' Competition remains strong for tendered bus routes in London.

Gwilliam (1989) notes that companies have tended to expand into areas where they have local knowledge; they have tended to avoid confrontation; they prefer to compete for tendered routes rather than lodge commercial registrations. In many areas operating territories are similar to those before deregulation and it is possible that there has been a tacit agreement not to trespass on each other's territory. Hills (1989) reports active competition on the road in Scotland.

It is too soon to conclude on this topic. Competition will increase if and when the investing institutions at home and abroad decide that there are profits to be made in the British bus industry. The firm prices at which the last few of the National Bus Companies were sold and the active trading in bus companies now going on may be an indicator that this is the case.

Gomez-Ibanez and Meyer's (1989) assessment was that 'neither the advocates nor the opponents of reform have been completely vindicated by subsequent events. However, as to whether or not competition would emerge, which was central in the prior debate, the advocates appear to have the better of the argument.'

Traffic congestion. A fear that is often expressed concerning bus deregulation is that a flood of vehicles in competition will cause road congestion. The White Paper acknowledged the worry and the legislation gave reserve powers to the Traffic Commissioners in the event that congestion caused by buses had to be controlled. Two standard counter arguments were given: that smaller buses are more agile in traffic and that they would provide a better substitute to private cars than conventional services and thereby reduce traffic congestion.

There has not generally been enough growth of service to cause traffic problems. The agility of minibuses is manifest and is illustrated by the greater speeds actually

152

achieved. There is also some isolated evidence of substitution for car use (Banister and Mackett, 1990, for evidence on both of these points). Traffic Commissioners have not had to use their powers.

Fares would fall and cross subsidy would be reduced. This was an oversimplification of a quite complex series of propositions. The system of quantity licensing had fostered uniform pricing-rates per kilometre that did not vary much by time or place. It also enforced cross subsidy - permission to run profitable services was granted contingent on the operator also agreeing to offer unremunerative services. Operators themselves introduced other kinds of cross subsidy.

The new arrangements for tendering for non-commercial services has greatly reduced some forms of cross subsidy and has forced the authorities responsible to consider what it is worthwhile paying for. But price competition has not developed to any great extent and much uniformity in fares scales has survived. There is discussion in the literature about why this might be (eg Evans 1990b, Dodgson and Katsoulacos 1990). A phenomenon which deserves explanation is the preservation of historically determined differences in average fares levels between apparently similar areas.

Tyson (1990) confirmed that 'in many instances vehicle mileage has, as would be expected, increased on potentially profitable routes and has diminished on less remunerative routes and at unremunerative times, for instance, in the evenings and on Sundays'.

Greater variety and responsiveness in services to demand and new opportunities for operators. An important part of the 'variety' proposition was the belief that in the UK bus size was too great and that the forces of competition would greatly encourage the use of smaller vehicles. Some simulation work I did at the time for the Government (Glaister 1985, 1986) suggested that this was the case. There is an interesting piece of research to be done on the reasons why bus size increased systematically over the decades. It is possible, of course, that the big bus is in fact optimal for many market circumstances, as argued by Gwilliam, Nash and Mackie (1985a, b). But my conclusion that capacities of the order of 30 to 40 would suit many circumstances better than the 70 or more of the conventional double decker was not inconsistent with the findings of several other, more recent authors (see Banister and Mackett for a summary). Note that this is a rather larger size than the 15 to 25 capacity vehicle which many companies bought in the early stages because that was what was available. Recent purchases are generally of the larger size predicted.

Some operators have taken advantage of opportunities to do things differently offered by the technology of small vehicles. For instance, in Exeter the entire workshop side of the business was closed down and the main technical activity was contracted out on a performance contract to the Ford dealer.

There are important effects on the markets for drivers. The driving licence requirements are less demanding. It is remarked that they enjoy the better social contact with their passengers and achieve better job satisfaction. The vehicles are less daunting to drive and so new labour markets have opened up. More importantly, the minibus has been the hook on which to hang substantially less advantageous terms and conditions of work, both in the London case and under deregulation (Banister and Mackett 1990). It is unclear to what extent these effects have anything to do with the technology of vehicle size. Nor is it necessarily to do with deregulation: sceptics point out that minibus experiments pre-dated deregulation and minibuses are being introduced in a regulated London. However, I would conjecture that it has been the commercial pressure brought to bear by deregulation which has changed attitudes and speeded change.

Patronage will increase. The official statistics indicate that patronage did not increase during the first few years after deregulation.. Gomez-Ibanez and Meyer (1989) and White and Turner (1990) both argue that, after standardising for the fares increases the decline in patronage is much as it would have been on the basis of secular trends, so the increase in vehicle kilometres appears to have been unproductive. We have seen that costs per vehicle kilometre have fallen considerably. But vehicle kilometres have increased whilst passenger kilometres have remained stagnant - so load factors have fallen and costs per passenger kilometre have fallen little.

This is the great disappointment of the policy. It is also a mystery. The explanation given by White (1990) is that the potential benefit of the extra vehicle kilometrage was not converted into better service quality. This was because of irregular running, or vehicle bunching, lack of service coordination, or confusion amongst passengers because of frequent changes, or some other factor. There can be no doubt that some of these factors played a part. For instance, some authorities put a great deal of effort into opposing deregulation and none into preparing for it with most unfortunate short term consequences for passengers.

However, it is not at all clear that this is a complete explanation. In most detailed case studies of which I am aware bus output increase was accompanied by an improvement in observed or estimated service quality. Banister and Mackett document the favourable small vehicle experience so far in terms of patronage (although they can find little direct evidence on delivered service quality) and note that the full market potential for minibus operations had not yet been identified. Evans (1990) estimates 'scheduling efficiency' in two case studies, defined as the theoretical average passenger waiting time if buses had regular headway on every route as a percent of the corresponding figure with bus times as they were. He estimates a 5 or 6 percentage point fall in efficiency since competition started which is not enough to vitiate the considerable increase in bus kilometres - yet measured patronage did not respond. He surveys other examples and he notes that 'This gap between estimated and expected patronage is a puzzle, both at the national level and at the level of the case-study towns'.

One problem is that outside the metropolitan areas the pre-deregulation patronage data are often of poor quality and after deregulation they became commercially sensitive with all the difficulties that implies. In many cases the 'before' data is the outcome of a single day's observation. In all cases 'after' data is difficult because of problems of grossing up samples when the universe of bus routes is changing rapidly. To state the obvious, if a fundamental change like deregulation is to be evaluated then it is essential to ensure that good statistics are recorded both before and after the event - particularly passenger usage. It seems that we failed in this respect in the case of UK bus deregulation.

Evans (1990) finds that the most convincing explanation of the unexpected patronage results, and the one accepted by other commentators, is that a known infrequent service has been replaced by an unknown frequent one, so that effective waiting times have not been reduced. It is interesting to note that software houses report an unanticipated boom in sales of vehicle routing and scheduling routines, and no sales of the real-time passenger information systems they were successfully developing before deregulation.

If this diagnosis is correct then the remedy is simple: inform passengers about the services. The White Paper foresaw some of these problems but took the line that providing good information would be in the operators' own commercial self-interest. However, a precaution was taken: the purpose of the system of registration of commercial services and the 42 day rule was to provide a central source of information and to constrain the rate of change as a source of confusion to passengers. We have noted that managers seem to have been slow to adopt good marketing practice and commercial pricing. In 1984 the UK bus industry spent less than one percent of its revenue on marketing (Wooton, 1984) and there is little sign that this proportion has increased greatly. If there really is a dysfunction of the normal commercial incentives then there may be a case for some short term action by public authorities. To a degree this has been done by some local authorities from the beginning, where they have accepted this as one of their functions (see Tyson, 1989, 1990).

This is a point of some importance in the context of the British Rail privatisation proposals.

Recent developments. There are now some indications that the industry is beginning to respond in the way that the White Paper originally envisaged. There is a considerable quantity of active trading of bus companies, including purchases of companies by overseas capital. Some of the larger companies are now publicly quoted on the stock exchange and their share prices have been buoyant. *Bus Briefing* of July 1995 says:

'It is clear that fewer passengers across the country as a whole have been lost under the deregulated regime than under any other'.

'And in some areas, where bus operators, working with local authorities, have actually delivered the sort of services that the public wants, that passenger numbers have increased, in some cases dramatically. Patronage in Exeter is claimed to be more than 300% higher than in 1985; it is 26% higher in Bristol, and significantly greater in Oxford... There are indications, too, from other parts of the country that the decline in passenger numbers may have been halted, for the first time in 45 years'.

'Profits are rising, too. In 1993/94, according to the latest *Bus Industry Monitor* figures, the industry as a whole recorded a profit margin before interest and taxation of 7.2% - up from 5.8% in 1992/93. Outside London, the same margin increased from 6.3% to 7.8%, which is easily the best result achieved since deregulation...'

'Capital investment increased too, up from £118.4m in 1992/93 to £165m outside London...'

'The picture which emerges from the new *BIM* report is of an industry which is coming to terms with its new regulatory regime and ownership structure, is increasingly profitable, and thus able to fund its investment requirement, and may have learned how to win passengers back'.

Perhaps the time was under-estimated for the industry to transform itself from a regulated, state-planned activity to a mature market-driven commercial and competitive one.

Coordination and integration would be provided by the market. The White Paper took a strong, free market line on the matters of coordination and integration of services. To the extent that these things are in passengers' interests they would command a price and would automatically be provided by the normal commercial process. Of course, this was a controversial proposition because it attacks the heart of the case for intervention in route planning and in ticketing systems.

It was always accepted that some central agency would be required to administer concessionary fares schemes. Local authorities have undertaken this and the schemes seem to have worked surprisingly well, with participating operators being willing to settle on the strength of sample survey information on usage of their services.

Other forms of integration, notably the integrated travel pass, have had a more mixed experience as one would expect, since some gave more advantageous terms than others to pass purchasers. Tyson (1989, 1990) has reported developments in the metropolitan areas, which are particularly interesting because of their size and complexity, and because the former authorities had specific duties to integrate.

This is another area where change and the emergence of market forces have been slower than was expected. In his 1990 paper Tyson notes that for many passengers, the impact of any reduction in co-ordination of services has been lessened by the increase in the volume of service provided... there have been commercial opportunities for integration between bus and rail, although it has taken time for them to be recognised and the market to react. The role of the Passenger Transport Executives in securing services under contact has been crucial to the continuation of integrated services and has, in some cases, only had to be temporary until the services

156

became commercially viable.

After a period in which many schemes were withdrawn the inter-availability of tickets between modes and operators has now been substantially restored (see Tyson, 1990 Table 3). A development of particular interest and reassurance to those sympathetic with the White Paper is the development in Tyne and Wear of a separate company - jointly owned by the Passenger Transport Executive and the bus operators - to administer a travelcard scheme. It issues tickets and allocates revenues in accordance with agreements amongst its members on the strength of survey data.

Safety. Safety was a subject of great debate when deregulation was proposed. It was alleged that competition would lead to neglect of vehicle maintenance and personnel training. Foster (1985) lists the various irregular driving practices it is alleged took place before regulation in 1930. It is difficult to know how common they actually were then; there does not appear to be any evidence on the point. Some predicted that they would reappear. The operator licensing system and extra vehicle inspection resources were two responses.

In the event there are few reports of serious problems of this kind. The official accident statistics show a steady continuation of the previous decline in injuries and deaths per passenger kilometre. It seems that the quality regulation has been sufficient so far. Further, one should note that times are different and, in the UK, drivers are now better educated, trained and generally more responsible than they were in the 1920s.

Barriers to competition: collusion, predation, merger

The White Paper took a simple line on competition. Regulation itself was the important barrier. Technical conditions in the bus industry were thought to be such that economies of scale, network effects, information asymmetries etc. would not enable significant barriers to be sustained.

This was not to deny that predatory practices had been observed in the trial areas, but it was argued that it would not be commercially sensible, or even possible, to ward off competition on many fronts simultaneously without the sustenance provided by a protected, regulated sector. Nor was it to deny the historical experience that under competition there was a tendency for territorial companies to form and that in the dense urban areas operators had formed associations.

The lack of concern about these matters was founded on several observations. We now have sophisticated pro-competitive legislation; corruption and criminal enforcement of cartels is not likely to be as much of a problem in the UK as it might be elsewhere in the world; and combines, associations and territorial monopolies would be so constrained in their behaviour by the threat of competitive entry that they would have to behave almost as if the industry were perfectly competitive - the market would be contestable, to use the modern terminology.

The propositions to the effect that the market is contestable were strongly questioned at the time by opponents of deregulation (see for example Gwilliam, Nash and Mackie, 1985a, b). It is certainly true that as the primary, binding constraint to competition was removed, other, less important constraints have become binding.

Some of the present barriers were created deliberately for well-meaning reasons: for example, the 42 day rule for entry and exit, the registration system and the requirements for an operator's licence all conspire to ensure that an operator is large enough to operate a whole route himself and to sustain the risk of having to run a misjudged service for a period of time. Owner drivers are not encouraged by the operator's licence requirement. Gwilliam (1989) and Beesley (1990a) have argued that the operation of concessionary fares schemes has constituted a barrier.

In spite of the confidence that company size would not matter it was decided, as a precaution, that the National Bus Company would be broken up into relatively small companies (some 200 to 300 vehicles each) and privatised in such a way as 'to promote sustained and fair competition' (section 48(1) of the 1985 Act). Privatisation was not a necessary accompaniment to deregulation as the situation in Scotland illustrates; there the industry was deregulated but not privatised.

The market value of the NBC was recognised to be small in the absence of regulation. Little official information has been given about the proceeds from the sale of individual companies. Press reports suggest that the early sales did indeed realise rather little. It seems that the later sales realised more than had been hoped for. Recently there has been much talk of the trading in ex-NBC companies and other companies. It has been alleged that one or two companies are aggressively buying up companies, leading towards concentration of ownership and auguring badly for competition. The general view seems to be that there is a clear tendency towards concentration in the bus industry.

The wheels of the system for appraising mergers grind slowly but the Monopolies and Mergers Commission has now ruled on several cases establishing that two geographically contiguous companies would form a 'substantial part' of the UK within the meaning of the legislation and that such mergers would be viewed with concern. Conversely, mergers not involving contiguous bus companies - of which there have been several - are regarded as being of little concern.

The 1985 Act made the local bus industry subject to UK and EC competition law, like any other industry. Relevant questions are:

1 Is the *general* competition law deficient?

2 Is there some feature of local passenger transport markets which means either that the law should be applied in a *special* way, or that the law should be changed in some way to suit?

3 If the present system is deficient, how damaging are the deficiencies? If a change is proposed, will the new regime be less damaging than the current one?

The relevant competition legislation. The three relevant pieces of domestic legislation are the Fair Trading Act 1973, the Restrictive Trade Practices Act 1976 and the

Competition Act 1980. This legislation is enforced by the Director General of Fair Trading, The Monopolies and Mergers Commission and the Secretary of State for Trade and Industry. Most of the sectoral regulators have concurrent jurisdiction with the DGFT under both the Fair Trading Act and the Competition Act.

The procedures these bodies follow in working together are complex. They are set out clearly in the OFT's guide, *Monopolies and Anti-competitive Practices* (OFT, 1995).

The gist of the legislation is quite simple. The test is always whether some action can be shown to be against the public interest. In the case of the Fair Trading Act and the Competition Act any action is presumed not to be against the public interest until it has been shown to be so. In the case of the Restrictive Trades Practices Act any registerable agreement is presumed to be against the public interest, it is an offence to fail to register it and it must be approved by the Director General of Fair Trading or the Restrictive Trades Practices Court.

In all cases, if an action has been found to have been against the public interest there is no penalty in respect of the action *before* the determination. Either it will become prohibited under an order issued by the Secretary of State, or it will be condoned by him, or an undertaking to suitably moderate the behaviour will be given by the offender. Unlike US anti-trust law there is no system of fines or damages to be paid to parties injured by the offending behaviour before the decision of the Secretary of State.

To qualify for investigation the alleged offender must have a turnover above a threshold (£10 m pa) and supply a significant portion of the relevant market (in many cases at least 25% - the 1989 MMC ruling on the Badger Line merger case established a precedent that the local territory occupied by two bus companies could constitute a substantial part of the UK, even though it is much less than 25% of the UK bus market). Thus small bus companies may fall below one or other of these thresholds.

The UK is subject to the competition provisions of the Treaty of Rome, in particular Articles 85 (prevention, restriction or distortion of competition) and 86 (abuse of dominant position). However they are of little direct relevance in the case of the local passenger transport markets because Community law applies only where practices may have an effect on trade between Member States.

When an offence may occur. Smoothly-working competition is presumed by the authorities to make behaviour contrary to the public interest impossible or unlikely. Thus the presence of a degree of monopoly power is a *necessary* condition for offensive behaviour.

However, the existence of monopoly is certainly not *sufficient* to indicate a situation contrary to the public interest. If the technological circumstances create a natural monopoly, then, by definition, it will be cheaper for a single enterprise to produce than for several. Monopoly is then in the public interest, providing there is sufficient control over prices, quantity and quality of output to prevent abuse of the dominant position. This was the logic behind the creation of some of the newly privatised network-based utilities as monopolists under the control of a specialist regulator.

During the development of the bus deregulation policy it was argued that the evidence was against the existence of significant natural monopoly in bus markets, at least in terms of the nature of operating costs. I am not aware that there has been any new evidence since to question that view.

A monopoly may exist where there is no natural monopoly. It may be benign: although there is only one supplier or only a few, they do not act in a way contrary to the public interest.

Barriers to entry. In particular, this will be the case if the barriers to entry to the industry by competitors exist but are not of great substance. In the bus industry, exploitation of monopoly power will involve raising fares, reducing the quantum of service, or reducing other dimensions of service quality, either to make excess profits or to feather-bed inefficiency. If barriers to entry are negligible then this cannot happen because sooner or later a competitor will enter, taking advantage of the opportunity created.

Somebody who wishes to argue that agglomeration in the bus industry is a bad thing must, as a minimum, demonstrate that there are *significant* barriers to competitive entry and that the new disadvantages that may come with intervention by the authorities are not greater than those associated with the offending practices.

Some attempts to erect barriers have been detected and prevented after intervention by the competition authorities. For instance the attempt to restrict the use of bus terminals by the bus companies that control them.

Other barriers are alleged to have appeared since deregulation. Beesley (1992 chapter 11) suggests that the existence of payments for concessionary fares, the 42 day rule, the under-development of the leasing market for vehicles and the prohibition on self-employed drivers from hiring themselves out to an operator unless they themselves hold operator's licences all constitute secondary barriers to entry.

Predatory behaviour. Predatory behaviour has been alleged in the bus industry. This may involve one operator reducing fares or increasing capacity in the hope of driving another operator out of the business. Although behaviour that looks predatory is not uncommon, it is notoriously difficult to demonstrate objectively that it has occurred. The OFT have usefully defined their test for this which has three components:

1 whether it is feasible for an alleged predator to recover his lost profit after dispatching the prey (and that must imply some source of super-competitive profit),

2 whether the alleged predator actually incurs short term losses as a result of his conduct, and

3 that there was an intent to predate.

A number of the allegations of predation dealt with by the OFT have involved the bus industry (see OFT, 1995, p. 20). Typically, either an offender has simply agreed to desist, or no action is required because, by the time the decision has been taken, the prey has disappeared from the scene and market circumstances are quite different.

It has been alleged that large companies have worked to establish a reputation that they would behave aggressively towards an entrant, even to the extent of damaging their own *long term* profitability - in other words to behave irrationally. A barrier is thus created because potential entrants give credence to this threat.

It has been argued that there are special features of the local passenger transport market which either imply a different interpretation of the existing laws or amendments to them. The leading argument is that transport markets need to be coordinated and integrated. In drafting the 1985 Act the Government took the view that private, for profit operators would recognise the need to inform passengers of their services, to market them and to relate them in a sensible way to those of others. Otherwise they would lose business. But many commentators attribute the disappointing failure of the increase in the total number of bus miles to generate a commensurate amount of new patronage to a failure of the system to deliver the information and service stability and timetable coordination which passengers require. This may well be correct, although I have not seen hard evidence to support the proposition. Nor have I seen any analysis of why this should come about if it is true.

One possibility is that there is simply a shortage of the right kind of entrepreneurial skill in the bus industry, an enduring result of a regulated system in which marketing skills were less important. If this view is correct then there may be a positive advantage in agglomeration of companies because the rare, specialist skills in short supply can be used to advantage over a larger market.

Failure of price competition. There are some sophisticated technical arguments which carry some weight to suggest that in these kinds of markets price competition will not work as it should, and that it will be replaced by excessive provision of services. This is suggested to be an inherent market failure (see Mackie *et al*, 1995).

This is one rigorous interpretation of the old, but much-abused notion of 'wasteful competition'. But a theoretical demonstration of a tendency to over-supply the market, compared with a theoretical optimum, does not of itself demonstrate a case for restriction of output by regulation. That would imply that, in practice, an omniscient regulator could determine what the optimum actually was, and could enforce it without sacrificing other important benefits of competition or falling foul of the classic dangers associated with regulation - especially regulation which restricts quantity offered. In other words, proposed new regulation would have to do better than the system abolished under the 1985 Act.

It has also been argued that there are revenue benefits from service regularity which are external to the individual operator but internal to the market as a whole. That is, it may be to the individual's short term commercial advantage to disrupt service regularity, but this is against passengers' interests and in the long run this damages the industry as a whole. If so there will be an inadequate incentive on the individual firm to cooperate for the benefit of the passenger. This argument carries some weight. It is interesting to note that in the 19th century the horse bus Associations - local cartels of operators - husbanded their passenger markets carefully and took a great deal of trouble to achieve regular services. Operators who caused perturbations suffered severe penalties.

Even if the requisite degree of coordination is achieved in the open market there is a risk that scheduling and timetabling agreements, which would be registerable under the Restrictive Trades Practices Act, would be adjudged to be anti-competitive and against the public interest. Worse, a fear that this might be the outcome may discourage operators from even considering attempting to come to sensible arrangements. A similar problem may arise concerning market-driven attempts to cooperate over the acceptance of a competitor's tickets and travel cards.

The development of rail privatisation will emphasise this problem. Obvious candidates for ownership of rail franchises are some of the larger companies which now operate buses. One can imagine that in sparsely populated areas of the country it will be in the public interest for a common owner of bus and rail services to coordinate them, subject to the Franchising Director's minimum rail service specifications. Yet this may well risk being seen as an undesirable, anti-competitive move by conventional standards.

This may be one area where special treatment of local transport markets is justified.

Slowness and lack of penalties. One of the weaknesses of the existing procedures is general, but seems to be particularly serious in the case of the bus industry because entry and exit of firms can happen so quickly. This is the slowness of the processes coupled with the fact that there is no penalty imposed on a party judged to have offended in respect of his behaviour up until the judgement: no fine and no payment of damages to an injured party. All that is required is an agreement to desist. Bus markets can change so quickly that serious or fatal damage can be inflicted upon a complainant before his complaint is upheld. Equally, an aggressive operator can 'try on' a dubious practice in the knowledge that, at worst, he will be told to stop it after a substantial delay.

One response to this has been to suggest something on the lines of the US system of triple damages (see Beesley, 1994 and Lipworth, 1994), though there are obvious difficulties in the assessment of such damage in a context where, for instance, it has proved so difficult to demonstrate that alleged predators have been incurring loses.

A final feature which may be more important in the case of bus markets is the prospect that there may be companies which underestimate the skills involved in running a commercially successful bus service. They exploit the lack of barriers to entry in the industry and damage both themselves and the established operator. They then leave having sustained a loss. It is not clear that this is a sufficient problem to merit special action, nor that it is worse in the bus industry than many others. It would be difficult for a regulatory authority to distinguish this kind of operation from a well informed operator who intended to take normal commercial risks in entering a new market. For the authorities to attempt to prevent the taking of this kind of risk could be very damaging to the essential process of trial and error which prevents ossification in a rapidly changing market.

Is there a sufficient case for change? In practice there is no such thing as perfect or optimum regulation. The relevant question is always whether an imperfect system of regulation will achieve a better outcome than an imperfect, less-regulated market over a long period of time. The experience is that regulation usually has outcomes different from those originally intended. In particular administrative barriers to entry risk creating the opportunity for the very exploitation of monopoly positions that worry some commentators about the current situation.

The emergence of local monopoly in the bus industry is not in itself a bad thing, and it could offer some advantages in terms of making service coordination easier.

One of the shortcomings of the present system is intrinsic to the UK competition law in general - the absence of penalties and the slowness of the process of investigation. Whilst it may be the case that the bus industry is more severely affected by this it must also affect other industries and it would be better to address the problem in the context of general reform.

One possibility would be the creation of a specialist regulator with powers concurrent with those of the existing authorities - on the analogy of the privatised utilities. This would foster the development of specialist understanding of the issues, including a full consideration of special features of the local public transport markets which might lead to a more appropriate understanding of where the public interest lies. However, a significant amount of the work of the existing competition authorities has involved bus cases in recent years, and there is no reason to think that such specialist expertise cannot be - or has not been - developed within the OFT and the MMC.

The creation of a specialist independent regulator would provide an opportunity for one fundamental and far-reaching change. If, on the analogy of the Rail Regulator, he was given the function of issuing licences for access to the road network then the burden of proof of behaviour against the public interest could be effectively reversed. Good behaviour would be defined as part of the conditions of the licence and these would be enforced by the new regulator. If the regulator considered that bad behaviour warranted it he could revoke a licence and it would then be up to the operator to demonstrate that he had not contravened the conditions of his licence, perhaps on appeal to the MMC.

Note that this need not be, and probably should not be, route-specific licensing. Also, the regulator could be given a primary duty to promote competition, along side other, possibly conflicting, duties. In these respects such a new system would be different from the system of regulation which was, rightly, abolished in 1985.

If this line were taken then it would be for consideration how the regulator's functions would relate to those of the Traffic Commissioners who still look after safety regulation and operator licensing. It would be an option for the Traffic Commissioners to take on these new functions and duties themselves. The economic regulation of competitive markets in the spirit of modern, general UK competition law would be quite a new kind of activity for them, and it would arguably be better to leave them with their current functions and to create a new office to deal with economic regulation.

Some of the options are:

1 Do nothing special. Rely on the present authorities to judge the public interest of localised transport monopolies and their behaviour. Continue to develop expertise and case experience relevant to the special public interest characteristics of local transport markets. Campaign for reform of general competition law to rectify some of the shortcomings which may be particularly important in the case of local passenger transport markets.

2 Create a new regulator with powers and duties similar to those of the Rail Regulator. An overriding duty to promote competition would help to prevent a slide into the undesirable state of affairs which the 1985 Act abolished.

3 As in 2, but, in addition give the regulator duties to collect and publish consistent information about timetables. Possibly also to pro-actively coordinate timetables, to enforce interchangeable ticketing and to enforce regularity and predictability of services (but not to control fares or limit total quantity offered, except in special circumstances, or where he judges the public interest to be at risk by the normal criteria of competition law).

4 Revert to something close to the London model, in which a planning authority determines all services and fares, and procures these services under competitive tendering.

Whilst the London alternative has worked surprisingly well (see below) this would be a drastic change at the national level, involving much new bureaucracy. It creates less pressure for cost efficiency than the 1985 Act system and it creates a convenient target for manipulation by political authorities and others with consequences not necessarily in the (travelling) public interest as conventionally defined under competition law. It would be an unnecessarily draconian measure, unless its proponents can demonstrate that the present system has gone badly wrong and that it could not be adequately improved by one of the alternative options.

The conclusion would seem to be that the White Paper did under estimate the importance of *potential* failures of competition and that UK competition law is presently not ideally suited to dealing with problems that may occur. However, so far it is unclear how important competitive failures have been *in practice*. It seems unlikely that a great deal of damage has been done. A particularly difficult aspect is the framing of legislation and implementation which will not unintentionally hinder desirable, market led integration and co-ordination.

London bus tendering

In the period before 1984 bus services in London were provided by London Transport (LT). This body was answerable to the Greater London Council (GLC) under legislation passed in 1969.

As Figure 5.8 shows, between 1963 and 1979 costs per bus mile in the London Bus industry rose in real terms by a factor of 2.3. During the period 1970-1982 they rose by more than 68% and over the same period the annual grant paid to London Transport (the Underground and buses) rose from £6.5 million to nearly £370 million: a thirteen fold increase in real terms. The Government presented these figures in the white paper *Public Transport in London* (Department of Transport, 1983) and stated that 'new arrangements are needed to secure the cost effective delivery of services from both the public and the private sector'.

In the 1985 White Paper *Buses* (Department of Transport, 1984) the Conservative Government stated its proposal to deregulate the bus industry outside London. Deregulation in London was deferred 'while the changes, so recently instituted, bear fruit' (*Buses*, para. 4.18). The changes referred to were a consequence of the 1984 London Regional Transport Act. Under this Act, London Regional Transport (LRT, or LT) is constituted as a conventional nationalised industry but it has a statutory obligation to 'in the case of such activities carried on by them as they may determine to be appropriate invite other persons to submit tenders to carry on those activities for such period and on such basis as may be specified in the invitation to tender' (LRT Act, section 6(1)). London Transport responded to this obligation by putting many of its bus services out to competitive tender. London Buses Ltd. and London Underground Ltd. were created as wholly-owned subsidiaries.

By 1993/94 the annual turnover of the tendered bus operation had grown to nearly £200 million out of a total of £457 million for buses in London as a whole. Tendering was introduced as a part of LT's strategy to improve the efficiency of bus operations in London. Between 1984 and 1993 bus costs were reduced from £4.11 per bus mile to £2.98 at constant 1992 prices, in a labour intensive industry against a background of rising real earnings. Tendering has led to improved service quality: crude performance statistics show consistently higher proportions of service actually delivered on tendered services.

Until mid 1994 three year contracts were competed for in a sealed bid auction administered by the Tendered Bus Division of LT (TBD). Independent bus operators made bids in competition with the twelve subsidiaries of London Buses Limited (LBL), which is itself a subsidiary of LT. LBL was therefore an 'in-house', public sector supplier which provided non-tendered ('block grant network') services as well as services on contracts won in competition with the private sector. In several cases it has operated the same route as part of the network and then under contract to a similar specification. By 1994 London had 60% of its bus service provided by a fully regulated public sector operator, a further 20% operated by the same operator under competitive contract and the remainder by private sector operators under competitive contract. The private sector operators could, and often did, also operate in the unregulated bus industry outside London.

Under tendering a new set of principal-agent relationships between London Transport and operators were established. Opportunities for private sector firms to supply services were introduced. Monopoly provision was replaced by competition to supply services. In these circumstances one would expect tendering to lead to cost savings. Tendering has indeed led to reduced overhead costs: management slack allegedly present before tendering has been eroded and many jobs have been lost in this area; there have been efficiency gains in engineering; it is common for buses to be housed in yards located out of the city as opposed to the former covered inner city depots; expenditure on staff facilities has fallen under tendering.

Since mid 1994 there have been significant changes in the organisation of the London Bus industry. In 1993 all routes operated on the block grant network were put onto negotiated route-by-route contracts. In 1994 the TBD was replaced by a new body named London Transport Buses Procurement. The LBL operating units were privatised. The present is an assessment of a regime which started in 1984 and ended in late 1993.

The bus tendering process

The process adopted for the first package of tendered routes involved the following steps:

1 selection of routes to be tendered, evaluation of optimum service levels and preparation of service specifications;

2 advertising of the intention to invite tenders and presentation of outline information to operators;

3 operators to submit information about their companies, including a company profile, financial summary, resources available, licences held, experience and an indication of the routes which interested them;

4 service specification and draft contract sent to operators deemed acceptable;

5 formal opening of tenders and evaluation of bids;

6 contract awarded;

7 services operated.

The first proposals were launched in October 1984, with the first tendered routes in operation in July/August 1985. The contracts management team involved five LT staff, though with others involved from time to time. The equivalent of two years of staff time was involved in the first round of tendering (Newton and Rigby, 1985 paragraph 4.10).

The October 1984 package involved the tendering of 13 individual routes. This was followed by a second round, including 10 individual routes to be tendered during 1985-86. The relatively tentative approach was designed to test the impact of tendering. LT believed that if they went too quickly into the new arrangements, their Group Planning Office would have been unable to cope. There was a need to review routes thoroughly prior to contracting, especially in the light of the reduced need for rebooking following the introduction of Travelcards. Moreover, it was believed that a sudden move to mass tendering of routes would swamp the market, possibly leaving no competition for many services.

Routes initially identified as candidates for tendering were those where another operator would be likely to run the route more cost effectively than London Buses. It was decided to avoid tendering routes where crew-operated buses were used on the grounds that such a move could lead to complications if operators proposed to switch to one-person operation. Additional criteria used to select a list of routes were:

1 low average passenger load per bus;

2 high cost (per bus hour);

3 small number of buses required to operate the service;

4 secure an even spread around outer London;

5 avoid routes with particular complexities.

LT managers were concerned that tendering would 'freeze' the bus network for the three years of the contracts. There would be little possibility of innovation in the way services were provided, for example involving minibus services. Orpington (in south east London) was selected to pilot an experiment in different kinds of provision, involving more local routes serving Orpington itself and a simpler network of trunk routes linking Orpington with other suburban centres. LT consulted about proposed changes in the area, then put a proportion of the proposed new route system out to tender. It began operation in May 1986.

Early experience

Of the 13 routes put out to tender in October 1984, successful tenderers were selected for 12. LT's subsidiary (London Buses Limited (LBL)) won six of the routes, National Bus Company subsidiaries won four and independent operators two routes. The agreed total contract prices for the 12 routes were some £1 million (25 per cent) below the previous total costs of £4 million. As the estimated total costs per annum of the tendering process were £200,000, the net saving was estimated to be £800,000 per annum. Where LBL lost a route only certain costs could be saved immediately.

Others, such as fixed overheads, would require reduction over a longer period. LT officers expected overall savings (ie taking account of the need to slim down LBL) to build up over the three year life of contracts (Newton and Rigby, 1985 pages 22 to 24).

The reliability of services on the 12 tendered routes varied from one to another, but overall improvements were achieved. In particular the two independent operators and one of the NBC subsidiaries achieved significant improvements. Revenues increased significantly on three routes, with an overall revenue rise on the 12 services.

Thus the first impacts of tendering were generally positive, in terms of cost savings, revenues and reliability. As tendering in London got under way, preparations were being made for deregulation in the rest of the country. It was still the Government's stated intention to move to deregulation in due course. But the move to tender routes in London had implications for the possibility of the move to deregulation. LT contracts had no provision for early termination. The lack of such a 'break clause' was deliberate: contract prices would have been higher if contractors believed there was a risk contracts might be broken early.

Contracting under the prospect of deregulation. LT looked at a number of ways of coping with the interaction between contracting and deregulation.

In fact the Government has never introduced deregulation in London. Although ministers reiterated their intention to do so from time to time between 1984 and 1993, a number of pressures conspired to prevent the deregulation of bus services that had taken place in the rest of the country. One of these pressures was the public's strongly expressed concern that the Travelcard would not survive. Another may have been the realisation that competition in a deregulated bus market would have destroyed the existing system whereby profitable routes cross subsidised unprofitable ones, so that increased direct subsidy might have been needed to replace it.

LT themselves believed there were four main differences between London and the rest of the country. These differences helped to explain why the Government did not move to deregulation in the capital:

1 acute and widespread traffic congestion;

2 an extensive rail network whose intensive use could relieve congestion;

3 a high volume of bus services run at high cost, with network infrastructure owned by London Buses Limited;

4 a bus market totally dominated by one company.

These reasons - and doubtless the Government's concerns about possible political fall-out from deregulation - were clearly sufficient to keep deregulation at bay in the capital. The success of tendering encouraged LT to go further, and over the years from 1985 to 1995, the proportion of routes put out to tender rose from under 5 per cent to 50 per cent.

Tendering expands. This expansion inevitably meant that LBL lost routes. As they did so, pressure intensified on a number of fronts. It was in LT's interests that LBL won as many contracts as possible, otherwise it would be necessary to slim down the LBL companies, leading to industrial relations difficulties and the need to dispose of fixed assets. Some private tenderers feared that LT would skew the tendering arrangements so as to favour its subsidiary. LT conceded that comparisons of costs between tenders submitted by LBL and those submitted by private contactors would have to be calculated in such a way as to allow for fair comparisons. Tenders should be transparent so as to avoid the risk that LBL would cross-subsidise bids and thus under-cut private companies. LT was faced with a difficult problem: by ruling out cross-subsidy of this kind, it was making it more likely that LBL would lose a number of contracts and thus there would be a greater need to slim-down LBL.

There were a number of difficulties for LT as LBL companies had to slim down after contracts were lost. The need to merge and then close bus maintenance works, such as those at Aldenham and Chiswick, proved particularly fraught during 1985 and 1986 - though this would, in fact, have occurred independently of the expansion of bus tendering.

Contract conditions. LT also had to review its 'good employer' policy. In common with many parts of the public sector, LT had offered more generous employment and welfare conditions than a number of private organisations. Outside employers would be able, it was recognised, to achieve lower costs simply by being less generous employers. LT had also to decide whether or not to insist on maintaining existing conditions of employment. By abandoning such conditions, tender price reductions could be achieved, with any adverse reaction being deflected towards the contractors.

LT also had to decide which kind of contract to use. Contracts for bus services could (and can) take broadly two forms:

1 'bottom line' contracts, in which, after making a bid for support (which is accepted as part of the contracting process), the contractor has responsibility for and is financially affected by the level of receipts collected;

2 'cost' contracts, in which the operator is simply paid by LT for supplying a specified service: receipts are handed over to LT.

Up till an announcement by the Secretary of State in 1993, LT used only 'cost' contracts. Future contracts are to be on a 'bottom line' basis.

LRT noted that preferences amongst operators, both in the UK and abroad, were for 5 to 7 year contracts, in order to provide stability for investment decisions. It was decided however that contracts in London tendering would run for three years in order to retain continuous competitive pressure. As regards the type of vehicle, no specification was made in the early days of tendering.

The reactions of those who tendered for routes were monitored by LT. Tenderers were largely content with the fairness of the process and also that planning staff at 55, Broadway (LT headquarters offices) were generally helpful. Some of the smaller contractors questioned the need for so much statistical information, arguing that for small companies such demands were onerous. Most tenderers said nothing had occurred during 1984 to 1986 that would put them off bidding in future rounds.

A welfare balance

The impact of tendering. The welfare impact of tendering is calculated as its net effect on producer and consumer surpluses. Tendering has been associated with cost reductions and service quality improvements. Cost reductions and revenue generating service quality improvements both have a positive effect on producer surplus. Service quality improvements also increase consumer surpluses. These effects are considered in greater detail and quantified below.

Cost savings. We will proceed in the present analysis by assuming that bus tendering resulted in a 14% net cost saving. This was the (weighted) estimated cost saving due to tendering. We apply this figure to the total annual cost of operating the tendered network each year over the period 1987-1992. Total annual operating cost data are taken from London Transport accounts. Total annual operating costs on the tendered network and associated cost savings calculated on the basis that tendering led to a 14% reduction are listed in columns *a* and *b* of Table 5.1[6].

Table 5.1
Cost savings from tendering in 1992 prices

year	a. Cost (£mill)	b. Cost saving (£mill)	c. Labour cost (£mill)	d. Reduced wages (£mill)	e. Net cost saving (£mill)
1987	56.5	9.2	47.1	7.5	1.7
1988	87.4	14.2	72.9	11.7	2.5
1989	117.8	19.2	98.2	15.7	3.5
1990	136.8	22.3	114.0	18.2	4.1
1991	170.6	27.8	142.1	22.7	5.1
1992	189.0	30.8	157.5	25.2	5.6

Total cost savings from tendering calculated on this basis over the period 1987-1992 are £123.5 million in 1992 prices. This figure relates only to savings on the tendered network. Tendering may also have led to cost savings on the block grant network: managers may have tried to ensure good performance on the block grant network in order to avoid routes being put out to tender. There are other factors however which have contributed to cost savings on the block grant network: we did not feel that it is possible to identify the effect that tendering as opposed to other factors has had on block grant network costs.

The bus industry is labour intensive. Further cost savings have been achieved through reductions in labour costs. Some labour cost savings have stemmed from changed working practices leading to increased productivity. On the other hand a large part of labour cost savings has accrued through reductions in wages. In evidence presented to the House of Commons Transport Committee one LBL manager stated that a typical wage fall due to tendering is 16% of the basic weekly rate (House of Commons 1993). At the same time the hours associated with the basic week have not fallen. This implies that the hourly rate has fallen by at least 16%. Overtime enhancements have been reduced so that hourly overtime rates must also have fallen by at least 16%. These figures were put to LBL managers during a series of interviews and there was general agreement that they are reasonable estimates.

White (1992) argues that wage reductions represent transfers and as such should be excluded from the cost benefit calculation. In order to allow for this two welfare balances - one based on total cost savings, one based on cost savings net of wage reductions - will be estimated. We proceed to estimate cost savings net of wage reductions by first estimating labour costs on the tendered network. We assume that labour costs make up 70% of total operation costs: this is consistent with the ratio of the LT wage bill to total operation cost as calculated from LT accounts. Tendered network labour costs calculated on this basis are listed in column c of Table 5.1. Wage reductions are calculated on the basis that hourly wages have fallen by 16%. The value of reduced wages is listed in column d of Table 5.1. Total estimated wage reductions are £101 million in 1992 prices over the period 1987-1992. The cost saving net of wage reductions is listed in column e of Table 5.1. Over the period 1987-1992 the total cost saving net of wage reductions is £22.5 million in 1992 prices.

Revenue gained. We estimate the revenue impact of tendering based on the increased bus miles attributed to tendering and the elasticity of demand for bus travel with respect to bus miles run. The increase in demand, which as a percentage is equivalent to the increase in revenue, is calculated using an estimated a 0.78 elasticity of demand with respect to bus miles run.

Estimated revenue gains are presented in Table 5.2. The revenue figures are inflated by an index of London bus fares using 1992 as a base year. The total revenue gained between 1987 and 1992 estimated in this way is around £10 million.

Table 5.2

Revenue gains from tendering in 1992 prices

Year	a. tendered schedule coverage (%)	b. block grant schedule coverage (%)	c. revenue gain lower bound (£mill)	d. revenue gain upper bound (£mill)
1987	94.3	91.8	1.0	1.0
1988	96.3	93.9	1.5	8.9
1989	96.4	92.9	2.6	6.3
1990	97.6	95.7	1.7	13.6
1991	98.5	97.2	1.6	21.3
1992	98.8	98.0	1.2	21.1

Now consider an alternative scenario: increased schedule coverage on the block grant network is a result of tendering. A route on the block grant network may be put out to tender if schedule coverage is low. Hence tendering creates incentives to perform well on the block grant network. In this case, when calculating gained tendered miles in a given year it is more appropriate to consider the difference between tendered schedule coverage in that year and block grant coverage in the initial year. We can argue that in this case block grant miles have also increased as a result of tendering. Then we calculate the gained block grant miles in a given year based on the difference between block grant schedule coverage in that year and the initial year. We follow the same method as above for calculating revenue generated and we do this for both the block grant and tendered networks. The revenue generated by tendering, which is the sum of revenue generated on the tendered and block grant networks, is approximately £70 million over the period 1987-92 in 1992 prices.

Revenue gains are estimated based on revenue and mileage data taken from LT accounts and are presented in columns *c* and *d* of Table 5.2[7].

Gains to consumers. A fall in price leads to an increase in consumer surplus. There is an analogous result regarding changes in the service quality of transport; an increase in service quality raises the level of consumer surplus (see Jones 1977 pp.95-98, Glaister 1981 pp.31-32). For every service quality change there is an equivalent price change which yields the same increase in demand and the same increase in consumer surplus. Generalised cost can be defined as the sum of price of travel and the cost to the consumer of journey time. Price and service quality changes which yield equivalent changes in demand yield equal changes in consumer surplus if generalised cost is a linear function of travel time. See MVA (1994) consultancy for

172

derivation of a generalised cost function which is linear in travel time.

We have argued that bus tendering led to an increase in service quality. We estimate the increased consumer surplus that has resulted from this. The methodology we adopt is to first estimate the equivalent price change to the service quality increase and then use this to estimate the increase in consumer surplus.

Consumer surplus gains attributed to tendering are presented in table 5.3. The lower bound for consumer surplus gains corresponds to the scenario in the previous section where tendering led to increased service quality on the tendered network. The upper bound for consumer surplus gains corresponds to the scenario in the previous section where tendering led to increased service quality on both the tendered and block grant networks.

Table 5.3
Consumer benefits of tendering in 1992 prices[8]

year	Gains to present users lower bound (£mill)	Gains to new users lower bound (£mill)	Total gains lower bound (£mill)	Gains to present users upper bound (£mill)	Gains to new users upper bound (£mill)	Total gains upper bound (£mill)
1987	1.2	-	1.2	1.2	-	1.2
1988	2.1	-	2.1	12.2	-	12.1
1989	3.8	-	3.8	9.1	0.1	9.2
1990	2.2	-	2.2	17.8	0.3	18.1
1991	1.9	-	1.9	27.7	1.4	29.1
1992	1.4	-	1.4	26.0	1.3	27.3

The total gain in consumer surplus is the sum of the gains to existing and new users. The lower bound for total gain over the period 1987-1992 is £12.6 million in 1992 prices. The upper bound for total gain over the period 1987-1992 is approoximately £95 million.

The welfare impact of tendering. The welfare impact of tendering is calculated as the sum of resulting changes in producer and consumer surpluses. This is presented in Table 5.4. The change in producer surplus is equal to the sum of cost reductions and generated revenue. The lower and upper bounds for change in producer surplus in Table 5.4 correspond to the lower and upper bounds for generated revenue. The lower bound for welfare change is the sum of the lower bounds for changes in producer and consumer surpluses (similarly for the upper bound).

Two upper and two lower bounds are presented: the lower/upper bound for producer surplus I and corresponding lower/upper bound for welfare change I regard wage reductions as transfers; the lower/upper bounds for producer surplus II and corresponding welfare change II regard wage reductions as efficiency gains.

Producer surplus changes are weighted by the shadow price of public funds: increased producer surplus has allowed a reduction in the level of subsidy to the London bus industry. A weight of 1.21 as suggested by Dodgson and Topham (1983) for use in the appraisal of transport projects is used.

The lowest bound for total welfare gain through tendering over the period 1987-1992 is approximately £50 million in 1992 prices. We note that this figure understates the actual welfare gain. The lowest bound is based on the assumption that wage reductions represent transfers as opposed to changes in welfare. We proceeded by deducting wage reductions from cost savings to get a net cost saving. We did not at this stage take into account the fact that wage reductions allow the freeing of public funds and thus have an impact on welfare. Assuming a shadow price of public funds equal to 1.21 the deadweight losses avoided due to wage reductions total £21 million in 1992 prices over the period 1987-1992. This figure can be added to the lowest bound for welfare change which then becomes approximately £70 million. The highest bound for total welfare gain through tendering over the period 1987-1992 is approximately £330 million in 1992 prices.

This figure actually overstates the welfare gain. There have been severance payments made due to tendering. Although severance payments represent transfers they affect welfare through deadweight losses associated with raising public money. Detailed data relating to severance payments through tendering are confidential and have not been made available to us. London Transport accounts show total severance payments (*ie* due to tendering and other factors) over the period 1987-1992 were approximately £60 million in 1992 prices. The deadweight loss associated with this figure is £10 million in 1992 prices. This represents an upper bound for the impact of severance payments on welfare.

Welfare gains can be adjusted so that they represent the estimated present value of tendering. Assume the standard 8% discount rate for public sector projects. The lower bound for the present value of net benefits (taking into account deadweight losses avoided through wage reductions) from tendering over the period 1987-1992 is approximately £90 million. Over the same period the upper bound for the present value of net benefits is approximately £380 million.

Table 5.4
The welfare impact of tendering in 1992 prices

Year	Change in producer surplus lower bound I (£mill)	Change in producer surplus upper bound I (£mill)	Change in producer surplus lower bound II (£ mill)	Change in producer surplus upper bound II (£ mill)	Change in consumer surplus lower bound (£mill)	Change in consumer surplus upper bound (£mill)	Change in welfare lower bound I (£mill)	Change in welfare upper bound I (£ mill)	Change in welfare lower bound II £mill)	Change in welfare upper bound II (£mill)
1987	3.3	3.3	12.3	12.3	1.2	1.2	4.5	4.5	13.5	13.5
1988	4.8	13.8	19.0	28.0	2.1	12.2	6.9	26.0	21.1	40.2
1989	7.4	11.9	26.4	30.9	3.8	9.2	11.2	21.1	30.2	40.1
1990	7.0	21.4	29.0	43.4	2.2	18.1	9.2	39.5	31.2	61.5
1991	8.1	29.1	35.6	59.4	1.9	29.1	10.0	61	37.5	88.5
1992	8.2	31.8	38.7	62.8	1.4	27.3	9.6	59.1	40.1	90.1

The estimated cost saving from putting a given route out to tender was confirmed to be 20% on average. It is the same as London Transport's own (non-statistical) estimate and is of the same order as those previously estimated in the contexts of refuse collection and ancilliary hospital services. After allowing for costs of administration the estimated cost saving was 16%. This is on a like-for-like basis. But as part of tendering it was often the case that old buses were replaced by more expensive new buses. The estimated cost saving net of administration costs after taking this factor into account is 14%, against which one should set any passenger benefits associated with new vehicles.

A part of the cost reduction has stemmed from wage reductions: a typical wage fall due to tendering is 16% of the basic weekly rate. The Transport and General Workers Union felt that it has been powerless to act because in a competitive environment an industrial dispute results in members' job loss. Fragmentation of LBL through the formation of subsidiaries and lack of awareness over the potential impact of tendering further contributed to the lack of industrial action. The union and managers of bus companies suggest that worker morale is low and that this may make bus service quality poorer than it would otherwise have been.

Our estimate of the financial impact of tendering is based on the analysis of cost and revenue data. The total cost saving from tendering, assuming that tendering has led to a 14% net cost reduction *on tendered routes*, is approximately £125 million in 1992 prices over the period 1987-1992.

Estimated revenue gains attributed to tendering are approximately £10 million in 1992 prices over the period 1987-1992. Service quality increased on the block grant network after the introduction of tendering. If service quality increases on the block grant network are attributed to tendering then estimated revenue gains rise to approximately £70 million.

The service quality increases generate consumer welfare gains. We estimated increased consumers' surplus corresponding to the two scenarios for revenue generated by tendering. The estimated increase in consumers' surplus in 1992 prices over the period 1987-1992 total around £12 million on the tendered network and £90 million in the case where tendering is credited with service quality increases on the block grant network.

Finally we estimated an overall welfare balance for tendering. Producer surplus gains are the sum of cost savings and revenue gains. We estimated two welfare balances corresponding to the two scenarios for revenue generated by tendering as above. The welfare gains corresponding to the worst-case scenario, in which we take the cost saving net of estimated wage rate reduction together with the lower bound for revenue generated, is £90 million. For the best-case scenario the gain is £380 million. Both of these figures relate to the period 1987-1992 in 1992 prices and assume compounding at a rate of 8% pa.

If a 14% cost saving had been realised across the *whole* network, then, *ceteris paribus* costs would have been reduced (in 1992 prices) by £84 million per year since

1986, yielding a cumulated cost reduction of £588 million by the end of 1992. The present value of this cost reduction, based on an 8% compounding rate, is approximately £744 million, as opposed to the £125 million (or £170 million when compounded at 8%) we have attributed to cost saving on the tendered network alone.

A source of possible over-estimation of welfare gains is severance payments made due to tendering. Although severance payments represent transfers they affect welfare through deadweight losses associated with raising public money. Detailed data relating to severance payments through tendering have not been made available to us. London Transport accounts show that total severance payments (*ie* due to tendering and other factors) over the period 1987-1992 were approximately £60 million in 1992 prices. The deadweight loss associated with this figure is £10 million in 1992 prices. This represents an upper bound for the detriment to the welfare balance due to severance payments associated with tendering.

The process of tendering bus services in London was not introduced entirely without problems. However, they were managed successfully by staff at LT, LBL and in the private companies. Given the politically-charged nature of some of the early debates about the future of bus provision in London, it is a tribute to the professionalism of those involved that the system worked as well as it did. The notion of a publicly-organised and accountable bus system in the capital has remained intact, yet savings were achieved and services improved. What London now has is a system that embraces all the benefits of an organised route network with most of the benefits of private sector management. It is an arrangement that is likely to survive.

British rail privatisation[9]

This section mainly relates to the first full year of the separation of operations from infrastructure, April 1994 to March 1995. So far as the average passenger is concerned nothing much appears to have happened. The trains look the same and have the same owners. Fares and services have not varied any more than usual. But behind the scenes at British Rail, the Office of the Franchising Director, Railtrack and the Office of the Rail Regulator there has been frantic activity, revolutionising the administrative and legal basis on which the railway runs.

The new railway organisation in brief[10]

Railtrack owns the signalling and fixed infrastructure, including the land and stations. It was initially a Government-Owned Company with all the issued shares held by the Secretary of State; these shares were sold to the private sector in the spring of 1996. Railtrack covers all costs from access charges to users (which are subject to regulation) except that the Secretary of State retains the power to give direct capital grants in respect of freight facilities if justified on public interest grounds. Note that this differs from the Swedish arrangement, where the track authority receives direct government grant. Railtrack will 'buy in' most of its services under competition and will employ only about 12,000 people.

The Franchising Director. All of the financial support to the railway will pass through the Franchising Director with the exception of certain freight grants. He has defined passenger service groups which are being offered as 25 franchise agreements to train operators under competitive tender. Arrangements for through ticketing and concessionary fares will be enforced through these agreements.

The British Railways Board will continue for a period providing operations and infrastructure services. The Government will continue to exercise the regime of normal public sector scrutiny. British Rail Infrastructure Services was created as a set of companies which were then privatised. This will create new markets in infrastructure services (including track maintenance work) and sell its trading activities to the private sector. Passenger services have been divided into Train Operating Units corresponding to the passenger franchises and these are progressively being vested as separate Train Operating Companies and franchised out. Rolling stock is now managed by three Rolling Stock Companies which have been privatised; they lease the rolling stock assets to the train operators.

The Regulator is independent. He approves all access agreements between Railtrack and passenger and freight train operators. Railtrack has a network licence which is administered by the Regulator. Any party wishing to operate trains will require an operator licence. These operators will be British Rail residual passenger services; franchised passenger service operators; open access passenger service operators; freight train operators.

The Regulator can vary licences by agreement: if not agreed he can refer the matter to the Monopolies and Mergers Commission.

The Regulator will ensure that arrangements for allocating train paths and settling timetable disputes are fair and reasonable. The Act transfers to the Railway Regulator a number of the functions of the Director General of Fair Trading in respect of monopoly situations in the supply of railway services.

Creating the new legal structure

The Rail Regulator. This privatisation is different from the previous major utility privatisations in the United Kingdom in a number of significant respects. One of the most important is the fact that the industry had its independent regulator in place, with the sections of the primary legislation which confer his powers on him fully in force, well in advance of the sale of the publicly owned assets in question. In other cases the sponsoring government department managed the flotation or trade sales first, and only then did the industry regulator take over the public interest oversight and regulation of the industry.

Another significant difference is the role which Parliament has given to the Regulator in relation to the commercial contracts under which users of the

178

infrastructure obtain permission to use it. In the other industries, the regulator's role is very much a function of the licences which the industry players hold. Railway licences are much simpler documents. Much of the most important economic regulation of the industry - particularly the control of prices charged for the use of railway assets - is a function of access agreements not licences. And the Regulator's approval of every access agreement is required. If it is not approved, it is void. The Regulator has duties to monitor the Railtrack and the British Railways Board licences which were issued by the Secretary of State.

The Regulator has established a clear and consistent procedure in considering a number of major policy issues. In each case he will sound out views, issue a consultation document, consider the responses and then issue a firm policy statement.

The Regulator has considerable powers and he has started to demonstrate his independence in his exercise of them. However, it is important to understand that there are many things over which he has no power at all. Some of these may come as a surprise to those familiar with the other regulated utilities: most of them stem from the more complicated regulatory structure which the railways have. That, in turn, ultimately derives from the fact that the railway receives, and will continue to receive, substantial subsidy from central government

Many contracts are not regulated, such as the terms of leases for rolling stock, station leases and the contracts between Railtrack and British Rail Infrastructure Services (the greater part of the Railtrack expenditures). The Regulator cannot make agreements: they must be made by the parties and, where he has the duty, he must approve them. He does not enforce contracts: they are enforced by the parties themselves using normal legal process, like any other contract. The Regulator must act in accordance with a General Authority. This places many constraints on what the Regulator can insist upon in the licences he issues and in the contracts he approves. Most importantly, and most surprisingly to the general public, he is not allowed to regulate passenger fares. The power to do this is given to the Franchising Director through the contracts he offers for passenger franchises, presumably on the grounds that fares regulation has direct implications for subsidy and therefore for the Exchequer.

The Regulator has a similar degree of independence to those of the four previous major privatised utilities, except that the Regulator has a duty 'until 31st December 1996, to take into account any guidance given to him from time to time by the Secretary of State...' (Railways Act 1993, 4(5)(a)). That is one of the critical distinctions between the Regulator and the Franchising Director who does not have the same degree of independence: he must exercise his functions 'in the manner which he considers best calculated to fulfil, in accordance with such instructions and guidance as may be given to him from time to time by the Secretary of State, any objectives given to him from time to time by the Secretary of State...' (Railways Act 1993, 5(1)(a)). To have to take guidance into account is very different to having to fulfil instructions.

The Regulator has statutory *functions* in four main areas: the granting, monitoring and enforcement of licences to operate railway assets; the approval of access agreements between facility owners and dependent users of those railway facilities; the enforcement of domestic competition law; and closures.

The Regulator's *duties* are set out in Section 4 of the Railways Act 1993. In brief, they are to protect the interests of users of the railways, to promote competition, to promote the use of the network, to ensure that Railtrack does not find it unduly difficult to finance its activities. This wording presumably reflects the recognition that a large portion of Railtrack's income ultimately will derive from public expenditure decisions. The duties are also to take into account the position of the Franchising Director, because he has his own budget, and that budget is voted to him as a government department.

As Winsor (1995) notes, the Regulator's Office has been working hard at developing good quality standard - template - documentation which the players in the restructured industry can use. As with the other privatised industries which have at their centre a monopoly owner and operator of infrastructure, there is a need for a universally binding commercial code which governs commercial access to the network and a wide range of operational matters.

Throughout all the Regulator's decisions the general thrust has been to create structures which allow parties to negotiate, rather than to attempt to impose solutions.

The consultative committees. The Railways Act fundamentally changes the consultative committees. There is now the Central Rail Users Consultative Committee and several area-based Rail Users' Consultative Committees. Although the Regulator appoints their members (the Secretary of State appoints the Chairmen) and is responsible for their funding and administrative support, they have a statutory existence independent of the Regulator. Their dealings are with the independent Regulator rather than with the Department of Transport as in the past. Potentially this gives them much more opportunity for real influence, if they persuade the Regulator to take up matters which concern them. The Regulator has said that his Office will not have a regionally based organisation and that he will be relying on the Committees for local intelligence. Thus, as 'the eyes and ears' of the Regulator they have a fundamental role in the regulatory process.

The Franchising Director. The Franchising Director's function is to define rail passenger franchises and to sell them to train operating companies using a competitive tendering procedure. Given the charges for track and station access it is generally anticipated that costs will exceed passenger revenues for most of the franchises, in which case these bids will be negative. In other words prospective train operators will be bidding for the lowest subsidy for which they would be willing to operate the defined services. The Franchising Director will be using a budget fixed by the Government to fund the subsidies. He has to ensure that the franchise agreements that he enters into promote the interests of the passengers. But he also has to ensure that Railtrack is engaging in negotiations with the train operators which produce access agreements which the Franchising Director can sell to the market. The Regulator in turn has to ensure that those access agreements promote the public interest.

The Franchising Director has stated that the Passenger Service Requirement lies at the core of the franchising agreement. It comprises two components: a minimum level of services to be provided by the operator which will be safeguarded and a degree of flexibility above this level which will allow the operator room to develop and improve his services further. The Office of Passenger Rail Franchising has specified certain mandatory service characteristics, such as train frequency, stations to be served, first and last trains and peak train capacity requirements. Franchise agreements will allow for adjustments of these over time, subject to consultation and a veto held by the Franchising Director.

The Franchising Director is hopeful that operators will generally find it in their own commercial interests to offer a better service than the minimum specified in the Passenger Service Requirement. Of course, the extent to which this is in fact the case will depend upon commercial judgements on the extra revenues to be won in relation to the magnitudes of the variable components of access charges and the precise way that they depend upon additional services.

The Office of Passenger Rail Franchising's other responsibilities include encouraging investment, improving services and developing arrangements to ensure the continuation of such matters as concessionary travel for staff, through ticketing and certain travelcards and railcards.

Although the Franchising Director has started to commit himself to particular patterns of expenditure by publishing Passenger Service Requirements he has not yet published any indication of the criteria he has been using to reach these allocations of public funds.

The other new companies. A large number of companies and agreements are being created outside the powers of the Regulator. These include the three rolling stock-owning companies. Train Operating Companies will initially lease rolling stock from the three Rolling Stock Leasing Companies. The leases will allocate responsibilities for matters such as maintenance and safety. The terms of the leases under which operators will acquire the use of their vehicles are unregulated - and heavily influenced by Government. Similarly, the terms of the contracts under which Railtrack will procure engineering services from the British Rail Infrastructure Services companies are unregulated - even though they form the core of Railtrack's cost base which in turn determines the regulated charges for access to Railtrack's assets.

Railtrack is responsible for central timetabling and co-ordination of all train movements, signalling and planning and securing investment in infrastructure. It is also responsible for safe operation of the network under the supervision of The Health and Safety Executive.

Railtrack's property portfolio includes stations' railway land, buildings, installations and light maintenance depots, many of which will be leased to train operators. However, 14 large mainline stations will initially remain under Railtrack's direct control.

Structure of charges

Unlike the regulators of other utilities, the Rail Regulator does not set overall price limits for Railtrack in its licence; instead, his function involves approving the terms and conditions - price as well as other matters - on which access is gained to the railway network by each individual operator. He needs to reach a view on the broad principles on which access charges should be established and to ensure that these principles are reflected consistently in trading agreements between two commercial parties.

The track access charges set by the Government for 1994-95 comprised

1 track usage charges: maintenance and renewal costs attributable to the passage of trains;

2 traction current charges: passed-through charges for electric power.

These two items account for some 9% of total track access charges. The remainder is in the form of a fixed charge made up from:

3 'long run incremental costs': that part of the fixed charge which indicates the long run costs imposed on Railtrack in delivering the total access rights of a train operator and

4 apportionment of common costs.

The latter is the remainder of the fixed charge. It is designed to recover the rest of Railtrack's costs. It is apportioned on the basis of passenger vehicle miles for costs below the level of one of the dozen or so geographical zones and passenger revenues for costs at zonal and national level.

The main concerns addressed in the Regulator's *Structure of Charges* policy statement are

1 that there is a need for greater transparency of charges;

2 that operators face significant risks of reduced profits if revenues fall, since they will not be able to escape access charges by reducing services, and that there should be some mechanism for sharing this risk between Railtrack and operators; and

3 that, with on average over 90 per cent of the access charge in the form of a fixed sum, it is desirable to achieve greater variability.

The Regulator concluded that some changes can be made to short run variable costs so as to base these charges more on actual costs, relying less on assumptions. But this does not address the main concerns. Changes that can be achieved in respect of those charges which are currently fixed are limited in the short term. So he laid down a process for allowing the structure of charges to develop during the period of the access agreements, with the aims of greater transparency and greater variability in response to changes in operators' rights for access.

The charges as they stand are essentially cost-based, as distinct from reflecting the value to users. He has therefore proposed a mechanism that will allow value-base pricing for changes in access to develop within a clearly defined regulatory framework, rather than attempting to impose administered charges for such access and quality premia. The key idea is that the parties to the agreements are commercial entities who should be encouraged to negotiate changes to their common satisfaction. The terms on which agreements are reached will deliver benefits to both parties, but the distribution of those benefits between them will, as in the outcome of any negotiation, depend upon the circumstances of the case.

The level of charges

The charges levied by Railtrack and set by the Government for 1994-95 had three principal components: operating costs, current cost depreciation and a return on capital.

Railtrack's operating costs (£1,500 m in 1994-95) comprise infrastructure maintenance, the greater part of which is covered by the contracts with British Rail Infrastructure Services (BRIS), Railtrack's own day-to-day operating costs and external costs such as rates and power. The Regulator accepted the general principles involved here, but concluded that there is scope for Railtrack to reduce its own operating costs by 3% real pa. It will also be able to secure substantial cost savings in its procurement of engineering services. But these contracts are not regulated and the degree of saving will depend on the nature of the competition for these contracts.

Asset renewals (£560 m in 1994-95) are more difficult. In principle, if the railway's capital stock were in equilibrium (that is, in a proper state of repair and, on average, half-way through its useful life), then actual expenditure on renewals necessary to maintain the network in modern equivalent form would equal the current cost depreciation charge. In practice, the actual age and condition of many of the assets are uncertain and it is not clear that Railtrack's customers will continue in the long term to wish to pay for the maintenance of exactly the same set of assets. It is claimed that in a general sense the average age of the assets is greater than half their expected lives - that is, there is a backlog of investment to be recovered.

The Regulator identified 'pay as you go' as an alternative strategy to charging current cost depreciation. This is the basis on which road costs have been computed by the Department of Transport in the past. Under this approach Railtrack would undertake expenditure for which its customers were willing to pay or had contracted to pay for in the sense that there was a contractual level of service to be maintained, and no operator would pay in advance of such spending. However, this would cause significant fluctuations, both geographically and over time, and it would complicate investment funding.

In the event the Regulator concluded that he would allow charges to cover current cost depreciation. This reflects the assurances that charges would be sufficient broadly to sustain the present national timetable of services. One consequence is that the Regulator will have to be satisfied that Railtrack does not inflate profits by allowing actual expenditure to fall below the level needed to renew the network in modern equivalent form.

Return on capital (£350 m in 1994-95). In order to construct a value for the assets the basic principle employed by The Department of Transport, in consultation with the Treasury, was the Modern Equivalent Asset Value (MEAV: the fundamental reference on the application of this to public sector industries is the Byatt Report, 1986). 'A Modern Equivalent Asset is one which provides the same service potential as the existing asset, but takes account of up to date technology and the likely demand for future capacity. It may not therefore involve a like for like replacement' (ORR, January 1995, page 5).

The approach is *cost* based. The Government sought to answer the question, 'what is the cost to the economy of keeping the railway running whilst in the public sector?' That, they argued, is what the charges should be whilst in the public sector. The relevant concept is economic opportunity cost. The capital expenditure spent on railways each year is capital that would have an alternative use in some other, public sector investment, where, by assumption, it would yield a real return of 8% pa.

The **market** valuation of Railtrack was quite another matter, and clearly depended upon the market's view of future earning power as well as renewal costs. There are many reasons that MEAV would diverge from market values.

The Department's method had been to calculate an MEA valuation of the assets and then require an 8% real return (the current standard required rate of return on this kind of capital asset in the public sector) on that value. As a concession, the return was reduced to 5.1% in the first year in recognition of the efficiency gains available to Railtrack, the full rate to be earned after three years.

The Regulator was not convinced of the need to earn a full return on MEA values in order for the business to be sustained. Further, he took the view that 8% was an unduly high rate in current market circumstances.

In his policy statement the Regulator did not express a view of what an appropriate capital value for Railtrack might be. He simply determined that all charges for 1995-96 should be rebased by reducing them by 8% from the Department's starting point, and that they should be reduced by a further 2% below the Retail Price Index between 1996-97 and 2000-01, when the next periodic review will take effect. (The Regulator took the view that Railtrack's own operating costs should be reduced by 3% pa, but charges contain other elements - hence the net requirement of 2% pa.)

The Regulator's conclusions on future levels of access charges for franchised passenger services are implemented through the approval of individual access agreements, rather than through a price control provision in Railtrack's network licence. Therefore, the Regulator will issue a review notice under the terms of access agreements already entered into to require the parties to come forward with amendments. Similar provision will be included in future access agreements.

There is a further complication. Railtrack's total costs are to be covered not only by passenger franchise access charges, but also by open access charges (see below), station and depot lease income. The Regulator has firmly stated that he will enforce a 'single till' principle by which all income from ancillary activities - such as rentals from retailing - must be set against Railtrack's costs when calculating track access charges. However, there is an exception in that he has determined that there should be a provision to allow that variations in net income from property from the levels assumed by Railtrack in the projections submitted to the Regulator should be shared between Railtrack and its customers through variations in access charges.

He wishes to change the basis of allocation of the non-variable charges from that adopted in 1994-95 in order to improve the incentives to use and develop the whole of the existing network.

The next periodic review of access charges will take place in 2000, to be implemented from 1 April 2001. A parallel review of competition will take longer and be implemented one year later.

Access agreements include provisions which involve Railtrack making payments to, or receiving payments from, operators in respect of variations in performance. There is similar compensation payable by Railtrack for additional possessions of track for maintenance purposes required beyond the provision in access agreements.

Open access charges

Train operators who are not passenger franchise operators are said to be open access operators. These could be operators of neighbouring passenger franchises, free-standing passenger operators or freight train operators. The policy on moderation of competition (see below) means that the largest category is freight.

Freight access charges. The most important principle here is that freight operators should not be a financial burden on passenger operations and that Railtrack should not unreasonably exploit its monopoly position. Given the view that the costs attributable to freight movements are relatively low - especially in cases where the infrastructure is not provided for freight alone - but that there are substantial invariant costs to be recovered, one immediately thinks of some form of cost recovery where price margins above avoidable cost are higher in markets where there is greater monopoly power (such as Ramsey pricing). Then charges vary according to willingness to pay: each traffic is required to contribute towards the non-variable costs in such a way that the charges reduce their traffic by a similar amount. So a traffic which is only just viable at variable cost will be charged variable cost whereas one which is profitable will be asked to bear a higher proportion of the non-variable costs.

In practice it is impossible for a regulator to attempt a literal interpretation of this principle, as is nicely explained in the US Interstate Commerce Commission's August 1985 discussion of its *Coal Rate Guideline, Nationwide*, which embodied

'Constrained Market Pricing', a sophisticated application of relevant economic principles to practical regulation of rate-making.

In his policy statement on this (ORR, February 1995) the Regulator decided that he would not attempt to specify detailed regulated tariffs. Rather, he adopted the principle that the operators and Railtrack are those who will have the best information and that the most practical solution is to simply allow the parties to negotiate their own rates - as has happened in the past. Once agreed the rates must be approved by the Regulator as part of the access contract.

The Regulator will apply several tests. He will require to be satisfied that the rate is not below avoidable cost. And it must not be above a cost ceiling which is the 'standalone cost' which would be incurred by a notional efficient competitor. This last condition is the interpretation of prevention of exploitation of monopoly power (again, as discussed by the ICC in *Coal Rate Guideline*). If a charge comes within 50% of an average notional upper limit calculated by Railtrack the charge will be individually reviewed by the Regulator.

Allowing negotiated charges implies a degree of price discrimination between operators (but not cross-subsidy). But the Regulator will not permit undue discrimination, nor prices which significantly distort competition between freight users in the final markets in which they themselves compete.

Having established the principles there is some way to go in refining their application. The policy document contains some guidelines for calculation of relevant costs. These include a requirement that all unit costs be adjusted each year by RPI - 2 per cent. Costs are to be calculated specifically for the respective flow and the particular vehicles in question, rather than using broad national averages. Avoidability is to be assessed over an appropriate timescale. No return on existing assets is to be included in the cost floor.

In recent years the freight businesses have been given the objective of avoiding losses, on the old accounting basis. However, they have failed in this. It is therefore quite possible that the Regulator's prohibition on cross subsidy from the passenger side together with the changes in costing will lead to a substantial increase in average charges to rail freight. The Government has made some direct subsidies available, but the amounts appear to be relatively small. They may have to be increased if the Government's declared aim of reversing the dramatic historical shift of freight from rail to road is to be achieved.

Competition between passenger services

The railways policy originally envisaged that in due course there would be competing passenger services on significant sections of the network. This was one of the main reasons for separating ownership of the fixed infrastructure from the operation of trains: it would avoid the problems of achieving fair competition which have arisen in other regulated industries where the infrastructure owner is also a service provider.

However, there has been a long tradition of using cross-subsidy to finance public service obligations, especially in the non-commercial sectors: Network South East and

Regional Railways. Even within the commercial InterCity sector there has been cross subsidy.

The wish to introduce competition creates a familiar problem: profits will be competed away in the form of lower fares and higher service levels (elimination of monopoly profit to the benefit of consumers). So if the public service obligations are to be preserved these internally generated profits must be replaced by an increase in external support. This was clearly illustrated by the privatisation and deregulation of the bus industry outside London.

However, there has been no sign of a willingness on the part of the Government to fund any such increase in support - for instance in the official public expenditure plans. The Franchising Director has felt this problem particularly keenly, being acutely aware that the budget he expects to win is unlikely to be generous enough to keep all services going in addition to replacing the lost monopoly profits. He has therefore argued strongly that the Regulator should grant exclusive rights of access to franchised train operators in order to help him sell the franchises with the least possible financial support. The Regulator does have a duty to take into account the financial position of the Franchising Director but he has to balance this with his duties to promote competition and to promote the use of the network.

This conflict had to be resolved before the franchises could be offered for sale. After consultation, the Regulator made his policy statement (ORR, December, 1994). It is a complex policy - understandably so in the circumstances. For the immediate future the point is simply that there will be no new competitive services allowed - although it is implicit that much of the considerable competition that exists in the inherited service patterns will continue. There will be scope for increased competition here in terms of the marketing of the services. This will put pressure on the veracity of the revenue allocation systems which, in the past, have in some cases been based on modelled estimates of what passengers will do, rather than direct observations of what they have actually done.

It is too early to judge the response of the market to the longer-term implications of the competition policy. This will be reflected in the bids for franchises which are likely to have a 7 year term. Its complexity will have the inevitable consequence that some of the outcomes will not have been predicted. But, equally, it has always been impossible to predict the outcome of any regime other than 'no change', including complete freedom of entry.

Whatever the outcome, there will have been a different kind of competition - one '*for* the market' when the franchises are sold.

Conclusion on rail privatisation

By the end of March 1995 the regulatory framework was in place (albeit with some gaps to be filled), so as to facilitate the start of the franchising process. In the year 1995-96 the first passenger franchises were let, the freight companies Rolling Stock Companies and many other companies were privatised.

The signs are that the political conflicts inherent in creating greater transparency in costs and subsidies are beginning to show. For the first time changes will become apparent to passengers and taxpayers (local and national) which will be clearly attributable to the railways policy. The temptation for the Government to intervene for the sake of short term expediency has so far proved to be irresistible. There is a risk that the new structure, so expensively created, will be prevented from functioning, the result being a more directly state-run industry than it was in the past. The British Railways Board certainly used to be subject to pressures from government. But it did preserve a real degree of independence on fares setting, service levels and investment strategy - especially in the commercial sectors. These freedoms were hard-won over several decades. Now the Government has taken over more or less direct control of many passenger fares and minimum service levels. The fear of exposing monopoly profits to the benefits of competition because of the implied substitution of extra, visible direct subsidy has led to the moderation (that is, abandonment) of new competition in the short term.

Overall conclusion

The British experiences of deregulation and privatisation in the transport sector almost have the appearance of having been specifically designed to be part of a systematically designed laboratory experiment. As yet it is too soon to come to a rounded conclusion. But there are some indications.

First, most systems can be made to work - the world does not come to an end if a transport service is deregulated or privatised. Second, the evidence is pretty clear that competition in input markets - and especially labour markets - produces substantial operating cost reductions compared with conventional regulated, publicly owned provision. Third, competition in final markets for passengers and freight throws up difficult political issues which essentially derive from the past tendencies to use internal cross-subsidies to secure universal service provision.

In my view it is a good thing that these debates be brought into the open so that the appropriate politically accountable bodies are forced to take explicit decisions on the use of public money. But this may imply increased direct subsidy. Whilst this can often be justified, the case will need to be skilfully argued in a climate of public expenditure reductions. Fourth, adjustments in the market can take place extremely quickly in some cases (as with London bus tendering), but in others they can take much longer that one might have expected (as with bus deregulation out of London). Fifth, one cannot expect the 'forces of competition' to operate unaided by the normal protections offered by pro-competitive legislation which applies to all goods and services. One must review whether the general State and Community legislation is fit for the purpose, and one must also take care not inadvertently to leave or create barriers to competition specific to the industry in question.

Finally, and perhaps most importantly of all, if a government decides to go down the route of deregulation or privatisation or both, then it must discipline itself to follow the logic of the policy through: not to interfere unduly for political expediency.

Transport is an area where governments seem to find this particularly difficult. But if the discipline is not adequate then the markets will not be able to work in the intended fashion and there is a risk of a thoroughly confused and undesirable outcome.

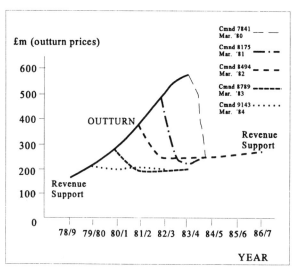

Figure 5.1   **Local authority subsidy for buses compared with public expenditure provision (England only)**

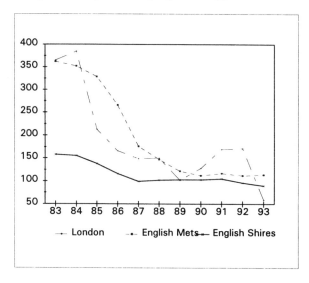

Figure 5.2   **Financial support for buses (£m at constant 1993 prices)**

189

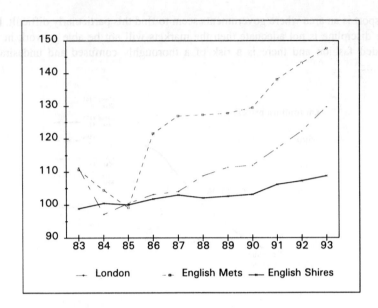

Figure 5.3   Passenger fares indices (relative to manual earnings)

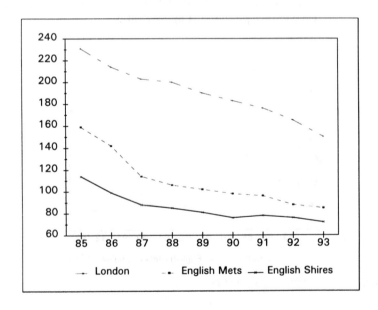

Figure 5.4   Cost per bus km (pence at constant 1993 prices)

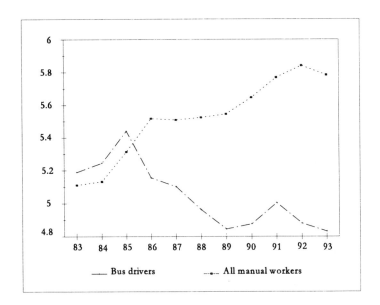

Figure 5.5   **Hourly earnings (£ per hour at 1994 prices)**

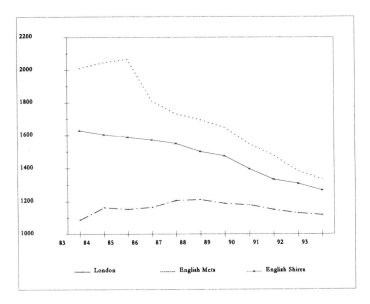

Figure 5.6   **Passenger journeys by area**

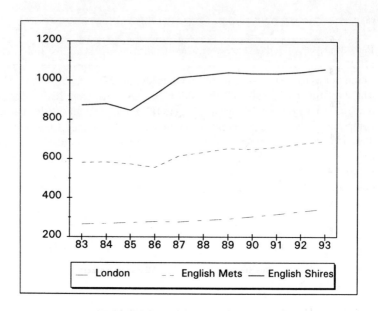

Figure 5.7   **Bus kilometers by area**

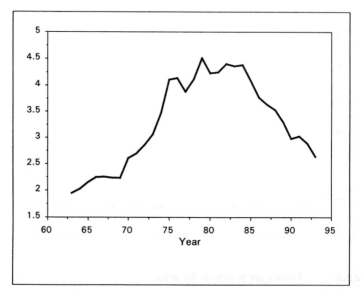

Figure 5.8   **Bus costs in London (£ per bus mile at 1992 prices)**

192

Notes

1 Parts of the following text are abstracted from Kennedy, Glaister and Travers (1995).
2 Some of this section is abstracted from Glaister (1991).
3 These estimates, and many others in this paper, are made from *Bus and Coach Statistics Great Britain.* White and Turner (1990) note that alternative ways of computing these average increases can increase the estimates somewhat.
4 Tyson has noted the effects of changes in accounting conventions in the case of the Passenger Transport Executives, contemporaneous with deregulation, which reduced the apparent operating costs. In particular some historic pensions liabilities are now not borne by the bus operating companies.
5 In a personal communication and Hibbs (1990).
6 The cost benefit calculation relates to the period 1987-1992. All figures are in 1992 prices.
7 Mileage gains estimated in this way are sensitive to the mileage elasticity. Based on data from the period 1971-1990 London Transport estimate that the upper bound for mileage elasticity of demand for bus travel is 0.3 (London Transport 1994). Estimated revenue gains based on this elasticity are approximately 40% of those in Table 5.2.
8 Where there is no entry in the table consumer surplus gain is negligible.
9 This section is abstracted from Glaister (1995).
10 A detailed and comprehensive statement will be found in OPRAF, May 1995.

References

Banister, D. J., 1985. 'Deregulating the Bus Industry - the Proposals'. *Transport Reviews.*
Bannister, D.J. and R. L. Mackett, 1990. 'The Minibus: theory and experience, and their implications'. *Transport Reviews*, Vol.10, No.2.
Barker, T. C. and M. Robbins, 1974. *A History of London Transport*, George Allen and Unwin.
Bayliss, D. and W. J. Tyson, 1988. 'Competition for local bus services in Great Britain'. International Commission on Transport Economics, UITP.
Beesley, M.E., 1985. 'Deregulating the Bus Industry in Britain: a reply'. *Transport Reviews,* Vol.5, No.3.
Beesley, M.E., 1989. *The Role of Government in a Deregulated Market.* ECMT, Paris.
Beesley, M. E. and Littlechild, S. C., 1983. 'Privatisation: principles, problems and priorities'. *Lloyds Bank Review*, 149.
Beesley, M. E., *Privatisation, regulation and deregulation*, IEA 1992.

Beesley, M.E., 1990b. 'Collusion, Predation and Merger in the UK Bus Industry'. *Journal of Transport Economics and Policy*, special issue, September.

Beesley, M. E. and Lipworth, S., 'Abuse of monopoly power', in Beesley (editor) *Regulating Utilities: the way forward*, IEA Readings 41, 1994.

Beesley, M.E. 1990a. 'Bus Deregulation: Lessons from the UK' In: *Proceedings of an International Conference on Competition and Ownership of Bus and Coach Services* (ed: D. Hensher), *Transportation Planning and Technology*, Gordon and Breach, London.

Bennathan, E., L. Escobar and G. Panagakos, 1989. *Deregulation of Shipping: What is to Be Learned from Chile. World Bank Discussion Papers*. No. 67.

Bös, D., 1993. 'Privatisation in Europe: a comparison of approaches'. *Oxford Review of Economic Policy*, 9(1), pp. 95-111.

Byatt, I. (Chairman), *Accounting for Economic Costs and Changing Prices*, A report to HM Treasury by an Advisory Group, HMSO, 1986.

Cross, A. K. and R. P. Kilvington, 1985. 'Deregulation of inter-city coach services in Britain'. *Transport Reviews,* Vol.5, No.3.

Department of Transport: *Bus and Coach Statistics*, Great Britain, 1993-94.

Department of Transport, *Britain's Railways: a New Era*, March 1994.

Department of Transport, 1984. *Buses*. HMSO, Cmnd 9300.

Dodgson, J. S. and Y. Katsoulacos, 1990. 'Competition, Contestability and Predation; the Economics of Competition in Deregulated Bus Markets'. In: *Proceedings of an International Conference on Competition and Ownership of Bus and Coach Services* (ed: D. Hensher), *Transportation Planning and Technology*, Gordon and Breach, London.

Dodgson, J. S. and N. Topham, 1987. 'Shadow Price of Public Funds: a Survey', in *Transport Subsidy*, Policy Journals (1987).

Domberger, S., Meadowcroft, S. A. and Thompson, D. J., 1986. 'Competitive tendering and efficiency: The case of refuse collection'. *Fiscal Studies,* 7(4) pp. 69-87.

Domberger, S., 1987. 'Franchising in Competitive Tendering' in Estrin, S. and Whitehead, C. eds. *Privatisation and the Nationalised Industries*. Sticerd, London School of Economics.

Domberger, S., Meadowcroft, S. A. and Thompson, D. J., 1987. 'The impact of competitive tendering on the cost of hospital domestic services'. *Fiscal Studies,* pp. 39-53.

Evans, A., 1987. 'A Theoretical Comparison of Competition with the Economic Regimes for Bus Services'. *Journal of Transport Economics and Policy*.

Evans, A., 1990a. 'Bus Competition: Economic Theories and Empirical Evidence'. In: *Proceedings of an International Conference on Competition and Ownership of Bus and Coach Services* (ed: D. Hensher), *Transportation Planning and Technology,* Gordon and Breach, London.

Evans, A., 1990b. 'Competition and the Structure of Local Bus Markets'. *Journal of Transport Economics and Policy*, special issue, September.

Foster, C., D., 1985. 'The economics of bus deregulation in Britain'. *Transport*

Reviews, Vol.5, No.3.

Foster, C. D., 1992. *Privatisation, public ownership and the regulation of natural monopoly.* Oxford: Blackwell.

Glaister, S., 1986. 'Bus Deregulation, Competition and Vehicle Size'. *Journal of Transport Economics and Policy.*

Glaister, S. 'UK Bus Deregulation: the Reasons and the Experience', *Investigaciones Economicas,* May 1991.

Glaister, S. and C. Mulley, 1983. *Public control of the British bus industry.* Gower (Aldershot).

Glaister, S., 1985. 'Competition on an Urban Bus Route'. *Journal of Transport Economics and Policy.*

Glaister, S. and Mulley, C.M., *Public Control of the Bus and Coach Industry,* Gower Press, 1983.

Glaister, S. and M. E. Beesley, 1990. 'Bidding for Tendered Bus Routes in London'. In: *Proceedings of an International Conference on Competition and Ownership of Bus and Coach Services* (ed: D. Hensher), *Transportation Planning and Technology*, Gordon and Breach, London.

Glaister, S., *Public Transport Subsidy*, Policy Journals, 1987.

Glaister, S., 'The New Rail Industry 1994/95' CRI *Regulatory Review*, CRI, 1995.

Gomez-Ibanez, J., and J. R. Meyer with P. Kerin, and L. Dean, 1989. *Deregulating and Privatizing Urban Bus Services: Lessons from Britain.* Report for US Department of Transportation, Urban Mass Transportation Administration, Office of Private Sector Initiatives, Washington, DC 20590.

Gwilliam, K. M., 1990. (Editor of special issue*), Journal of Transport Economics and Policy*, September.

Gwilliam, K.M., C.A. Nash and P.J. Mackie, 1985b. 'Deregulating the bus industry in Britain: a rejoinder'. *Transport Reviews,* Vol.5, No.3.

Gwilliam, K. M., 1989. 'Setting the market free. Deregulation of the Bus Industry'. *Journal of Transport Economics and Policy*, January.

Gwilliam, K.M., C.A. Nash and P.J. Mackie, 1985a. 'Deregulating the bus industry in Britain - (B) The Case Against'. *Transport Reviews*, Vol.5, No.2.

Haskel, J. and Szymanski, S. 1993. 'Privatisation'. *Economica,* pp.161-181.

Hay, D. and Morris, D., 1991. *Industrial Economics and Organisation.* Oxford University Press.

Hesseltine and Silckock, D., 1990. 'The effects of bus deregulatin on costs', *Journal of Transport Economics and Policy,* special issue, September.

Hibbs, J. 1990. *A survey of managers in the bus industry.*

Higginson, M P, 1984 'The activities and intentions of independent bus and coach operators'. Unpublished research for LRT.

Hills, P., 1989. Early Consequences of the Deregulation of Services in Scotland'. Conference on Competition and Ownership of Bus and Coach Services, Thredbo, Australia, May 1989.

Kay, J. A. and Thompson, D. J., 1986. 'Privatisation: a policy in search of rationale'. *Economic Journal.*

Kennedy, D., S. Glaister, T. Travers, *London Bus Tendering*, Greater London Group, LSE, March 1995.

Mackie, P., Preston, J. and Nash C., 'Bus deregulation: ten years on', *Transport Reviews*, forthcoming.

Nash, C. 'Rail Transport Regulation', in *Regulatory Review 1994*, Gilland and Vass (eds), CRI., 1994.

Office of the Rail Regulator:

Penalty fares rules, April 1994

Guidance on third party liability and insurance, April 1994

Guidance on licensing of non-passenger operators, July 1994

Competition for railway passenger services: a consultation document, July 1994

Guidance on licensing of passenger operators, July 1994

Guidance on licensing of light maintenance depot operators, July 1994

Competition for railway passenger services: a consultation document, July 1994

Framework for the approval of Railtrack's track access charges for franchised passenger services: a consultation document, July 1994

Guidance on licensing of station operators, July 1994

Railway operations and the environment: environmental guidance: a consultation document, July 1994

Meeting the needs of disabled passengers: a code of practice, August 1994

Criteria for the approval of passenger track access agreements, September 1994

Framework for the approval of Railtrack's track access charges for freight services: a consultation document, October 1994

Annual Report 1993/94, October 1994, HMSO

Railtrack's track access charges for franchised passenger services: developing the structure of charges: a policy statement, November 1994

Criteria and procedures for the approval of freight track access agreements, December 1994

Competition for railway passenger services: a policy statement, December 1994

Retailing of tickets at stations: a consultation document, January 1995

Framework for the approval of railtrack's track access charges for freight services: a policy statement, February 1995

Ticket retailing: a policy statement, April 1995

Railtrack's track access charges for franchised passenger services: the future level of charges: a policy statement, January 1995

Office of Passenger Rail Franchising, *Passenger Rail Industry Overview*, May 1995.

Pinsent & Co., *Rail Privatisation*, no 5, January 1995.

Rees, R., 1985. 'The theory of principal and agent. Part 1'. *Bulletin of Economic Research,* 37(1), pp.3-26.

Swift, J., 'The role of the Rail Regulator', Sir Robert Reid Memorial Lecture, Office of the Rail Regulator, January 1995.

Thomas, C. 'Contracting out: managerial strategy or political dogma?' In Ramanadham, V. V. (ed), *Privatisation in the U.K.* Routledge.

Turner, R. and White, P., 1987. 'NBC's urban Minibuses. A review and financial

196

Appraisal'. TRRL Contractor Report CR42 Crowthorne.

Tyson, W.J., 1989. *A Review of the Second Year of Bus Deregulation*, Report to Association of Metropolitan Authorities and Passenger Transport Executive Group.

Tyson, W.J., 1990. 'Effects of Deregulation on Service Co-ordination in the Metropolitan Areas'. *Journal of Transport Economics and Policy*, special issue, September.

Vickers, J. and Yarrow, G., 1988. *Privatisation: an economic analysis*. MIT Press.

White, P. and Turner R., 1990. In: *Proceedings of an International Conference on Competition and Ownership of Bus and Coach Services* (ed: D. Hensher), *Transportation Planning and Technology*, Gordon and Breach, London.

White, P., 'Bus deregulation: a welfare balance sheet'. *Journal of Transport Economics and Policy*, special issue, September.

White, P., 1990a. 'Change Outside the Mets. Conference on Public Transport: the Second Year of Deregulation in the Metropolitan Areas', at Institute of Mechanical Engineers, London, March 1990.

Winsor, T., 'The Strategic Aims of the Rail Regulator', Office of the Rail Regulator, April 1995.

Wooton, J. 1984. 'Overview and Information Technology in Public Transport'. Conference, University of Newcastle, April.

6   Evaluating transport projects and policies

John Dodgson

Introduction

This paper aims to review the public evaluation of projects and policies within the transport sector. The primary tool for evaluation is (social) cost-benefit analysis. This tool aims to measure, value and compare **all** the costs and benefits of a particular proposal. One of the main themes of this paper is the extent to which the rules of cost-benefit analysis provide an objective framework within which the costs and benefits of a particular scheme can be compared. This in particular will lead us to consider the welfare economics foundations of cost-benefit analysis and in particular the conflict between economic efficiency criteria, on which cost-benefit analysis in practice is most often based, and distributional considerations.

The paper's title indicates that we will not just be concerned with traditional investment projects like the construction of a new highway or a high-speed rail line. Evaluation can be concerned with a wide range of policies as well as traditional construction projects. Thus we might wish to evaluate alternative subsidisation policies for urban public transport (Dodgson, 1986; Glaister, 1994), the costs and benefits of the introduction of congestion pricing schemes for urban roads (Newbery, 1990), different transport safety programmes (Evans, 1994), or alternative measures to deal with environmental problems of transport. These last measures can encompass major international collaborative policies to tackle the very long-term problems of global warming (see Cline, 1992), to which the transport sector plays its part through the burning of fossil fuels.

Efficiency benefits

Attainment of economic efficiency in the economy as a whole occurs where no individual can be made better off without making another worse off, even when resources are rearranged so as to allow for all technologically-possible mixes of goods and services produced. However there will be one such economically-efficient position for each possible distribution of welfare between all the individuals making up society. The global optimum position for the economy depends on some form of Samuelson-Bergson social welfare function which provides a ranking over all the possible 'social states', that is all possible combinations of individual utility.

If we wish to assess the contribution that an individual project or policy will have, we have a choice. We could concentrate purely on the contribution that that project makes to economic efficiency, or we could consider its effect on distribution, or we could combine the two. Only the last of these three approaches would guarantee that we could judge whether social welfare had been improved or not. Nevertheless, we might instead consider the impact of the project on economic efficiency as a first step, on the grounds that if efficiency is improved then society **could** take steps to ameliorate any adverse distributional consequences of the project should they be found to arise. (The clear danger, of course, is that society might not choose to ameliorate such adverse consequences, or might simply remain in ignorance of them.)

The basic idea here is that of compensation tests: if a policy leads to a situation where the gainers could potentially compensate the losers, then the policy is judged to be desirable. Although initially proposed as an objective test, it might be hard nowadays to find advocates of the approach who would argue that the test is an objective criterion for improvement in social welfare, since the whole idea is that compensation does not actually have to be paid. It does however form the basis of most practical cost-benefit analysis, on the (often implicit) ground that we seek to measure overall costs and benefits given willingness to pay (that is, given the existing distribution of purchasing power). This enables us to contrast the net benefits of a project in a wider framework than that of financial analysis where we consider willingness to pay (again on the basis of the existing distribution of purchasing power) for project benefits via revenue to the investing agency, and the agency's willingness to pay for the costs that it itself will have to incur in carrying out the project. Because of market imperfections and externalities the former type of social cost-benefit evaluation will often encompass wider definitions of benefits and costs than the latter financial one. However we still have the problem that social welfare will depend on both efficiency and equity considerations.

The next question is how we measure willingness to pay. The initial idea is that the area under a normal (ie constant money income, or Marshallian, demand) curve measures the consumer's surplus utility from a good. Marshallian surplus in fact gives a crude measure of willingness to pay because although Marshall wanted his surplus to measure **surplus utility** this is not possible unless the measuring rod, namely money, has constant marginal utility. Many years ago Samuelson (1942) showed that this is not possible except in exceptional circumstances. The marginal utility of money is equal to the marginal utility of each good divided by its price, that is to say, it is equal to the Lagrangean constant in the constrained utility maximization problem where the consumer maximizes utility subject to his/her budget constraint. If a consumer is maximizing utility, then if income and all prices double, consumption of all goods will remain unchanged (ie the Marshallian demand functions are homogeneous of degree zero in prices and money income). But if all quantities remain unchanged, their marginal utilities will also remain unchanged. Consequently the marginal utility of money will be halved and, generally speaking, the marginal utility of money cannot remain constant with respect to everything, ie with respect to all prices and income. Samuelson then considered two cases (discussion of which in textbooks has confused generations of students). The first is the case where the marginal utility of money is constant with respect to all prices but not income - a special case of homothetic preferences where indifference curves are parallel along any ray through the origin - and the second is the case where the marginal utility of money is constant with respect to income and all prices but one - in this case indifference curves are vertically parallel for this **numeraire** good.

In any case, we cannot interpret the Marshallian surplus as a measure of surplus utility unless we are prepared to interpret preferences in terms of cardinal utility, that is, we have to say something about the levels of utility along successive indifference curves as well as about the curves' shapes. Since economists these days are not prepared to do this, we have to interpret preferences simply in terms of willingness to pay. This is what Hicksian surplus does (Hicks, 1942). The compensating variation (CV) measures the maximum amount that the consumer is prepared to pay once a price change (or a number of price changes) has occurred rather than go without the price change. If the price change(s) make the consumer better off, then the CV is a measure of the consumer's benefits from the change, while if the price change(s) make the consumer worse off, then the negative CV measures the consumer's loss from the change.

An example of the first case is illustrated in Figure 6.1. Here the initial price of good 1 is p_{11}, and the consumer purchases q_{11} units. The price then falls to p_{12}, and demand increases to q_{12}. The consumer achieves a higher level of satisfaction on indifference curve u_2. Given the new prices, the consumer would be better off as long as he/she did not have to give up more than the amount ad of the numeraire good q_2. This amount is equal to the difference between the minimum expenditure required to achieve the final utility u_2 at the final relative prices and the minimum expenditure required to achieve the initial utility u_1 at the final prices. This difference is the compensating variation as defined in the previous paragraph. Because the Hicksian, compensated, quantities associated with the original level of utility u_1 can be derived by differentiating the expenditure function (a result known as Shephard's lemma) the CV can also be measured in Figure 6.1 by the area under the Hicksian demand curve between the two prices: this area is $p_{12}p_{11}\alpha'\gamma'$ in the diagram.

The main alternative Hicksian measure, the equivalent variation (EV), measures the maximum amount that the consumer will accept instead of a price change (or changes). If this sum is positive, then the consumer gains from the changes, whereas if it is negative he/she loses. Alternative, and much less commonly encountered, Hicksian measures consider compensation when consumers are constrained to consume fixed quantities of goods.

Compensating variation and equivalent variation measures of price changes will differ from each other (and from Marshallian surplus) unless there are no income effects - in which case all three measures will be equal. It seems intuitive that if the sum of compensating variations, or the sum of equivalent variations, are positive, then a project will be desirable. Actually, the relationship between compensating variations, equivalent variations, and compensation tests is a little more complicated than this. Boadway (1974) showed that if the sum of compensating variations was negative, then gainers would certainly not be able to compensate losers (so that in this sense the project was not desirable): on the contrary it is possible for the sum of compensating variations to be positive, but for compensation still not to be possible. However, I also showed (Dodgson, 1977) that if the sum of equivalent variations is positive then the losers could not compensate the gainers for a reverse move back to the initial situation. There is an anomaly here too, in that if the sum of the equivalent variations is negative, then we cannot be certain that losers cannot still not compensate the gainers for a reverse move. These anomalies are directly related to the so-called Scitovsky paradox in compensation tests, which arises whenever utility functions are not of the quasi-homothetic, Gorman polar form type. With the Scitovsky paradox utility possibility curves can intersect, so that the fact that the gainers from a move can potentially compensate the losers does not **guarantee** that reverse compensation is not also possible.

There is also a reason for preferring the EV to the CV. This is that for an individual consumer the EV will rank alternative policies in the same way as will the consumer - in this sense it is, in Morey's (1984, p.166) words 'a money index of utility that is a strictly monotonic transformation of the utility function'. This is as close as we can get to cardinal utility: in other words, if the EV for a particular consumer for a move from an initial position is greater than the EV for a second move **from the same initial position**, then we can be sure that the cardinal utility gain from the first move is greater than that from the second (however, whatever the values of the EVs, we cannot say **how much** greater). EV can do this because it is based on the fixed set of initial prices. However CV does not have this property because each of the CVs for policy moves from an initial position will be based on a different set of final prices: hence we cannot be sure that the CVs from different policy moves will rank the moves in the same way that the consumer would.

We turn now to measurement. Given the difficulties of measuring demand it may not be so crucial in practice to measure CV or EV rather than Marshallian surplus. In the past it may have been said that Marshallian surplus was superior to the Hicksian measures because Marshallian demand curves are observable. However, developments in demand theory mean that it may be just as straightforward to measure Hicksian surplus. When demand functions are derived by an explicit utility-maximizing procedure, then the Hicksian demand functions can be derived from the underlying expenditure function by Shephard's lemma (or we can just measure CV or EV as the difference between minimum expenditure levels required to achieve specified levels of utility at pre- and post-project prices). When the utility function is of the Stone-Geary Linear Expenditure function type (an example of Gorman polar-form preferences), there are explicit formulations of CV and EV in terms of incomes, prices and the parameters of the Linear Expenditure System demand functions:

Labeaga and Angel Lopez (1994) provide an example for Spain. For the more satisfactory - and now widely estimated - Almost Ideal Demand System, which is itself derived from a particular functional form for the expenditure function, the minimum levels of expenditure required to achieve particular levels of utility at different sets of prices can also be solved.

An alternative approach to the one described above, where functional forms of demand to estimate are derived from an explicit formulation of the utility or expenditure function, involves starting with the Marshallian demands and integrating back to the indirect utility function (and hence the expenditure function) via the partial differential equation of Roy's identity:

$$q_i = - [\partial v / \partial p_i / \partial v / \partial m]$$

This approach has been used by Hausman (1981). Although it is extremely difficult to solve for the n-good case, Hausman has derived closed-form solutions for the two-good case for both linear and log-linear Marshallian demand functions. For the linear demand function

$$q_1 = \alpha p_1 + \delta m + \gamma z$$

(where z is a set of socio-economic characteristics, and p_1 and m are deflated by the price of the other good p_2), Hausman solves for the expenditure function as

$$m(pu) = e^{\delta p_1} - \frac{1}{\delta} (\alpha p_1 + \frac{\alpha}{\delta} \gamma z)$$

For the log-linear demand function

$$\ln q_1 = \alpha \ln p_1 + \delta \ln m + \gamma z$$

the expenditure function is derived as

$$m(pu) = \left[(1-\delta) (u + e^{\gamma z}) \frac{p_1^{1+\alpha}}{1+\alpha} \right]^{1/1-\delta}$$

These results for the most conveniently and commonly estimated forms of single-equation demand function have been used by a number of economists in empirical work where the benefits of price or wage changes need to be valued.

Other empirical work in the transport sector has used the Hausman method, but not to explicitly value benefits of price changes. De Jong (1990) modelled motorists' decisions on the ownership and use of cars simultaneously. To do this he used Hausman's log-linear results, with parameters from a log-linear estimate of the demand for car use in terms of annual kilometres as a function of income, fixed car costs, and running costs. These were used to derive indirect utility values in order to determine whether utility would be higher with or without a car. If utility would be higher if a car were owned, then the model also determined optimal use.

Demand modelling in transport frequently uses discrete choice models, for example to model the household's decision as to whether or not to own a car, or the choice of which mode to use for a particular type of trip such as the journey to work. Small and Rosen (1981) extended the standard result in the continuous choice case, that welfare benefits can be measured by areas under compensated demand curves, to the discrete choice case. Although there is a discontinuity in demand curves at the price at which the consumer switches from one discrete choice to another, the minimum expenditure function is continuous. This is because, at the point of switching, the minimum expenditure required to achieve the particular level of utility under consideration is the same whichever of the two discrete options is chosen: any further price change will then lead to one particular option being chosen, and the expenditure function will then be differentiable in the normal way with respect to the price of the good chosen, yielding the usual Hicksian demand functions which can be used to measure CV and EV.

In models of discrete choice conditional utility depends on prices and qualities of the discrete goods and on other measurable characteristics of both goods and consumers, and on a stochastic 'taste' variable. The consumer makes the choice which yields the greatest utility. Small and Rosen derive a general formula for the Hicksian surplus in such discrete choice cases - though to do so they have to assume that income effects are negligible for the good whose price or quality has changed, and that the consumer's marginal utility of income is approximately constant. The resulting welfare measure is the negative of the integral of the probability of choosing the good evaluated at initial and final conditional utility levels, divided by the marginal utility of income.

Small and Rosen then derive specific expressions for this benefit measure for two widely-used discrete choice models, the binary probit and the logit. In the case of the logit model where the probability of choosing good 1 is:

$$\exp W_1 / \sum_i \exp W$$

their measure of benefits is:

$$-(1/\lambda)\ [\ln \sum_i \exp(W_i)\ ]_{W_1^0}^{W_1^f}$$

The value of the marginal utility of income can be derived if the demand for the commodity is known, and the conditional utility function for good 1, W_1, depends on its own price, P_1, so that W/P is also known. In these circumstances it can be solved from Roy's identity.

An example of the application of this approach is to the evaluation of the benefits of US airline deregulation by Morrison and Winston (1987). Morrison and Winston compare the difference in CV between the actual and optimal fares and frequencies on 769 airline routes using this measure. We consider this study later in the paper.

Another issue in consumer surplus measurement is that of dynamic adjustments in demand. Dargay and Goodwin (1995) investigate the implications for transport evaluation of the situation where, perhaps because of adjustment costs or habit, consumer responses to transport price changes are not instantaneous. Many studies have found that long-run price elasticities exceed short-run elasticities. In these circumstances the first period benefits of a transport improvement that lowers transport costs will be measured as the benefits of a demand curve based on the short-run elasticity. In successive periods the demand curve will become more elastic, so undiscounted benefits will rise. Consequently, if benefits are evaluated on the basis of short-run responses, overall benefits will be understated. The reverse holds for the costs of policies which increase prices.

Dargay and Goodwin investigate the value of a 'pivot elasticity', somewhere between the hort- and long-run values, whose value is such that the present value of future benefits evaluated at this elasticity will be equal to the present value of actual benefits in each period of time. This investigation considers the case of the most commonly used form of dynamic adjustment model, the distributed lag model. Whatever the form of the dynamic demand model, the 'pivot' value of elasticity will depend on the short- and long-run elasticities, the speed of adjustment of demand to the long run equilibrium, the value of the discount rate, and the length of time over which total benefits are evaluated.

The relevance of shadow pricing

In undertaking economic evaluation, how far can we take market prices to reflect the true resource costs of economic activities? A major complication which arises in appraisal is that which follows from the theory of second-best. Lipsey and Lancaster (1956) sought to derive the conditions for economic efficiency when one or more of the Pareto conditions do not hold. In general, the second-best optimum would involve all the other Paretian conditions in the economy being broken:

> The general theorem for the second best optimum states that if there is introduced into a general equilibrium system a constraint which prevents the attainment of one of the Paretian conditions, the other Paretian conditions, although still attainable, are, in general, no longer desirable. In other words, given that one of the Paretian optimum conditions cannot be fulfilled, then an optimum situation can be achieved only by departing from all the other Paretian conditions (Lipsey and Lancaster, 1956, p.11).

Moreover:

> Specifically, it is **not** true that a situation in which more, but not all, of the optimum conditions are fulfilled is necessarily, or is even likely to be, superior to a situation in which fewer are fulfilled (Lipsey and Lancaster, 1956, p.12).

This has serious implications for attempts to improve economic efficiency because by attempting to improve the situation in one part of the economy we may be reducing efficiency in the economy as a whole.

The implication for the valuation of the outputs and inputs of projects is that in the extreme case no market prices may reflect the prices required for second-best optimisation. There are two approaches to deal with this problem. One is to adopt a general equilibrium approach to cost-benefit analysis and consider all the impacts throughout the economy of a particular project. This approach has been considered by Boadway (1975), Hammond (1980) and Diewert (1983). The approach is theoretically correct, but likely to be impossible to implement in practice. The alternative approach is to consider only those price distortions thought to be most relevant for the project or policy under consideration.

This second approach follows from attempts to limit the damage caused to piecemeal welfare economics by the general theorem of second best. These attempts started with Davis and Whinston's (1965) paper which argued that some sectors of the economy might be isolated (in terms of having low or zero values of the cross-derivatives of costs and utilities with respect to prices which cause the problems in Lancaster and Lipsey's second-best optimum equation) from those with the initial distortions. In such circumstances prices in the isolated sectors might still be regarded as reflecting correct valuations. Cost-benefit analysis of this partial equilibrium type could then proceed on the basis that the analyst should identify the most important outputs and inputs for the project or policy under consideration, and should then concentrate on deriving appropriate prices for these outputs and inputs.

How might such **shadow prices** be derived in the presence of distortions? To illustrate this, we consider the case where a public project uses an input which is produced in a distorted market. Given the frequency with which concrete manufacturers are accused of colluding to fix prices, and given the importance of concrete in major transport construction projects, concrete might be a good example.

If concrete were produced by a perfectly competitive industry, then the price of concrete would equal its marginal costs of production, and the market price of concrete would reflect its resource costs to the economy as long as it were used by competitive industries. This is because the demand curve for concrete would reflect the value of its marginal product, which would in turn reflect the valuation which consumers place on the contribution which the concrete makes to the production of final output. The supply curve of concrete in a competitive market would reflect the marginal cost of producing concrete in terms of the economy's valuation of the alternative uses of the inputs (labour, plant, etc) used to produce concrete.

However, if concrete were produced by a cartel which was successful in raising prices above marginal costs of production, then a distortion arises. This is illustrated in Figure 6.2, where we assume that the cartel operates like a pure monopolist, and so produces output Q_1 at price P_1 given an initial pre-project demand curve of D_1 (Similar expositions can be found in many texts on cost-benefit analysis, including Boadway and Bruce, 1984, pp.297-312, and Sugden and Williams, 1978, 99-112.)

The relevant question in determining the shadow price of the concrete is that of what the economy foregoes if extra units of the concrete are used in a public project. If there are increases in the production of concrete then the economy foregoes the next-best alternative uses of the inputs needed to produce the extra concrete. These uses are valued at the marginal cost per tonne of concrete. If instead concrete is diverted from other uses to the public project, then the economy loses its valuation of concrete in these other uses. This valuation is equal to the market price, which is what the marginally-excluded other users would have been prepared to pay.

In practice, if a project requires increased inputs such as concrete, some of the extra input will be supplied from increased production and some will be diverted from other uses as the increased demand for the input increases market price. This is shown in Figure 6.2 where we assume that the project shifts the demand curve for concrete horizontally to the left to D_2. (For simplicity we presume that our project's demand for concrete, the horizontal shift in the demand curve, is not sensitive to price rises so we have a parallel shift in demand.) Output of concrete increases from Q_1 to Q_2, so that the distance aQ_1 indicates the amount of concrete diverted from other uses. The appropriate shadow price per tonne of concrete is therefore:

$$SP = \frac{Q_1 Q_2}{aQ_2} MC + \frac{aQ_1}{aQ_2} P$$

(You can think about the complications that emerge when we return to a full general equilibrium framework by worrying about what happens to this formula if some of the users of concrete are not operating in fully competitive product markets, and if some of the inputs in concrete manufacture are not supplied competitively.)

Shadow pricing of inputs may also be necessary where the inputs are subject to a distortionary tax, in the sense of a tax which aims to raise revenue, as opposed to an externality-correcting tax whose objective is to correct an existing distortion. In the absence of freely-floating exchange rates, scarce foreign exchange needed to purchase imported project inputs such as specialised machinery might also need to be shadow priced. Finally where project labour might otherwise be unemployed because of imperfections in the working of the labour market, shadow prices might also need to be used.

Valuation issues

A major issue in transport appraisal is that of the valuation of unmarketed outputs and consequences of projects and policies. The major problems of valuation in the transport sector are of travel time, accident risk (particularly risk of loss of life), and environmental costs. Environmental costs include the costs of noise, localised air pollution, and globalised air pollution, as well as impacts on landscape and townscape, and on flora, fauna and biological diversity.

Generally, economists have been more successful at valuing time and accident costs than at valuing environmental costs. There have been very many studies of the value of time (for a recent worldwide survey and comparison of results see Waters, 1995). Many studies start from the principle of utility maximisation, where the consumer faces not only a monetary budget constraint but also total and travel time constraints. This yields an indirect utility function where utility is a function of income, travel times, travel costs, the overall time constraint and (implicitly) the prices of non-transport goods and services. When a first-order approximation is taken for the direct utility function this yields the linear form of the indirect utility function. In turn this yields the value of time as the ratio between the time and cost parameters in the indirect utility function (for a derivation see MVA Consultancy, et al, 1994). The parameters of the utility of travel functions are estimated using a discrete choice model, in particular the multinomial logit, to model traveller choice. The travel choice data are derived both from revealed traveller preferences and, increasingly, from stated preference experiments. (See John Bates' paper in the present volume for discussion of travel modelling, and Hensher, 1994, for a survey of stated preference techniques.)

Valuation of risk of loss of life (and of injury) can now be based on consumers' evaluations of small changes in risk. Mishan (1971) argued that the correct valuation of fatalities was not the lost output measure commonly used (and still used even today in some countries), but the sum of the compensating variations of all the individuals whose risks of death had changed. If a project reduces the expected number of fatal accidents, then each individual's compensating variation is the maximum amount he or she would for the reduction in risk. If the project increases the risk of death then an individual's compensating variation is the minimum amount of money they would accept instead of returning to the original lower risk level.

This approach has been made operational both through behaviourial studies of willingness to accept payments for differential risk in the labour market (see in particular Marin and Psacharopoulos, 1982), and through surveys of individuals' willingness to pay for changes to risk in different risky situations. Jones-Lee (1994) surveys the literature. After using the gross output method in the valuation of fatal road accidents for many years, the British Government adopted results estimated using the willingness-to-pay method in 1988.

Both behaviourial and stated preference methods have also been used to value environmental effects. The main behaviourial approach is that of hedonic house price estimation (or simply surveys of realters/estate agents). There are large numbers of studies using contingent valuation methods to try to elicit individuals' valuations of environmental effects using stated preference techniques. Neither of these approaches is considered further in the present paper because environmental valuation is the subject of Chris Nash's paper in this volume.

Comparing benefits at different points in time: the choice of discount rate

Where projects, such as investment projects, involve benefits and costs which accrue in different time periods, a discount rate has to be used to discount these costs and benefits to a common point in time. For social cost-benefit analysis the appropriate discount rate is the social discount rate, which reflects society's relative valuations of benefits and costs at different points in time. This social discount rate might be interpreted simply in efficiency terms, or it might also try to take account of equity considerations. In that case, it raises important questions of inter-generational equity. Such considerations are particularly relevant for policies, such as actions to slow down global warming or reduce species' extinction and preserve biological diversity, which not only have particularly long-term effects but are also irreversible.

There are two main contenders for the social discount rate. These are the social opportunity cost (SOC) rate and the social time preference (STP) rate. The SOC rate shows the marginal social rate of return from investment in the private sector. If the SOC rate were eight per cent, it would mean that the marginal private sector investment yielded a social rate of return of eight per cent. This would be likely to differ from the private rate of return from this investment because the private firm might have to pay taxes on its profits, and these taxes then represent a transfer of real benefits to the rest of society, and because the project might create negative or positive technological external effects such as environmental pollution. The private sector might also make sub-optimal allowance for risk.

The STP rate shows society's relative valuation of present versus future consumption. If the STP rate were four per cent, this would mean that society was indifferent between $100 of consumption this year and $104 of consumption (at constant real prices) next year.

With perfect capital markets, no capital taxation, perfect information and no external effects, the SOC and STP rates would be equated at the market rate of interest, and this market rate could be interpreted as the social rate of discount in efficiency terms. In practice the two will not be equal. Although it is not necessarily so, it is often assumed that the SOC rate will exceed the STP rate, so we will consider the consequences of using one or the other rate to evaluate projects under these circumstances, using our example where the SOC rate is eight per cent and the STP rate is four per cent.

If the government used the SOC rate in public project appraisal, it would only accept projects with a social rate of return in excess of eight per cent. This would be acceptable if all project funds were to be diverted from private sector investment since the marginal yield on such investments in social terms is eight per cent. However, if all of the public project funds were to be diverted from private consumption, then use of the SOC rate might lead us to reject some desirable projects. Any public project with a rate of return below eight per cent would be rejected, but if such a project yields a return above four per cent, it would be desirable because it adds to the present value of private consumption (which must be calculated by discounting at the STP rate, which is four per cent in our example). The problem with using the SOC rate is therefore that we might **reject** some **desirable** public projects.

If the government instead used the STP rate in our example this would imply accepting all projects which yield a return in excess of four per cent. This is fine if all the funds are diverted from private consumption, but not if some are diverted from private investment. This is because private investments yield a return of at least eight per cent, so society could be made worse off by accepting public projects with a lower rate of return. Consequently, the problem with using the STP rate is that we might **accept** some undesirable public projects.

One solution to this problem is to derive a synthetic discount rate which takes account of the source of funds. Thus we could use a form of shadow pricing to allow for the impact on efficiency of different sources of funds. The social opportunity cost of the amount of capital, K, incurred in the project can be written as:

$$SOC = K[(\theta)(\rho/r) + (1 - \theta)]$$

where

θ = the marginal propensity to save from disposable income
ρ = the SOC rate
r = the STP rate.

Once allowance for the opportunity cost of capital has been made for in this way, costs and benefits can be discounted at the STP rate. (In practice, the situation will be much more complicated, since we have to allow for the extent to which the government will reinvest those returns from the public sector investment which accrue to itself).

A recent debate (Birdsall and Steer, 1993; Cline, 1993) over the correct rate of discount to use to measure the costs and benefits of greenhouse gas abatement policies illustrates the use of this kind of synthetic approach, the practical problems in measuring STP and SOC rates, the particular differences in dealing with inter-generational transfers, and the way in which benefits of very long-lived projects are especially sensitive to the choice of discount rate. Cline (1992) conducted a major cost-benefit analysis of actions to ameliorate global warming. This study calculated costs and benefits over a three hundred year time horizon. That the choice of discount rate is critical can be gauged by the fact that the present value of one million dollars received two hundred years in the future is $19,000 at a discount rate of two per cent, $58 at a discount rate of five per cent, and 20 cents at a discount rate of eight per cent.

Cline considered the costs and benefits of action to reduce carbon dioxide emissions by one-third and to hold them at that level indefinitely. He estimated the costs of taking such action as rising to about 3.5 per cent of world GDP in the first few decades of the twenty-first century, and then tapering off to around 2.5 per cent of GDP for the rest of the time period considered. Benefits of this action in Cline's 'central case' rise fairly steadily, but annual benefits only exceed annual costs around the middle of the twenty-second century. Annual benefits exceed annual costs around the year 2060 in Cline's 'high damage' case.

Cline uses a weighted, or synthetic, discount rate equal to

$$[(\theta)(SPK)(r) + (1-\theta)(r)]$$

where SPK is the opportunity cost of capital, to discount these costs and benefits.

Cline argues that 'pure' time preference, the preference of individuals for present versus future consumption because they are mortal, is not relevant for such policies because the benefits accrue to future generations and society is not mortal. However, future generations are expected to be better off than present generations, so on the basis of declining marginal utility of income, Cline adopts a positive STP rate of 1.5 per cent based on his projection of long-run annual per capita income growth in the USA of one per cent per annum, and a value for the elasticity of the marginal utility of income of -1.5.

The opportunity cost of capital term attempts to measure the opportunity cost of expenditure on greenhouse gas abatement diverted from private sector investment by estimating the present value of the consumption stream that would have occurred if the private investment had earned the social rate of return (which Cline takes as eight per cent) for society. This calculation is based on an assumption that private investment projects yield benefits for a fifteen year time period. Hence benefits of private sector investment are compounded forward for fifteen years at eight per cent, and discounted back to the present at the social time preference rate of 1.5 per cent. This is equivalent to calculating the shadow price of capital as the ratio of the fifteen year annuity factor at 1.5 per cent, to the fifteen year annuity factor at eight per cent. These calculations yield a shadow price of capital of around 1.5.

Given an assumption that twenty per cent of the costs of greenhouse gas restrictions will be financed by displacing private investment, and the rest through reductions in private consumption, this yields a social discount rate of 1.5 per cent. Even with such a low discount rate, Cline finds a benefit-cost ratio for aggressive abatement of 0.74 in his central case. Nevertheless, Cline argues that policy makers may still wish to take out 'greenhouse insurance' because of the fear of the consequence of high-damage or catastrophic scenarios if they are risk-averse.

However, Cline's choice of discount rate has been criticized by World Bank economists Birdsall and Steer (1993). The World Bank uses a much higher discount rate in its own project appraisal, and much of Birdsall and Steer's argument is concerned with the opportunity cost of capital. If society can use the funds invested in greenhouse gas abatement in alternative projects with higher rates of return then it does seem sensible that they should do so. In addition, although not mentioned by Birdsall and Steer, Cline's assumption that private sector projects only last fifteen years and that none of the benefits are re-invested, also reduces his implied opportunity cost of capital. Birdsall and Steer also suggest that there should be some pure time preference (otherwise why don't we simply transfer income to low income countries - in practice we clearly do prefer our own consumption to that of others), and believe that Cline's assumption of a one per cent real per capita growth rate is unduly pessimistic in the light of historic growth performance. They suggest one per cent for pure time preference, and two per cent for annual per capita income growth. On these grounds the benefits of greenhouse gas abatement would be much reduced.

Such abatement policies indicate the sensitivity of evaluation results to choice of discount rate to an extreme degree, but choice of discount rate will also be crucial for many transport infrastructure projects which, as the next section on uncertainty indicates, are much longer-lived than many other investment schemes.

Incorporating uncertainty

In an uncertain world, economic evaluation must take account of risk and uncertainty. Nijkamp and Rienstra (1995) consider why transport infrastructure projects are particularly risky. First, they have long lives in relation to most investment projects. Secondly, they require large amounts of capital. Thirdly, there is usually a long period of time before construction can actually start because of the need to plan projects and gain the necessary permissions to acquire land and meet environmental standards, often in the face of strong objections. Fourthly, actual construction itself takes a long period of time. Finally, the investments are irreversible, and most of the capital cannot be recovered if the project is unsuccessful. Projects face political, financial, construction, operational and commercial risks. These risks will impact on the social cost-benefit returns from the projects as well as on financial returns.

How should uncertainty be built into project appraisal? The rule of thumb of adding a risk premium to the discount rate to reflect the subjective uncertainty of the project is not generally regarded as acceptable. Such an approach does lead to greater proportionate reductions in the present value of benefits the further in the future those benefits are expected to accrue, and we might expect future events to be more uncertain the further in the future they occur. Nevertheless, there are no objective criteria for deciding the size of the discount factor to be used for any particular project. Furthermore, we may have more information about the sources and nature of uncertainty faced by a particular project than the simple discount factor is able to reflect.

A very common approach is to test the sensitivity of project results both to particular assumptions, for example about traffic growth or competitors' expected responses, and to particular valuations, such as the value of travel time or of accident savings or of the discount rate. This approach enables the analyst to judge what particular aspects of the project have the largest influence on its outcome. It may also indicate those aspects of the evaluation where more detailed work is needed. Sensitivity analysis can also be modified by weighting different outcomes differently, either in a formal way by using von Neumann-Morgenstern cardinal utility concepts, or in a less formal way as in Cline's different treatment of his alternative scenarios for global warming.

Sensitivity analysis can be made much more powerful if it is combined with risk analysis. Here a Monte Carlo simulation is carried out of project Net Present Values. First explained by Pouliquen (1970), the method involves associating a probability distribution to each of the elements of the appraisal, such as traffic forecasts, time savings, labour costs or competitors' responses. The user can choose from among different alternative forms of distribution function, and can choose the mean and appropriate measure of dispersion for each item. The risk program then runs by selecting a value of each variable at random, but according to the specified probability distribution. These values for all the project components are then combined in a single NPV calculation.

By itself, this single NPV value would be of no use, but the process is repeated several hundred times. This yields a probability distribution of NPVs for the particular project under consideration. The analyst can then assess the probability that the project has a positive NPV, or the probability that the NPV exceeds some minimum acceptable figure. Probability distributions of NPVs for different projects can also be compared to contrast the mean expected NPVs with the degree of risk as measured by the distributions of calculated NPVs.

One problem identified with early applications of the risk analysis technique is that different individual elements of a project might have risks which are correlated with each other, so variations in one would not be randomly distributed with respect to variations in another. However, modern risk computer packages (such as Palisade Corporation's @RISK package) can allow for such inter-correlation between risks. Like any technique, however, the results can only be as good as the data input, and the individual probability distributions of risk are themselves likely to be subjective: however project analysts are likely to have more information about the sources and nature of uncertainty than are implied in simple risk premia calculations, so risk analysis can help to utilise what information is available in the most effective way.

Income distribution, social welfare maximization and the problem of identifying ultimate beneficiaries

We can consider the integration of efficiency and equity effects by reference to the concept of the social welfare function. Here we do not interpret the social welfare function in terms of an aggregation of individual preferences, but in terms of some judgement about the social welfare to be obtained from different social states. (Social states are defined as combinations of levels of economic activity and distributions of the outcomes of such activity.) These judgements might be viewed as the judgements of policy makers: in turn their judgements might reflect the values of some voters imperfectly through the voting system by which they are elected.

Suppose that social welfare depends only on individual utilities. We can then write:

$$Z = f(\mathbf{U})$$

and the change in social welfare, dZ, is equal to:

$$dZ = \sum_i (\partial Z / \partial U_i)\, dU_i$$

If individual utility then depends only on individual income (which is implicit in the idea of the expenditure function) then:

$$Z = g(\mathbf{M})$$

and the change in social welfare is equal to:

$$dZ = \sum_i (\partial Z / \partial M_i)\, dM_i$$

The terms $(\partial Z / \partial M_i)$ can be interpreted as welfare weights to be applied to the benefits to different individuals. They can also be interpreted as the 'social marginal utility of income'.

A special case is that of the utilitarian, or Benthamite, social welfare function. Here social welfare is equal to the sum of individual utilities, that is:

$$Z = \sum_i U_i = \sum_i h_i(M_i)$$

and

$$dZ = \sum_i (\partial U_i / \partial M_i)\, dM_i i$$

where the welfare weights are now equal to the marginal utilities of income.

In these kinds of analysis it is normal to adopt the assumption that the social welfare function is symmetrical in individual incomes. This means that the contribution of an individual to social welfare will depend on that individual's income, and not on other factors such as his/her race or sex, or family relationship with the Minister of Transport. In these circumstances we can drop the i subscript on the h utility of income function. (In practice a complication often arises because income data relate to households rather than individuals, and households contain different numbers of individuals. To deal with this problem household income data can be adjusted to take account of family structure using 'equivalence scales'. Equivalence scales are factors intended to convert household income of households of different sizes to equivalent income that yields the same utility. A common use would be in deciding what basic pension for a married couple would be equivalent in utility terms to a particular single person's pension, given that there are economies of scale in household consumption. Economies of scale mean that although two people can't live as cheaply as one, they do not need double a single person's income to maintain the same standard of living.)

A particular case of the symmetric utilitarian social welfare function is that where the elasticity of the marginal utility of income is assumed to be constant. In this case the individual utility function takes the form:

$$U_i = \frac{1}{1+\eta} M_i^{1+\eta}$$

The marginal utility of income is

$$\partial U_i / \partial M_i = M_i^{\eta}$$

and the elasticity of the marginal utility of income with respect to income is

$$\frac{\partial(\partial U_i / \partial M_i)}{\partial M_i} \frac{M_i}{\partial U_i / \partial M_i} = \eta$$

The distributional weight of individual i relative to that of an individual with mean income is then:

$$w_i / \bar{w} = M_i^{\eta} / \bar{M}^{\eta} = (\bar{M} / M_i)^{-\eta}$$

that is to say, benefits are weighted by average income divided by the income of the beneficiary, raised to a power equal to the negative of the elasticity of the marginal utility of income. Remember that η is negative, so that individuals with lower than average incomes have higher than average weights. Although there have been claims that the elasticity of the marginal utility of income is measurable, this is not in fact so (see Deaton and Muellbauer, 1980, pp.140-141, 217-218).

A related social welfare function is that in which social welfare is symmetrical with respect to individual incomes (but is not equal to the sum of individual utilities) and in which society is concerned only with **relative** rather than absolute inequality (ie society has 'constant relative inequality aversion'). Atkinson (1970) showed that in such circumstances the social welfare function takes the form:

$$Z = \sum_i \left[\frac{1}{1-\epsilon} \right] M_i^{1-\epsilon} \quad ; \quad \epsilon > 0$$

and

$$dZ = \sum_i (M_i^{-\epsilon} . dM_i)$$

The parameter ϵ is referred to by Atkinson as the 'degree of relative inequality aversion', but it is also equal to the negative of the elasticity of the social marginal utility of income. If ϵ takes a value of zero then social welfare is simply equal to the sum of individual incomes, and society is therefore concerned only with the total level of income and not at all with its distribution. All the welfare weights in this case equal one.

In the more general case where ϵ does not equal zero, the resulting distributional weight for individual i relative to an individual with mean income is equal to the ratio of average income to individual i's income, raised to a power equal to the degree of relative inequality aversion. (Remember that the degree of inequality aversion is a positive number.) Thus the relative distributional weights are:

$$w_i / \bar{w} \;=\; M_i^{-\epsilon} / \bar{M}^{-\epsilon} \;=\; (\bar{M} / M_i)^{\epsilon}$$

The parameter ϵ cannot generally be estimated but depends on value judgements. Consequently studies of the distributional consequences of policies which use Atkinson's measure of inequality typically use a range of values to test the sensitivity of results (see for example Newbery, 1995).

In a transport evaluation context, Hau (1986) has set out the different forms of welfare weighting systems described above, and used them to evaluate the distributional consequences of alternative transport policy options in the Interstate 580 corridor of the San Francisco Bay area. A discrete choice model was used to consider the benefits to three different income groups (low, medium and high) of different policies with regard to a variety of modes, including bus, BART with bus access, carpool, and own-drive.

One of the major problems of fully incorporating distributional consequences into project and policy analysis is to determine the ultimate beneficiaries (and losers). For example, where benefits of transport investment projects are capitalised in changes in land and property prices, the income levels of those who ultimately gain and lose may differ from those of the immediate gainers and losers. A full distributional analysis of a project which benefitted freight traffic would require us to know the incomes of the consumers of the transported goods whose prices fell as a result of reductions in transport costs.

Highway investment appraisal: a traditional application of cost-benefit analysis

One of the earliest cost-benefit analysis studies in Britain was that of the London to Birmingham motorway published in 1960. Highways provided an ideal subject for cost-benefit evaluation because their use was not charged in Britain, so there was a need to evaluate project output in a different way. In addition, users of related parts of the road network could gain or lose because of changes in traffic congestion as a result of switches of traffic to the new or improved road. Furthermore, the main benefits, the benefits to road users, could be measured in terms of savings in operating

215

costs, reductions in travel time, and reductions in the expected numbers of accidents. Not only could the expected impacts of new roads be measured, but valuations of time savings and accident reductions - albeit crude at first - could be derived. (Environmental consequences have proved to be more difficult to value.)

In Britain procedures for evaluating road schemes using cost-benefit analysis were standardized in the COBA computer package as long ago as 1973. COBA and the valuations it incorporates have been revised since, but the basic structure remains unchanged. However, from an early date it had been criticized, both because it did not include environmental effects, and because of concern about the way it incorporated traffic forecasting procedures. To attempt to allay these concerns the Government appointed an Advisory Committee on Trunk Road Assessment which reported in 1977. This Leitch Committee argued that evaluation needed to take account of environmental impacts in a formal way, even if they could not be valued in monetary terms. (There had been a flurry of activity in valuing the environmental costs of transport - and particularly noise - in Britain at the end of the 1960s and the beginning of the 1970s, but consistent monetary valuations did not emerge.)

This led to the current 'framework' approach, a fairly informal variant of multi-criteria analysis, in which non-monetary impacts of road projects are measured and included in the final balance-sheet alongside the monetary results from the COBA part of the evaluation. It is then up to the decision-maker's 'judgement' as to which project is actually selected.

After the publication of the Leitch Report in 1977, the advisory committee arrangement was made permanent as the Standing Advisory Committee on Trunk Road Assessment (SACTRA). SACTRA's 1992 report revisited the issue of environmental valuation. Its terms of reference were to review the methods used to assess environmental costs and benefits, and to consider whether a greater degree of valuation was desirable. SACTRA believed that there was no legitimate objection to monetary valuation, and that attempts should be made to value some of the environmental effects of road schemes using both the hedonic house price method and contingent valuation/stated preference methods. As a consequence the government commissioned a programme of research on environmental valuation. SACTRA also recommended that the government should consider the environmental effects of its roadbuilding programme at a more strategic national and regional level, as well as just at the level of individual schemes.

The most recent SACTRA report, published in December 1994, considered the impact of road construction on traffic levels. COBA had always been based on the idea of a fixed-trip matrix, with user benefits in terms of savings in time and operating costs being measured for traffic flows which were forecast to occur **in the absence of the road scheme being evaluated**. This means that benefits to traffic generated by the scheme were not considered. This had two consequences, one more serious than the other. The first consequence is that new road schemes might generate new traffic, which would create benefits to this newly-generated traffic. These could be measured by the consumer surplus benefits of the extra trips. Exclusion of these benefits would lead to an underestimate of measured benefits.

Of greater concern, particularly to those opposed to roadbuilding, was the possibility that, if the new road was congested, the generated traffic could increase travel costs and time for existing traffic. This would mean that the benefits measured by COBA would overstate the true benefits to existing traffic. Moreover, depending on the elasticities of demand and the elasticity of vehicle generalised costs with respect to traffic flow, actual benefits could be less than the benefits measured by COBA.

This is illustrated in Figure 6.3. The MPC_1 curve shows the generalised cost per trip as a function of traffic flow in the absence of investment. The equilibrium traffic flow would be F_1, and generalised cost per trip g_1. Now if the road is improved so that the curve relating generalised cost to traffic flow falls to MPC_2 then **in the absence of traffic generation**, generalised cost per trip would fall to g_2 and the benefits of reduced generalised costs to pre-investment road users would be measured by the area g_2g_1ab. These are the benefits measured by COBA because of its assumption of a fixed trip matrix.

However the fall in generalised cost from g_1 to g_2 leads to traffic generation. As traffic levels increase, so does congestion on the improved road. The new equilibrium is at point c on the diagram, with traffic flow F_2 and generalised cost per trip g_3. There are now benefits equal to area dac for the generated traffic, but to be offset against these are losses of benefits to existing traffic because of the impacts of increased traffic flows on travel time and operating costs. These lost benefits are measured by the area g_2g_3db.

Williams and Moore (1990) consider the relationship between these two areas, and the circumstances where the COBA method can understate the true user benefits. In the limit, where the elasticity of demand for an improved link is infinite, **all** the benefits of improved roads would be lost. (There are also circumstances in which overall travel costs will worsen as a result of road investment -see Arnott and Small, 1994; Mogridge, 1990.) It should be noted that these results presume the absence of efficient road pricing.

This illustrates an important feature of cost-benefit analysis, namely that unforeseen **economic** consequences of projects might reduce measured benefits. For example, in cost-benefit analyses of rail closures it is often assumed that transfers of former rail users to cars will increase traffic congestion, but it is less common to measure the second-round effects through behaviourial responses of existing road users to the increased congestion.

A further issue in road investment appraisal (and in appraisal of other transport infrastructure) is that of whether such investment generates additional benefits to industry and the economy in general which are not captured in the appraisal process. Both Dodgson (1973) and Jara-Diaz (1986) show that in a competitive economy the ultimate benefits of transport investment in reducing industrial costs and the prices of final goods and services will be correctly measured by the benefits to freight traffic provided that generated traffic is correctly forecast. (Where there is monopoly power in the economy, the situation is more complicated.)

This view seemed to have been generally accepted, though the issue of the role of infrastructure investment has re-emerged with the publication of aggregate studies which show a correlation between aggregate public investment and productivity growth (see in particular Aschauer, 1989).

Over the years a number of studies have tried to develop a microeconomic link between particular transport infrastructure investments and regional or local economic growth. My own study of the M62 motorway suggested a modest relationship (Dodgson, 1974). This and other studies have been surveyed by Button et al (1995). They conclude:

'... perhaps the most objective position is to say that the role of adequate transport and other infrastructure is now seen by many as being a necessary but not sufficient condition for economic development. In this sense one can think of transport and similar infrastructure as not exerting a primary effect on development but rather as a facilitator which assists and reinforces other, more immediate instruments such as the release of land for construction and the direct provision of new buildings.... What these aggregate studies, and criticisms of them, seem to imply is that micro, sectoral studies are necessary to isolate the role of specific types of infrastructure, if high levels of intra-public infrastructure efficiency are to be attained' (Button, et al, 1995, p.192).

Measuring the benefits of introducing road congestion charging

Economists may wish to evaluate pricing schemes as well as investment schemes. Indeed although investment is often seen as the solution to transport capacity problems, such as shortage of airport runway capacity, improvements in the efficiency of pricing may often be a more cost-efficient alternative to major infrastructure construction. In addition, there is an important inter-relationship between pricing and investment, since the social benefits of any project will depend on the pricing scheme to be implemented: prices will determine project demand, and hence benefits, while there may also be feedback effects of project demand on project operating and/or congestion costs. It would, for example, be foolish to try to evaluate the social benefits of a bridge scheme, and **then afterwards try to decide what pricing policy should be implemented for the bridge**.

In this section we consider the evaluation of proposals to implement highway congestion charging schemes. The economics of such first-best pricing schemes have been familiar to economists for many years. Newbery (1990) provides a clear exposition. However, an investigation of the distributional consequences of such schemes also indicates a major reason why attempts to persuade politicians to implement such schemes have not been successful.

The net benefits of road pricing are shown in Figure 6.4, which is the standard road pricing diagram. The MPC curve shows the marginal private costs of car use. These are equal to average private costs (APC) of car use because each user ignores the external congestion costs he imposes on other road users. The MSC curve shows marginal social costs, and includes both marginal private costs and marginal congestion costs. (We ignore environmental costs in this exposition.) In the absence of congestion charging each motorist travels as long as his benefits from the trip, as measured along the aggregate demand curve D, exceed his own private costs. The equilibrium is therefore at point c, with traffic flow F_1 and generalised cost per trip g_1. This is not economically efficient because at the equilibrium traffic flow marginal social costs exceed marginal benefits. The optimal traffic flow is at F_2, where marginal social costs are equal to marginal benefits. This economically-efficient flow can be achieved by charging each car user a price equal to ab.

The benefits and costs of this policy can then be measured in terms of areas on the diagram. The real resource cost per trip falls from g_1 to g_3, so there are benefits in savings in the cost of resources used to provide the remaining trips equal to the area g_3g_1db. However, there is a loss of benefits because of the reduction in traffic flow from F_1 to F_2: this loss is equal to the area F_2acF_1 under the demand curve between F_1 and F_2 (this measures these displaced car travellers' valuations of their trips) minus the resource costs of providing these trips, F_1dcF_2. This net loss of displaced trips, dac, needs to be offset against the resource savings g_3g_1db, to give the overall efficiency benefits of congestion charging.

On the basis of these kinds of arguments, economists have been almost united in advocating congestion charging as a sensible economic solution to the problem of urban road congestion. However, an investigation of the distributional consequences of the policy shows why politicians have been reluctant to follow this policy prescription. The benefits of road pricing are achieved by charging motorists **more** for the use of roads. Consequently the generalised cost per trip rises to g_2. A part of this (g_3) represents real resource use, while the remainder (g_2g_3) represents a tax, which is a transfer to the government. In practice both represent a real cost to the motorist, who is unlikely to distinguish between them. The overall benefits of road pricing are therefore achieved by imposing a total cost on initial road users equal to area g_1g_2ac, by means of a transfer of resources to government equal to area g_3g_2ab.

Although in practice some road users might gain from road pricing because they have a relatively high value of time and therefore would be happy to trade off a time saving from reduced traffic congestion against the charge they have to pay, most road users are likely to be worse off. The government then does have resource savings that it can use to make others in society better off, but it will be much more difficult to identify the beneficiaries from road pricing. This is particularly so ex ante, when policy is being deciding in the face of opposition from those who can see that they are likely to lose.

Evaluating urban public transport subsidies

Another application of economic appraisal techniques has been in the evaluation of the benefits of urban public transport subsidies, including both the optimal level of subsidy and the balance between fare and service frequency levels. In Britain this led to the development of the Glaister model (Glaister, 1994), which was used first in London and then in the other main conurbations. The Glaister model was a computer model which evaluated changes in a particular city from the existing (base) fares and service levels on both bus and rail modes. The model included data on the length and type of the road network, speed-flow characteristics, road vehicle operating costs, and traffic flows on each city's base network. Combined with own-elasticities for public transport, cross-elasticities between public transport fares and car traffic flows, and time values, this enabled the model to assess the effects of public transport fares and service levels on road transport demand and congestion costs. The model also calculated user benefits to existing and newly-generated public transport trips when fares or frequencies changed. An increase in frequency would reduce waiting time for existing passengers both through the direct effects of reduced headways between buses or trains, and because a waiting passenger would be less likely to find the next bus full.

Because cross-elasticities were low (and also because increases in bus service levels would themselves add to congestion) the model discovered that the main benefits of public transport subsidies were those to public transport passengers, rather than those which - as had been widely supposed before - arose because of reductions in the costs of road congestion. The model was used in the early 1980s to assess the allocation of public transport subsidies but, with rising subsidies the Government adopted an alternative strategy which was to try to reduce subsidies by deregulating bus services. The methods were also used to assess benefits and costs of urban transport subsidies in Australia, first by comparing benefits in different cities (Dodgson, 1986), and then by developing a computer model for Sydney.

Measuring the benefits of deregulation

White (1990) used a cost-benefit framework to evaluate the benefits of local bus service deregulation in Great Britain. Local bus services outside London were deregulated in 1986. After this date any operator can provide any commercial service they wish as long as they register the service at least 42 days in advance. Fares do not need to be registered, and can be changed at any time.

The Government hoped that deregulation and the resulting competition would reduce costs, improve service quality and put downward pressure on fares. In particular the Government had been concerned about rapidly escalating subsidies. Deregulation certainly did lead to a reduction in costs, partly because wages in the industry fell - both in nominal and in real terms - and partly because there were real productivity improvements. Competition led to an increase in service levels, while there was considerable innovation through the introduction of minibus services.

However the impact on passengers was less clear. Fares in the larger cities rose as subsidies from government were cut, while there was considerable service instability. Even after the initial changes in routes and services, bus services continued to be subject to changes as operators jostled for market position. Indeed the industry has still not settled down nearly ten years after deregulation, and timetables are still subject to continuous revisions. The outcome was that passenger demand (which had been subject to decline before deregulation) continued to decline, **but at a faster rate than might have been expected given the fare and bus-kilometre changes that occurred and our knowledge of the relevant fare and service level elasticities**.

White ascribes this more rapid decline to the impact of instability in the industry in deterring passengers. His cost-benefit study compares the pre-deregulation situation outside London in 1985/86 with the position three years later in 1988/89. The study compares cost levels before and after deregulation. Real costs per bus-km outside London fell by 30 per cent over the period. White excludes that part of the decline which is due to a fall in the real price of fuel which would have occurred in any event. More contentiously, he also excludes as a benefit of deregulation the reductions in earnings in the bus industry, arguing that these are simply a transfer from one section of the community to another. The problem with doing this is that it would omit important dynamic effects of reform in improving long-term efficiency in the economy.

White also estimates the impact of deregulation on passengers. Figure 6.5 of the present paper illustrates the problem, and presents an approach which indicates the logic of the method White uses, but differs in some details of exposition. Before deregulation the fare per trip is F_1 and the number of journeys is T_1. After deregulation the fare has risen to F_2 and the number of journeys has fallen to T_2. Service quality is also presumed to have changed, partly as a result of an increase in bus-kms, and partly because of the impact of instability. Consequently the demand curve will have shifted because of both sets of factors, and is represented on the diagram by D_3, which passes through point a.

The problem is to disentangle the impact of the decline in demand which is due to those external factors such as increasing car ownership which would have reduced the demand for bus services in any event, from those factors due to bus deregulation. The demand curve D_2 shows the demand curve which could have been expected in the post-deregulation year due to the underlying decline in the demand for bus services **but with no changes in service quality**. If deregulation had simply increased fares then demand would be higher than T_2, and we could evaluate the impact of deregulation as the area under D_2 between fares F_2 and F_1. However demand has fallen more than we would expect on the basis of the fares increase, so we should ascribe the remaining fall to the combined effect of different changes in service quality. We can measure the cost in money terms by asking what fare would induce passengers to make T_2 trips when the demand curve is D_2. The answer, as the diagram shows, is F_3. Consequently the overall loss to travellers is the area F_1F_3dc. (This measure of loss is related to the distance function-based concept of the inverse demand curve, which shows the price which would induce the consumer to consume a certain quantity of a good: see Schwab, 1985.)

White's cost-benefit approach has been used more recently in a study of the impact of policies in the one area of Great Britain which was not subject to bus deregulation, namely Greater London. In London a programme of competitive tendering was introduced for the provision of bus services. Different operators competed with the existing London bus operators for the right to provide specified services planned by London Transport, in return for subsidies. Costs were reduced and, because competitive tendering also led to an improvement in service standards, revenue was increased. Kennedy Glaister and Travers (1995, pp.85-94) have calculated the welfare gains as part of an overall study of the impact of competitive bus service tendering in London. They considered alternative assumptions as to whether real wage changes should be treated as a transfer or as a real benefit of the process (see the paper by Glaister in this volume for details).

Morrison and Winston have evaluated both the economic effects of US airline deregulation (Morrison and Winston, 1986) and the difference between the resulting situation and the contestable ideal (Morrison and Winston, 1987). If the airline industry were perfectly contestable firms would set prices equal to marginal costs and provide economically efficient service levels. Morrison and Winston (1987) compare the level of consumer welfare that would be achieved in this situation on 769 city-pair routes in the US with the welfare from the actual fare-frequency combinations faced by air travellers on the routes in 1983. These welfare effects are evaluated using their multinomial logit model of intercity demand, and Small and Rosen's compensating variation formula for this type of discrete choice model.

Since the welfare differences are not equal to zero for any route on which there is at least one potential competitor, the hypothesis of perfect contestability is rejected. The difference between actual and optimal welfare was evaluated at $2.5 billion. The CVs for individual routes were then regressed on numbers of actual and potential competitors to test the hypothesis that the industry is imperfectly competitive. Morrison and Winston's results show that the numbers of actual and potential competitors do matter, with one actual competitor on a route having the same impact as three potential competitors. They therefore conclude that the market is imperfectly competitive.

Assessing strategic interdependence

In an age where the transport sector in many countries is increasingly deregulated and/or privatized, cost-benefit evaluations increasingly need to allow for assessments of the responses of independent organisations to the project or policy under review. A good example of a cost-benefit appraisal which tried to take account of such strategic interaction was the study by Kay, Manning and Szymanski (1989) of the Channel Tunnel between Britain and France. (The Channel Tunnel also provides an excellent example of the major other risks faced in transport infrastructure appraisal.) Construction of the Tunnel commenced in 1987, and the Tunnel opened in 1994, although a full range of services was not provided until 1995. Previously there had been a number of abortive attempts to build the Tunnel, and a number of officially-sponsored cost-benefit studies. These studies had indicated that the Tunnel would yield net social benefits, but nevertheless construction with public funds had not been approved. The British Thatcher Government of the 1980s was opposed to public funding, but agreed with the French to sanction a tunnel to be built with private funds. The private scheme involved an assessment of the financial worth of the project (part of which was made public in the share issue prospectus), together with environmental impact statements, but there was no need for a full cost-benefit analysis given that the criterion for going ahead was the (expected) net financial benefits of the project to the investors.

Kay et al (1989) try to estimate the discounted present value of both private and social benefits of the Tunnel over a fifty year life. A major problem is to estimate the fares and freight rates charged by the Tunnel in the light of the response of the main competitor to the Tunnel, namely the cross-Channel ferries. These fares will in turn determine both Tunnel and ferry revenue, and also the numbers of users and hence the user benefits. The ferries' response is complicated by the fact that some ferry routes, known as the short-sea routes, closely parallel the Tunnel and so are very close substitutes for it, whereas others are further away and are therefore less close substitutes.

Kay et al determine a Nash-equilibrium where each firm maximizes its profits given the fares of its competitors. The reaction curves which are solved to determine this equilibrium depend on marginal costs, and on three features believed to determine demand: these are (1) the attractiveness of each mode in terms of its expected market share given equality of prices with its rival, (2) the elasticity of substitution in terms of the extent to which **differences** in fares alter these base market shares, and (3) the extent of collusion between the two dominant ferry operators. Plausible values were taken for each of these three variables.

The resulting equilibria are primarily driven by the much lower marginal costs of the Tunnel operator in comparison with the ferries. Consequently it is profitable in the model for the Tunnel to cut prices and to capture a high proportion of short-sea passenger and freight traffic. The resulting profit-maximizing prices are then used to predict demand and to measure revenue, operator profits, and user benefits in comparison with pre-Tunnel fares and freight rates. The study shows that the Tunnel could be expected to be profitable given its anticipated construction costs (but actual costs have turned out to be very much greater than expected), and that social benefits can be expected to be very great. When it was opened Eurotunnel denied that it would engage in the predicted price war, but there was severe price competition in the first full Summer (1995) of Tunnel operation, despite Eurotunnel's short-term need to keep revenue up in order to meet its immediate debt-financing problems.

Strategic interaction issues are relevant elsewhere in the transport sector. Ex ante appraisals of airline and bus deregulation - in contrast to the ex post evaluations of Morrison and Winston (1987) and White (1990) respectively - would have needed to anticipate the response of newly-deregulated and entrant firms, a very difficult task. In Britain appraisal of major new rail infrastructure investment has been considerably complicated by the form of railway privatisation adopted. Rail infrastructure has been separated from operations and has become the responsibility of a new organisation called Railtrack. The Government plans to float Railtrack on the stock market in 1996.

Railtrack will provide access to rail operators at commercial rates, and will therefore have to ensure that investment in new infrastructure generates a commercial rate of return (though there may be some government assistance where the investment yields social benefits, such as reduction in road traffic congestion, not captured in railway operator revenue). The main railway operators will be operators of passenger services franchised for specified periods of time (perhaps as little as seven years, but this has not been settled). Moreover, any particular section of route to be improved may have a number of train operators, each with different time horizons. It is clear that investment appraisal must take account of reactions of the different train operators, especially because the benefits of infrastructure investment involving high-speed improvements will depend on decisions which operators make about rolling stock investment. These complications have already delayed the franchising of the route where major infrastructure renewal is urgently needed, the West Coast Main Line.

Conclusions

This paper has reviewed methods of economic appraisal of projects and policies in the transport sector. In particular we have been concerned to show the theoretical foundations of social cost-benefit analysis. These theoretical foundations provide an external frame of reference to which disputes, for example about which benefits and costs should be included in evaluation and which involve double-counting, can be referred. This is important because there is often a danger with public sector evaluation that project benefits might be overstated, or costs understated, in order to secure approval of projects whose primary aim is to achieve political objectives, such as re-election, or to satisfy bureaucratic objectives, such as the construction of particular types of project which are favoured personally by the bureaucratic decision-makers. If the private sector makes mistakes, which it often does, the consequences of these mistakes are at least reflected in profits. However such constraints are not present for public-sector decision-makers, whether they be politicians or officials, so that temptations to overstate net benefits of public schemes and engage in 'appraisal optimism' are greater than they are in the private sector. At least cost-benefit theory provides some frame of reference, though it must be doubted whether its influence is nearly so strong as is the threat of direct loss for the consequences of incorrect decisions.

Although cost-benefit analysis has an important role in appraising individual projects, it also has a strategic role in checking on the overall validity of spending plans. Thus if projects of a particular type or in particular sectors appear to be producing low rates of return, then this would suggest a change be made in the direction of the public spending strategy. Hence there is an important feedback from the appraisal of individual projects to the allocation of investment funds between different types of transport projects, or between transport projects and projects in other sectors of the economy. In order for this feedback to be effective it is necessary that the performance of projects be monitored in order to discover whether expected costs and benefits are actually realised in practice. If they are not, then this in turn needs to influence future decision-making.

In practice, for many types of scheme there will be problems because not all of the identified consequences of the project will be quantified in monetary terms. These remaining items must not be left out of the appraisal, but should be listed or described in such a way that they are brought to the attention of the decision maker. It may be that this will be done through some formal type of multi-criteria analysis, or a less formal method may be used. The conflicting dangers are either that factors not valued in monetary terms will simply be ignored, or that they will be allowed to influence decisions in a way that bears no consistency from project to project.

Finally we return to distributional issues. The paper showed how equity considerations could be built into project appraisal in a formal way, but in practice such a detailed evaluation of the costs and benefits to individual groups will be difficult to achieve. Probably what is most important is that decision-makers do not forget that projects and policies will have distributional consequences, and that serious adverse distributional consequences should not be overlooked when final decisions are taken.

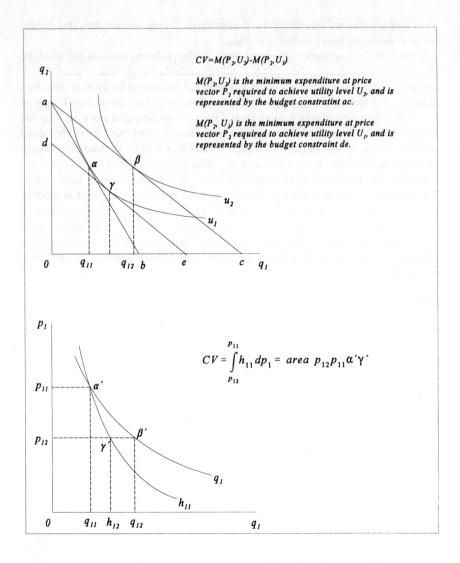

Figure 6.1   Compensating variation (CV) benefits of a price fall

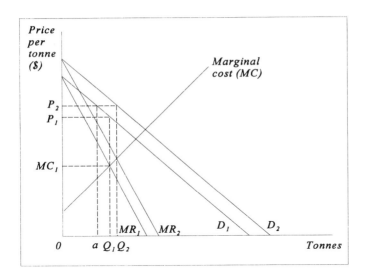

Figure 6.2   The shadow price of concrete

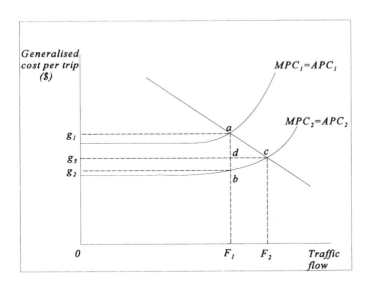

Figure 6.3   The impacts of generated traffic on highway investment benefits

227

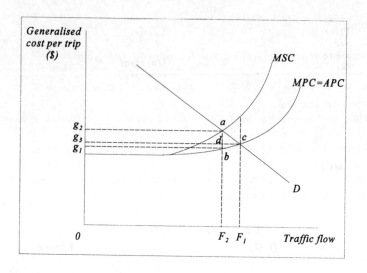

Figure 6.4   The benefits and cost of road congestion pricing

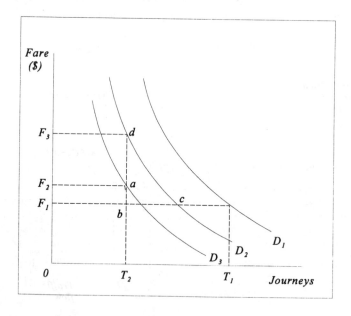

Figure 6.5   Welfare impact of bus deregulation

228

References

Advisory Committee on Trunk Road Assessment (1978) *Report of the Advisory Committee on Trunk Road Assessment* (the Leitch Report) HMSO, London

Arnott, R, and Small, K (1994) 'The economics of traffic congestion' *American Scientist* 82, 446-455

Aschauer, D A (1989) 'Is public expenditure productive?' *Journal of Monetary Economics* 23, 177-200

Atkinson, A B (1970) 'On the measurement of inequality' *Journal of Economic Theory* 2, 244-263

Birdsall, N, and Steer, A (1993) 'El calentamiento de la atmosfera: actuemos ya, pero sin falsear las cifras' *Finanzas y Desarrollo* 30(1), 6-8

Boadway, R W (1974) 'The welfare foundations of cost-benefit analysis' *Economic Journal* 84, 926-939

Boadway, R W (1975) 'Cost-benefit rules in general equilibrium' *Review of Economic Studies* 42, 361-374

Boadway, R W, and Bruce, N (1984) *Welfare Economics* Basil Blackwell, Oxford

Button, K J, Leitham, S, McQuaid, R W, and Nelson, J D (1995) 'Transport and industrial and commercial location' *Annals of Regional Science* 29, 189-206

Cline, W R (1992) *The Economics of Global Warming* Institute for International Economics, Washington DC

Cline, W R (1993) 'Demos una oportunidad a la atenuacion del efecto de invernadero' *Finanzas y Desarrollo* 30(1), 3-5

Dargay, J M, and Goodwin, P B (1995) 'Evaluation of consumer surplus with dynamic demand' *Journal of Transport Economics and Policy* 29, 179-193

Davis, O A, and Whinston, A B (1965) 'Welfare economics and the theory of second best' *Review of Economic Studies* 32, 1-14

Deaton, A, and Muellbauer, J (1980) *Economics and Consumer Behaviour* Cambridge University Press, Cambridge

de Jong, G C (1990) 'An indirect utility model of car ownership and private car use' *European Economic Review* 34, 971-985

Diewert, W E (1983) 'Cost-benefit analysis and project evaluation: a comparison of alternative approaches' *Journal of Public Economics* 22, 265-302

Dodgson, J S (1973) 'External effects and secondary benefits in road investment appraisal' *Journal of Transport Economics and Policy* 7, 169-185

Dodgson, J S (1974) 'Motorway investment, industrial transport costs, and sub-regional growth: a case study of the M62' *Regional Studies* 8, 75-91

Dodgson, J S (1977) 'Consumer surplus and compensation tests' *Public Finance* 32, 312-320

Dodgson, J S (1986) 'Benefits of urban public transport subsidies in the major Australian cities' *Economic Record* 62, 224-235

Evans, A W (1994) 'Evaluating public transport and road safety measures' *Accident Analysis and Prevention* 26, 411-428

Glaister, S (1994) 'Public transport: the allocation of urban public transport subsidy' in Layard, R, and Glaister, S (eds) *Cost-Benefit Analysis* Cambridge University Press, Cambridge

Hammond, P J (1970) 'Cost-benefit analysis as a planning procedure' in Currie, D A, and Peters, W (eds) *Contemporary Economic Analysis* Vol II Croom Helm, London

Hau, T D (1986) 'Distributional cost-benefit analysis in discrete choice' *Journal of Transport Economics and Policy* 20, 313-338

Hausman, J A (1981) 'Exact consumer's surplus and deadweight loss' *American Economic Review* 71, 662-676

Hensher, D A (1994) 'Stated preference analysis of travel choices: the state of practice *Transportation* 21, 107-133

Hicks, J R (1943) 'The four consumer's surpluses' *Review of Economic Studies* 11, 31-41

Jara-Diaz, S R (1986) 'On the relation between users' benefits and the economic effects of transportation activities' *Journal of Regional Science* 26, 379-391

Jones-Lee, M (1994) 'Safety and the saving of life: the economics of safety and physical risk' in Layard, R, and Glaister, S (eds) *Cost-Benefit Analysis* Cambridge University Press, Cambridge

Kay, J, Manning, A, Szymanski, S (1989) 'The economic benefits of the Channel Tunnel' *Economic Policy* 9, 212-234

Kennedy, D, Glaister, S, and Travers, T (1995) *London Bus Tendering* The Greater London Group at the London School of Economics, London

Labeaga, J M, and Angel Lopez (1994) 'Estimation of the welfare effects of indirect tax changes on Spanish households' *Investigaciones Economicas* 18(2)

Lipsey, R G, and Lancaster, K (1956) 'The general theory of second best' *Review of Economic Studies* 24, 11-32

Marin, A, and Psacharopoulos, G (1982) 'The reward for risk in the labor market: evidence from the United Kingdom and a reconciliation with other studies' *Journal of Political Economy* 90, 827-853

Mishan, E J (1971) 'Evaluation of life and limb: a theoretical approach' *Journal of Political Economy* 79, 687-705

Mogridge, M J H (1990) *Travel in Towns: Jam Yesterday, Jam Today and Jam Tomorrow?* Macmillan, Basingstoke

Morey, E (1984) 'Confuser surplus' *American Economic Review* 74, 163-173

Morrison, S, and Winston, C (1986) *The Economic Effects of Airline Deregulation* Brookings Institution, Washington DC

Morrison, S, and Winston, C (1987) 'Empirical implications and tests of the contestability hypothesis' *Journal of Law and Economics* 30, 53-66

MVA Consultancy, Institute for Transport Studies at Leeds University, Transport Studies Unit at Oxford University (1994) 'Time savings: research into the value of time' in Layard, R, and Glaister, S (eds) *Cost-Benefit Analysis* Cambridge University Press, Cambridge

Newbery, D M (1990) 'Pricing and congestion: economic principles relevant to pricing roads' *Oxford Review of Economic Policy* 6, 22-38

Newbery, D M (1995) 'The distributional impact of price changes in Britain and

Hungary' *Economic Journal* 105, 847-863

Nijkamp, P, and Rienstra, S A (1995) 'Private sector involvement in financing operating transport infrastructure' *Annals of Regional Science* 29, 221-235

Pearce, D W, and Nash, C A (1981) *The Social Appraisal of Projects* Macmillan, London

Pearce, D W, and Markandya, A (1989) *Environmental Policy Benefits: Monetary Valuation* OECD, Paris

Pouliquen, L (1970) *Risk Analysis in Project Appraisal* World Bank Staff Occasional Paper no 11, Washington DC

Samuelson, P (1942) 'Constancy of the marginal utility of income' in O Lange et al, eds, *Studies in Mathematical Economics and Econometrics in Memory of Henry Schultz* University of Chicago Press, Chicago

Schwab, R M (1985) 'The benefits of in-kind Government programs' *Journal of Public Economics* 27, 195-210

Small, K A, and Rosen, H S (1981) 'Applied welfare economics with discrete choice models' *Econometrica* 49, 105-130

Standing Advisory Committee on Trunk Road Assessment (SACTRA) (1992) *Assessing the Environmental Impact of Road Schemes* HMSO, London

Standing Advisory Committee on Trunk Road Assessment (SACTRA) (1994) *Trunk Roads and the Generation of Traffic* HMSO, London

Sugden, R, and Williams, A (1978) *The Principles of Practical Cost-Benefit Analysis* Oxford University Press, Oxford

Waters, W G II (1995) 'Values of travel time savings in road transport project evaluation: research review and directions'. Paper presented at the Seventh World Conference on Transport Research, Sydney

White, P R (1990) 'Bus deregulation: a welfare balance sheet' *Journal of Transport Economics and Policy* 24, 311-332

Williams, H C W L, and Moore, L A R (1990) 'The appraisal of highway investments under fixed and variable demand' *Journal of Transport Economics and Policy* 24, 61-81

Transport externalities: does monetary valuation make sense?

Chris Nash

Introduction

Transport was one of the first sectors in which the importance of externalities was recognised with respect to traffic congestion, and the proposed solution in the form of a congestion tax formulated. More recently attention has been paid to a range of other externalities arising from the activities of the transport sector, of which the most important are accidents and a wide range of environmental effects. At the same time, argument has arisen as to whether all of these factors should really be seen as external disbenefits from transport systems and whether they may be balanced by external benefits.

To the extent that such externalities do indeed exist, it is generally recommended that they should be taken into account both in pricing policy, generally through the medium of a Pigovian tax, and in project appraisal by means of quantification and valuation in a social cost-benefit analysis. Both of these recommendations clearly require that the externalities in question be valued in money terms. However, despite several decades of research, no unanimity exists on the methodologies to do this, or on the results such methodologies give. Doubts have consequently arisen in some quarters as to the practical value of this whole approach to the problem.

In this paper we shall seek first to give a brief account of the externalities arising from the transport system, also discussing the counter argument that many of these factors should not be considered as externalities at all. We then turn to the argument concerning positive externalities. We discuss both the principles and practice of the valuation of transport externalities, and the relevance of such valuations for practical policy issues. Finally we examine some recent attempts to value the external costs of transport systems, and seek to understand why the values differ so widely, before reaching our conclusions on whether monetary valuation makes sense. Where arguments affect different modes of transport differently, we shall concentrate on road transport, as this is widely recognised as the major cause of externalities in the transport sector (Mauch and Rothengatter, 1995).

Externalities arising from the transport sector

Externalities are commonly described as impacts on the utility, cost or production function of one economic agent by variables under the control of another economic agent and where the effect is not the subject of a market transaction. Whilst other definitions may exist, it is this definition that is useful in the analysis of cases of market failure, for it is only in these circumstances that intervention is needed to ensure that the cost or benefit in question is taken into account by relevant decision-takers.

Table 7.1
Principal environmental effects of transport systems

Resource	Effects
Land	Land take, property destruction, extraction of building materials, visual intrusion, waste disposal
Air	Local pollutants (C0, HC, NO_x, lead, particulates) Acid rain (NO_x, SO_x) Global warming ($CO2$)
Water	Pollution by run off; oil extraction and transportation
Other	Noise and vibration

Source: Adapted from OECD (1988)

It is often argued, following Coase (1960), that the prime - or indeed the only - cause of such effects is the inadequate definition and policing of property rights, since otherwise externalities would always be eliminated by market activity in the form of bargaining. However, as here defined, externalities are frequently also public goods (or bads); in other words they are both non-rival (that is to say that consumption by one economic agent does not prevent their simultaneous consumption by others) and non-excludable (it is not possible to prevent their consumption by others). Therefore even if property rights were adequately defined and enforced, market failure might still occur as a result of the free-rider problem. For instance, if it were possible for residents of a particular area to trade with motorists in order to reduce levels of noise or air pollution, each individual resident would have an incentive not to pay, in the hope of benefitting from the trading of others without having to pay themselves. In addition, bargaining has transaction costs and therefore may not occur even if it is in principle possible. Consider for instance the problem that has just been suggested. It is hard to see how a market could be established in which motorists and residents traded over the amount of noise and air pollution they emit and suffer whatever the legal position regarding property rights, given the number of people involved and the difficulties in identifying them. Therefore, externalities may remain as a cause of market failure even if property rights are adequately defined, and other measures therefore remain potentially desirable. At the same time, it must be borne in mind that government intervention is neither perfect nor costless, and that the risk exists of replacing market failure by government failure.

The most longstanding example of an externality in the transport sector to be found in the literature is that of congestion (Pigou, 1924). The entry of an additional vehicle on to the road system will, if traffic is already sufficiently dense to prevent free flow conditions, lead to a further reduction in speed for all traffic. Thus, as well as the delays suffered by the additional vehicle, all other vehicles on the road system will suffer delays. At the margin, the external congestion cost caused by one more vehicle is the additional delay to all other vehicles it causes. This must be distinguished from the average delay compared with free flow conditions, which may be a much greater number.

Remember that:

$$g = M + vT$$

where

> g = generalised cost per km
> M = money cost per km
> v = value of time
> T = journey time per km.

Assume that speed is a decreasing function of flow, or:

$$S = S(F)$$

where

> S = speed
> F = flow.

Thus generalised cost per kilometre may be written:

$$g = m + \frac{v}{S(F)}$$

Total user cost per kilometre is given by generalised cost times flow:

$$TC = g.F = M.F + \frac{v.F}{S(F)}$$

Differentiating this to obtain the marginal social cost gives:

$$\frac{\delta TC}{\delta F} = M + \frac{S(F).v - v.F.S'(F)}{[S(F)]^2}$$

$$= M + \frac{v}{S(F)} - \frac{v.F.S'(F)}{[S(F)]^2}$$

The externality per kilometre is therefore the difference between the generalised cost paid by the users and the marginal social cost they impose, namely:

$$\frac{v}{S(F)} \cdot |e_{SF}|$$

where e_{SF} is the elasticity of speed with respect to flow.

Some controversy has arisen over whether congestion should in fact be regarded as an externality, since it is experienced by the same group of people as cause it - namely road users. On an everyday definition of an externality as an effect by one sector of the economy on another, it would not be an externality. It is hoped that the above explanation makes clear why, in terms of the definition which is relevant to examining issues of market failure, congestion is clearly an externality. It should be noted, however, that it is not the total cost of congestion that is an externality, but rather the difference between the marginal and the average cost. Again, this point is not often understood in public debate on this issue.

In its simplistic form, then, the argument that congestion is not an externality fails to stand up. However, there is a more sophisticated argument which has a greater degree of relevance. This is that motoring is to be seen as a club good, where the participants finance the infrastructure by means of user charges. If these charges are set at an appropriate level and are used to provide an appropriate amount of additional capacity as traffic expands, then there is in fact no externality in the form of additional congestion; each additional motorist has paid for the infrastructure to be provided to prevent this from happening. For in this situation, price will be equal to long run marginal social cost, and at optimal capacity long run and short run marginal cost will be equal. Such an outcome could be produced by the market mechanism if road space were produced in a competitive market; given the strong natural monopoly element in transport infrastructure in practice it would appear that such a solution would undoubtedly require government regulation, at least of the charges for the use of roads.

But even so, is this a reasonable portrayal of reality? In practice, it is not currently the case that roads are charged for at the point of use, except for a minority of toll roads. There is a big gap between payment of motoring taxes and the provision of additional infrastructure. By no means all the receipts of motoring taxes are used to provide additional infrastructure; nor, given the external costs of road building is it necessarily desirable that they should be. Even if they were, this would not prevent congestion worsening in some locations (especially in urban areas) where provision of additional road space is particularly expensive and there is no guarantee that 'on the average' congestion is not worsening. There are many parts of the network where it may be considered unacceptable - whether for justifiable environmental reasons or for political expediency - to expand the capacity of the road system. Although this may be offset by the effect of other policy measures, such as parking restrictions or traffic restraint, these measures also have their costs. There seems no reason in practice to suppose that the external costs of road congestion are in fact exactly balanced by charges levied to fund new roads, or that in any feasible state of the world they could be.

Thus in most circumstances it will be appropriate to regard the additional congestion caused by extra traffic as a true externality. It must be remembered that by the same token, however, any excess of tax paid over the out of pocket costs of maintaining and operating the road system must be regarded as a surplus which already goes at least part way towards offsetting these external costs. It is not correct simultaneously to regard these charges as covering the capital cost of providing the road system and to add marginal congestion costs to them to obtain marginal social cost.

A second major externality takes the form of accident costs. But here again the identification of the externality involved requires care. When a driver is involved in an accident, part of the cost is borne by the driver him or herself. This may be directly in terms of pain or suffering, as well as financially in terms of damage, loss of income or in terms of what they pay in insurance premiums. These costs are not necessarily externalities; they may simply be part of the user cost of road transport, although it may be doubted whether users are always fully informed about the risks they run, suggesting a possible alternative form of market failure in terms of imperfect knowledge. For a vehicle to be deemed to be imposing an externality in this case requires the simultaneous presence of two conditions. The first is that the accident should not have taken place or should have been less serious in the absence of the vehicle in question, and the second that some of the costs should have been borne by individuals other than the driver of the vehicle in question. It follows that by no means all the costs of accidents may be regarded as external costs.

In fact current Department of Transport practice in Britain assumes that marginal changes in traffic levels do not alter the accident rate per mile for motorised vehicles. On this assumption the only external cost of an accident involving only motorised vehicles is that part of the cost that is not borne by the user (i.e. medical, policing or damage costs borne by third parties), and this is estimated to be approximately 7%. On the other hand, it is assumed that accidents involving a motor vehicle and a pedestrian or cyclist would not have happened in the absence of the motor vehicle, and that therefore all the costs imposed on the pedestrian or cyclist are to be regarded as external. In aggregate, this leads to the conclusion that 39% of the costs of urban road accidents are externalities.

These assumptions as to the external costs of accidents may be seen as something of a lower bound. It seems reasonable to assume in practice that an increase in traffic flows adds to the number of conflicting movements, and that the chance of one vehicle being involved in an accident is indeed raised by the presence of additional vehicles on the road. An alternative extreme assumption would be that as traffic increases, the number of conflicting movements increases in proportion, so the accident rate for each vehicle might be expected to rise in proportion to the increase in traffic (Newbury, 1988). On this argument the number of accidents in total would rise with the square of the traffic level, and there would be an externality involved at least equal to the total cost of accidents. Having surveyed the (in his opinion) inadequate evidence, Newbury concludes that the truth is somewhere in between the two; that whilst as traffic rises, motorists might be expected to offset some of the increased risk by driving more carefully (itself presumably involving costs in terms of effort and lower speeds), it is unlikely that they would totally offset the increased risk. Nevertheless even on the Department of Transport assumptions accident costs turn out to be a very substantial element in the external costs of road transport in Great Britain.

More recently most attention has shifted to environmental effects as externalities. Here there are a wide variety of effects, as listed in Table 7.1. Transport is a very significant source of most of these pollutants. For instance, in Great Britain over a million people are exposed to road noise in excess of 70 dB(A), and around 15 million in excess of 60 dB(A). In Western Europe as a whole, transport accounts for 61% of emissions of nitrogen oxides, 49% of volatile organic compounds and 26% of carbon dioxide (Mauch and Rothengatter, 1995).

The impact of these externalities varies from purely local, in the form of land take, property destruction, noise and local air pollution, to regional in the case of acid rain and its impact on wildlife, forests and buildings and to global in the case of greenhouse gases. Whilst some, such as certain local air pollutants, may be expected to reduce over the coming few years as the use of catalytic convertors - now compulsory for all new cars within the European Union - grows, others such as emissions of particulates and greenhouse gases, continue to worsen.

Whilst land take, property destruction and the extraction of building materials may be seen as not being external costs, since they are generally the subject of market transactions, the transactions in question are frequently not entered into voluntarily as market transactions but rather as a result of compulsory purchase orders, and they frequently have an effect on third parties through changing the amenity level of the environment in which they live and work, or indeed through more drastic implications such as the elimination of jobs. Thus there may well be externalities associated with these effects. In all other cases, the effect concerned is quite clearly an externality.

It is worth commenting also that these effects may have a variety of impacts. For instance, local air pollution may be a direct disamenity (i.e. perceived as unpleasant), and it may have indirect effects (e.g. damage to property or damage to health). In the latter case the indirect effect may be perceived without the recipient knowing the cause of it, a matter of some importance when it comes to valuation procedures.

Thus it is clear that the transport sector is the producer of many external effects which are the cause of serious concern. In the next section we consider briefly whether there are offsetting external benefits to consider when seeking to correct for these external costs.

Does the transport sector create positive externalities?

Recently the argument has emerged that, whilst the transport sector may create negative externalities, there are also strong positive externalities which offset these (e.g. Willeke, 1992). It is clear that improved transport facilities have permitted the development of patterns of production and distribution that in turn lead to provision of a wider range of goods at lower prices. Thus transport improvements may well have positive impacts on third parties other than the producers and consumers of the transport facilities in question. However, as Rothengatter (1993) argues, these effects do not satisfy the other condition to be regarded as an externality - namely of not having been processed through the market. The demand curve for transport as an intermediate good reflects the final demand for its products and provided that the market is competitive there can be no net benefit from reducing the price of transport below its marginal social cost in order to provide those final goods more cheaply. In this case, the externality is what is known as a pecuniary externality, and these externalities have long been recognised as irrelevant from the point of view of intervention to improve economic efficiency (Scitovsky, 1969). Given market imperfections such as regional unemployment there may in principle be a case for subsidising transport in particular circumstances, but such a case cannot be established by comparing the social benefits of cheaper transport with its external costs; the comparison must be of external benefits with external costs or of social benefits with social costs.

Principles of valuation of transport externalities

The reason why externalities interfere with the efficient working of the economy is that those taking the decisions leading to their creation have no incentive to take them into account. Therefore, the most obvious way of achieving economic efficiency is to ensure that a price be charged which represents the compensation required by those adversely affected by negative externalities (or a payment be made representing the willingness to pay of those benefitting from positive externalities). Implementing such a pricing structure costs money, however, particularly in terms of the degree of monitoring required to establish the scale of the externality each agent is creating and - to the extent that those affected by it may not be in possession of perfect information or act rationally - it may not be the most effective solution in any particular situation. A cost-benefit analysis is required to consider whether pricing, or some other form of intervention, is the most efficient approach and whether it is worth the costs. Nevertheless, the principles and the need for valuing externalities remain unchanged. If the aim is to establish whether a particular measure will be economically efficient, then the approach should be to try to measure the compensation required for tolerating negative externalities and the willingness to pay for positive ones.

This is far from easy to establish, however. Firstly, as stated above most externalities are public goods, and suffer from the usual difficulties in achieving unbiased preference revelation. Secondly, some external effects (global warming for example) stretch well into the future, and it is difficult to forecast the circumstances in which they will be experienced and the preferences of those affected by them. Valuation of such effects also runs straight into the continuing debate about social discount rates; many studies find such externalities to be insignificant because they are discounted at relatively high opportunity cost based discount rates. Others argue that placing a very low value on such future effects on these grounds is unjustified when there is no good reason to suppose that the resources saved by ignoring them will be ploughed into other investments which will in fact compensate future generations for the damage caused. Thirdly many external effects are poorly understood both by the population at large and even by specialists in the fields in question. For this reason, environmentalists frequently invoke the 'precautionary principle' whereby emissions suspected of being dangerous are more strictly controlled than would be justified on the basis of hard evidence of their harmful effects. Fourthly, but by no means least, many would argue that environmental problems should not be seen solely in terms of barriers to economic efficiency, but as ethical issues concerning the survival of species, and ultimately of the planet as we know it. In approaching such issues, people may not regard them as goods which can be traded off against money.

These problems point to an alternative approach to handling the externalities of transport systems which may be preferable in many cases (Bowers, 1991). This consists of determining standards in terms of emissions levels or other externalities which must not be exceeded. The standards based approach is particularly helpful in dealing with the problems of international negotiations on global pollutants, where an approach based on willingness to pay measures may be seen as exceptionally unfair in that it gives little weight to the preferences of the poor countries of the world. Of course the standards must rest on views on the benefits of restricting the level of the externality relative to the cost of so doing. But standards tend to rest more firmly on the views of experts in the field rather than willingness to pay or willingness to accept

239

compensation. Once a standard has been established, it may be translated into a money value by means of an opportunity cost argument. This relies on the fact that if the emission in question is allowed to increase from one source then it must be reduced from another. The cost of achieving a reduction in the level of the emission from the most cost-effective alternative source then becomes the cost of additional emissions.

Thus we have two broad principles on which the valuation of externalities may be based, either of which may be deemed appropriate in any particular context. There is nothing wrong in principle with mixing the two forms of valuation in a single study. It may be that for some externalities, where the effect is readily perceived and immediate (noise for instance) a direct willingness to accept compensation type of measure is seen as appropriate, whilst for others with long term and little understood effects (such as global warming, for instance) the opportunity cost argument is deemed appropriate. What is not acceptable is to adopt whichever approach is most convenient in terms of availability of data, unless it is believed that the economy is already at an optimum in terms of levels of externalities, when the two approaches should yield equivalent results.

Valuation of transport externalities in practice

The previous discussion of principles of valuation will be irrelevant if it is not possible to devise ways of implementing them with a reasonable degree of reliability in practice. A comprehensive review is contained in Nash and Bowers (1988). It is possible to divide the methods used to value externalities broadly into three groups:

Revealed preference methods

These methods rely on finding a market in which members of the population reveal the value (in terms of willingness to pay for or to accept compensation for) they attach to the attribute in question. For instance in the case of time savings, a long established approach is to apply discrete choice modelling techniques to circumstances in which people have a choice which involves a trade-off between time and money costs of travel (most commonly mode choice decisions). Slightly more heroically, the same approach has been applied to decisions involving safety (for instance by modelling whether people choose to use a seat belt or not). The heroism here is in the assumption that people are fully aware of the consequences of their choice and decide rationally. This may be a reasonable assumption in the case of the choice of mode of transport for a regular journey to work, although many would dispute even this; that people are well informed on the quantitative risks involved in not wearing a seat belt is less plausible.

Turning to environmental issues, there are two long standing revealed preference approaches in use: hedonic pricing and the Clawson approach. Hedonic pricing is most often used in the context of house price models, although it is also used for instance in the estimation of the value placed on accidents via wage rate studies. The approach is to estimate the relationship between house prices and the environmental characteristics of houses, controlling for other factors such as the physical characteristics of the house and its accessibility (for results of some such studies see Table 7.2). The estimated hedonic price for environmental characteristics, such as the level of noise and air pollution, is often taken as some sort of mean valuation of the characteristics in question, although it is possible to apply a two stage procedure which goes on to estimate the relationship between this value and characteristics of the population such as age and income (see Rosen, 1974).

The house price approach has been subject to many criticisms. For instance, as usually applied, it assumes a perfect market in which buyers with perfect knowledge can obtain any combination of characteristics they wish. In that situation, the implicit price of each characteristic would represent the value placed on it by all who trade in that characteristic. At best it can obviously only be used to value attributes experienced in the home, and where people correctly perceive the effect on themselves. Thus it is likely to be more appropriate as a way of valuing noise nuisance than of valuing the health impacts of air pollution. A further problem is that it effectively represents some sort of present value of a stream of future benefits, discounted at an unknown discount rate which may differ from that used in project appraisals.

Table 7.2
Results of US house price models

% reduction in house prices from:

1 unit increase in Leq measure of noise nuisance	0.08 - 0.88
1% increase in sulphur deposition	0.06 - 0.12
1% increase in particulates	0.05 - 0.14

Source: Pearce and Markyanda (1989)

The Clawson, or travel cost, approach by contrast is only applicable for valuing the benefits of visiting facilities (e.g. country parks, nature reserves, forests, beaches). It relies on estimating a demand curve relating the frequency of visit to the travel cost involved (see example in Table 7.3). Again there are many practical problems involved, of which the frequent occurrence of multi-purpose trips with no easy way of determining the degree to which the cost is incurred on behalf of any one purpose may be the most prevalent. Again it is a very partial technique; at best it can only measure the benefit from visiting a site rather than the benefit the site may hold in terms of scientific research, in terms of forming the subject of books and films or simply because people are willing to pay to preserve it.

In general then it appears that revealed preference methods are likely to be of value only in measuring amenity values of benefits readily perceived and understood and experienced in a limited number of locations; even there many problems exist. Use of the revealed preference approach might fit well with a policy in which the more complex environmental effects are valued on the opportunity cost approach in accordance with environmental standards.

Table 7.3
Example of the travel cost approach
Everett's study of visitors to Dalby Forest (N. York Moors)

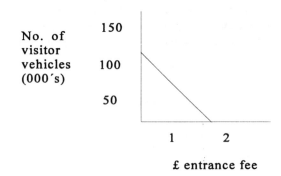

TOTAL WILLINGNESS TO PAY = £103,116 p.a.

(+ £10,700 actual revenue)
1976 prices

Source: Everett (1979)

242

An alternative to finding markets in which people reveal their valuations by the choices they make is to use surveys to ask them about hypothetical decisions. We shall refer to such hypothetical methods as stated preference methods.

In recent years, stated preference methods have taken over from revealed preference as the dominant method used in overcoming valuation problems in cost-benefit analysis. In some contexts, such as the value of time savings, the reason is simply one of cost-effectiveness. By asking a respondent to choose between a number of hypothetical alternative pairs of options (often 12-16), estimates may be obtained of the relative value they attach to different attributes of the options with much smaller and therefore cheaper samples than if revealed preference data were used, since in a revealed preference survey only one response is obtained per respondent. An example of a single stated preference question is given in Table 7.4. Moreover the values in the questions may be framed to yield the maximum information, and problems such as multicollinearity may be avoided. A second reason for preferring stated preference methods is that uncertainty about perceptions may be reduced by the provision of information; for instance the journey times and costs of the alternative modes (MVA et al., 1987).

Table 7.4
Example of a stated preference question

OPTION A

LONDON, dep	250	320	350	420	450
Stockport...	510	540	610	640	710
Manchester, arr.	520	550	620	650	720

Fares: One way £12, Return £24
Scheduled Journey Time; 2 hrs 30 mins

OPTION B

LONDON, dep	250	●	350	●	450
Stockport...	540	●	640	●	740
Manchester, arr.	550	●	650	●	750

Fares: One way £10, Return £20
Scheduled Journey Time: 3 hrs
Up to 30 mins late

In this situation I would:

Definitely Prefer A   [   ]
Probably Prefer A   [   ]
Like A & B Equally   [   ]
Probably Prefer B   [   ]
Definitely Prefer B   [   ]

Source: Fowkes and Nash (1991)

Similar stated preference exercises have now become used for valuing the 'human' costs of accidents. As discussed above, accident costs take a number of different forms. Some - damage to property, loss of output, medical expenses - are clearly 'economic' costs, readily valued in money terms. But over and above that there is clearly a desire to avoid the pain and suffering associated with injury or death in an accident that would still exist even if there were no 'economic' loss. Whilst there are circumstances in which this can be valued using revealed preference data, there is always a concern about the respondent's perception of the risks they are running. Thus again stated preference methods have become used in this context (Jones-Lee, 1987). Whilst there may remain concerns about respondents abilities to answer questions involving changes in very small probabilities of death or injury in an accidents, such studies do appear to produce consistent results and to have led to a big increase in the values used in practice in Britain (Table 7.5).

However, stated preference methods also exist in a number of different forms. The one which has become most popular in the environmental field is the contingent valuation method. This actually asks a straight 'willingness to pay' to achieve or avoid some particular result, such as to protect a forest from destruction or to prevent building of a power station in a particular location.(see the example in Table 7.6). The attraction of this approach is that in principle it can be used to value anything, whether it can readily be quantified or not, whether it has actually been experienced or not. It can estimate not just use values, but option (the value people place on having a resource available in case they want to use it), existence (the value people attach to the existence of a resource even though they never expect to use it) and bequest (the value people attach to being able to make a resource available to future generations) values as well. With the aid of this technique it would appear possible to quantify all the externalities involved in the transport sector.

Table 7.5

DOT values - average cost per casualty in Great Britain by severity

(1985 prices)

	Pre-revision	Post 1987 revision	Post 1988 revision
Fatal	180330	252500	*500000
Serious	8280	13500	13500
Slight	200	280	280

* 1987 prices

Source: Department of Transport

But again there are a number of problems. There has been concern ever since the approach was first formulated with the likely biases that may creep in (Mitchell and Carson, 1989). The most important of these may be listed as:

1 Information bias. By providing incomplete or partial information, a biased result may be obtained (whether accidentally or by design).
2 Strategic bias. We are usually using these techniques to value public goods, and there is a large literature on the incentive people will have to distort their valuations of public goods according to the payment mechanisms they expect to be used.
3 Instrument bias. People are usually asked their willingness to pay in terms of some particular tax or charge, and their views on whether that particular payment mechanism is fair or not may distort their answer.
4 Starting point bias. If people are simply asked, unprompted, what is the most they would be willing to pay for a particular benefit, they find it very difficult to answer. Therefore the interview usually proceeds in the form of a 'bidding game', in which a figure (e.g. £1 per week) is named and then is increased or decreased according to whether the respondent is willing to pay it or not. Starting point bias occurs if the first named figure influences the final outcome.

245

Table 7.6
Example of a contingent valuation question

A firm proposes to undertake a major tourist development in your neighbourhood (details are attached). Without the revenue from this development, your local tax bill will have to increase.

What is the maximum increase in taxes you would be willing to pay to avoid the necessity for this development to go ahead?

Source: Adapted from Mitchell and Carson (1989)

There is conflicting evidence on the seriousness of all these problems, and in part this reflects the fact that they are likely to be much more serious in a badly designed survey than in a well designed one. But it is also the case that despite the apparent universality of the technique some issues are easier to deal with than others. For instance it is likely to be easier to tackle the preservation of a feature which is well known but about which feelings do not run strong, than either a very controversial issue or one which is complicated and poorly understood. It is also the case that strategic bias is likely to be less severe if the study is seen as a hypothetical academic study rather than part of the appraisal for an actual decision. This means it is easier to research values which may be measured in one location and applied in another than to obtain values for unique assets, such as a particular nature reserve, park or view, which are known to be under threat.

Alternative or opportunity cost approach

This approach is quite different from both stated and revealed preference approaches in that it does not attempt to estimate willingness to pay for the benefit or to avoid the cost. Rather it asks what expenditure would be needed to offset it. In general the problem with this approach is that if we do not know the value placed by the population on the effect in question then we do not know whether in fact it is worth offsetting it. In some circumstances we may be clear that it is worthwhile offsetting it (for instance, where air pollution damages a building and it is cheaper to repair it than to replace it, or where it destroys crops and we know their market value is at least as great as the cost of replacing them).

As explained in the previous section, a version of this approach which may more appropriately be termed the opportunity cost approach has become much more common in recent years as a result of two developments. The first is a tendency in the face of uncertainty about the true damage costs caused by different pollutants to adopt a precautionary principle of limiting the level of the pollutant to what is considered a safe level. In this situation, any project which pushes pollution above the limit must be balanced by another (shadow) project to offset this effect. For instance if we are already at the limit and greenhouse gas emissions in transport are to be allowed to rise, then emissions must be reduced elsewhere. In this context, the cost of reducing greenhouse gas emissions elsewhere by one unit becomes the opportunity cost of allowing them to rise in transport. Quantification of this opportunity cost is also not without its problems; strictly it requires examination of all possible ways of reducing greenhouse gas emissions elsewhere in the economy in order to identify the one with the least cost.

In principle, then, methods exist which may be used for valuing all the external costs of road schemes, but all have their problems and the reliability of all is open to doubt. In order to consider whether monetary valuation of externalities is useful in practice, it may be useful now to examine and compare the results of a few of the many studies that have been conducted on this topic.

Some practical examples of valuation studies

One of the biggest problems facing work in this area is the fact that different studies tend to come up with totally different results for the external costs of transport. Having discussed the principles, it may be of interest to examine some actual examples of attempts to quantify the external costs of transport to try to understand why these differences occur.

Table 7.7 shows two recent estimates of the accident and environmental costs of transport in the UK. It will be seen that Mauch and Rothengatter's estimates are consistently much higher than those of Pearce, with the biggest difference being in the category of air pollution/climate change. Table 7.8 presents another comparison, this time between estimates of external costs of car transport produced by Peirson, Skinner and Vickerman and by Mauch and Rothengatter. The range given by Peirson et al varies between urban and inter-urban, so one would expect the mean (as estimated by Mauch and Rothengatter) to lie between the two. But only for noise is that true. Elsewhere, the estimate of Rothengatter is higher, and in the case of climate change an order of magnitude higher. Why is this?

Table 7.7
UK external costs of transport 1991 (£b)

	Pearce	Mauch and Rothengatter
Accidents	4.7 to 7.5	13.3
Noise	0.6	3.4
Air Pollution } Climate Change	2.8	10.3
Total	**8.1 to 10.9**	**27.0**

Note: Mauch and Rothengatter's results have been converted from ECUs to pounds using an exchange rate of 1.4284 (Source: *Economic Trends Annual Supplement*, 1994 Edition. HMSO London. Table 5-1).

Source: Pearce (1993); Mauch and Rothengatter (1995)

A detailed examination of the differences makes it clear that there are differences not just of detailed methods but also of principle in the way the costs are assessed. In the case of climate change, both Pearce and Peirson et al rely on studies which have attempted to predict the cost of climate change over the next 200-300 years and thus work out the marginal external cost of the emissions which cause it. Generally these costs are found to be relatively small when discounted (even at low rates of discount) and expressed per unit of emissions. According to their methodology, it is only worth incurring a very small increase in costs or loss of benefit from reduced travel to offset the effects of climate change. In other words, according to the results of Pearce and Peirson et al, climate change should be a very minor consideration in transport policy (although the latter devote considerable attention to the question of whether there are reasons not encompassed in their estimates for taking this effect much more seriously).

Table 7.8
UK unit external cost 1991
(car) (p/pass km)

	Peirson, Skinner and Vickerman	Mauch and Rothengatter
Accidents	0.58 - 1.33	1.84
Noise	0.08 - 0.39	0.28
Air Pollution	0.17 - 0.43	0.70
Climate Change	0.03	0.46
Total	**0.86 - 2.18**	**3.28**

Note: Mauch and Rothengatter's results have been converted from ECUs to pounds using an exchange rate of 1.4284 (Source: *Economic Trends Annual Supplement*, 1994 Edition. HMSO London. Table 5-1).

Source: Peirson, Skinner and Vickerman (1994); Mauch and Rothengatter (1995)

Mauch and Rothengatter adopt a totally different approach. They do not attempt to cost climate change. Rather they take the view that, in the light of the uncertainties involved, the precautionary principle should rule and targets for the reduction of greenhouse gases should be achieved. They select the fairly stringent target of a reduction in greenhouse gas emissions for Western Europe of 50% by the year 2040, this target being met 50% by an equiproportionate reduction and 50% by a move towards an equal emissions allowance per capita. In this case the costs of additional transport emissions of greenhouse gases, in terms of the need to offset these by reductions in greenhouse gas emissions elsewhere in the economy, are very much greater than the direct damage cost estimates used by Pearce and by Peirson et al.

Thus whilst there may be problems resulting from different studies giving different results which derive from inadequacies in valuation methodology, the differences in this case derive from a far more fundamental source. The basic issue is whether it is appropriate to seek to value directly effects which may be poorly understood and remote in time, or to derive values which result from an environmental policy which put forward standards in the form of constraints within which conventional economic analysis may proceed. The notion of sustainability as most commonly defined (i.e. seeking to meet the needs of the current generation without compromising the ability of future generations to meet their needs) might be taken, in the face of uncertainty, as lending support to the second view.

Relevance of values for practical policy decisions

In practice, there are two main ways in which valuations of externalities might be used. These are in transport pricing policy and in cost-benefit analysis of transport investments or other transport projects (such as regulatory measures).

In an ideal world, vehicles would be charged in accordance with the externalities they created. This would require a pricing structure in which a price per kilometre was charged which varied with:

1 the characteristics of the vehicle, which determine the noise, emissions, delay to other vehicles and accident risk involved. Strictly these obviously depend not just on the characteristics of the vehicle when new, but also on its condition and the way it is driven; accurate measurement would therefore require continuous monitoring of every vehicle on the road.

2 the characteristics of the road it is being driven on, including physical features (width, gradient, curvature) of the road itself and the surrounding land use (housing, countryside etc). These again influence both the congestion effects and the environmental impact.

3 the time at which it is being driven (which is important in terms of the degree to which noise is a nuisance) and the traffic conditions on the road at that time.

Such a pricing structure, in which the price per kilometre is adjusted in accordance with continuous monitoring of the location and condition of the vehicle and the road conditions in which it is being driven is currently still in the world of science fiction, although the road pricing proposals recently considered in Cambridge, in which the charge would depend on traffic speeds, would if implemented represent a significant move towards fulfilling it for a particular city. Even if it were technically feasible, one would still need to consider whether it was worth the cost of implementation, and whether people would actually adjust more effectively to a simpler more understandable tariff than one where one would not know the price one was going to be charged for a journey at the time of setting out on it.

What most countries have at the moment is a very different structure consisting of a fuel tax, which may vary with the type of fuel (diesel, leaded/unleaded petrol) and an annual fee which varies with the type of vehicle. Additional tolls may be charged on motorways (where one might expect that typically external costs would be less than on other types of road). This offers some possibility for influencing both the type of vehicle people buy and the extent to which it is used, but can only charge for external costs on the average in each case. The case remains then for using a variety of other means to influence the way in which vehicles are used in specific circumstances. These means might include pricing measures (e.g. electronic road pricing in particular areas) and physical measures (bans on particular types of vehicles, parking controls, traffic management). There is no prospect in the foreseeable future of being able to handle transport externalities solely through pricing measures even if that were clearly seen as the most efficient approach. Nevertheless, having information on the value attached to the externality in question is an essential element in the appraisal of any measure to overcome the problem of transport externalities.

Suppose that it is accepted that, even with the existing pricing instruments at the disposal of governments, the combined sum of fuel taxes and annual licence duty should at least equal the sum of relevant marginal costs incurred by the road authorities and marginal external costs for each individual vehicle type. There is generally no agreement even on the direction of movement of individual prices required. The British government for many years argued that, by ensuring that taxes for each vehicle type cover the road provision costs allocated to that type, with a margin ranging from some 30% for the heaviest goods vehicles to 100% for cars and light vans, it is ensuring that no vehicles are undercharged, whilst some are making contribution to tax revenue considerably in excess of the relevant costs.

However, the methodology used in this comparison is simply to take the total capital and current expenditure on roads and to allocate it between vehicles on a 'fair' basis. The inclusion of capital costs suggests that if this procedure has any economic significance, it must be as some form of long run costing. However, simply allocating the capital expenditure of the year in question, rather than making some estimate of depreciation and interest on capital, is an unusual and unjustified approach. The British government has now withdrawn this methodology and is in the process of examining alternatives. When Newbery (1988) explored alternative long and short run marginal cost pricing approaches using data from the mid-1980s, including accident externalities but not environmental costs, he concluded that all types of vehicle were being undercharged, the surplus on cars revealed by the Department of Transport approach being offset by allowing for their disproportionate use on congested urban roads (Table 7.9). Including of environmental costs would obviously add to this discrepancy. Similar debates about the methods used to allocate the costs of road provision and maintenance to vehicles are to be found in many other countries around Western Europe, with the road lobby arguing that motorists are already paying a surplus more than sufficient to cover any environmental costs.

Table 7.9
Relationship between road taxes and road costs by vehicle
class in Great Britain 1986

Vehicle Class	Road taxes	Road costs including accident	Ratio of tax: cost including accident
Motorcycles	65	748	0.09
Cars, light vans	8260*	10129	0.82
Buses and coaches	50 **	604	0.08
LGVs	65	609	0.11
HGVs	1320	1833	0.72
Total	9760	13973	0.70

* Includes car tax of £980 mn.
** Includes fuel tax rebate on stage services of £125 mn deducted
Source: Newbery (1988)

If the application of money values of externalities in pricing is not straightforward, what about the position regarding project appraisal? The current position in Britain is that environmental effects of road building are not explicitly valued in money terms, but are considered along with those items (construction and maintenance costs, operating cost savings, time savings and accidents) in a table of impacts based on that originally recommended by the report of the Advisory Committee on Trunk Road assessment back in 1978, and still often referred to, after the Chairman of that committee, as the 'Leitch framework'. Some idea of the range of effects taken into account in this approach is given in Table 7.10. This permits the full consideration of local environmental impacts (regional and global effects are not considered) of a particular road scheme when the individual decision is taken. But because the formal cost-benefit analysis is undertaken excluding valuation of environmental impacts, it does not contribute to more strategic decisions about road investment. Benefit cost ratios for individual schemes are quite misleading as a guide to the extent to which resources should be diverted from elsewhere in the economy into building roads, partly because of the omission of environmental costs but also because they are assessed as the rate of return on short stretches of new road and on the assumption that traffic growth is going to be allowed to continue at a substantial rate - i.e. they fail to look strategically at alternative policies for corridors or areas as a whole.

Table 7.10
Costs and benefits of road schemes
THE LEITCH FRAMEWORK

Incidence	Nature of effect	No of measures	Other
Road users	Accidents Comfort/convenience Operating costs Amenity	1 6 5 	3 2
Non-road users directly affected	Demolition disamenity (houses, shops, offices, factories, schools, churches, public open space) Land take, severance, disamenity to farmers		37 7
Those concerned	Landscape, scientific, historical value, land-use, other transport operators		9 (+ verbal description)
Financing authority	Costs and benefits in money terms	7	
TOTAL		19	59

Source: Leitch (1978)

Given the above discussion of the difficulties of environmental valuation, would the introduction of money values for environmental effects in investment appraisal be beneficial? In favour of such a move would be the fact that it would permit a more accurate assessment of the overall rate of return on road building to be assessed; that it would ensure that regional and global environmental externalities were taken into account as well as local, and that it would promote clarity and consistency at the level of decisions on individual schemes. Against it are the arguments that environmental valuation remains very uncertain, that as we have seen above there is no consensus even about the basic principles on which it should be based, and that it is usually incomplete. At the project appraisal level, valuation of local environmental effects is particularly problematic, in that it is dealing with the value to be placed on particular assets such as parks, buildings and the aesthetic amenity of the townscape or landscape.

If values for factors which are, in principle, readily measured such as noise and air pollution are to be used in pricing decisions - and arguably here there is no choice - then there seems no good reason not to use them in project appraisal as well. What is of more doubt is whether it makes sense to introduce values of unique local features into project appraisal. But it must always be remembered that if this is not done, then any benefit cost ratios quoted are incomplete and misleading.

Conclusion

The orthodox view of transport externalities is that they are a relatively simple case of market failure, to be resolved by valuing them in money terms and charging a tax which will lead decision takers to place appropriate weight on them when making transport decisions. In reality the position is much more complex than this. Firstly we have found that there is no consensus on the principles that should be used in environmental appraisal, and in particular on when it is appropriate to use willingness to pay type measures and when opportunity cost derived from environmental standards. Secondly we have found that even if there is agreement in principle existing methods of valuation are not adequate to reliably value all the relevant externalities. Thirdly we have found that it is not possible actually to devise pricing structures which fully reflect the way in which external costs vary across vehicles, times and places.

Does this add up to a conclusion that, in practice at least, monetary valuation of environmental externalities does not make sense? In the view of the current author, the answer is no. Both in pricing decisions and in the cost-benefit analysis of alternative projects and regulatory measures, a view has to be taken on how much it is worth paying to avoid particular external costs. Although existing methods are not capable of producing a definitive answer to the issue they do provide guidance. They should be used, but they should be used in the context of a full understanding of their limitations and of the controversies which remain, and in particular in the context of clear and explicit statements on the crucial issue of the degree to which environmental standards are seen as more appropriate than willingness to pay type studies as an approach to valuation.

References

Bowers, J K (1991). 'Pricing the Environment. A Conspectus and a Critique'. Working Paper G91/25, School of Business and Economic Studies, University of Leeds.

Coase, R H (1960). 'The Problem of Social Cost'. *Journal of Law and Economics*.

Everett, R D (1979). 'The Monetary Value of the Recreational Benefits of Wildlife'. *Journal of Environmental Management.*

Fowkes, A S and Nash C A (1991), Eds, *Analysing Demand for Rail Travel.* Avebury, Aldershot.

Jones-lee, M. (1987), 'The Value of Transport Safety', *Policy Journals*, Newbury, Berks.

Leitch, Sir George, Chairman (1978) *Report of the Advisory Committee on Trunk Road Appraisal* HMSO, London.

Mauch, S P and Rothengatter, W (1995) *External Effects of Transport.* Union International des Chemins der Fer, Paris.

Mitchell, R C and Carson, R T (1989). *Using Surveys to Value Public Goods. Resources for the Future,* Washington.

MVA consultants; Institute for Transport Studies, University of Leeds; Transport Studies Unit, University of Oxford (1987), 'The Value of Travel Time Savings'. *Policy Journals, Newbury*, Berks.

Nash, C and Bowers, J (1988). 'Alternative Approaches to the Valuation of Environmental Resources'. In Turner, R K, Ed. *Sustainable Environmental Management* Belhaven.

Newbery, D M (1988) ' Road User Charges in Britain.' *Economic Journal.*

OECD (1988). *Transport and the Environment.* OECD, Paris.

Pearce, D W and Markyanda (1989). *Environmental Policy Benefits* - Monetary Valuation. OECD, Paris.

Pearce, D (1993). *Blueprint 3. Measuring Sustainable Development.* Earthscan, London.

Peirson, J, Skinner, I and Vickerman, R (1994). 'Estimating the External Costs of UK Passenger Transport: The First Step Towards an Efficient Transport Market.' Discussion Paper 94/2. Centre for European, Regional and Transport Economics, University of Kent.

Pigou, A C (1924). *The Economics of Welfare.* London, AMS Press.

Rosen, S (1974). 'Hedonistic Prices and Implicit Markets'. *Journal of Political Economy.*

Rothengatter, W. (1993). 'Externalities of Transport' (In Polak, J and Heertje, A (Eds), *European Transport Economics*, Blackwell, Oxford).

Scitovsky, T (1969). 'Two Concepts of External Economics'. *Journal of Political Economy.*

Willeke, R (1992). In Round Table 92, *Benefits of Different Transport Modes.* European Conference of Ministers of Transport, Paris, OECD.

8   The economics of transport and development[1]

K. M. Gwilliam

Introduction

The purpose of this paper is to consider the transport policies necessary for furthering the sustainable development of transitional and developing countries. Section two considers the nature of sustainable development and the different dimensions of the concept applied to the transport sector. Sections three and four consider the role of transport in economic development and the impediments to economically sustainable transport. Section five assesses the role of private and public agencies in the sector in the future. Sections six and seven discuss the environmental and social dimensions of policy. Finally section eight recapitulates the requirements of a reformed economic order for sustainable transport. The discussion concentrates particularly on the respects in which the transport problems of the lower income countries differ from those of the rich countries, and on the role that economic analysis instruments can play in resolving those problems.

Sustainable development

The concept of sustainability

The process of sustainable development is interpreted in this paper as having three major dimensions. First, it involves a continuing capability to support improved quality of life. Infrastructure and services must be financed in such a way as to allow the necessary capital to be maintained and the operating costs met. This corresponds to the concept of **economic sustainability**. Second, it involves an **improvement in the general quality of life**, and not merely an increase in traded goods. Whilst the possibility of trade-off between the various aspects of quality of life does not rigidly exclude a path of development involving some use of non-renewable assets, the path of development should be one in which the outcome occurs by choice and not through the unforeseen long-term consequences of policies. This is our interpretation of the concept of **environmental sustainability**. Third, it must be **shared by all categories of population**, particularly those with the very lowest life quality. In particular, it is desirable to avoid patterns of development imposing uncompensated losses on those who are already very poor. This we term social sustainability.

Transport trends in the developing world

The background to our discussion of the sustainability of transport developments in the lower income countries is an observation of recent trends, together with an extrapolation of those trends to indicate likely futures in the absence of any substantial change in sector policies.

Demand for personal transport is growing faster than population or GDP in most developing and transitional economies. The worldwide motor vehicle fleet has already grown more than six fold since 1950 and is expected to grow 34 percent from 557 million (1989) to 745 million (2000)—over 10 times its size in 1950 (Figure 8.1). The developing countries, which owned a fleet of 178 million in 1989, will probably extend this fleet to 262 million (+47 percent) by the year 2000. This rapid growth will occur particularly in countries which are beginning to industrialize rapidly. For example, if the continued rapid economic growth in China is accompanied by a liberalization in transport market policy one can expect a tripling of the vehicle fleet in the decade 1990 to 2000. Car miles traveled tends to grow even faster than the growth of car ownership.

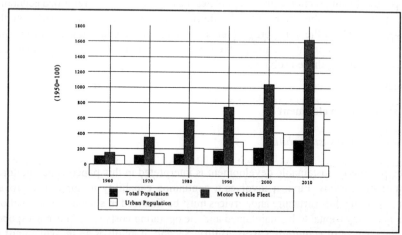

Figure 8.1   **Growth of population and vehicle fleet since 1950**
Source: A.Faiz. 1993. 'Automotive emissions in developing countries - Relative implications for global warming, acidification, and urban air quality.' *Transportation Research* 27A(3):167-186

Demand for freight transport typically grows less rapidly with GDP than that for personal transport. However, in the developing countries the expected growth rate is close to that expected in the auto fleet, largely because of the effects of transport liberalization on choice of mode. The highest growth rates for the truck fleets are expected in the countries of Eastern Europe; for the former socialist countries as a whole trucking is expected to triple in the next two decades, though ton kms are likely to grow more rapidly than truck kilometers because of increasing average truck size.

Aviation is expected to grow world wide by six percent per year, though much more rapid growth may occur in some countries. In China the annual growth rate is currently 20 percent. The maritime sector is expected to grow moderately at average annual rates around three percent, as an aggregate for all cargo classifications. This is in stark contrast to the post-WWII period when seatrade volumes doubled about every ten years. The trans-Pacific and trans-Atlantic routes will maintain their prominence, although further significant increases in the Europe-Asia sector can be expected. Inland water transport is likely to increase in Western Europe, Russia, and China; in each case annual freight volumes of 350-400 million tons of waterborne freight are likely by the end of the 1990s.

For rail transport the CEE and CIS countries experienced substantial losses of both rail and passenger traffic in the five year period between 1988 and 1992. Though this decline has 'bottomed out' in most countries economic restructuring means that the former volumes of rail traffic are unlikely to be recovered. Rail traffic may also decline in some developing countries as their economic balance of activity shifts from primary product export towards industrial production both for domestic consumption and export. The main counter effect is the recovery of traffic in some countries of Latin America and Africa associated with concessioning of systems to the private sector.

Trends in non-motorized sectors are variable. Animal drawn transport is generally decreasing, personal bicycle ownership is high, and its use as a main mode of transport increasing in China and some other Asian countries, low and stable in Latin America, but declining in Africa over the last decade. In poorer countries the use of cycles as public transport modes has been increasing.

Synergy and conflict

Economic, social and environmental sustainability are compatible in many contexts (Figure 8.2). Road or public transport systems which are economically unsustainable fall into disrepair. Such depletion of facilities fails to serve the needs of the poor and often has adverse environmental consequences.

Such convenient synergy between economic, environmental and social sustainability is not all embracing. Increased mobility, particularly private motorized mobility, typically increases measured wealth but damages the environment. In practice the environmental and social consequences of transport emerge in indirect and diffused ways and are very difficult to redeem once they are embodied in the fixed capital of residential and employment location and the social capital of habitual life styles[2]. Because environmental damage in transport is largely uncharged for, private incentives tend to produce development concentrating on the maximization of the market good elements in total life quality. This will differ from the 'environmentally sustainable development path', which best converts increased wealth producing capability into total quality of life, by a 'sustainability gap' which will tend to increase over time, and with income growth.

The need to ensure transport provision which is economically, environmentally and socially sustainable has important policy implications. Economic sustainability requires that the core infrastructure should be maintained in effective operational condition and that the infrastructure should be efficiently operated for the provision of transport services. Environmental sustainability requires that transport sector activities do not endanger the long term availability and quality of the physical environment (water, air, soil and bio-diversity). Social sustainability requires that all groups of the population should benefit from the process of development.

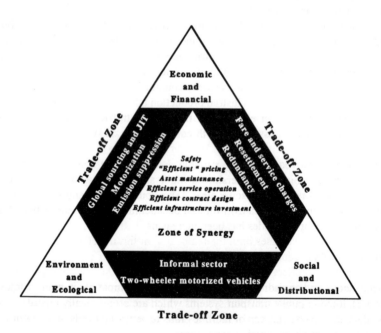

Figure 8.2   Sustainability, synergies and trade-offs
Source: Sustainable transport: sector review and lessons of experience. World Bank 1995.

258

In many developing countries the transport sector exhibits the very antithesis of these conditions. Much infrastructure has been allowed to deteriorate to an unusable condition, partly as a consequence of shortsightedness in the allocation of adequate funds for routine maintenance. Furthermore, low cost transport services of good quality have not been provided by state owned or state regulated enterprises, partly as a consequence of government imposed objectives or constraints which have made it impossible to maintain the equipment necessary to provide service. Transport has become a major contributor to environmental problems of the most polluted megacities in the developing world. Some groups of the very poorest may actually suffer rather than benefit in the process of securing national income growth.

The core of the problem has been a persistent failure to secure consistency between the high level objectives of the society and the actions of individuals and public agencies. This occurs partly because individuals are not confronted with the appropriate incentives and partly because governments do not possess adequate skills to design policies and to perform the planning and control tasks required to implement them. The quest for sustainability thus calls for both policy and institutional reform in many developing countries.

Transport and economic development

Transport, economic growth and poverty

Whilst there remains substantial controversy as to whether inequality is harmful to growth, or whether growth necessarily reduces inequality, there is a growing consensus that economic growth nearly always reduces absolute poverty. The link between growth and transport is equally clear. It has long been recognized that economic development is enhanced by trade. Hence the process of development generates an increasing demand for transport to give physical access to ever larger markets for products and raw materials. The evidence of the positive effect of growth on poverty is clearly demonstrated in the experience of the high performing East Asian economies (Table 8.1).

Transport sector weaknesses limit the realization of this development potential in two ways. First, bad transport facilities restrict the ability to gain from trade. For traditional primary product exporters high cost, low quality domestic transport has sometimes led to loss of traditional export markets to competitive sources of supply or excluded countries from new markets of high potential. For example, the lack of accessibility to markets has contributed to slow growth of exports of countries of central and southern Africa (particularly those that are landlocked). A recent study in Cameroon, Mali and Côte d'Ivoire revealed that transport costs per ton kilometer for their internationally traded goods was twice that of France and five times that of Pakistan.

Second, bad infrastructure, including transport facilities, appears to adversely affect the growth of productivity in other sectors. Recent macro-level studies have indicated that transport and communication investment is highly correlated with growth, but uncorrelated with private investment. This suggests, (a) that investment in this sector is not 'crowding out' other productive investment and, (b) that it raises growth by increasing the social return to private investment.

Table 8.1
Changes in selected indicators of poverty

Economy	Period	Percentage of population below the poverty line			Number of people (millions)		
		First year	Last year	Change	First year	Last year	Change
HPAEs							
Indonesia	1972-82	58	17	-41	67. 9	30.0	-56
Malaysia [a]	1973-87	37	14	-23	4. 1	2. 2	-46
Singapore	1972-82	31	10	-21	0. 7	0. 2	-71
Thailand [a,b]	1962-86	59	26	-30	16. 7	13.6	-18
Others							
Brazil [a,b]	1960-80	50	21	-29	36.1	25.4	29.6
Colombia	1971-88	41	25	-16	8.9	7. 5	-15.7
Costa Rica	1971-86	45	24	-19	0. 8	0. 6	-25
Côte d'Ivoire	1985-86	30	31	1	3. 1	3. 3	6.4
India	1972-83	54	43	-9	311.4	315	1
Morocco	1970-84	43	34	-9	6.6	7. 4	12
Pakistan	1963-82	54	23	-31	26.5	21. 3	-19
Sri Lanka [a]	1963-82	37	27	-10	3. 9	4. 1	5

Note: This table uses economy-specific poverty lines. Official or commonly used poverty lines have been used when available. In other cases the poverty line has been set at 30 percent of mean income or expenditure. The range of poverty lines, expressed in terms of expenditure per household member and in terms of purchasing power parity (PPP) dollars, is approximately $300-$700 a year in 1985 except for Costa Rica ($960), Malaysia ($1,420), and Singapore ($860). Unless otherwise indicated, the table is based on expenditure per household member.

a. Measures for these entries use income rather than expenditure.

b. Measures for these entries are by household rather than by household member.

Source: *The East Asian Miracle; Economic Growth and Public Policy.* World Bank, 1993.

The mechanisms through which transport impacts on productive activity are complex. For rural agricultural production, transport improvement lowers input prices and hence production costs, improves access to credit, facilitates technological diffusion, increases the area of land under cultivation, and increases the availability of 'incentive' goods. Sector studies, such as that of crop production in Egypt, support the hypothesis that inadequate transport infrastructure was an important constraint on aggregate agricultural productivity. This is confirmed by cross country studies in developing countries.

As productivity increases in agriculture the demand for agricultural labor decreases. Migration to the towns creates a supply of cheap labor for manufacturing employment in the developing countries. For the new urban industrial and service activities, the quality of transportation infrastructure and public transport service affect location decisions, the efficiency of the labor market, and the costs at which labor is obtained. Taken in conjunction with decreasing real costs of trunk haul international transport this has contributed to dramatic changes in the structure of trade and transport. International trade in merchandise has been observed to grow more rapidly than National Income (a world average of 4.9 percent per annum between 1980 and 1992 compared with an income growth of 3 percent). The share of raw materials movement between traditional primary producing and manufacturing regions has declined and the share of cross movements of manufactures and semi-manufactures throughout the world has increased. Over 50 percent of the exports of the low income developing countries, more than 60 percent of those of middle income countries and in excess of 90 percent of those of Asia's newly industrialized economies are manufactures.

Taiwan, Malaysia, and Thailand have already followed the example of Japan and Korea in basing rapid growth on the export of their manufactures. Where this process of industrialization takes the form of participation in globally integrated production and assembly chains high quality transport and communication links are essential. Country studies, such as that of economic policy and development in Indonesia, stress the continued importance of infrastructure to country growth at the later stage when private sector industrial growth is beginning to strain available capacity.

The freight transport pre-requisites for growth

As the globalization of markets continues, manufacturers in the industrialized countries seek strategic alliances with partners in developing countries to take advantage of attractive factor cost differentials. The lure of low labor costs is a necessary, but no longer sufficient element of attractiveness. Efficient transport is essential. India lost much of its textile and garment exports to competing neighbors in Southeast Asia where governments had adopted more liberal transport and trade facilitation policies. European clients of Ivoirian cocoa bean growers turned to Central American suppliers who had been able to containerize their products for effective door-to-door transport. Tanzania lost much of its market for sisal exports to Europe to Brazilian suppliers able to deliver small consignments in short intervals with a high degree of reliability.

This process has had substantial effect on the nature of the port and shipping industry. As vessels have grown in size, the economies of containership size while at sea and the diseconomies while in port have driven carriers toward new network structures. To justify a port call by a jumbo, a relatively large port consignment size is needed. A linear pricing structure has developed, 'absorption pricing', under which shippers are charged a door-to-door rate independent of port choice. Under absorption pricing the choice of port has shifted from the shipper to the shipping line, and natural hinterlands have dissipated. The decision to call at a port now hinges on economic trade-offs between diverting a large mainline ship, using a feeder vessel, or using an intermodal transport system. Ports must compete for roles within this global structure.

Modern port facilities are only part of the requirement. With increasing vessel size and improved port handling, shipping costs have already been brought down to a level at which the major savings are now to be found in the land transportation links. Shipping lines are therefore increasingly involved in land transport. For example, 80 percent of the turnover of the French national shipping line CGM arises outside the sea transport business proper. Efficient inland distribution networks, physically and administratively well integrated with ports, are essential. For example, the failure of San Pedro in Côte d'Ivoire to develop as anticipated is the consequence of the failure to complete the road network towards the north of the country and the landlocked Mali and Burkina Faso.

Box 1. Customs practices and their effect on transport

Customs procedures in many developing countries remain entrenched in traditional practices and constitute a major impediment to trade and the provision of related transport. A World Bank survey in 1989 revealed that in India three weeks were incurred, on average, for customs clearance of traded goods. Because of such delays and the associated risks of transport equipment holdup the through-transport rates for containers between Indian origins and overseas destinations were up to 40 percent higher than those experienced in other regional economies.

Similar circumstances prevailed in Mexico in the late 1980s when the Government embarked on a program to gain control of the customs process and to improve efficiency. Several measures were taken. Line responsibilities in the Ministry of Finance were streamlined. The regulatory framework applicable to Customs, which had proliferated over the years, was simplified and made transparent. Customs inspection of traded consignments was made random whereby the decision was left to computers. Only in cases of suspected contraband can the authorities intervene. Discretionary involvement of customs officers was further reduced through duty collection by commercial banks. The number of steps in the customs process has been reduced from twelve to four. The new system has led to the closure of several inspection facilities. Customs clearance must now be carried out at the frontier or at an interior site within the jurisdiction of a trader's local fiscal office. This measure removed the past need for lengthy detours to clear customs at interior sites with no obvious geographical relation to the shipper.

The effects of all these measures have been dramatic. For instance, the average delay of roughly 1,200 daily truck movements across the US-Mexican border at Nuevo Laredo has been reduced from three days to 20 minutes. Substantial reductions in customs-induced waiting times have also materialized in the case of air freight, as well as waterborne or rail-based trade. The World Bank has estimated that the annualized cost savings due to the custom reforms would amount to more than US$2 billion, of which US$300-350 million could be ascribed to better utilization of transport infrastructure and equipment.

Source: H.J. Peters Service: *The Nex Focus in International Manufacturing and Trade Policy.* Policy Research Working Paper 950. World Bank. 1992.

In many countries the domestic regulatory environment and restrictive international aviation and maritime policies may also preclude the development of customer responsive transport (Box 1). For example, simplified customs and trade facilitation procedures are often particularly difficult to achieve because of the vested interests in existing arrangements in large and complex administrations such as those in India.

Examination of recent trends in trade and transport thus indicates that economic sustainability is crucial for traditionally measured economic growth. Eliminating the impediments to economic sustainability thus remains a cornerstone of policy, necessary also to permit the achievement of the further objectives of environmental and social sustainability.

Impediments to economically sustainable transport

The problem of maintenance

Inadequate maintenance of infrastructure is seen as the primary transport problem in most African and Latin American countries. It is increasingly becoming so in Eastern Europe and the former Soviet Union.

Maintenance of road infrastructure. Road infrastructure presents the greatest problem. About 1,500 kilometers of road are being lost each year in Kazakhstan alone due to inadequate maintenance. Priority is being given to road investment over road maintenance in Eastern Europe, despite the higher returns available on maintenance. This myopia is partly a technical failure to recognize the high cost of restoring roads allowed to deteriorate to the point at which reconstruction is required, estimated in research on Costa Rica and Chile at two and a half times that associated with a policy of timely and effective maintenance. Short term political pressures and/or the electoral cycle may also cause decision makers to implicitly adopt a very high rate of discount of the future (Box 2).

Box 2. The economics of road maintenance in Africa

Poor maintenance raises the long term costs of maintaining the road network. Maintaining a paved road for fifteen years costs about $60,000 per km. If the road is not maintained and allowed to deteriorate over the fifteen year period, it will then cost about $200,000 per km to rehabilitate it. This is three times as expensive in cash terms, and 35 percent more expensive in terms of NPVs discounted at 12 percent. However, at a discount rate above 16 percent it will appear sensible to defer maintenance in terms of the road agency costs.

But poor maintenance also has an impact on vehicle operating costs. An analysis of alternative maintenance strategies showed benefit cost ratios varying from 3.4 to 22.1 according to traffic volumes and initial road conditions. These costs are immediate, and hence the advantage is independent of the discount rate. It is thus the fact that the costs to road users do not enter into the calculations of the road agency which is the major reason for the low priority accorded to maintenance.

Source: Based on I.G. Heggie. *Management and Financing of Roads: An Agenda for Reform.* World Bank. 1994.

Earmarking of taxes. In the absence of direct user charges the provision of more secure finance for road maintenance typically involves the appropriation of part of the fuel tax. This is a very controversial issue for many multilateral agencies, most notably IMF and the World Bank.

The general *macroeconomic* argument against earmarking is that it reduces overall fiscal flexibility. This implicitly assumes a unitary state with homogeneous preferences in which an omniscient and benevolent government continually reviews expenditures to ensure that allocations are optimal. If the government system is not capable of delivering that control one of the main arguments against earmarking falls. For example, in Colombia, extensive earmarking is a reflection of poor budgeting and expenditure control practices. At the *microeconomic* level the major criticism of earmarking has been that it is ineffective as a protection of a particular expenditure line, especially where the earmarked tax covers only part of the funding requirement[3]. In the case of Colombia although the earmarked funds for National Road Fund grew at the same rate as GDP, the total funding grew more slowly than GDP, and more slowly than government investment in other sectors. Wherever the government retains control over the tax rates or over the allocation of complementary funds form the total level of funding may be just as vulnerable with earmarking as without it.

The main arguments for earmarking concern its beneficial effects on *resource allocation* and on *efficiency of service provision.*

On *resource allocation* there are two main issues. Firstly, earmarking allows those who value a particular service to direct payments to secure its supply. Especially where management of the funds is partly under the control of paying users of services

264

it also reduces the tendency of competing interest groups to argue for over provision of services which particularly favor them. Secondly, earmarking funds for maintenance but not investment may counter a systematic bias against maintenance in regimes where both are funded through the same channels.

With respect *to efficiency of provision* the greater security of funding associated with earmarking facilitates improved work scheduling and more efficient utilization of equipment and manpower. Studies in Latin America indicate that part of the reason why force account maintenance is little more than half as efficient as contracted maintenance is that equipment utilization rates and number of kilometers maintained per employee are very low, as a consequence of the insecurity or untimely availability of the funding to maintain regular work schedules and to buy fuel and supplies. Earmarking may also facilitate contracting out of maintenance. In Ghana the greater certainty of funding associated with earmarking allowed effective competitive bidding to be introduced, avoiding the necessity to award small continuation contracts to contractors, giving a significant boost to contractor cash flow, and enabling unit costs to be reduced by 15-20 percent.

In summary, if government budgetary procedures are good, and operational implementation is effective, there is no justification for earmarking. At the other extreme, where governance is bad and the government lacks self discipline, earmarked funds will not be secure, and earmarking is redundant. But many countries may fall in the middle ground where the benefits of better service provision outweigh any possible adverse effects on inter sectoral resource allocation.

The complexity of the arguments suggests that the issue must be decided on a case by case basis. Three criteria seem paramount, namely:

1 Whether there is a substantial overlap between beneficiaries and taxpayers in general.

2 Whether the tax/price mechanism appears to generate an appropriate level of resources.

3 Whether these resources are likely to be effectively used for the purpose intended.

Earmarking funds for roads is thus particularly appropriate where there is a well recognized need for protection of a budget line as one of high productivity (e.g. there is a crisis in road deterioration) and/or the efficiency of highway maintenance planning and implementation has been adversely affected by insecurity of funding (i.e. productivity in road maintenance is low). It should be approached particularly cautiously where taxation on road use is a high proportion of total tax revenue and there are many sectors making similar claims for special fiscal treatment. In all cases it must be associated with an institutional organization embodying adequate efficiency incentives (see below).

Maintenance of operational assets. Maintenance of operational assets is also a serious problem. Attempts to protect the poor by maintaining bus fares at low levels may be counterproductive unless supported by direct subsidy. Inadequate finance for vehicle replacement has led to physical deterioration of the bus fleet and ultimately the reduction in service provided to the poor as well as the middle classes in such cities as Dakar, Panama, and El Salvador. Unrealistic control of passenger fares has also damaged many railway companies. Similarly, foreign exchange controls often impact most heavily on services to the poor. For example, inability to purchase spare parts has seriously hindered the provision of public bus and rail services in a number of African countries, and has decimated the bicycle stock in Mozambique and Kenya.

Box 3. The fiscal burden of state enterprises

A recent study of state owned transport enterprises in fifteen countries found that 26 recorded profits and 49 recorded losses; whilst airlines, airports and ports showed a roughly even split between profit makers and loss makers, none of the railways in the study were adjudged profitable. At its peak the deficit of the Argentine railways was 1 percent of GDP. In Tanzania, when the shortfall in regular road maintenance was added to the transport sector budget, the overall drain on government's fiscal revenues rose from 2.5 percent of total current revenues in FY85/86 to 17.4 percent in FY86/87. The total transport sector drain on central government revenues can be significant--in some cases accounting for as much as 20 percent of government expenditures.

Source: Ian G. Heggie. op. cit.

State ownership of public transport undertakings does not necessarily solve the problem if governments are unable to sustain the fiscal burden that their parastatals impose (Box 3). In the absence of adequate government funding parastatal public transport companies typically respond by deferring maintenance activities, not paying bills, and running down working capital. These methods cannot be used to finance current operations indefinitely. Thus, wherever this kind of problem of incompatibility between aspirations and reality arises, the solution must be found in policies which either increase revenues (which might include improved attention to eliminate fare evasion or reduction of concessionary fare availability as well as fare increases) or reduce costs (which might include reductions in service frequency or coverage, but must primarily concentrate on reduction in operating costs). The failures to maintain assets in public transport service provision are thus closely related to the questions of efficiency of supply, to which we now turn.

Government intervention and economic efficiency

Throughout the world governments have regulated the transport sector, imposing constraints on entry accompanied by the prescription of quality norms, price levels and maximum profit rates. The institutions used have been either statutory monopoly

266

public enterprises or regulatory commissions, which also usually constrain entry to give some degree of monopoly power to the regulated suppliers.

The consequences of regulation. Regulation has occurred partly on economic grounds. Many government have believed that there were such extensive economies of scale or scope in the transport sector that they needed to intervene to secure those economies without exploitation of monopoly power. The sector has also been regulated for social policy reasons. Safety regulation is common for all modes and governments have also increasingly set operational standards designed to protect the environment. Public transport fares have been controlled ostensibly to protect the poor, whilst maritime cargo has been reserved for national carriers for balance of payments and national employment reasons. National airlines and shipping fleets are also protected in some countries for strategic defense reasons.

Most of these reasons for intervention have some prima facie plausibility. But they all involve the interposition of some arbiter of the public interest, either political or administrative, between consumer and supplier. The achievement of a desirable outcome thus depends both on the regulatory agency properly reflecting the public interest and on its ability to induce the supplier to work in that public interest. In practice regulation has frequently taken the form of protection of a monopoly supplier, without the existence of any structure of incentives to align the private interests of the supplier with the public interest. As in developed countries, whilst suppliers and their employees have usually benefited, the effects of regulation on users have generally been very detrimental.

1 *Transport operating costs.* There is ample evidence from the developing countries of the efficiency differences between private enterprises in competitive situations and protected (usually public sector) enterprises. In shipping it has been estimated that elimination of cargo reservation in Venezuela could reduce national shipping costs by 30 percent. In Argentina, privatization of the railways reduced labor costs by 60 percent, and further savings in maintenance expenditures are expected. These savings occur irrespective of whether privatization is associated with fragmented intra-modal competition or not. Even in road maintenance there is evidence that force account activities of government departments are less efficient than competitive private sector contractors. In Brazil routine road maintenance costs by contract were 25 percent lower than by force account and in Colombia 50 percent lower.

2 *National trading costs.* Many developing countries have practised cargo reservation under a Liner Shipping Code, arising from the UNCTAD V meeting at Manila which condoned developing countries' reservation of 40 percent of their export or import traffics for their own national fleets. Whilst ostensibly aimed at assisting the Balance of Payments of the developing countries the benefits are very doubtful. The direct gains to balance of payments from using domestic shipping are usually much less than their freight revenues because the maintenance and operation of a national

fleet are usually very foreign exchange-intensive. Few developing countries have domestic oil resources, steel making, and an efficient shipbuilding industry. Thus the only savings that materialize are the cost of crewing and vessel management—assuming that these functions would be fulfilled by nationals. Against this must be set the loss to domestic importers and exporters, which is the difference between what they pay for carriage of cargo and what they would have to pay in a free market. In a study of Venezuela it was concluded that freight rates were 30 percent higher than would have been the case in a free market and losses were 9.4 times as high as gains.

3 *Innovation.* This may also be inhibited by monopoly franchising as managers concentrate on satisfying the regulator in supplying the traditional services. It is common in developing countries for new public transport demands (for example, from peripheral new shanty settlements in such cities as Caracas, Venezuela) to be met by the informal sector. This is accentuated by the greater ability of the informal sector to tailor service type and quality to the needs and ability to pay of users.

4 *Poverty alleviation.* Although income distribution is often the ostensible reason for regulation, the outcome is often the very opposite. The effects of price regulation on service levels have already been noted. Concessionary fares in many countries apply to the privileged rather than the poor. This problem also applies where metros (which are often relatively expensive forms of transport, in some cases used disproportionately by the middle class) are being subsidized whilst bus and informal transport modes deteriorate.

Creating competitive pressure. There is an increasing body of experience of reintroducing competition into the transport sector in the industrialized countries. The general forms of competition adopted — between modes or between operators in the same mode competing 'in the market', or between alternative suppliers competing for tendered franchises or concessions 'for the market' — are equally relevant for the developing world. What differ are the conditions into which competition is being introduced, and hence the ease with which different forms of competition can be established. It is on these differences that we concentrate here.

Competition in the market —free entry. Completely *free entry* is typical of the road passenger transport and trucking markets in many low income countries. Where it occurs it is usually associated with a completely private sector supply, a wide range of alternative forms of transport, and an important role for the informal sector. But effective competition depends on the creation of a 'level playing field'. There are several components to this, which may be absent in the developing world.

1 *The rule of law must prevail to exclude the use (or threat) of physical violence.* In the Chilean bus market new entrants who attempted to undercut prevailing fares were liable to suffer physical damage to their vehicles. The emergence of Mafia

control of some sectors in Russia and the violent 'turf wars' between operators' associations in the black taxi business in South Africa are prime examples of the dangers of a complete regulatory vacuum.

2 *All special advantages or disadvantages of incumbents should be eliminated.* Following trucking deregulation in Ethiopia the parastatal has been able to maintain its market by operating at a deficit, using private companies as affiliates, because of its preferential access to traffic of other parastatals. Similarly, the publicly owned bus company in Odessa in the Ukraine responded to private sector competition with commercially unsustainable predation (though in this case there was sufficient public and political opposition to cause the practice to be controlled). In such circumstances there is no incentive for new entrants to compete.

3 *Predatory commercial behavior must be controlled.* A major danger of government disengagement from regulation of transport operations in developing countries is that of a strong private sector monopoly emerging. Controls over cartellization, normally inadequate in developing countries, need to be constructed. Collaborative arrangements, such as the operators' associations in the public transport sector in Latin America, the liner conferences in the international maritime industry or the strategic alliances of companies in distribution, must be carefully designed to avoid dangers of cartel exploitation. This is no simple matter. The boundaries between acceptable vertical integration and unacceptable monopolization of supply, or between acceptable strategic alliances and unacceptable cartellization may be very blurred, especially for more unsophisticated administrations.

4 *Any remaining military or social service obligations should be subject to specific, costed, contractual compensation.* This is a particular problem in eastern Europe where it is not uncommon for less than half the passengers to be paying fares, often on the basis of (unfunded) legal rights granted by central or federal governments.

5 *There must be an actual or potential source of competitive pressure.* Where demand is dense, and particularly where the nature of that demand is varied, competition can occur as a result of the entry of new modes to compete with the existing regulated modes. This was the origin of the public light buses in Hong Kong and the minibus in Dakar. Some flexibility towards the introduction of new categories of services at higher prices may also be a means of reconciling the maintenance of a basic low fare provision with the provision of adequate total capacity and a sufficiently varied range of price/quality combinations to meet demand. Such segmentation may occur through the (often illegal) activities of the informal sector (as in the case of shared taxis in many African and Latin American cities). Even within highly controlled situations it may be the means of allowing effective fare increases for existing operators without abandoning the controlled basic fare (as in the 'two tier' systems of both taxi and bus licensing in Seoul). The provision of new modes, or at least

new qualities of service to supplement the existing public sector companies, may also be the route through which the private sector may first be given a role in developing or transitional economies.

Competition for the market—franchises and concessions. Private participation can be mobilized even where the economies of scale are considered to be sufficiently large to wish to limit the number of suppliers in the market at any one time. It can take a number of forms, including competition for limited period monopoly rights to provide specific services within a specified network structure (which we refer to as 'franchising'); competition for the longer term monopoly right to provide all service within a given area or mode (which is referred to as 'concessioning').

Franchising service provision allows government to retain control over the nature, quality and price of services to be provided to the public, whilst using competition for franchises of short duration as a means of obtaining cost efficient supply. Competition for the market may be viewed as involving government as the sole customer of a competitive transport supply sector, acting on behalf of, and in the interests of, both consumers and taxpayers. Competition can either be for unremunerative services only (as in the U.K.), or for all services (as in Costa Rica). It requires an administrative competence to design the franchising system, plan networks, enforce fair conditions of competition and monitor and enforce contracts. This competence may not initially exist in the government sector. Possible solutions to this are the use of subcontracting by the state owned enterprise, as in Delhi urban buses.

Even within a licensed franchise system it may be possible to generate substantial competitive pressure by overlapping franchises. This approach is practised to secure competition in the taxi markets in many countries where single vehicle ownership is the rule, but operators combine in competing marketing groups, or in the use of competing radio dispatching circuits; between different bus operators' associations in Buenos Aires; and between operators of different kinds of public transport vehicles in some African countries.This form of competition makes it possible to obtain the cost advantages of small scale operation in sectors where scale economies in the traditional sense are absent, whilst at the same time allowing some degree of organization of supply. The essential requirements for this form of competition to work is that there is a competent franchising authority to orchestrate the competition, and that there is either sufficient initial fragmentation or sufficiently effective control over cartellization to prevent the emergence of a 'grand cartel'.

Longer term concessioning of the provision of facilities has been practised in developing countries for toll roads (for example, in Mexico); for freight railways (for example in Argentina and several African countries) and even for metros (for example, one line of Buenos Aires metro in Argentina). Port and airport management has been commercialized in this way (for example in the port of Conakry and airports of Libreville, Conakry, Lome and Madagascar). In a number of francophone African countries the management of whole urban bus systems has also been concessioned.

Private sector companies will normally wish to maximize profit and minimize risk. This will lead to demands for freedom to set prices, guarantees of minimum traffic or revenue, security from competitive provision and immunity from operators liability. Whilst competition at the concessioning stage (via auctions of a single feature such as price of an otherwise common set of specifications) may be a way of limiting these requirements, there is always the possibility that a defaulting franchisee will be able to secure a favorable renegotiation. That possibility may encourage over-optimistic assumptions to be adopted about traffic demand and construction costs especially if concession periods are short and permitted prices too constrained (as appears to have been the case with several of the Mexican toll roads).

Choosing a competitive form for developing countries. The appropriate choice of a competitive form and the path adopted to achieve that form will thus depend not only on the technological characteristics of the subsector, but also on the regulatory history, nature of social objectives, and the administrative and entrepreneurial capabilities of the country concerned. There is no 'one size that fits all' in the wardrobe of transport regulation. The main determinants of that choice are likely to be:

1 *Social objectives and competition.* Franchising arrangements appear to be more easily managed to pursue congestion management, environment and distributional objectives.

2 *Regulatory history.* The greater the dominance of a single organization the more difficult it may be to escape from it. For example, some countries (CEE economies, China, India) are highly dependent on rail networks which are in place and likely to remain the backbone of the surface transport system for many more decades.

3 *Administrative and entrepreneurial capabilities.* Where there is competent administration and an entrepreneurial basis for more fragmented competition, competitively tendered franchising can work well. Where local entrepreneurial skills are limited the periodic management contract, as used in many port and airports in Africa, may be better in the short term, though its long term desirability will depend on the extent to which local capability is developed. However, in cases where indigenous administrative skills are scarce, or corruption in administration is prevalent, as in many African countries, free entry may be preferable.

The problem of international transport protectionism

In both international shipping and aviation markets competition usually exists. Two steps are necessary in order to obtain the benefits of competition in these circumstances. First, privatization of state owned national flag carriers may be required to eliminate constraints on commercial freedom of operation which would unduly burden them in international competition and hence distort the market. But even private sector national flag carriers are not necessarily efficient. Secondly, therefore, there would need to be a self denying ordinance by government to eliminate historic practices of cargo reservation or of administrative market sharing. The extent

271

to which these steps are taken appears to depend partly on the perception in the developing world of the behavior of the developed countries (Box 4).

Box 4. Transport protectionism in Latin America

At the second meeting of the Conference of Ministers of Transport, Communications and Public Works of South America, in June, 1994, Argentina and Peru both reported improved quality and frequency of shipping services and reductions of rates of up to 50 percent after the abolition of cargo reservation schemes. Similarly Chile, Peru and Venezuela advocated open competition in the air. But in both sectors there remained substantial support for continued cargo reservation and flag protection, for two reasons. Firstly, it was believed that in both air and maritime sectors the North American and European carriers were in receipt of government subsidies which gave them unfair competitive advantage over regional carriers. Secondly, it was believed,

particularly in the maritime sector, that developed country cartels would be able to use market power to eliminate regional carriers and ultimately exploit their monopoly. Unless both the reality and the perception of such anti-competitive behavior by the OECD countries can be assuaged countries like Brazil will continue to resist moves to increase reliance on international competitive market processes.

Source: H. J. Peters private communication.

Public and private sector roles

There is a growing belief in some countries that the provision of both transport infrastructure and services can be left entirely to the private sector. The implication of that view is that neither governments nor the international lending and aid agencies need do more than address the problems of creating the necessary commercial environment for private involvement. That perspective is disarmingly false.

The private sector role in service provision

In most land transport modes the absence of scale economies makes it appropriate to depend primarily on competitive private sector operation. But that still imposes substantial public sector responsibilities.

First, the establishment of credible competitive pressures requires the existence or introduction of profit seeking potential suppliers. That typically requires action by government to restructure formerly monopolistic sectors. International institutions can help in the creation of a private sector. For example, in the trucking industry the World Bank has assisted both in the transfer of ownership (in Hungary and Russia) and in releasing the constraints on private initiative (in Mexico). In international air transport, in contrast, even a private national monopoly may be too small to take advantage of scale economies, and it may be appropriate to form international groupings or consortia. Various forms of consolidation or merger have occurred after liberalization in the airline industry in the US and Europe. Air Afrique is an example of such a grouping in the developing world, and the World Bank has been encouraging further regional airline consortia both in West and Central Africa and in Southern Africa.

Second, where a private monopoly is being created it is important to prevent the subsequent exploitation of private monopoly power. In the case of privatization of air and maritime transport, international competition is intense. In the case of railway companies, competition from the road haulage sector is usually sufficiently intense to be confident that the primary incentives to management will be to improve efficiency in order to compete rather than to restrict output. For example, the Argentine railways´ share of the freight market (in ton-mile terms) prior to concessioning was only 8 percent. In situations where external competition is less constraining, as for example in the franchising of the suburban rail services in Argentina, the control has to be built in to the concession arrangement (for example, by specifying maximum fares chargeable in dollar terms).

Third, the problem of potential monopoly exploitation is not confined to cases of unitary ownership. Cartellization has occurred amongst fragmented operators, for example, in the black taxi operations in South Africa, in the bus industry in Chile and in the trucking associations of Sub-Saharan Africa. These cartels are often associated with criminal elements of control. Control of illegal cartellization and predatory practice is particularly difficult in countries which lack a tradition of competitive private enterprise.

Three issues are of particular significance in limiting the expansion of private sector participation in transport operations in developing and traditional economies.

1 *Conglomeracy*. Only 40 percent of the employees of the state port authorities in the transitional economies were engaged in direct port or transport activities. Without divestiture of these historic responsibilities a privatized parastatal would always be vulnerable to lose its markets to new entrants, or international competitors, not carrying the same obligations. It was estimated that the cost of providing the 'safety nets' for the Russian Federation would be $75 billion.

2 *Traditional social obligations.* Even in non-socialist countries privatization may be impossible without the prior clearing of historic obligations such as unremunerative routes, excess labor, the debt obligations associated with mistaken past investments. However, great care is needed to ensure that the preparation process does not involve the refurbishment of capacity which may not, in the different future market situation, be economically justifiable.

3 *Traditional inter-company linkages within the state sector*. If remaining state enterprises continue to uneconomically favor their own account haulage or a privatized SOE, private competition will not emerge, and much of the benefit of commercialization will be lost. For example, 75 percent of the traffic generated by

SOEs in Egypt is handled by other SOEs on administrative rather than market criteria.

The private sector role in infrastructure

The private sector already participates in transport infrastructure provision in a number of ways:

1 *Supplying goods or services* as a subcontractor to publicly owned infrastructure authorities., often procured through specialized construction management agencies for contracting out (common in developed countries and in the AGETIP system in several African countries).

2 *Managing infrastructure under management contracts.* This is quite common in Africa where local entrepreneurial and management skills are scarce. For example, the port of Conakry is managed by the Port of Hamburg and a number of airports have been concessioned (Libreville, Conakry, Lome, Bamako, Douala).

3 *Financing transport infrastructure under concessions* covering whole networks, such as the railways of Argentina, single links, such as the toll roads of Mexico, or major interchanges such as airport or bus terminals. It is often the case, as with the recent development of major highway systems in China, Mexico, and the Hungarian autoroute concessions, that new facilities are being provided within the private sector whilst the basic network remains public.

4 *Private ownership* of infrastructure is less common as government may be unwilling to cede ownership for strategic planning reasons, whilst the private sector may be loathe to take ownership for legal liability reasons[4].

Private sector financing of infrastructure is attractive to government because it allows infrastructure to be expanded without increasing government debt. Between 1982 and 1994 it is estimated that there has been about US$25 billion of private investment in transport infrastructure. The majority of this has been in toll motorways in Latin America (notably Mexico) and Asia (notably Malaysia and Thailand). Private sector investment in ports has also been increasing and over 50 countries were considering some kind of privatization of their airport systems by 1994. Private sector financing facilitates the mobilization of skills not available in the public sector in capital assembly, planning and management for major projects. Build, operate and transfer concessions also act as 'enclave' arrangements allowing more flexible procurement and contracting in circumstances where a more general reform of public sector arrangements is not possible.

Those benefits do not always come cheap. The private sector typically asks either for direct government guarantee of minimum traffics at specified prices, or for exclusive rights to exploit the revenue potential of a secure and buoyant market.

274

Potential concessionaires may share the revenue risk with the financial sector through revenue insurance schemes, as in the case of the Mexican ports, though these inevitably involve increased costs for the concessionaire which are ultimately passed on to government in the terms of the contracts reached. Backsliding by government on guarantees is not uncommon, and the transfer of asset ownership may appear to be the strongest way of locking in the gains of commercialization. The international institutions can facilitate private finance by guaranteeing the private sector against government non-performance. Penetrating cost/benefit analysis of the long term public funding implications may reduce the enthusiasm for private finance, as has happened in the case of some private projects in Hungary.

There is undoubtedly scope for further expansion of private sector involvement in infrastructure, exemplified by the interest that is now being shown in urban rail projects in Bangkok. But it is equally clear that there are substantial parts of the transport infrastructure, including all rural and most urban roads, where the difficulties of collecting adequate revenues make the introduction of genuine private risk capital improbable.

The continuing role of state enterprises

State ownership remains the norm in some sectors in most countries (notably road and rail infrastructure) and in most sectors in some countries (for example China). Municipal ownership of public transport service provision is also still the case in most eastern European cities such as Budapest and Moscow. The parastatals are not always inefficient. For example, the technical performance of transport SOEs such as Ethiopian Airways, Chinese Railways or the Port of Singapore, matches the best in the world in many respects. But some problems generally prevail even in technically competent enterprises. Underlying the almost universally poor record of state owned railways in developing countries has been the interfering relationship between the government and the enterprise which has led to poorly defined goals, relatively passive management unresponsive to changing market conditions, political interference in management decisions, and inadequate funding. Similar experience is common also in other modes; for example, the financial failures of the Cameroon bus enterprise SOTUC and air company CAMAIR can be largely attributed to the effects of persistent government intervention.

The obvious conclusion, that the path to improvement is through commercialization, is supported by comparisons between publicly and privately owned transport enterprises in different countries and sectors. For example, amongst the publicly owned bus enterprises in India those which have the greatest degree of commercial autonomy, such as in Tamil Nadu, are the most successful in providing cheap efficient service. Increasing efficiency by reducing political intervention in operational management is thus the primary reason for setting the SOEs on a more commercial footing.

It is also the common experience in cities in the transitional economies that the previously high levels of subsidy and uneconomically low levels of fares cannot be sustained in a liberalized economy. Similar problems have already been noted for the maintenance of roads in many African and Latin American countries. Commercialization may thus become a political necessity.

Commercializing public sector service provision

It is equally the case for service provision and infrastructure that commercialization involves reconsideration both of the principles of pricing and financing and of the organizational arrangements.

Pricing. Incorrect price signals have been at the heart of inefficient use of resources in the transport sector. In the FSU the combination of a policy of extremely specialized industrial concentration and transport prices administered at too low a level led to excessive amounts of freight transport. FSU freight ton kilometers per dollar of GDP is far greater than that of countries of similar size (four and a half times that of China, five times that of Canada, six times that of the US and seven times that of India). The shift away from this structure, which would have resulted in any event as a more market oriented economic system developed, has been compounded by the economic nationalism associated with fragmentation.

Excessive demand is not only a characteristic of the former socialist countries. For example, in Korea, the demand for all transport modes, and hence the pressure on infrastructure, is accentuated by a systematic undercharging for transport in comparison to other services and commodities.

As in developed countries, there may be distributional issues at stake, or there may be 'second best' reasons for using public enterprise pricing to compensate for the adverse efficiency or environmental impacts of underpricing of road use. This is inherently problematical in developing countries because charges set in such a way as to achieve a given distributional objective, or to compensate for a given degree of undercharging of private road transport, may not yield levels of revenue sufficient to meet full operational and vehicle replacement costs. In those circumstances sustainability must be the pre-eminent objective, as failure to sustain the service will also involve failure to meet distributional or system efficiency objectives. Hence the minimum requirement is the achievement of a secure revenue to meet full operating and equipment replacement costs.

Organization

1 *Performance agreements.* Opportunistic intervention in operational management has been a particular problem in the transport sector in developing countries. As in the industrialized countries this can be avoided by separating the strategic direction functions from the operational management functions, and establishing clear procedures and channels of responsibility for both. This is frequently done by using performance agreement contract arrangements as the channel for achieving the politically determined objectives while giving the enterprise

managements commercial objectives (and freedoms) in meeting the contract requirements. Such arrangements have been commonly used in the railway sector, in such countries as Bolivia, Mexico, Morocco, Tunisia, Gabon and Ghana. They have also been used, though less frequently in urban public transport, air transport and ports, particularly in West Africa (for example, performance agreements have been signed between the government and the state owned railways, urban public transport company and airline in Cameroon).

Performance agreement systems have not always achieved their objective. Enforcement problems commonly arise both because of the political difficulty for management in taking a legal action against government, and because of the frequently dominant market power of government as sole buyer. Many SOEs (for example, in Kenya and Cameroon) have encountered problems precisely because government was not paying its bills on time. In Senegal the government failed to carry out its commitments under the agreement because it did not have the administrative capacity to coordinate all of the contracts which were being signed in order to ensure that they were within the financial capability of the country. In Mexico a series of 'convenios' have failed to noticeably improve railway performance because of a continuing lack of adequate definition and decision concerning a valid and clear role for the railways on which clear financial targets and responsibilities could be based.

2 *Subcontracting supply functions.* Commercial competitive pressure can also be exploited in a public monopoly supply organization by 'unbundling' the supply function to identify those elements which can be subcontracted to the private sector on a competitive tendering basis. This is common in respect of rail track maintenance and in port operations. For example, the Philippine Ports Authority has a statutory monopoly power to own and operate port facilities, but contracts out warehousing and stevedoring to the private sector. Because both management and labor have a strong vested interest in maintaining as much activity as possible within the public enterprise there should be a clear legal obligation to test the market by putting work out to competitive tender. This will also require independent auditing of public sector bids. In some cases new public sector activities may also be required for an interim period to assist the development of an effective private market (for example, public equipment pools to facilitate private sector competition for road maintenance contracts).

Commercializing public sector infrastructure provision

Both patent inefficiency of operation and increasing inability to sustain the fiscal burden of traditional infrastructure supply arrangements has led many governments to begin to seek alternative mechanisms of a more commercial kind. As for operations this has highlighted problems both of an economic and institutional nature.

Pricing and financing. The economic problems arise primarily from the traditional treatment of infrastructure as a free good. While in the case of many developing countries it is the fiscal rather than the resource allocational implications that have brought the issue to the forefront of political attention, the relevant pricing prescriptions apply to developed and developing countries alike.

1 *Congestion and short run marginal social cost pricing.* The economic case for congestion pricing is just as cogent for developing as developed cities. Singapore pioneered a simple form of peak period cordon pricing in its area licensing scheme in 1973. 20 years later, that experience has not been replicated in developing countries. Schemes have been considered, but abandoned, in Hong Kong, Bangkok and Kuala Lumpur.

   In the past the problem has been partly technological. The available technologies of manual or electronic cordon charging are only suitable when there are a limited number of arterial roads entering the city carrying traffic which is a major cause of urban congestion, and can be intercepted by a small number of tolling points. Of the twenty to thirty major congested cities in the developing world only a few (Algiers, Bangkok, Bombay, Lagos, Nairobi, Tunis and Seoul) satisfy these conditions.

   New electronic technologies are now available. Whilst the investment costs and administrative requirements for successful implementation of an electronic pricing scheme make it likely to remain the exception in developing countries for some time, technology is no longer the real barrier. In the developing as in the developed countries road pricing will have to be seen as distributionally acceptable before it can be implemented. This will involve tax restructuring which would make it part of a more comprehensive package involving the commitment of more than transport ministries alone. There are also problems concerning jurisdiction and financial transfers to be overcome in many countries.

2 *Road infrastructure cost recovery.* Fixed costs of paved roads are about 50 percent of the total on main arterial roads, and may be as high as 75 percent on local roads. Outside the major urban areas in developing countries the relatively low level of congestion over much of the networks thus means that, even if it were possible to set prices equal to short run marginal costs, total costs would not be covered. The issue is therefore to devise mechanisms which recoup costs in a way which also stimulates efficient user decisions.

The charging devices practically available have limited versatility. Direct tolls can be varied both by vehicle type and by distance traveled, and are hence the preferred cost recovery instrument so long as no internal distortions are introduced in the use of the network. Taxes on vehicles may be varied by vehicle type both to correct for imperfections of fuel taxation in allocating variable costs and to distribute fixed costs. Nowhere in the developing world is the vehicle related tax also varied by distance traveled. Taxes on fuel vary fairly directly with use, but do not adequately reflect the different cost responsibility of different vehicle types or their differential impact according to initial road design. However, they are often the only instrument of cost recovery immediately available.

In those circumstances the principles for setting fuel taxes are simple. For road users as a whole taxes plus tolls should cover all of the costs imposed by infrastructure use. In many developing countries (Ethiopia, Ghana, Zaire, Myanmar, Colombia, Indonesia) that is not the case (Figure 8.3). In some, such as Venezuela and Russia for example, road transport fuel is even sold below its border price. If allowance is made for environmental costs many more would be seen to be underpaying in total. Amongst those covering costs in total, there will be many for whom charges do not cover costs for specific vehicle categories—particularly heavy freight vehicles.

In many countries with a weak direct tax base, there is heavy reliance on indirect taxation. Particularly high taxation on transport fuel makes sense in that context both because the inelasticity of demand for gasoline limits the distortion it causes and because it is consumed disproportionately by higher income groups so the distributional effect of the tax is likely to be relatively progressive. In looking at tax/cost ratios these considerations may suggest ratios considerably higher than unity, particularly for the private car. Despite this there remains a widespread resistance to use this instrument in developing countries because of the fear that it may be inflationary, have adverse effects on economic development and cause immediate hardship to the poor. One of the most pressing challenges to the economist is to demonstrate convincingly the fallacy of these presumptions.

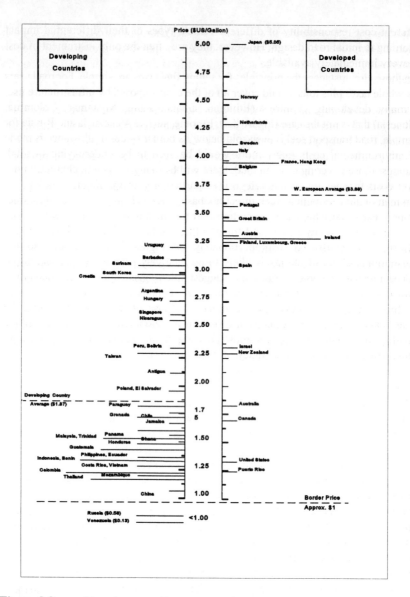

Figure 8.3   **Premium gasoline pump prices**
Source: Energy Detente (February 1994) and World Bank Data

Organization. In many countries the most pressing problem is the inefficiency of administration of infrastructure maintenance. Even where the infrastructure responsibility does remain in the public sector, and where taxation on fuel has an

280

important general revenue raising as well as a user charging function, efficiency can often be improved by organizational devices to introduce greater incentives to economic efficiency. This can be achieved in different ways at national, regional and local levels.

1 *National roads organization.* Where possible the introduction of greater market discipline in infrastructure provision is best achieved by full corporatization, giving the supply agencies commercial freedom and a commercial remit. This is both possible and allocationally efficient where there is a method of pricing directly for use and there are no externalities. These conditions appear to hold for inter-urban railways and, in sparse networks, to inter-urban roads; to a lesser extent for airports and seaports (because of water, air and noise pollution); but not for urban rail (where externality effects are large) or for urban and rural secondary roads (where both pricing feasibility and externality problems occur). In the case of urban rail systems, commercial structures for supply have been common with farebox revenues supplemented by deficit financing by municipal or national governments. In all cases the revenues accruing are viewed as charges for use.

In contrast, taxes on road users have not been viewed as charges for road use but as part of general (sumptuary) taxation. But governments have shown a low willingness to allocate, and high temptation to defer funding, particularly for road maintenance. The completion of this vicious circle is a high resistance by users to taxation on use. Piecemeal commercialization has existed for many years in the US turnpikes and the French and Italian autoroutes. More recently a number of African countries have begun to introduce commercial concepts in the management of roads and the Economic Commission for Latin America and the Caribbean has urged its members to corporatize their road systems.

The corporatized road agencies, as currently being developed under the Sub-Saharan Africa Road Maintenance Initiative, are promising examples of this type of arrangement, though they are not necessarily a panacea, as the unsatisfactory experience of the Office des Routes in Zaire demonstrates. There are several requirements for a successful commercialization. First, the accounts and performance of the road agency must be made transparent, with the amount of money spent on roads, the efficiency with which it is expended and the effects of that expenditure on performance clearly visible. Second, there must be a clear indication of what is a charge for roads, with charges separately specified from general taxation on use. Charges must be directly transferred to the Roads Authority. Third, the level of charges and expenditures must be linked. Finally, the determination of the level of charges and expenditures should be under a management representing users interests.

2 *Regional and municipal transport.* The functions of infrastructure planning, environmental protection and urban transport network planning require detailed local implementation. Decentralization of responsibilities is therefore desirable

to levels at which users' voices are likely to be effective. This generally implies responsibility for urban transport being assigned to city or city region governments, and responsibility for rural infrastructure being assigned to the lowest level of government at which effective implementation can be managed. It also requires modally specific interests to be represented in the processes of management of the modes.

The probability of a comprehensive policy surviving over time depends on the robustness of the institutions concerned. Adequately trained administrative and professional staff are required at the operational level. Very successful packages of institutional reform have been linked to packages of technical assistance to aid the development of urban transport planning capability in several cities in Brazil (Recife, Curitiba, Port Alegre, Belo Horizonte), in medium sized cities in Mexico and in some North African cities such as Tunis. This requires not only an initiating decision but also a continued political commitment to the maintenance of the local capability. For example, a program of technical assistance in transport planning for Bombay was successful for a period of ten years, but much of the gain was lost following changes of government which eroded political commitment to it. EBTU in Brazil also died, despite its initial success in stimulating integrated transport planning.

Good implementation has several dimensions. The hierarchical separation of functions must be very clearly specified, with the local responsibility for execution accompanied by an adequate system of accountability and incentives for efficient performance. Transfer of responsibilities must be accompanied by the transfer of either an appropriate secure financial provision or appropriate powers of taxation if services are to be maintained. Current steps to decentralize planning responsibility in countries as different as Russia and Korea will depend crucially on the extent to which funding and responsibility transfers can be matched.

3 *Local roads and paths.* At the most local level, particularly in rural areas, the problem is often one of ownership. The presumption that local authorities exist which have an interest and capability to maintain the infrastructure is often unfounded. A number of steps are necessary to overcome this problem. Ownership of the local roads and paths must be clearly vested in the local authority or community council. Local roads should only be constructed after local consultation on facility design. Particularly in the case of subsidiary road and path networks, more direct user involvement in the implementation of road works will also assist the sense of ownership. Common to all these extensions of user participation is a need for institutional change and more diffused training in the necessary technical and administrative skills. This also highlights the importance of locally based non-governmental organizations.

Environmental sustainability and economic instruments

Environmental sustainability is beginning to be recognized as important by the developing countries. But the nature of what is recognized, and the means of addressing the perceived problems, often differ substantially between the developing and developed world.

The perception of the environmental problem

Greenhouse warming and the depletion of the ozone layer are widely regarded in the developed world as the two most challenging long term issues in the developed world. While global warming is at present primarily a result of the industrialization and motorization levels in the OECD-countries in a scenario of a 'rapidly changing world,' *by the year 2010 the presently developing countries will be the largest emittents of CO_2 and CH_4.* Nevertheless, despite the great vulnerability of such countries as Bangladesh to the effects of global warming, it is not generally regarded by them as 'their' problem or responsibility. The adoption of policies to limit their contribution to global warming thus depends heavily on the extent to which effective action can be linked to policies to ameliorate problems which they do recognize (such as local air pollution or the economic burden of fuel imports).

In respect of *local environmental impacts*, road traffic accounts for as much as 90-95 percent of CO and lead, 60-70 percent of NOx and HC, and a major share of particulate matter in megacity centers. In many cities in developing countries levels of SO_x and particulates exceed World Health Organization (WHO) guidelines by very large amounts (in the late 1980s about 1.3 billion people worldwide lived in urban areas that did not meet WHO standards for particulate matter). Above all, over half a million people die each year as a result of road traffic accidents alone. Road traffic also causes noise, visual intrusion, severance of community activity and communication. Moreover, the creation of infrastructure to carry the traffic can also have severe effects on local amenity by physically dividing neighborhoods. While the local conditions have improved in developed countries there is a drastic decline in urban living conditions in many developing country cities. This is now beginning to be recognized as a high policy priority in cities where the impacts have already occurred (Mexico, Bangkok, Seoul, etc.) but it still remains difficult to convince rapidly developing city and national administrations that there is an incipient problem of great magnitude.

The adverse effects of the heavy concentration of motorized traffic in agglomerations is further aggravated by some special features of road transport which exacerbate pollution in developing and transitional economy countries:

1 The large proportion of motorcycles and three wheelers in the vehicle population in many Asian countries and cities.

2 Large fleets of highly-polluting old technology 2-stroke engine automobiles (in

particular in countries of Central and Eastern Europe).

3 The high proportion of buses, taxis and trucks in the traffic stream, often mixed with tractors and slow-moving non-motorized vehicles.

4 Higher average age of the vehicle fleet and very low scrappage rates (average age of the vehicle fleet in many Asian countries in excess of 10-15 years).

5 Indigenous production of obsolete vehicle models (typically in developing countries manufactured automobiles are half as fuel efficient compared to the 'best practice').

6 Poor fuel quality, particularly the high lead content of gasoline and the high sulfur content of diesel.

The role of technology

Wherever possible it is sensible to adopt technological means to overcome problems. We distinguish three complementary approaches to use technology to control the impact of motor vehicles on the environment; improving fuels, improving vehicles, and improving traffic management.

Improving fuel. Automotive fuels in developing countries are among the dirtiest in the world. Lead content of gasoline may be as high as 0.8 to 1.1 gm/liter, compared with .15 gm/liter for leaded (!) fuel in industrialized countries and the sulfur content of diesel is often in excess of 1.0 percent by weight, compared to 0.5 percent or less in industrialized countries.

Introduction of unleaded gasoline and the substitution of CNG for gasoline were both shown to be economic in Indonesia on the basis of their effects on health related costs. But a pilot program to substitute CNG for gasoline in public transport vehicles in Jakarta was retarded by the absence of adequate infrastructure (filling stations) and the perception of only a marginal advantage to the operator. Hence, technological innovations must be supported by appropriate economic incentives. That is not always the case. For example, in Mexico until November 1991 the price of leaded petrol was only 70 percent of unleaded fuel. As a consequence it was more economical to use leaded fuel which destroyed the catalytic converter (thus increasing noxious emissions) and to incur the additional cost of a replacement catalytic converter to comply with legal provisions at the annual test, rather than to use unleaded fuel for which the device is designed.

Improving vehicle type and condition. Typical domestically manufactured automobiles in India, China, Eastern Europe and Latin America are only half as fuel efficient as 'best practice' vehicles in Japan and other OECD countries, and have emission characteristics of 1950/60 vintage motor vehicles, particularly with respect

284

to crankcase and evaporative emissions. As national governments are interested in keeping the jobs in their automobile industry they have little reason to tighten the environmental standards. High average age and poor standard of vehicle maintenance also lead to much higher toxic exhausts per car mile than in developed countries. In countries of Eastern Europe medium size gasoline driven trucks of low fuel efficiency are still prevalent. In the South and East Asian countries two stroke engine motor bikes and three-wheelers account for up to three-quarters of the vehicle population, and hence the vast majority of the emissions; in many cities such as Hanoi, Ho Chi Minh City and Pnom Penh these most polluting vehicles are at present rapidly replacing the least polluting vehicles, the pedal cycle.

In developing countries which import vehicles manufactured in OECD countries it is not too difficult to adopt the highest standards for new vehicles, though it is not clear that adoption of such high standards represents a cost effective strategy in low income countries where other sources of pollution might be attacked more cheaply. Domestic production can also be adjusted step by step to these standards because most producers assemble components licensed by OECD country manufacturers. A start can be made by policies to accelerate the scrapping of high pollution, high mileage vehicles such as older taxis, buses and trucks, as in the Taxi Modernization Program in Mexico City. This is supplemented by a large-scale emissions retrofit program which includes more than 100,000 gasoline minibuses and gasoline trucks. In Santiago an action program has been started to renew the bus fleet; for new cars catalytic converters have been obligatory since September 1992. For existing, often aged, vehicles, maintenance control is the most challenging issue. Substantial efforts are now being made in some countries (for example, Chile, Indonesia and Costa Rica). These measures require the creation of specialist institutions with adequate equipment and trained staff, which typically do not exist in the poorer countries.

Improving traffic management. Some environmentally beneficial improvements are relatively easy to introduce and have achieved success. For example, recognition of the environmentally benign nature of bicycles, both as main and supplementary modes, has resulted in schemes to segregate cycles from motorized modes in circumstances as diverse as Shanghai, Ghana and Mexico, which have increased cyclists' safety and increased average traffic speed.

As gaseous emission rates per motor vehicle kilometer vary inversely with speed control of congestion is frequently seen as the main potential source of environmental improvement. In many countries traffic control systems have been undermined by lack of enforcement and inadequately trained staff for design and implementation. In cities of developing countries, where no coordinated traffic signal schedules have been implemented, traffic management can increase road capacity by as much as 30 percent. Recent developments in electronics have reduced both the initial cost and maintenance needs for such applications as selective bus detection for priority at traffic signals, on-line computerized traffic control, traffic enforcement, and electronic charging. Technology is thus seen as having an important role to play in improved traffic management. More general strategies of reducing congestion through infrastructure expansion are also often supported on environmental grounds.

While these management and investment measures may be justifiable for economic reasons of transport cost reduction, they must not be assumed to be necessarily environmentally beneficial. In this respect 'the devil is in the detail'. The air quality impact of infrastructure improvement will depend critically on the detail of its effect on traffic patterns. This not only includes its effect on where traffic is diverted and what distribution of traffic speeds results, but also its effect on the total volume of travel which will typically increase in response to increased speeds. There remains an important challenge to be able to bring together the environmental and economic resource impacts of such schemes in a way which allows their cost effectiveness to be more fully assessed.

Policy instruments for a better environment

Improvements in vehicles and fuels can undoubtedly attenuate most local air polluting effects of road traffic. However, other environmental impacts — such as noise, visual intrusion, safety, and global pollution effects — are more directly related to traffic volume per se, and require a demand control strategy. The spotlight therefore falls on the development of policy instruments which can restrain the quantities of the most damaging transport activities, by traffic restraint, shifts to less damaging modes, or actions to reduce the amount of transport demanded. These are all policy areas which have attracted much professional attention in the developed countries in recent years, but where achievement has been very variable.

Environment and mode choice in developing countries. For long distances over which a substitution is possible, a fully loaded train requires one third the energy per passenger kilometer of a loaded car and one tenth that of a loaded aircraft. For more local movements non-motorized transport has an equivalent energy advantage over motorized modes. Mode choice is thus often seen as central to environmental policy.

1 *Long distance movement —the role of rail transport.* Railways continue to play an important role in the economy of many developing countries. Railways in China and India employ respectively, 3.4 and 1.6 million people and carry 70 percent and 50 percent of freight traffic respectively. The former Soviet Union railways were even more dominant. But most railways in developing countries have steadily lost traffic to road and air competition. As a consequence they have often become an insupportable drain on the national budget (the Argentine railway deficit in the mid-1980s was US$600 million, equivalent to one percent of GDP or 9 percent of the entire public sector deficit). The key to achieving the potential environmental benefits associated with rail transport is thus to find a basis on which they can establish a commercial market position.

In practice, only where railroads have rationalized their operations have they been able to define a competitive niche for themselves. The 'niches' are not insubstantial. In the case of freight, rail can have a clear competitive role for non-containerized, long-distance, bulk movement of low value products. With the advent of containerization, railroads can also play a significant complementary role in an integrated, multimodal (including ports/maritime and roads/trucking) container system for freight. In the case of passenger transport the role is more circumscribed. In high density population corridors (as in China and India) rail can have a commercial role. High speed rail also requires sufficient occupancy to counterbalance the higher energy consumption and the high cost of the infrastructure. Demand may be sufficient in some densely populated and relatively high income countries such as South Korea. Even in China the population density is such that a first high speed route is planned to link Beijing to Shanghai.

There are two major impediments preventing railways from occupying their appropriate role. First, there is the deadening effect that the lack of commercial freedom has had on managerial initiative. Second, there is often distortion arising from the undercharging of their competitors for the use of publicly provided infrastructure. In the inter-urban context this is largely a matter of levels of fuel taxation that do not cover the sum of the real costs of the fuels and the real costs, by traffic category, of the use of roads. In the urban context, the failure to internalize congestion and environmental externalities is even more critical. In the case of most predominantly, passenger railways (Bangladesh, Egypt and Sri Lanka), as well as urban metro systems, the achievement of potential externality reduction and affordability benefits is likely to require continuing targeted subsidies. Only railways with primarily freight traffic (Mexico, Zimbabwe, China) are likely to be able to maintain commercial viability in the absence of broader institutional and policy reform to internalize externalities.

2 *Non-motorized transport and the local environment.* For passenger movement the bicycle is the most energy efficient of all mechanized modes a ten mile commute requiring only 350 calories. Particularly for low income countries an adequate provision for non-motorized transport is therefore a good economic proposition. Bicycles can achieve nearly 2000 persons per lane per hour at a maximum speed of about 15 km/hr, though that capacity is reduced considerably, as is the speed, as traffic is mixed. In urban areas, autos can achieve little more than 1200 persons per lane hour, albeit at speeds up to 40 kms per hour. Buses can achieve up to 3-4000 per lane hour in mixed traffic situations and up to 20,000 per lane hour at up to about 25 km per hour on separated busways, whilst LRT and metro can do better both in capacity and speed. Hence, if either the road conditions or the level of congestion is such as to keep motorized vehicle speeds down, and separation of vehicles can keep non-motorized vehicle speeds and capacities up, there may be a continuing role for bicycles even with high personal values of time. In particular that is likely to occur for shorter trips or for the local distribution function in conjunction with mass rapid transit linehaul. The impediments to

developing this potential, and recent attempts to overcome them are discussed later.

Improving urban structure. Central to the issue of sustainability is the fact that the process of development is so closely associated with the process of urbanization. In 1950 urban areas accounted for 16 percent of the population of Africa and Asia, 42 percent in Eastern Europe and 41 percent in Latin America. With a tripling of world population in the following half century, it is estimated that by the year 2000 38 percent of the population of Asia and Africa will live in urban areas, 67 percent of Eastern Europe and 77 percent of Latin America. In the developing world, a large proportion of this urban population will live in the megacities. Of 23 cities expected to have populations of over 10 million by the year 2000, 17 will be in developing countries, which are expected to have a further 18 cities with populations over 5 million.

Of itself, urbanization is not the problem. The productivity of most countries is driven by the productivity of their cities, achieved through agglomeration economies. And the productivity of the cities is a function of their size and the efficiency of their transport networks. But the growth of most of the major cities in the developing world has been rapid and uncontrolled. They are frequently characterized by a low proportion of urban space devoted to roads (e.g., 11 percent in Bangkok compared with 20-25 percent in most European cities with well functioning transit systems and 30 percent in some American cities dominated by the car), very mixed traffic composition; inadequate separation between working and living space and moving space (as occurs in most of the larger Indian cities); and an aging and ill maintained vehicle stock (as experienced in Cuba before the current shift to bicycles). These characteristics generate three transport related problems. Firstly, roads are very congested despite moderate per capita car ownership levels (e.g., Mexico City, Buenos Aires and Seoul are saturated at car ownership levels only one third of those of Western Europe). Secondly, traffic contributes to a polluted urban environment (e.g., Mexico, Bangkok, Teheran). Thirdly, journeys to work for the poor are of long duration and often high cost, absolutely and as a proportion of income.

1 *Structure planning.* Distance traveled by private car per capita, and hence fuel consumption per capita, is highly dependent on urban form. Increased net residential density, and linear nucleated urban forms, are sometimes advocated as being more environmentally desirable both because they reduce the total distances that individuals travel and because they are conducive to high density (and hence more viable) public transport systems which attract traffic from the car. The strong negative correlation of urban density with gasoline consumption has been dramatically demonstrated in recent research. High density often means low personal space availability (Figure 8.4). Many of the cities which rank high as 'transport energy efficient cities' rank low in terms of housing quality indicators (for example, Tokyo) or vice versa (most North American cities). Reducing fuel by urban densification may thus be viewed as trading off the internal environment for the external environment. The willingness to plan for one type of city rather than

the other is partly a matter of preferred life style and partly a matter of inherent space availability.

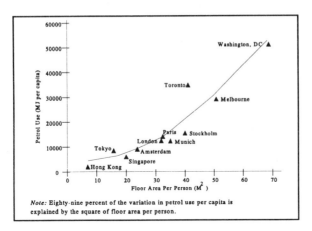

Figure 8.4   Energy consumption vs. housing space in major world cities

In any event, it may seem paradoxical to promote planning of land use whilst at the same time promoting market processes as the means of improving transport service provision. The problem is that, in the absence of prices which reflect all social and environmental costs, incorrect incentives are given for land use decisions. But today's land use decisions determine tomorrow's social and environmental costs. Many secondary cities, and rapidly growing countries such as Vietnam, still have land use patterns which retain the option of development structured around public transport. Given the difficulty of introducing optimal prices, and the extended time period over which the consequences of mistaken past policies might survive market processes, it is highly desirable that governments attempt to shape the developing structure of the city[5].

The operationalization of that prescription is not easy, however. Land use planning and control in developing countries is typically either non-existent, or inadequately enforced. The development of adequate land use planning functions and skills is thus of critical importance to sensible transport facility provision, particularly in fast growing cities with rapidly increasing income levels. But it can be done, as the experience of Curitiba in Brazil shows. The essential requirements for that kind of success are strong political vision, commitment and stability and efficient technical planning support.

Whatever urban structure is adopted, it must be recognized that, especially in very fast growing cities, traffic and demand management are a complement to, and not a substitute for, the creation of infrastructure. Government must plan, and in most cases finance and implement, the major transport infrastructure. Foresighted planning in the early stages of development is essential.

289

Superimposition of extra transport infrastructure capacity in a city in which too small a proportion of land space is allocated to such infrastructure (Bangkok is an extreme example) is inordinately costly, disruptive, and environmentally damaging, whether done at grade, elevated or underground.

2 *Urban mass rapid transit.* For corridors with high traffic volumes mass rapid transit is more economical in the use of space, and less environmentally damaging, than urban transport dependent exclusively on the automobile. But there is a curious 'Catch 22' situation that has afflicted many mass rapid transit proposals. When cities are small the corridor flows are not sufficient to justify mass rapid transit systems. By the time they have grown to the size at which the likely traffic volumes seem adequate, the urban structure has already developed to the stage at which the superimposition of a MRT network is too costly. It is not merely that the capital costs are high, but that the burden on the fisc of maintaining the system is not tolerable under conventional taxation and financial management systems. Particularly where that burden falls directly on the municipality the consequence may be ruinous (as in the case of Pusan where the municipality was bankrupted by the burden of its metro with very adverse consequences on other municipal services).

Caution is particularly appropriate where there are more viable alternatives. For medium and large cities in countries where the bus is the backbone of mass urban movement, such as Bogota, Sao Paulo, Lima and Abidjan, segregated busways have proved able to carry high volumes (up to 20,000 persons per hour per lane) at acceptable speed and at a fraction of the cost of metros. The greater affordability of the busway solution is a great advantage where the potential users are poor and the municipality is unable to bear the subsidy costs necessary to keep fares down to acceptable levels. But that choice is not without its costs. Buses, at street level, not only emit more air pollutants than grade separated rail systems, but also have other adverse environmental impacts, such as the severance of local community linkages. The most famous of all busways, that on the Avenida 9 Julio in Sao Paulo, has severely blighted properties close to it.

Those effects might be minimized by grade separation. That suggests the possibility of a phased approach in which, at an early stage in development rights of way are protected which could be used initially for busways, but eventually for LRT or full metros if volumes justified it. That approach was suggested in Santiago (where in fact the government decided to move directly to full metro on cheap bilateral funding) and in Karachi. It does require, however, considerable foresight, capacity to plan, and willingness to commit to an urban structure.

Part of the reason for financial non-viability of MRT is that, in the absence of appropriate charges for road use, reflecting both congestion and environmental externalities, MRT systems are not able to generate adequate volumes of traffic at prices which are sufficiently high to cover their full costs. Various approaches have been adopted as a 'second best' to optimal pricing. In Korea auto purchasers must also purchase a public transport bond, which, for the cities with metros, is used as a source of capital finance for the metro. There is no logical reason why support should be restricted to capital expenditures. The implicit subsidization of the private auto might be confronted by an explicit recognition that part of the funds raised through taxation on vehicles or fuel, yields of central area parking charges, or from road congestion charges, should be devoted to public transport expenditures to reflect the contribution of metros to the control of congestion.

Increased emphasis on rail based transit also requires its integration into land use schemes. Modal interfaces have to be prepared to make the transfer to other modes feasible. In the case of passenger transport park-and-ride or bike-and-ride facilities can help to stimulate demand for public transport. Bike-and-ride may be a workable strategy also in low income countries, but may require supporting investments in cycle paths because of the high risk of cycling on roads.

Reducing the ecological impact of transport infrastructure. Much of the public concern about the impacts of infrastructure focuses not on the immediate and local impacts but on the much more dispersed and diffused impacts on the nature of development. For example, the transport investments associated with the Carajas Iron Ore Project and the POLONOROESTE program in Brazil, opened up large areas of Amazonia to developments which had some significantly adverse environmental and social effects. The difficulty with these types of program is that whilst they impose costs they may also confer very substantial benefits. A number of lessons were learned from the Amazonia projects experience. Firstly, environmental protection requires an adequate policy, legal and regulatory framework, together with technical capabilities for inspection and enforcement, appropriate legal and economic instruments, and a political commitment (including NGO participation) to achieve the environmental goals. Secondly, there is a need for a full ex ante environmental assessment, having clear spatial units of account so that concentrated problem areas can be identified and treated. This should embody a cross-sectoral and multidisciplinary approach, taking into account induced as well as direct development effects and inter-regional interactions.

Directly restraining road traffic. Given the limited extent to which either improved technology within the sector, shift of traffic to other modes or the use of planning measures to reduce traffic demand can reduce the environmental impact of traffic in large cities the management of demand becomes critical. Rapid 'spreading out' of congestion and environmental impact is to be observed in Asian cities such as Seoul. General non-price attempts to limit traffic have usually been ineffective and may even induce counter-productive effects. 'Non-auto days' as in Mexico City ('hoy no circulo'), or selective license plate availability as in Athens, have shown perverse effects in rescheduling activities or encouraging increased car ownership rather than restraining total amounts of traffic. The Santiago government attempt to keep 20 percent of the private cars off the streets on weekdays has been only partially successful because of difficulties of control. The common feature of these experiences is that attempts to restrain road traffic have usually failed due to lack of public transport alternatives, lack of staff for design and enforcement, and political unwillingness to implement and enforce. To be most effective a range of restraint instruments need to be planned as part of a comprehensive strategy, for which many governments are unprepared.

The role of pricing instruments. Market instruments in demand management have the advantage over more administrative policies in that they stimulate decentralized decision making to find the best way of adjustment according to individual preferences. The appropriate market mechanism oriented response to externalities would be to seek internalization of the effects in the decision processes of individuals through direct charges for environmental impacts. Because there are benefits associated with car use, and because the costs of suppressing emissions is not zero, the optimal level of auto generated pollution is also not zero. Ideally, the marginal pollution cost should be calculated, and an emission charge levied equal to this marginal cost. Although no developing country government has yet explicitly attempted to define an optimal price on these grounds because of difficulties of identifying marginal impacts and of attributing values to them, some countries have begun to move in the direction of using pricing instruments for environmental management purposes.

So far, the most common are uses of differential pricing to encourage the choice of less polluting alternatives, often combined with regulatory measures. These may include differentials in vehicle taxation to encourage the sale of cars with catalytic converters to reduce tailpipe emissions, differentials between diesel and gasoline, fuel price surcharges on the sulfur/heavy oil content of diesel, or lower taxes on clean fuels such as CNG. Perhaps the most commonly used and most successful differential has been that between leaded and unleaded fuels. Even in the absence of a consensus on how environmental impacts should be valued in monetary terms, economic calculations are important in environmental policy as means of selecting cost efficient instruments for the achievement of defined environmental targets and as means of making the most cost effective use of the physical instruments available, as demonstrated in the analysis of alternative instruments for the reduction of air pollution in Mexico City (Figure 8.5).

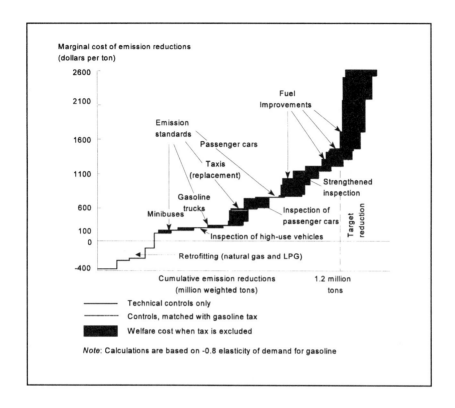

Marginal cost of emission reductions
(dollars per ton)

2600

2100

Fuel
Improvements

Emission
standards

1600

Passenger cars

Taxis
(replacement)

1100

Strengthened
inspection

Gasoline
trucks

600

Minibuses

Inspection of
passenger cars

Target
reduction

100
0

Inspection of high-use vehicles

Retrofitting (natural gas and LPG)

-400

Cumulative emission reductions
(million weighted tons)

1.2 million
tons

——————— Technical controls only

─ ─ ─ ─ ─ ─ Controls, matched with gasoline tax

███ Welfare cost when tax is excluded

Note: Calculations are based on -0.8 elasticity of demand for gasoline

Figure 8.5   **Program to reduce air pollution emissions from transport in Mexico City (with and without a gasoline tax)**

Source: 'A presumptive pigouvian tax on gasoline: complementing regulation to mimic an emission free'. *World Bank Economic Review* 8 (13): 373-94.

In the absence of a sophisticated technology to charge for emissions directly, the price of fuel may be the best available proxy. Increased fuel taxation has the advantage that it gives environmentally beneficial incentives in a number of dimensions, including not only short term responses concerning the number and length of trips made but also longer term decisions concerning choice of locations, modes and vehicle type. Whilst the calculation of 'right prices' of externalities for developing countries remains controversial the available evidence does suggest an optimal fuel price substantially above those prevailing at present even in high tax countries. Moreover, because the absolute value of income elasticity of demand for gasoline is greater than its price elasticity, the real value of this optimum charge should increase as incomes rises. Higher prices of fuel have been a component of comprehensive strategies for transport and the environment in countries such as Mexico, Thailand and Indonesia.

A logically equivalent approach to setting a price equal to an identified marginal pollution cost would be to identify the optimal level of emissions (that level at which marginal cost was just equal to marginal benefit) and to set prices to clear the market at that level. This is the 'tradeable permits' approach now being extensively discussed in OECD countries. The Singapore auctioning of permissions to purchase cars is the only notable example of this approach outside the OECD.

Safety

Over half a million people die each year from road traffic injuries. Seventy percent of these fatalities occur in developing countries. This represents between 30 and 80 annual traffic fatalities per 10,000 registered vehicles in developing countries compared with 2-5 per 10,000 vehicles in the developed world. Most of the victims in the developing world are pedestrians. In India, for instance, only 5 percent of those killed or critically injured were in cars. The economic cost of these accidents is high. In Kenya in 1990 it was estimated that the costs of traffic accidents were the equivalent of 1.3 percent of GDP.

Many factors contribute to accidents. One set relates to road users and their behavior, including the age, experience and training of drivers; excessive speed and a reluctance to use safety devices; the influence of alcohol, drugs, and stress, fatigue or illness; and in some cases a low value placed on human life. A second set relates to vehicles, including poor maintenance of vehicles and tires; lack of protection of passengers, particularly in trucks, and the prevalence of motor cycles in early stages of development. A third set relates to the infrastructure, including poor road design, alignment and surface conditions; frequent intersections and uncontrolled access; mixture of heavy and light traffic; and particularly lack of protection for non-motorized vehicles and pedestrians in mixed flows.

Conditions in many developing countries differ fundamentally from those in the developed countries. The predominance of non-motorized traffic and pedestrians, the lack of experience of drivers, and the unsuitability of much of the infrastructure for mixed traffic all suggest greater attention to protecting these vulnerable road users. The implication is that the most effective measures for improving safety in developing countries may be different from those in developed countries. In particular, separation of motor vehicles from other traffic, separation of living and working space from moving space, provision of separated space for pedestrians and non-motorized vehicles, and stronger protection of their rights of way at points of conflict need to be a high priority. Driver training and testing appear to be less effective in developing than developed countries. For example, a study of bus drivers in Pakistan found that though training improved their test scores, it did not change their behavior on the road or reduce accidents. Speed limits and alcohol regulations are often similarly ineffective due to poor enforcement.

Economic instruments are rarely used. More explicit treatment of safety impacts in economic appraisals of infrastructure projects could improve project design and selection. In principle, obligatory third party insurance associated with well enforced compensation liability systems should have the effect of making drivers more conscious of their external impact. In fact, however, the policing and legal systems are often inadequate for this purpose, with the result that there are no strong economic inducements to improve safety.

Social sustainability and economic instruments

Poverty reduction objectives in transport policy

It has been argued earlier that there is a strong correlation between economic growth and the reduction of absolute poverty at the national level. Notwithstanding this general 'trickle down' effect there can be some seriously perverse distributional impacts of transport improvement. Poorly designed transport provisions can perpetuate poverty by imposing on the poor a higher burden of time, effort and cost for mobility. For the rural poor, deprivation is largely associated with the inability to access materials and services essential to their (largely agricultural) activities and to market their products. For the urban poor the critical issue is an ability to access employment.

The transport related problems of the poor have two main causes. First, transport improvements have been inadequately targeted to the needs of the poor. Second, there has been inadequate protection for the poor against distributionally adverse consequences of otherwise desirable transport development. These problems are dealt with *seriatim*.

Targeting policy to help the poor

Rural roads. The allocation of scarce capital resources to activities promising the highest economic return can result in trunk and arterial transport networks and services bypassing large areas of the country (or globe) where the poor are concentrated. For example, a third of China's population and three-quarters of Ethiopia's population do not currently have access to paved roads (or all-weather transport), and gain little or nothing from the expansion of product and capital markets made possible by developments in the formal transport sector. It is the availability of adequate subsidiary networks that is crucial to these rural populations.

In fact, recent World Bank studies show a significant general deterioration in these assets, particularly in Sub-Saharan Africa, (including South Africa), where half of its 880,000 kilometers of rural roads are in poor condition. Rural roads were found to lack an overall policy framework, clear country strategies and coordination. Efforts to improve rural roads were not matched by attention to sustainable network-wide maintenance. Country capacities to plan, fund, implement and monitor rural road works were often inadequate, and efforts to improve institutional capacities have not always been successful. Improvement of that situation requires an appropriate institutional framework; a consistent plan for sustainable road maintenance; and effective implementation.

In establishing a strategy to improve the situation local beneficiary participation is crucial because local agencies have necessary information not available centrally and because local 'ownership' will improve the efficiency of implementation and maintenance. In many cases roads have been built by central government, often in agricultural or integrated rural development projects, with no one responsible for the maintenance. Participation should thus include involvement in needs assessment and prioritization. Simplified economic criteria can contribute to this assessment. District Development Committees have been set up in Uganda, Kenya and Ghana to strengthen local coordination and to give a degree of local autonomy in implementation. Even with improved institutional and planning capacity, there is a major need in many countries for strengthening implementation capability.

Non-motorized transport and the poor. Non-motorized transport plays a surprisingly large role even in industrialized countries where it accounts for nearly half of trips in some medium sized towns. In equivalently sized towns in India this proportion rises to between 50 and 80 percent. The cycle is dominant even in public passenger transport in some countries (for example, cycle rickshaws account for 50 percent of the vehicles, 70 percent of passengers and 43 percent of passenger mileage in Dhaka). Non-motorized vehicles account for a large proportion of urban traffic composition in many cities (Figure 8.6).

As in industrialized countries, mode choice is very income sensitive. Private transport is typically preferred to public and motorized to non-motorized. At very low incomes, or in periods of declining income, even the simplest form of mechanized transport, the bicycle, is beyond the means of many. For example, during the last decade in Africa as incomes collapsed the number of bicycles has diminished at a rather similar rate to that of motorized vehicles. On average, walking accounts for 25-50 percent of total daily trips in Central African and Asian cities, and more than 60 percent for the very poorest groups. In Delhi, 65 percent of people living in squatter areas walk to work, compared to 10 percent of low income and only 3 percent of middle income workers. Moreover, the average walking and cycling distances in developing countries are five times as great as those in developed countries. Because of this high level of dependence of the very poor on non-motorized transport, improvements of non-motorized transport are amongst the best focused ways of helping them.

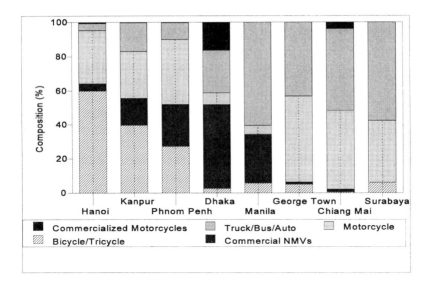

Figure 8.6   **Comparison of vehicle composition in eight Asian cities**
Source: Padeco Co. Ltd. 1995. 'Non-motorized vehicles in ten Asian cities: inventory of needs and opportunities'. Draft final report.

During the early stages of development, non-motorized transport also plays an important role in the freight market (Box 5). In Sub-Saharan Africa, where almost all rural transport is non-motorized, 90 percent is freight transport. The most dramatic improvement in this respect would be a shift from walking to cycling. For example, a study in Ghana showed that it takes 2 person days to move 1 ton-km by headloading, as against 1 person hour for a bicycle and trailer. What is more controversial is the role of non-motorized transport in longer term planning as incomes grow, particularly in urban areas. Non-motorized vehicles are unlikely to be able to exceed a productive capacity of 240 tons per hour per meter lane width, at a maximum speed of 10-15 km/ hour, whilst trucks can move over 1000 tons per lane hour at an average speed up to 40 km/hour.

The potential of non-motorized transport to assist both the poor and the urban environment tends to be very neglected for several reasons.

1 *Physical vulnerability.* This is largely due to the poor design of roads, with inadequate separation of fast and slow moving traffic on roads with insufficient capacity to safely sustain both at their free flow speeds.

2 *Fiscal discrimination.* Bicycles are often treated fiscally as a luxury good. Mark-ups on border prices have ranged between 200 and 500 percent in Tanzania, Ethiopia and Ghana. in Bangladesh in 1990 bicycles were subject to a 150 percent import duty. Maintaining the existing stock has been equally difficult; in 1992 in Zimbabwe only 17 percent of the available stock were in operation due to lack of spare parts or adequate local maintenance facilities.

3 *Non-local manufacture.* Production of bicycles remains concentrated in about a dozen countries which manufacture over 90 percent of the world's bicycles. Attempts to establish protected local cycle industries in the 1970s in Kenya, Tanzania and Mozambique failed due to low product quality and high cost of local parts manufacture.

4 *Lack of finance.* In 1992 a bicycle cost seven months average income in Uganda, ten months in Malawi and Tanzania and over three years income in Ethiopia. Informal sector credit arrangements are extremely expensive, whilst arrangements

to provide commercial credit to relatively poor people, such as those of the Grameen Bank in Bangladesh, are unusual. Risk of theft accentuates the problem.

Some of these issues are now being addressed. Safety is being improved by separation of motorized and non motorized traffic in a number of countries. For example, the first phase of a plan for a comprehensive cycle network in Pune, India, has involved construction of two lightweight river bridges for cyclists and pedestrians only. The World Bank is funding the creation of special bicycle routes in the cities of Shanghai and Ghuangzhou, and in rural areas in Ghana, Sierra Leone and Kenya. The development and application of composite economic and environmental appraisal procedures for non-motorized transport has been a very neglected area.

Novel schemes to assist the financing of a range of NMT vehicles have also been implemented recently. Government initiatives to finance rural vehicles as diverse as hand carts, bicycles, rickshaws and vehicle carts have come into operation in Burkina Faso, Zimbabwe and India, in all cases associated with rural development programs and using government credit institutions to finance or guarantee loans. NGOs have taken the initiative in developing credit schemes for bicycles and trailers in Sri Lanka and Bangladesh. Two features are common to these schemes. First, they are highly decentralized, with NGOs commonly involved in implementation. Second, successful schemes tend to lend through the intermediation of groups who assume liability for repayment of the loan.

Liberalization and the informal sector. In many cities in developing countries the areas housing the very poorest groups (often shanty settlements on the periphery) are beyond walking distance from the main locations of employment. In consequence governments have often relied on regulating the fares of a protected monopoly operator, in the belief that the service needs of the poor can be maintained by cross subsidy from profitable to unprofitable routes in the network. Unfortunately, fares set at affordable levels for the longer journeys of the poor frequently generate insufficient revenue for cross subsidy. The consequence is frequently that the regulated operators are unable to maintain vehicles, as in Yaounde and Douala where SOTUC is only able to keep about half of its vehicles on the road, and service, as in Dakar, where the regulated operator is now only able to supply one quarter of the demand. General fare control, without adequate financial provision for subsidy, is thus both wasteful (because it does not concentrate on those who need support most) and counterproductive (because it destroys service provision to the poor).

The common failure of government regulated public transport monopolies to maintain service affects the transitional as well as developing country cities. In Eastern Europe many public transport systems are facing severe problems as the richer obtain cars, patronage declines, and financial deficits mount to levels which are fiscally unsustainable. An extreme example is the Russian Republic where cost recovery was only a little over 10 percent, and where urban transport subsidies amounted to 6 percent of GDP in 1993. Many FSU municipal bus companies are unable to replace their vehicles.

Especially in countries where employment is scarce and wages very low, mobilization of the capability of the informal sector is often a way of ensuring that minimum cost, basic, service continues to be provided. Even without legal liberalization the informal sector often steps in to provide the service no longer available from the regulated operator (as in the case of the Blue Cars in Dakar). Legally liberalizing entry permits the informal sector to provide service which, though inferior in quality, is at affordably lower costs [e.g., matatus]. In many African cities these services have been the safety net which has provided the only available and affordable transport for the poor in the face of deterioration in the traditional urban public transport modes.

Increased scope for the informal sector can also have significant effects on direct poverty reduction because of the entrepreneurial and income generating possibilities that it offers for the relatively poor, as in the case of the rickshaws of Bangladesh or the black taxis of South Africa.

Choice of technology. Where labor is underemployed its money cost to an employer may exceed its real cost to the country. The market will therefore tend to choose methods of production which pay more attention to labor saving than is optimal, with adverse consequences for the very poorest. This problem can be addressed in infrastructure project selection and design. The intensive use of local labor in construction and maintenance of rural roads and the access they provide to markets typically have the most direct impact on some of the poorest groups in many countries. For example, the Maharashtra Employment Guarantee Scheme, which has been carrying out labor-intensive small scale rural public works since the mid-1970s, has been quite effective in reaching the poor; at its peak it accounted for about 3 percent of rural employment in the target areas. The Bangladesh Food For Work program has also successfully targeted the very poor for employment in expanding the rural road network.

In addition to being an important source of jobs, labor-based work methods can be cheaper and more reliable than capital-intensive works. In Ghana, small contractors with about four months of training in labor-based rehabilitation techniques and two months of trial contracts, were able to produce an average of 2 km of high quality gravel road per month at 15 percent less cost and up to 40 percent savings in foreign exchange over conventional capital-intensive methods. The Kenya Rural Access Roads Program established a rolling contract system with one-man contractors ('lengthmen') recruited from villages along local roads responsible for routine maintenance of a total of 7800 km of roads. The Gambia has had great success in the use of petty contracts for maintenance activities such as desilting of ditches, gravel excavation, grass-cutting and materials hauling. Small-scale village-based petty contractors were able to learn quickly the skills needed to organize workers to carry out tasks similar to the agricultural activities with which they were already familiar. Part-time routine maintenance work near their homes has been particularly popular among women.

Urban public transport. The case for a more commercial approach to urban public transport in developing and transitional economies has been discussed earlier. The most common concern about this approach is that commercialization, and particularly free competition, undermines the basis of traditional cross-subsidy, to the disadvantage of the poor. This may be the case in some circumstances, but there are several reasons why the concern should be treated very cautiously.

1 Elimination of cross subsidy may not be harmful to the poor. 'Public service obligations' have frequently disguised subsidy payments to already advantaged classes. In the Russian Federation where between 11 and 50 percent of passengers (including government servants, military personnel, transport staff, heroes of the state) have exemption and the existence of such a large category of exemptions encouraged fare evasion by up to 30 percent of those who should pay (again, not necessarily the most needy).

2 Low fares have in some cases resulted in uneconomically high trip rates (for example in Budapest). The reduction of such excessive demand may even allow cost recovery to be increased without fare increases where the overall capacity is determined by the all day demand rather than by the journey to work peak.

3 Extremely low fares in some of the transitional economies means that substantial fare increases, though politically unpopular, will still maintain journey to work transport costs at a low proportion of incomes, and hence have a relatively small effect in generating new poverty. The critical issues in these cases is often the pace of change, and the longer term effects on modal shifts, rather than the creation of substantial new poverty.

4 Liberalization may permit entry into the market of informal sector suppliers of transport service which is affordable to the poor. For example, deregulation of entry into the taxi (minibus) market in South Africa in 1987 allowed a rapid expansion of services to the black townships (albeit associated with much criminal violence). Similarly, after some years of sharply declining public transport supply and increasing fares in Lagos in the eighties, unregulated minibus services operated in a demand responsive manner ('kabu-kabu') have emerged since 1988 to become the dominant mode.

Whilst increased cost recovery associated with commercialization of public transport may be desirable in many cases, it is not always so. There are also situations, for example where high transport costs were the consequence of colonial land use and social policies, where the distributional consequences of commercial transport service are very adverse (as for example in Pretoria or Harare). In these circumstances direct measures may be necessary to provide affordable transport for the disadvantaged.

However, general subsidies are wasteful both because of their undiscriminating nature and because they encourage inefficient operation. Where subsidy is considered necessary it is therefore essential that it is (i) is precisely targeted and (ii) carefully administered to ensure that it is not captured by the suppliers or squandered in inefficient operation.

Where the problem is well defined geographically (as for example in the black townships in South Africa) subsidy may be efficiently targeted by route, with the maintenance of specific unremunerative services, whether subject to price control or not, designated as a public service obligation to be met by the operator. The costs of any public intervention should be fully financed through a service contract between the government and the operating agency. The service to be provided should be precisely specified and monitored. The duration of contracts and the associated subsidy should be limited to ensure frequent re-appraisal. Wherever possible competitive pressures should be employed to minimize the cost of providing the desired service.

Where deprivation is geographically more diffused, well targeted support may involve the use of subsidies on journey to work tickets channeled through either the employer or operator. Whilst in general income supplements are preferable to such payments in kind, the absence of an appropriate administrative framework for direct income transfers may make this difficult in many countries. Targeting individuals requires the identification of the category to benefit and the establishment of channels through which subsidies can be distributed and administered. Subsidies to workers, such as the Brazilian *vale de transport* can be handled through the employer where major employers are concerned, but create difficulty for the small enterprise and the informal sector. In contrast, the requirements of women, who frequently expend a larger proportion of their time on transport and suffer greater transport privation than men, tend to be relatively neglected.

Both of these approaches pose administrative capability requirements which may not be met in many developing countries, and where considerable inefficiency of service provision and misdirection of the subsidy may be the inevitable penalty of any attempt to organize subsidies. For that reason the most effective protection of the transport needs of the poor may consist of a combination of ensuring maximum freedom for the informal sector—which in many countries is the most significant supplier of transport to the very poor—and directing public investments into forms of transport (public transport, NMTs) most used by the poor.

Spatial relocation and resettlement. Adjustments in the scale and density of transport networks in response to locational changes in economic activity and demographic concentrations often results in spatial displacement. Because major transport infrastructure requires substantial amounts of land, they inevitably involve a substantial disturbance of activities (including agriculture) and of people. The adverse impacts of change may be disproportionately concentrated on the poor who are less well able to adjust to or to pre-empt them. In the case of physical resettlement of population governments have become increasingly sensitive to the great social and political damage that can be done. But there is still need to improve procedures and to ensure that efficient resettlement provisions are embodied in project designs rather than being left as conditions to be fulfilled.

Redundancy and severance. In many countries the transport sector employs significant quantities of redundant labor. For example, Indian Railways employ one tenth of all public servants, of whom 400,000 or more a quarter of the total may be redundant. Railways in Ghana, Brazil and Argentina and both ports and railways in Chile, were able to reduce staff by at least half on reorganization with little if any loss of output. This degree of redundancy is often caused by technological change in the sector, such as a shift from steam to diesel locomotion or innovations in signaling and traffic handling in railways, or containerization in ports. Trade unions seek protection against the adverse effects of change by enforcing the continuation of old staffing ratios (for example, 22 workers continued to be employed per container unloaded after containerization in the port of Bombay, although only one or two were needed), rigid craft divisions, and geographical areas of protection. Even where some staff reduction is accepted unions may be able to secure government commitments to protect outdated employment arrangements for those remaining, as in the case of the new bulk sugar terminal of the Mauritius Marine Authority which has been struggling ever since to overcome the costs imposed by the agreement.

The problem is compounded rather than resolved by government regulations and practices which increase or maintain employment in the public sector transport enterprises for social reasons, such as the system of guaranteed employment for life as found in Egypt and the former Soviet bloc countries, or laws limiting the private employer's right to fire workers in many other developing countries such as India, Sudan, Senegal and Côte d'Ivoire. For, in such circumstances, competition from other modes, such as road transport competition with rail, leads to loss of business, inadequate cash flow to maintain equipment, and failure of service quality. For example, the staff to bus ratio of the Ghana Omnibus Service Authority, unable to finance spare parts of new buses, but unwilling to shed labor, rose in 1988 to 55 to 1, compared to the ratio of 4 or 5 to one achievable by many public sector bus operators.

The consequences of redundancy are far reaching. Inability to shed labor may be a serious impediment to reorganization, and particularly to privatization. Within the enterprise it may lead to a low and compressed salary structure, impairing morale, encouraging moonlighting, and inhibiting the employment of higher skilled staff. The immediate costs for the national budget are high, for example, Argentine Railways prior to restructuring imposed a cost of 1 percent of GDP. The long term costs of unproductive public sector employment may be to crowd out productive investment, with an adverse dynamic effect on growth.

Although elimination of redundancy is of long term benefit, the short term effects may be to create a new, concentrated pocket of poverty. Even where 'ghost workers' are being eliminated from payrolls, as in the Gambia where 11 percent of the civil service payroll was eliminated following audit, there are some concentrated income losses. The establishment of a strategy to reconcile long term structural change with

303

the avoidance of new poverty is thus very important.

The least painful solution is to increase output so that labor is no longer surplus. In some cases, such as ports in Korea and Thailand, this is facilitated by general growth of the economy. In other cases, diversification of product or area of operation may obviate the need to shed labor. Redeployment of workers to other public sector employment, as in the Uruguayan and Costa Rican rail reorganizations may have a similar effect, though the usefulness of this strategy depends on the ability to match skills or retrain, and on the real need for labor in the receiving sectors. In some cases it may be possible to form a direct link between private sector development with the process of eliminating redundancy from public enterprises. This has been done by the transfer of assets to employees (as with buses in the winding up of JOC in Jamaica or trucks in the privatization of EFTA in Ethiopia), or the creation of workers' cooperatives in the fragmentation of parastatals (for example in the port of Vladivostock), which may achieve voluntary separation from previous employment whilst forming the basis for a market expansion resulting from increased efficiency.

Where these possibilities do not exist the process of structural change is more difficult. The use of voluntary retirement and limitations on recruitment may still be capable of yielding substantial reductions over a longer period. Brazilian railway staff was reduced by 60 percent over two decades in this way. But this approach may adversely affect efficiency as the better staff leave, and crucial skills cannot be replaced. And it may fail through loss of resolve by government, as in the case of the plan for staff reduction in the Sri Lanka Transport Boards after a period of staff reduction between 1982 and 1986. In Ethiopia staff retrenchment associated with the abolition of the Marine Transport Authority led to such public protest, including hunger strikes, that the government has been reluctant to restructure other transport parastatals.

Where voluntary solutions are not achievable the only way to avoid poverty creation is by compensation. For example, in the port sector in Chile and Benin, the railway sector in Argentina, Brazil, Chile, Ghana, Cameroon and Sudan, and to a lesser extent in urban public transport in Sri Lanka and Ghana that has been handled by severance pay arrangements. As shown in a study of state owned transport enterprises in six countries, the long run savings on the wage bill may enable governments to recoup costs in a short time (between 4 months and 4.5 years in the cases studied), despite high levels of severance payments. Although severance pay arrangements may pay for themselves, it is frequently the case that privatization will not be possible unless excess labor can be shed.

A reformed economic order for sustainable transport

Broadening the scope of transport objectives to encompass environmental and social sustainability potentially generates some conflicts with the traditional elements of material economic welfare. In practice, in the developing and transitional economies the synergy between the objectives is often more striking than the conflicts. A sound economic and financial basis is the *sine qua non* for the development of broader sustainability. Economic rationality is no less important to social and environmental improvement than it is to conventional material welfare. Extending the role of markets and the private sector is an important contributor to improving economic rationality, and much can be done to this end in the transport sector. That radically alters, but does not eliminate the role and responsibility of government.

In summary, the strategy for securing the best contribution of transport to sustainable development requires a revised economic order in which governments perform four main functions:

1 *The market creation function* involves identifying and establishing the appropriate competitive market form. Introducing competition is not just a matter of sweeping away traditional barriers to entry but also requires industrial restructuring (to create some potential competitors), administrative restructuring (to create markets and to monitor their performance), legal restructuring (to enforce a level playing field), and consumer restructuring (to prevent traditional linkages between state enterprises distorting opportunities for new entrants).

2 *The system management function* requires the development of instruments to reconcile private operation with public welfare where this will not automatically emerge from unmanaged private sector initiative. This implies getting infrastructure pricing right; developing efficient franchising and contracting mechanisms; setting environmental standards; and managing welfare transfers.

3 The *resource allocation functions* falling to government under a more commercial transport sector organization require interactive land use/transport planning instruments; coordinated infrastructure network planning: and budgeting for public infrastructure.

4 The *public sector re-organization function* requires the separation of political direction and operational management; and localizing responsibilities. It is usually the case that neither the state enterprise nor its sponsoring ministry, nor any other ministry acting alone, has full authority or political resources to insure such restructuring. Success therefore often requires involvement of central ministries (such as finance or planning) and understanding and commitment at the highest political levels. Even when political commitment is obtained there are problems concerned with the market structure to be created (whether to break up the parastatal into smaller units or not), and the pace of change (whether to commercialize before privatization or not).

Securing the environmental and social dimensions of sustainable growth must be integrated within these functions of government. The combination of these additional concerns with increasing reliance on market processes for service supply thus generates a set of new requirements for governments:

1 to better identify the real transport related environmental and poverty impacts;

2 to devise market compatible instruments to address targeted impacts;

3 to create the necessary institutional arrangements for the more locally responsive policy interventions involved in the new approach;

4 to provide appropriate and secure funding for the poverty related initiatives.

In many cases the necessary skills do not yet exist to respond to these challenges. For example, a targeted public transport service subsidy approach requires the initial specification of a route structure and associated fares and service levels, the development of contract letting, monitoring and enforcement skills. Similarly, resettlement requires new social survey and analysis as well as planning and implementation skills. Even labor based road maintenance requires new forms of technical and managerial capability. Because of the essentially local nature of the services being purchased these skills are also required at the local level. Improved economic skills and understanding are an essential element in all of these difficult areas.

Notes

1   This paper draws heavily from the recent World Bank paper 'Sustainable Transport.' I am grateful to my co-author Zmarak Shalizi and other colleagues, particularly Jerry Lebo, Lou Thompson and Hans Peters, for their contributions to the paper. However, the interpretations and conclusions expressed in this report are entirely those of the author and should not be attributed in any manner to the World Bank, to its affiliated organizations, or to the Members of its board of Executive Directors or the countries they represent.

2   Note that the observed association of the very highest income societies with a particular transport structure thus does not necessarily prove either that high income can only be achieved in that way, or that those who enjoy it would choose it in preference to all other possible outcome combinations if they were in a position to do so.

3   An early study of 37 developing countries, over the period 1955-65 showed a positive correlation between earmarked taxes as a proportion of gross investment, and road expenditure as a proportion of gross investment, supporting a tentative conclusion that there is a positive relationship and a likely causality between the amount earmarked and the amount spent on roads. However, the differences in the cross section analysis were not statistically significant. See Eklund, P. 1967 Earmarking of Taxes for Highways in Developing Countries. Economics Department Working Paper 1. World Bank, Economics Department, Washington, D.C.

4   The privatization of the New Zealand railway system was a rare case where the ownership of the track passed entirely into private ownership.

5   This was one of the three main thrusts in the 1975 World Bank Urban Transport Policy paper.

References

Antle, J.M. 1983. 'Infrastructure and Aggregate Agricultural Productivity: International Evidence'. *Economic Development and Cultural Change*. 31(3):609-619.

Binswanger, H., M-C. Cheng, A. Bowers and Y. Mundlak (1987). 'On the Determinants of Cross-Country Aggregate Agricultural Supply'. *Journal of Econometrics*. 36(1/2):111-131.

Bird, R. (1984). *Intergovernmental Finance in Colombia: Final Report of the Mission on Intergovernmental Finance*. Harvard University Law School: 87-115. Agriculture, 1964-1979. *World Development*. 15(9):1201-1217.

Creightney, C. (1993). *Transport and Economic Performance: A Survey of Developing Countries*. Technical Paper 232. World Bank, African Regional Office, Technical Department, Washington, D.C.

Daimler Benz A.G. (1990). Strategy for the Development of Road Transport in China until the Year 2000. Forschungsinstitut: Berlin.

Dick, M. (1989). 'Earmarking of Transport Funds in Colombia' *Earmarking, Road Funds and Toll Roads: A World Bank Symposium*. World Bank, Infrastructure and Urban Development Department, Washington, D.C.

Downing. A.,C. Baguley and B. Hills (1993). 'Road Safety in Developing Countries: An Overview' *Proceedings of the PTRC 19th Summer Annual Meeting*. London: PTRC.

Easterly, W. and S. Rebelo (1993). 'Fiscal Policy and Economic Growth' *Journal of Monetary Economics* 32 (2-3): 417-458.

Esfahani, H.S. (1987). 'Growth, Employment and Income Distribution in Egyptian Agriculture, 1964-1979'. *World Development*. 15(9): 1201-1217.

Faiz, A. (ed.) (1992). *Air Pollution from Motor Vehicles*. Draft. World Bank, Washington, D.C.

Fields, G. (1991). 'Growth and Income Distribution.' in *Essays on Poverty, Equity and Growth*. G. Psacharopoulos (ed.) New York: Pergamon Press.

Galenson, A. (1989). *Labor Redundancy in the Transport Sector*. Working Paper 158. World Bank, Infrastructure and Urban Development Department, Transport Division, Washington, D.C.

Gelb, A., J. Knight and R. Sabot (1988). *Lewis through a Looking Glass: Public Sector Employment, Rent Seeking and Economic Growth*. World Bank Working Paper 133. World Bank, Policy Research Department, Washington, D.C.

Goldstein, E. (1993). *The Impact of Rural Infrastructure on Rural Poverty: Lessons for South Asia*. Internal Discussion Paper IDP-131. World Bank, South Asia

Regional Office, Washington, D.C.

Guensler, R. and D. Sperling (1994). 'Congestion Pricing and Motor Vehicle Amazons: An Initial Review. *Curbing Gridlock: Peak Period Fees to Relieve Congestion.* National Research Council, Transportation Research Board. Washington, D.C. National Academy Press.

Gwilliam, K. (1993). *Urban Bus Operators' Associations.* Infrastructure Note UT-3. World Bank, Transportation, Water and Urban Development Department, Transport Division, Washington, D.C.

Gwilliam, K., S. Joy and R. Scurfield (1994). *Constructing a Competitive Environment in Urban Public Transport.* Draft. World Bank, Transportation, Water and Urban Development Department, Transport Division, Washington, D.C.

Gwilliam, K.M. and Z Shalizi (1995). *Road Funds, User Charges and Taxes* TWU Discussion Paper TWU 25. December, 1995. Washington, D.C.

Gyamfi, P. and G. Ruan (1992). *Infrastructure Maintenance in LAC: The Costs of Neglect and Options for Improvement.* Regional Studies Program Report 17. World Bank, Latin America and Caribbean Regional Office, Technical Department, Washington, D.C.

Hamer, A.M. (1986). *Urban Sub-Saharan Africa in Macro-Economic Perspective: Selected Issues and Options.* World Bank, Washington, D.C.

Harral, C. and J. Eaton (1986). *Improving Equipment Management in Highway Authorities in Developing Countries.* Transportation Issues Series 2. World Bank, Operations Policy Department, Transportation Division, Washington, D.C.

Harral, C. and A. Faiz (1988). *Road Deterioration in Developing Countries: Causes and Remedies.* World Bank, Infrastructure and Urban Development Department, Washington, D.C.

Heggie, I.G. (1991). *Improving Management and Charging Policies for Roads: An Agenda for Reform.* World Bank, Transportation, Water and Urban Development Department, Transport Division, Washington, D.C.

Heierli, U. (1993). *Environmental Limits to Motorization.* Switzerland: Neidermann, A. G.

Howe, J.D.F. (ed.) (1985). *Rural Transport in Developing Countries.* London: Intermediate Technology Publications.

Kessides, C. (1992). 'Note on the State of Knowledge and Experience with Labor Intensive Public Works Programs'. World Bank, Infrastructure and Urban Development Department, Urban Division, Washington, D.C.

Khosa, M. M. 'Transport and the 'Taxi Mafia' in South Africa' *The Urban Age* Vol. 2, No. 1. Fall, 1993.

Kogan, J. and L. Thompson. (1994). 'Reshaping Argentina's Railways' *East Japan Railway Culture Foundation.*

Lee, K.S., and A. Anas (1989). *Manufacturers' Responses to Infrastructure Deficiencies in Nigeria: Private Alternatives and Policy Options.* World Bank, Infrastructure and Urban Development Department, Washington, D.C.

Messerlin P. et al. (1990). 'The Uruguay Round—Services in the World Economy'. The World Bank. Washington, D.C.

308

Organization for Economic Cooperation and Development (OECD) (1992). *Climate Change: Designing a Tradeable Permit System*. Paris: OECD.

Organization for Economic Cooperation and Development (OECD) (1994). *Final Report of the Joint OECD/ECMT Project Group on Urban Travel and Sustainable Development*. Draft. Paris: OECD.

Pankaj, T. (1989). 'Road Fund Experience in Ghana'. *Earmarking, Road Funds and Toll Roads: A World Bank Symposium*. World Bank, Infrastructure and Urban Development Department, Washington, D.C.

Peters, H. J. (1990). *India's Growing Conflict Between Transport and Trade: Issues and Options*. Working Paper 346. World Bank, Transportation, Water and Urban Development Department, Transport Division, Washington, D.C.

Peters, H.J. (1993). *The Maritime Transport Crisis*. Discussion Paper 220. World Bank, Transportation, Water and Urban Development Department, Transport Division, Washington, D.C.

Persson, T. and G. Tabellini (1994). 'Is Inequality Harmful to Growth?' *American Economic Review*. 84(3):600-621.

Ravaillion, M. (1990). *Reaching the Poor through Rural Public Employment: A Survey of Theory and Evidence*. World Bank Discussion Paper 94. World Bank, South Asia Regional Office, Washington, D.C.

Ray, M., M. Mason, S. Thriscutt and M. Guerin (1992). *Road Rehabilitation and Maintenance in Central and Eastern Europe*. World Bank, Europe and Central Asia Regional Office, Technical Department, Infrastructure Division, Washington, D.C.

Riverson, J. and S. Carapetis (1991). *Intermediate Means of Transport in Sub-Saharan Africa: Its Potential for Improving Rural Travel and Transport*. World Bank Technical Paper 161. World Bank, Africa Regional Technical Department, Infrastructure Division, Washington, D.C.

Ross, A. and M. Mwiraria (1992). *Review of World Bank Experience in Road Safety*. World Bank, Infrastructure and Urban Development Department, Transport Division, Washington, D.C.

Shirley, M. and J. Nellis (1991). *Public Enterprise Reform: The Lessons of Experience*. World Bank, Policy Research Department, Finance and Private Sector Development Division, Washington, D.C.

Stein, L. (1989). 'Third World Poverty, Economic Growth and Income Distribution. *Canadian Journal of Development Studies* 10(2):225-240.

Svejar, J. and K. Terrell (1991). *Reducing Labor Redundancy in State Owned Enterprises*. Research and External Affairs Working Paper 792. World Bank, Research and External Affairs Department, Washington, D.C.

United Nations Centre for Human Settlements (HABITAT) (1987). *Global Report of Human Settlements 1986*. New York: Oxford University Press.

United Nations (1992). *United Nations Framework Convention on Climate Change*. New York: United Nations.

Urban Age Vol. 2, No. 1.

World Bank (1990). *Kenya Urban Transport Development Issues*. Africa Regional Office, Technical Department, Infrastructure Division, Washington, D.C.

World Bank (EDI) and Economic Commission for Africa (1991). 'The Road Maintenance Initiative: Building Capacity for Policy Reform'. *Readings and Case Studies*. Vol. 2. World Bank, Washington, D.C.

World Bank (1992). *World Development Report 1992: Development and the Environment*. New York: Oxford University Press.

World Bank (1992). *Rural Roads Maintenance: Review of Completed World Bank Operations*. Operations Evaluation Department, Infrastructure and Energy Division, Washington, D.C.

World Bank (1992). *Economic Policy and Development in Indonesia*. East Asia & Pacific Regional Office, Washington, D.C.

World Bank (1993). *Indonesia Energy and the Environment: A Plan of Action for Pollution Control*. Latin America and Caribbean Regional Office, Technical Department, Washington, D.C.

World Bank (1993). *The East Asian Miracle: Economic Growth and Public Policy*. New York: Oxford University Press.